Ferdinand II, Counter-Reformation Emperor, 1578–1637

Emperor Ferdinand II (1619–1637) stands out as a crucial figure in the Counter Reformation in Central Europe, a leading player in the Thirty Years War, the most important ruler in the consolidation of the Habsburg Monarchy, and the emperor who reinvigorated the office after its decline under his two predecessors. This is the first biography of Ferdinand since a long-outdated one written in German in 1978 and the first ever in English. It looks at his reign as territorial ruler of Inner Austria from 1598 until his election as emperor and especially at the influence of his mother, the formidable Archduchess Maria. Only against this background can one understand his later policies as emperor. This book focuses on the consistency of his policies and the profound influence of religion on them throughout his career. It also follows the contest at court between those who favored consolidation of the Habsburg lands and those who aimed for expansion in the Empire, as well as between those who favored a militant religious policy and those who advocated a moderate one.

ROBERT BIRELEY is Professor of History Emeritus at Loyola University Chicago. He has served as president of the American Catholic Historical Association and on the editorial boards of the *Catholic Historical Review* and the *Renaissance Quarterly*. Bireley has been a prolific author in the field of European religious history, with a special interest in the Reformation, Roman Catholicism, and Jesuit history. His books include *Politics and Religion in the Age of the Counter Reformation: Emperor Ferdinand II, William Lamormaini, S.J., and the Formation of Imperial Policy* (1981); *The Refashioning of Catholicism, 1450–1700: A Reassessment of the Counterreformation* (1999); and *The Jesuits and the Thirty Years War: Kings, Courts, and Confessors* (Cambridge, 2003). He is the recipient of numerous fellowships, including fellowships from the John Simon Guggenheim Memorial Foundation, the Institute for Advanced Study in Princeton, the National Humanities Center in Research Triangle Park in North Carolina, and the National Endowment for the Humanities.

Ferdinand II, Counter-Reformation Emperor, 1578–1637

ROBERT BIRELEY
Loyola University Chicago

CAMBRIDGE
UNIVERSITY PRESS

CAMBRIDGE
UNIVERSITY PRESS

University Printing House, Cambridge CB2 8BS, United Kingdom

One Liberty Plaza, 20th Floor, New York, NY 10006, USA

477 Williamstown Road, Port Melbourne, VIC 3207, Australia

4843/24, 2nd Floor, Ansari Road, Daryaganj, Delhi - 110002, India

79 Anson Road, #06-04/06, Singapore 079906

Cambridge University Press is part of the University of Cambridge.

It furthers the University's mission by disseminating knowledge in the pursuit of education, learning and research at the highest international levels of excellence.

www.cambridge.org
Information on this title: www.cambridge.org/9781107674400

© Robert Bireley 2014

This publication is in copyright. Subject to statutory exception and to the provisions of relevant collective licensing agreements, no reproduction of any part may take place without the written permission of Cambridge University Press.

First published 2014
First paperback edition 2017

A catalogue record for this publication is available from the British Library

Library of Congress Cataloging in Publication data
Bireley, Robert.
Ferdinand II, Counter-Reformation emperor, 1578–1637 / Robert Bireley (Loyola University Chicago).
    pages cm
Includes bibliographical references and index.
ISBN 978-1-107-06715-8 (Hardback)
1. Ferdinand II, Holy Roman Emperor, 1578–1637. 2. Ferdinand II, Holy Roman Emperor, 1578–1637–Political and social views. 3. Austria–Kings and rulers–Biography. 4. Holy Roman Empire–Kings and rulers–Biography. 5. Maria, Erzherzogin von Inner?sterreich, 1551–1608–Influence. 6. Habsburg, House of.
7. Counter-Reformation. 8. Thirty Years' War, 1618–1648. 9. Religion and politics–Europe, Central–History–17th century. 10. Europe, Central–History–17th century. I. Title.
DB65.75.B57 2014
973´.042092–dc23 [B]   2014020976

ISBN 978-1-107-06715-8 Hardback
ISBN 978-1-107-67440-0 Paperback

Cambridge University Press has no responsibility for the persistence or accuracy of URLs for external or third-party internet websites referred to in this publication, and does not guarantee that any content on such websites is, or will remain, accurate or appropriate.

Contents

List of illustrations and maps	*page* vi
Preface	vii
Abbreviations used in the notes	x
1 Boyhood and youth, 1578–1598	1
2 Early years in Inner Austria, 1598–1608	31
3 Toward the succession, 1608–1618	61
4 The Bohemian Rebellion, 1618–1621	90
5 Consolidation and expansion, 1621–1628	123
6 Overreach, 1628–1631	179
7 Setback, 1631–1632	216
8 Recovery, 1632–1634	248
9 Settlement and death, 1635–1637	273
Conclusion	305
Genealogy overview of the Austrian Habsburgs	314
Index	316

List of illustrations and maps

1. Pious Ferdinand born of pious parents *page* 167
2. Archduchess Maria at 26 168
3. Vow of Ferdinand at Loreto 169
4. Cardinal Melchior Klesl 170
5. Defenestration of Prague 171
6. Battle of the White Mountain (detail) 172
7. Maximilian of Bavaria 173
8. Hans Ulrich von Eggenberg 174
9. Empress Eleonore as widow 175
10. Ferdinand as member of the Marian Congregation in Vienna 176
11. Assassination of Wallenstein 177
12. Mausoleum of Ferdinand II in Graz 178

MAPS

Map of the Holy Roman Empire during the Thirty Years War 325
Map of the Inner Austrian-Croatian Military Border 326

Preface

Emperor Ferdinand II stands out as the most significant ruler in the Counter Reformation in Central Europe, a leading player in the Thirty Years War, and the most important individual in the consolidation of the Habsburg Monarchy, which completed its rise to the status of a European power at the Peace of Westphalia (1648) under his son, Ferdinand III. In addition, after a period of decline during the reigns of the weak Emperors Rudolf (1576–1612) and Matthias (1612–1619), Ferdinand restored the prestige of the imperial office. Magisterial studies have appeared in recent years of the major personalities of the Thirty Years War and the first half of the seventeenth century in Europe, such as J. H. Elliott's *The Count-Duke of Olivares: The Statesman in an Age of Decline* (1986) and Dieter Albrecht's *Maximilian I. von Bayern, 1573–1651* (1998) as well as many fine biographies of Louis XIII and Cardinal Richelieu of France, Philip III and Philip IV of Spain, Gustav Adolph of Sweden, James I of England, and others. Two biographies of Ferdinand's son, Ferdinand III, have recently appeared, Lothar Höbelt's *Ferdinand III. (1608-1657). Friedenskaiser wider Willen* (2008), and Mark Hengerer's, *Kaiser Ferdinand III (1608-1657). Eine Biographie* (2012).[1] There is nothing similar on Ferdinand II. Three extensive studies of the emperor have appeared in recent years. Johann Franzl's well, even entertainingly written biography, *Ferdinand II. Kaiser im Zwiespalt der Zeit* came out in 1978 (reissued without change, 1984). It was based on limited sources and is long out of date.[2] My own *Religion and Politics in the Age of the Counterreformation: Emperor Ferdinand II, William Lamormaini, S.J., and the Formation of Imperial Policy* appeared in 1981 and dealt with the period from 1624 to 1637, and Thomas Brockmann, *Dynastie, Kaiseramt und*

---

[1] This is soon to appear in an English translation published by the Purdue University Press.
[2] See also Steven Saunders, *Cross, Sword, and Lyre: Sacred Music at the Imperial Court of Ferdinand II (1619–1637)* (Oxford, 1995).

Konfession. Politik und Ordnungsvorstellungen Ferdinands II. im Dreissigjährigen Krieg (2011) covers only the years 1618 to 1630.

My book is meant to fill the gap for this influential Austrian Habsburg ruler, at least provisionally, and to argue for his place in European history. Assessments of Ferdinand have varied widely, for a long time dependent to some extent on whether the historian was Catholic, Protestant, or liberal. The historiography of Ferdinand begins with *Ferdinandi II. Romanorum Imperatoris Virtutes*, published by his Jesuit confessor, William Lamormaini, in 1638, the year after the emperor's death. The short volume became a Baroque classic, and it also appeared at the conclusion of the *Annales Ferdinandei* (12 vols., with two supplementary volumes, 1721–1726) by Franz Christoph von Khevenhüller, who had been a councillor and diplomat in the emperor's service.[3] Implicitly it called for Ferdinand's canonization. Friedrich Hurter in his *Geschichte Ferdinands II. und seiner Eltern* (11 vols. 1850–1864) maintained a similar tone.[4] Nineteenth-century historians of a nationalist and/or liberal persuasion, such as Felix Stieve in the *Allgemeine Deutsche Biographie* (1877), drawing upon a Protestant tradition and often acknowledging Ferdinand's personal qualities, represented him as an essentially passive character, wholly dependent upon his councillors, especially his ecclesiastical advisers, and constrained by an excessive religiosity.[5] But no such ruler could have accomplished all that he did. Others portrayed him as an aspiring tyrant who aimed to suppress German liberties. One still encounters these views occasionally in surveys of European or German history or of the Thirty Years War. Recent, limited studies, such as Dieter Albrecht, "Ferdinand II (1619–1637)" in *Die Kaiser der Neuzeit (1519–1918)* (1990) have produced a more balanced picture than either of these extremes.[6]

My own historical interest over the years has centered on the relationship between religion and politics in early modern Europe, not so much in theory as in the actual formation of policy. This was the case in my first book, *Maximilian von Bayern, Adam Contzen, S.J., und die Gegenreformation in Deutschland* (1975). I then crossed over to the broader stage of Habsburg Vienna for my earlier book on Ferdinand. Now after thirty years I return to Ferdinand with a much more complete study of this oft-neglected ruler. The focus remains on religion and politics, and I draw heavily on my earlier study especially in the later chapters, updating, revising, consolidating, expanding. But one cannot understand his later policies as emperor and ruler of the Habsburg lands without considering his early years, especially the

---

[3] A first edition came out in nine volumes from 1640–1646. See the Conclusion for a discussion of the *Virtutes Ferdinandi II.*
[4] Friedrich Hurter, *Geschichte Ferdinands II. und seiner Eltern* (11 vols., Schaffhausen, 1850–1864).
[5] *Allgemeine Deutsche Biographie* 6 (Leipzig, 1877): 661–4.
[6] (Munich, 1990), 125–41.

Preface

influence of his mother, the formidable Archduchess Maria (his father died in 1590 when he was only twelve), his long rule as archduke in Inner Austria, and his struggle to stabilize the succession in the Habsburg lands and in the Empire. It is fascinating to watch this deeply religious, conscientious, and genuinely humane ruler struggle to implement his goals amidst the morass of political reality and the sometimes contradictory views of his closest advisers. One sees emerge in his later years the conflict between those councillors who placed a priority on consolidation in the Habsburg territories and those who advocated expansion in the Empire, as well as the contest between his first minister, Hans Ulrich von Eggenberg, and his Jesuit confessor, William Lamormaini, both also friends dating from his early years in Graz, over the role Spain should play in Vienna's policy. Ferdinand certainly did not avoid failures; the Edict of Restitution of 1629 and his refusal to compromise on it proved to be a disaster and undoubtedly prolonged the long war. But in the end he deserves our admiration for his nearly forty years of rule from age eighteen to fifty-seven, so this book will contend. Readers will have to decide for themselves.

This book is based on extensive archival research principally in Vienna, Rome, and Munich, much of it undertaken long ago. A significant number of the documents that I first consulted in manuscript have now been published, chiefly in the two series *Briefe und Akten zur Geschichte des Dreissigjährigen Krieges* and the *Nuntiaturberichte aus Deutschland*. I normally cite them here in their published form.

The names of persons and places have posed many challenges. Generally I have tried to use the form most suitable in the context. For the most part this meant the anglicized form for rulers and major figures in the narrative, for example, *William* Lamormaini, not *Wilhelm*, and the foreign form for others, *Vilém* Slavata rather than *William*. Ranks and titles are given in the English form, as are place names. As to places for which there are two or more names in different languages, such as Pressburg, Bratislava, and Poszony, I have indicated the various names at the first mention in the text and again in the index and tried to find a compromise for use otherwise throughout the text between the name most commonly used in the seventeenth century and the one most familiar to today's reader.

Many people have supported me in the writing of this book. I want to single out several. Paula Fichtner, professor emerita of history at Brooklyn College and from the Graduate Center, City University of New York, herself a biographer of two Holy Roman Emperors, read an early version of the manuscript and gave me many valuable suggestions. Lewis Bateman and Shaun Vigil of the Cambridge University Press have been most helpful, as have the copy editor Randa Dubnick and project manager Bindu Vinod. I am also grateful to the anonymous readers of the Cambridge University Press for their helpful comments.

This book is dedicated to my colleagues in the Department of History at Loyola University Chicago where I have taught for forty years.

Abbreviations used in the notes

AF	Franz Christoph von Khevenhüller. *Annales Ferdinandei.* 12 vols. Leipzig, 1721–26.
AKGGI	*Acten und Korrespondenzen zur Geschichte der Gegenreformation in Innerösterreich unter Ferdinand II.* 2 vols. Ed. J. Loserth. Vienna, 1906–1907. Fontes Rerum Austriacarum, Section 2, 58, 60.
Albrecht 1	Dieter Albrecht. *Die auswärtige Politik Maximilians I. von Bayern 1618–1635.* Göttingen, 1962. Schriftenreihe der Historischen Kommission bei der bayerischen Akademie der Wissenschaften, 6.
Albrecht 2	Dieter Albrecht. *Maximilian I. von Bayern.* Munich, 1998.
ARSJ	Archivum Romanum Societatis Jesu, Rome
Aust.	Austria
Boh.	Bohemia
BA	*Briefe und Akten zur Geschichte des Dreissigjährigen Krieges in den Zeiten des vorwaltenden Einflusses der Wittelsbacher.* 12 vols. Munich, 1870–1978.
BAGW	*Briefe und Akten zur Geschichte Wallensteins 1630-1634.* 4 vols. Ed. Hermann Hallwich. Vienna, 1912. Fontes Rerum Austriacarum, Section 2, vols. 63–66.
BANF	*Briefe und Akten zur Geschichte des Dreissigjährigen Krieges,* Neue Folge: *Die Politik Maximilians I. von Bayern und seiner Verbündeten 1618–1651.* 10 vols. Munich, 1907–1997.
Bireley 1	Robert Bireley. *Maximilian von Bayern, Adam Contzen, S.J. und die Gegenreformation in Deutschland 1624–1635.* Göttingen, 1975. Schriftenreihe der Historischen Kommission bei der bayerischen Akademie der Wissenschaften, 17

Bireley 2	Robert Bireley. *Religion and Politics in the Age of the Counter Reformation: Emperor Ferdinand II, William Lamormaini, S.J., and the Formatiion of Imperial Policy.* Chapel Hill, 1981.
BL	Fondo Barberini Latini, Vatican Library, Rome
Brockmann	*Dynastie, Kaiseramt und Konfession. Politik und Ordnungsvorstellungen im Dreissigjährigen Krieg.* Paderborn, 2011. Quellen und Forschungen aus dem Gebiete der Geschichte, New Series 25
Casal	Peter Casal. "Das Tagebuch des Geheimsekretärs Peter Casal über die italienische Reise des Erzherzogs Ferdinand II. vom 22. April bis 28 Juni 1598." Ed. J. Loserth. *Mittheilungen des historischen Vereins für Steiermark* 48 (1900): 3–93.
Dudik	Beda Dudik. "Korrespondenz Kaiser Ferdinands II. und seiner erlauchten Familie mit P. Martinus Becanus und P. Wilhelm Lamormaini, kaiserliche Beichtväter, S.J.," *Archiv für österreichische Geschichte* 54 (1876) 219–350.
Franzl	Johann Franzl. *Ferdinand II. Kaiser im Zwiespalt der Zeit.* Graz, 1978.
Günter	Heinrich Günter. *Die Habsburgerliga, 1625–1635. Briefe und Akten aus dem General-Archiv zu Simancas.* Berlin, 1908.
HHStA	Haus- Hof- und Staatsarchiv, Österreichisches Staatarchiv, Vienna
Frieden.	Friedensakten
Krieg.	Kriegsakten
RTA	Reichtagsakten
Religion	Religionsakten
Hurter	Friedrich von Hurter. *Geschichte Ferdinands II. und seiner Eltern, bis zu seiner Krönung in Frankfurt. Personen-, Haus- und Landesgeschichte.* 11 vols. Schaffhausen, 1850–1864.
KSchw	Bayerisches Hauptstaatsarchiv, Munich, Geheimes Staatsarchiv, Kasten Schwarz
Lorenz	*Quellen zur Vorgeschichte und zu den Anfängen des Dreissigjährigen Krieges.* Ed. Gottfried Lorenz. Darmstadt, 1991
Mann	Golo Mann. *Wallenstein.* Frankfurt, 1971.
NBD	*Nuntiaturberichte aus Deutschland.* Abteilung 4: Siebzehntes Jahrhundert. Berlin/Tübingen, 1895–2013.
Pörtner	Regina Pörtner. *The Counter-Reformation in Central Europe. Styria 1580–1630*: Oxford, 2001.
Repgen	Konrad Repgen. *Die römische Kurie und der westfälische Friede. Idee und Wirklichkeit des Papsttums im 16. und 17.*

	Jahrhundert. Vol. 1: *Papst, Kaiser und Reich, 1521–1644*, 1: *Darstellung*, 2: *Analekten und Register*. Tübingen, 1962–1965. Bibliothek des deutschen historischen Instituts in Rom, 24, 25.
Rill	Bernd Rill. Kaiser Matthias. *Brüderzwist und Glaubenskampf*. Graz, 1999.
Ritter	Moriz Ritter. *Deutsche Geschichte im Zeitalter der Gegenreformation und des Dreissigjährigen Krieges*. Vols. 2–3. Stuttgart, 1895–1908 (rpt. Darmstadt, 1962).
Schwarz	Henry F. Schwarz. *The Imperial Privy Council in the Seventeenth Century*. Cambridge, MA, 1943.
Virtutes	William Lamormaini, S.J. *Ferdinandi II. Romanorum Imperatoris Virtutes*.Vienna, 1638.
Vita Lamormaini	"Vita Lamormaini," ARSJ, Vitae 139.
Wilson	Peter H. Wilson. *The Thirty Years War: Europe's Tragedy*. Cambridge, MA, 2009.

Chapter 1

Boyhood and youth, 1578–1598

The year 1578 marked the highwater mark for Protestantism in Inner Austria, the southernmost territory of the Austrian Habsburgs. In early February the combined estates of the duchies of Styria, Carinthia, and Carniola, which taken together made up most of the territory, assembled at Bruck an der Mur in Styria because of an outbreak of the plague in Graz, the provincial capital. There in the Pacification of Bruck they extorted from the Habsburg Archduke Carl widespread concessions for the practice of Protestantism. Later that same year, on July 9, to be exact, at 3:15 a.m. there was born in the castle of Graz the future archduke and emperor, Ferdinand II.[1] In due time he would complete the restoration of Catholicism in Inner Austria that his father, Archduke Carl, initiated shortly after agreeing under great pressure to the Pacification of Bruck.

Archduke Carl, born in 1540, descended from a grand Habsburg line dating back to Emperor Rudolf I in the thirteenth century. He was the youngest son of Emperor Ferdinand I, brother of Emperor Charles V. Born in 1500, Charles had become ruler of the Netherlands in 1515 and the following year King of Spain and with it the Spanish territories in Italy – that is Milan, Naples, and Sicily – and in the New World, and he reigned over the vast Holy Roman Empire from his election in 1519 to his abdication in 1556. The Empire stretched over most of Central Europe from the North and Baltic Seas (in the north) to the north of Italy (in the south), and from the French border in the west to Poland and Hungary in the east. It was composed of nearly 300 political units of three main types: secular principalities, ecclesiastical principalities governed by a prince-bishop or archbishop, and city-states that often included an extensive hinterland, and it was held together by a complicated structure with the emperor

---

[1] Hurter 2: 216

and a representative body, the diet (Reichstag) at the top. At his abdication, Charles divided his vast inheritance between his son Philip and his brother Ferdinand, thus initiating the two related lines of the Spanish and the Austrian Habsburgs. Ferdinand himself reigned as emperor from 1556 to 1564 after having governed the Austrian Habsburg lands in the Empire since 1521 and as king of Bohemia and of Hungary since 1526, both of which he claimed through his wife Anna. Bohemia belonged to the Empire; Hungary did not. So he brought together for the first time the three lands that would eventually constitute the heart of the Habsburg Monarchy: the Austrian lands, Bohemia, and Hungary.

Subsequently, Ferdinand I divided his territories among his three sons. Maximilian, the eldest, received Lower Austria with its capital in Vienna, Upper Austria with its capital at Linz, and the kingdoms of Bohemia and Hungary, and he followed his father as Holy Roman Emperor from 1564 to 1576. His son, in turn, Emperor Rudolf II (1576–1612) succeeded his father in all these lands. Emperor Ferdinand's second son, Archduke Ferdinand, received the Tyrol as well as Anterior Austria, the Habsburg lands along the Upper Rhine including Alsace, with his residence at Innsbruck. Inner Austria then fell to Carl, the third son. Inner Austria in addition to the three above-mentioned duchies also comprised to the south on the Adriatic Sea the county of Gorizia (Görz), Inner Istria, Fiume, Triest, and parts of Friuli. Inner Austria counted as the largest territory of the Empire with 18,446 square miles and a population of roughly one million.[2] According to Ferdinand I's testament, the three lines were to be equal. None of his sons was to marry or give his children in marriage without the knowledge and counsel of the others. The two younger brothers were to seek the emperor's advice in all important matters and to be bound by it with respect to alliances.[3] Otherwise the Inner Austrian government enjoyed full sovereignty.[4] Carl established his residence and a central administration for Inner Austria at Graz in Styria. For the coming years from 1564 to 1619, when Ferdinand as newly-elected emperor left for Vienna, Graz enjoyed the high point of its history as the seat of a flourishing and influential European court, only to sink back into provincial status after 1619.

Ferdinand's mother was the formidable, deeply religious Wittelsbach Maria of Bavaria, daughter of Duke Albrecht V (1550–1579). Her marriage to Carl in 1571 in Vienna united the two sometimes rival Catholic dynasties, Wittelsbach and Habsburg, that stood in the forefront of the Catholic restoration in

---

[2] Winfried Schulze, *Landesdefension und Staatsbildung. Studien zum Kriegswesen des innerösterreichischen Territorialstaates (1564–1619)*, Veröffentlichen der Kommission für die neuere Geschichte Österreichs, 60 (Vienna, 1973), 44–5. Bavaria's area in 1564 amounted to 10,579 square miles and Brandenburg's to 14,710. Carniola was awarded to the newly created Yugoslavia in 1919, and it now constitutes the Republic of Slovenia.

[3] *Graz als Residence. Innerösterreich 1564–1619. Katalog der Ausstellung*, Grazer Burg, 6. Mai bis 30 September 1964 (Graz, 1964), 56–7.

[4] Viktor Thiel, "Die innerösterreichische Zentralverwaltung 1564–1749, 1: Die Hof- und Zentralverwaltung Innerösterreichs, 1564–1625," *Archiv für österreichische Geschichte* 105 (1916): 4.

Germany. Altogether Maria presented her husband with fifteen children before his death in 1590, twelve of whom survived into adulthood, including three archdukes and among the daughters four queens, one grand duchess, and one princess.[5] Of these the future emperor was the sixth, preceded by the first child and first Ferdinand, who died shortly after birth, and then by four daughters.

Archduke Carl inherited two principal problems as he assumed rule of Inner Austria: the consistent advance into his lands of Protestantism in the form of the adherents of the Augsburg Confession or Lutherans, and the constant threat of invasion from the east by the Ottoman Turks who, starting in the late fourteenth century, had been moving up into southeastern Europe, nearly taking Vienna itself in 1529. A town of about 8,000 in 1582,[6] Graz with its formidable fortress stood as a bulwark to their advance. The two problems were linked. The Peace of Augsburg of 1555 legalized Christian practice in the Empire according to the Confession of Augsburg, and it conceded to the secular princes of the Empire the right to determine whether the established religion of their territory would be Catholicism or Lutheranism. In the Empire the Catholic Habsburg emperors depended upon financial support from Protestant states for defense against the Turkish threat from the southeast, and the Protestants exploited this dependence in order to secure concessions. Protestantism had spread into the Austrian lands, that is Upper and Lower as well as Inner Austria, long before the Peace of Augsburg, and Protestant nobles dominated the representative estates in all three by 1555. Anterior Austria and the Tyrol took a different path; after a brief experience of radical Protestantism in the 1520s and 1530s, it remained Catholic. In the Inner Austrian lands, the Catholic Archduke Carl required funds from estates largely Protestant in order to meet the Ottoman threat. Dependent upon them as he was, he made the religious concessions to them at Bruck in 1578. So the religious issue became intertwined with the struggle for superiority in the territory between the ruler and the representative estates who could exercise their power by withholding taxes. This contest between ruler and estates over ultimate authority or the upper hand was a feature of the growth of the state in the early modern period, and, generally,

---

[5] For a list of Maria's children, see Katrin Keller, *Erzherzogin Maria von Innerösterreich (1551–1608). Zwischen Habsburg und Wittelsbach* (Vienna, 2012), 294–7. The archdukes were Maximilian Ernst, Leopold who after serving as bishop of Passau and archbishop of Strasbourg, resigned his ecclesiastical dignities, assumed the rule of the Tyrol and Anterior Austria, and married Claudia de'Medici, and Carl who became bishop of Breslau and Brixen. The queens were Anna and Constance, both wives of King Sigismund of Poland, and two wives of Philip III, Gregoria Maximiliana who died in 1597 before her planned departure for Spain, and Margaret. Maria Christierna married Sigismund Bàthory, Prince of Transylvania in 1598, but their marriage lasted only several months, and Maria Magdelena married Cosimo de'Medici, the Grand Duke of Tuscany, in 1608.
[6] Franz Popelka, *Geschichte der Stadt Graz*, 2 (Graz, 1960): 289–90.

as eventually in the Habsburg lands under Ferdinand II, the ruler emerged as the winner, though not as a fully absolute ruler.

Emperor Maximilian II, while remaining Catholic, sympathized with the Protestant movement and hoped eventually to reconcile Catholic, Lutheran, and Calvinist. In 1568, in exchange for a generous grant of taxes to support the campaign against the Turks, he made concessions to the estates of Lower and Upper Austria. Allowed was the practice of the Confession of Augsburg by the nobility and by their subjects, not however in the cities, until the hoped-for reconciliation of the confessions. The concessions were given on condition that the Catholic Church was not to be insulted or maligned and its institutions were to be left untouched. Furthermore, a church order was to be drawn up for the Protestants. Such an order was prepared for Lower Austria and accepted by the emperor in 1571, but it was not accepted for Upper Austria, and so in the latter the status of the Protestants remained without a formal guarantee. In Lower, and especially in Upper Austria, the estates interpreted these concessions broadly, often overlooking the conditions. In 1574 Maximilian agreed, orally, to permit Protestant services in the seat of the Lower Austrian estates in Vienna, and a Protestant culture flourished that has retained its attraction up to the present day. A prominent school was founded in Linz in Upper Austria, and the University of Vienna came to be dominated by Protestants. Yet, according to the best estimates, although the nobility had for the most part gone over to Protestantism, less so in Lower than in Upper Austria, overall the population remained roughly equally divided between Protestants and Catholics, and the Protestants had not succeeded in creating an institutional framework. In Vienna, the major city of the Austrian lands, a slight majority remained in the old faith.[7]

Protestantism had spread continually and persistently in Inner Austria. Commercial and intellectual contacts with the German cities and Protestant universities such as Wittenberg and especially Tübingen fostered the advance of Lutheranism, and it benefitted from the widespread clerical abuses and pastoral neglect that had been revealed by visitations conducted by joint commissions of princely and ecclesiastical officials in 1528 and again in 1544–1545.[8] The nobility above all went over to the new evangelical teaching, using its rights of patronage and administration of church property to introduce Protestant pastors. The papal nuncio, Germanico Malaspina, reported in 1580 that not more than five members of the nobility remained Catholic in Inner Austria.[9] The new evangelical teaching gained many followers also in the towns and market towns (*Städte und Märkte)*; only seventeen of ninety-five of the latter were directly under the control of the ruler, the rest being subject to

---

[7] Walter Ziegler, "Nieder-und Oberösterreich," *Die Territorien des Reichs im Zeitalter der Reformation. Land und Konfession 1500–1650*, 2: *Der Südosten*, ed. Anton Schindling and Walter Ziegler (Münster, 1989): 124–7.
[8] Pörtner, 58–9.   [9] Ibid., 35.

nobility.[10] Protestants enjoyed relative peace in the 1550s, and the Protestant estates established schools in the provincial capitals Graz, Klagenfurt, and Ljubljana (Laibach), and in Judenburg. But the Protestants enjoyed no formal guarantee of toleration. In 1572, under pressure for funds to confront the Turks, Carl conceded to the Styrian nobility along with their subjects freedom of religion until a reconciliation of Protestants and Catholics took place. But this concession ignored the towns, and of course it did not apply to the domain lands of the ruler; nor was the concession fixed in written form.[11]

Six years later in 1578, Archduke Carl agreed to the Pacification of Bruck, which confirmed the earlier agreement of 1572 and then went beyond it, for the combined estates of Inner Austria. This document has remained controversial up to the present day. It has survived in two varying versions, one drawn up by the estates and one by the archducal chancery, neither of them signed by both parties. Once again it recognized the free exercise of religion for the nobility and their subjects, and it agreed that they could keep preachers in their residences, and since many nobles could not afford this, it also allowed for other preachers who would minister to a number of noble households and to their subjects. Protestant churches and schools were permitted in the same four cities – Graz, Klagenfurt, Ljubljana, and Judenburg – and subjects might attend these schools and churches as well as services on the grounds of noble landowners. The archduke reserved to himself the regulation of religion in the other towns and market towns, but he promised not to burden the consciences of his subjects, a phrase which the Protestants interpreted to mean freedom of worship while the archducal party limited it to a freedom of conscience which did not permit public worship. The ducal version then made the important point that Carl granted these concessions only for himself and so did not bind his successor. And to reiterate, there existed no formal document with the signature of both parties. The Pacification remained essentially an oral agreement which was open to interpretation.[12]

Why did the two parties accept this unsatisfactory agreement? Archduchess Maria later claimed that it burdened her husband's conscience and indeed drove a nail into his coffin.[13] Carl was desperate for funds. The new Emperor Rudolf had in 1577 entrusted him with further responsibility for the defense against the Turks by making him the supreme military commander for the Croatian-Slavonian Military Border east of Styria and Carinthia, while he himself retained the command of the Hungarian

---

[10] Ibid., 37–8.
[11] Karl Amon, "Innerösterreich," in *Die Territorien des Reichs im Zeitalter der Reformation und Konfessionalisierung: Land und Konfession 1500–1650*, 2: *Der Südosten*, ed. Anton Schindling and Walter Ziegler (Münster, 1989): 106–10.
[12] Pörtner, 30–3; *Acten und Korrespondenzen zur Geschichte der Gegenreformation in Innerösterreich unter Erzherzog Karl II. (1578–1590)*, ed. J. Loserth (Vienna, 1898), x–xi. Fontes Rerum Austriacarum, 50.
[13] *Graz als Residenz*, 196.

frontier to the north.[14] The estates, for their part, recognized the legitimacy of Carl's argument for funds for defense. They also were moved by a passive or "suffering" obedience that derived from their Lutheran theology and did not allow for a more active resistance to legitimate authority. At the imperial diets throughout this whole period representatives of the Inner Austrian estates found themselves in the "awkward position" of joining with their Catholic counterparts in petitioning for funds for defense against the Turks while at the same time calling upon the Protestant princes of the Empire to intercede with Carl or later Ferdinand on the religious issue.[15]

The second main issue for Carl was defense against the Ottoman Turks, "the hereditary enemy of Christianity." In the reign of Emperor Ferdinand I, a Military Border zone had been created in Croatia and Slavonia as a buffer between the lands under Habsburg suzerainty and the areas controlled by the Ottomans, and in the course of the 1530s and 1540s a line of fortresses had been constructed across the border from Inner Austria. In 1564 at Carl's accession, he and the Inner Austrian estates had agreed to accept the major burden for the defense of the Croatian-Slavonian border as opposed to the Hungarian border further to the north for which the emperor was responsible. After the death of Suleiman the Magnificent in 1566, when the Turks were perceived to be vulnerable, Emperor Maximilian undertook a new offensive which turned out to be disastrous and resulted in a humiliating peace in 1568.[16] Subsequently, Maximilian aimed to keep the peace with the Turks, refusing to enter the alliance of the pope, Venice, and Spain against them that resulted in the resounding naval victory at Lepanto in 1571. But the Turks did not consider raids and skirmishes along the border to violate the peace, and these continued regularly. In 1574 they conducted a major raid into Croatia where they inflicted a severe defeat upon Austrian forces. By 1577 roughly 7,000 imperial troops were stationed in the lands of the Military Border.[17] Much of this territory had been abandoned by noble and ecclesiastical landholders because of the constant fighting. The Habsburg authorities had then encouraged the settlement of refugees from areas conquered by the Turks such as the Vlachs or Walachians and the Uskoks who supplemented the sparse native population.[18] These peasants of the area of the Military Border received special privileges such as land free from feudal overlordship, a degree of self government at the local level, and reduced taxes in exchange for military

---

[14] Gunther Erich Rothenberg, *The Austrian Military Border in Croatia, 1522–1747* (Urbana, 1960), 46–50. Slavonia is here to be understood as a geographical rather than a political term designating eastern Croatia; see Ekkehard Völkl, "Militärgrenze und 'Statuta Valachorum,'" *Die österreichische Militärgrenze*, ed. Gerhard Ernst (Kallmünz, 1982), 1, n. 2.
[15] Pörtner, 31–3; citation on p. 33.
[16] Paula Sutter Fichtner, *Emperor Maximilian II* (New Haven, 2001), 125–34.
[17] Völkl, 10.   [18] On the Uskoks see Chapter 3.

obligations and other duties such as the maintenance of fortresses. Shortly after his accession in 1576, Emperor Rudolf placed Carl in charge of military operations along the Croatian-Slavonian border, as we have seen, and at the meeting at Bruck in 1578 the Inner Austrian estates consented as part of the arrangement to contribute nearly 550,000 florins annually for the defense of the border. In 1578, Carl established the war council (Hofkriegsrat) in Graz, which was partially under the control of the estates, and he began to reorganize the chain of border fortresses, constructing a new fortress at Karlovac (Karlstadt) which was to be the headquarters for the Military Border. But the emperor instructed him to remain on the defensive.[19]

The Pacification of Bruck sounded the alarm in Rome, partly because of fear that the concessions would lead to the advance of Protestantism into Gorizia, Triest, and Fiume, and from there into Venice and down into Italy. The Dominican Felician Ninguarda, a diplomat experienced in German affairs, was dispatched to Graz to inform Carl that he had incurred the excommunication imposed on those who aided heretics, and to urge the revocation of the Pacification. He arrived in early May 1578.[20] Whether Carl initially tended toward a more tolerant view similar to that of his brother Emperor Maximilian and only took on a militantly Catholic attitude under the influence of his wife Maria and the Jesuits – nearly all his privy councillors were Protestants –,[21] or whether from the beginning he was determined to restore Catholicism as he felt entitled to do by the Peace of Augsburg, is difficult to determine. The latter seems more likely. Prior to any negotiations concerning his marriage with Maria, he had taken steps to secure the dispatch of a Jesuit preacher to Graz for Lent in 1570 and soon envisioned a Jesuit college in Graz. To the Jesuit superior general in Rome he wrote in 1571 that he intended the restoration of Catholicism in his territory. So Carl followed the lead of his father, Emperor Ferdinand I, who had first brought the Jesuits to Vienna and to Prague in the mid-1550s, to found colleges. The college in Graz opened its doors in 1573, and the archduke henceforth vigorously fostered the work of the fathers, now undoubtedly supported by his wife Maria. Even before they began instruction in the school, the Jesuits staged the Corpus Christi procession in Graz for the first time in twenty years.[22]

To soothe Ninguarda's fears, Carl expelled Protestants from Gorizia, a territory surprisingly of little concern to the estates who had secured

---

[19] Rothenburg, 27–51.   [20] Pörtner, 72.
[21] Johannes Andritsch, "Landesfürstliche Berater," in *Innerösterreich 1564–1619*, ed. Alexander Novotny and Berthold Sutter (Graz, 1969): 88–9.
[22] Maximilian Liebmann, "Die Gründung der Grazer Universität und die Jesuiten," in *Katholische Reform und Gegenreformation in Innerösterreich 1564–1628*, ed. Franz M. Dolinar (Klagenfurt, 1994): 77–84; Bernhard Duhr, *Die Jesuiten an den deutschen Fürstenhöfen des 16. Jahrhunderts* (Freiburg, 1901): 23–5.

the Pacification.[23] Ninguarda traveled to Innsbruck and to Munich to discuss the situation in Inner Austria with Archduke Ferdinand of Tyrol and Duke Albrecht V of Bavaria. Both counseled against a direct revocation of the concessions of Bruck; such a drastic move might stir up a rebellion. From October 14 to 15, 1579 then, Archduke Carl, Archduke Ferdinand of Tyrol, and Duke William V of Bavaria – Maria's brother who had succeeded Albrecht V – met in the Munich Conference to draw up a plan to undermine the Pacification of Bruck in Inner Austria. They laid out a series of measures that aimed at a gradual process, carried out in deeds rather than in words, and avoided head-on confrontation. Carl was to secure control of the printing presses in order to prevent the heretics from publishing their propaganda and polemics, and polemical and seditious sermons were to be outlawed. The Pacification was to be interpreted narrowly, and nothing was to be permitted that was not explicitly granted in the document. This would greatly limit the activity of the preachers in the towns and market towns, including the four cities Graz, Klagenfurt, Ljubljana, and Judenburg. The construction of new Protestant churches was to be considered illegal. Eventually, all Protestant preachers would be expelled from the towns when they violated the aforementioned directives. In due course, then, Carl would exercise the right of reformation granted him by the Peace of Augsburg. The emperor, the rulers of the Tyrol and Bavaria, the king of Spain, and the pope could be expected to help the process along with counsel and with financial aid, especially in the case of a tax strike by the estates. Important for the implementation of this program was the introduction of Catholics into Carl's privy council and other major offices, and the gradual elimination of the Protestants. Measures were to be taken toward the reform of clergy and laity, and Pope Gregory XIII was requested to call upon the bishops to carry out their obligations. Carl was also urged to seek absolution from the pope from his excommunication, so as to quiet his conscience and obtain divine assistance for the program of action.[24] The princes also recommended that the pope establish a permanent nunciature in Graz, and indeed the following year Germanico Malaspina arrived as the first nuncio. Graz remained, then, the seat of a nunciature until Ferdinand moved to Vienna as emperor in 1619.

Archduke Carl soon began to take action, and he generally proceeded along the lines outlined at the Munich Conference. Shortly after his concessions at Bruck, he assured the prelates who held seats in the estates that he was ready to offer up his life for the faith. Morereover, the archduke was well aware of the connection between his authority and his right to determine the religion of his lands according to the Peace of Augsburg. Already in 1580 he shut down Protestant printing presses so that Protestant writers had to publish their

---

[23] Pörtner, 73.
[24] Ibid., 81–3; "Beschluss der Konsultation," 1579, October 14, Loserth, No. 11 (pp. 36–40).

Boyhood and youth, 1578–1598

materials outside Inner Austria. This became more significant after 1586 when the Jesuit college was elevated to the status of a university, and the Jesuit faculty members began to issue a steady stream of Catholic publications. He proceeded against the preachers in the towns where in his interpretation of the agreement of Bruck, he possessed the authority to do so, and in 1580 he imposed silence on Jeremias Homberger, director of the Protestant school in Graz. Later that same year, on December 10, departing from the procedure recommended by the Munich Conference, Carl decreed that in the towns and in his domain lands, only Catholic worship would be permitted. But this caused such an uproar that the decree had to be revoked the following February.[25] Homberger was now exiled for exhorting to resistance. Gradually, Protestants were dismissed from office but not from all their positions, especially in the military, and in 1582 Carl directed that only Catholics be placed in the lesser positions at court.[26] In 1582 Carl virtually repeated the edict of 1580 that prohibited Protestant worship in the towns and cities, and in its enforcement he concentrated on Graz itself where he then forbade the city's magistrates to attend Protestant worship. A wedge began to develop between the Protestant nobles with their overwhelming majority in the estates and the townspeople, especially the artisans. The two groups frequently disagreed on issues, for example, on the apportionment of taxes, and now their consensus on the religious question began to break down. The estates were not willing to go to the barricades to support the townspeople in their struggle.[27]

An inner council began to form to deal with the religious issue that included the nuncio, the rector of the Jesuit college Heinrich Blyssem, and two bishops, both brought over from Salzburg who were for years to serve as major figures in the Counter Reformation in Inner Austria: Martin Brenner, bishop of Seckau from 1585 to 1615; and Georg Stobäus von Palmburg, bishop of Lavant from 1584 to 1610. The Jesuit college was raised to the status of a university in 1586, a development that brought a much larger contingent of Jesuits to the city who, as we have seen, began to issue a flood of Catholic writings. In 1587 the archduke ordered that all the students from the cities and market towns should attend this university.[28] That same year the reformation commissions were introduced that were to serve an important function in the implementation of the Counter Reformation. These were commissions headed jointly by a prelate and a government official and accompanied by a squad of soldiers who moved from parish to parish restoring a Catholic pastor and pressuring parishioners to return to Catholic practice.[29] Reform measures were also underway as the nuncio Malaspina undertook visitations of monasteries and religious houses where he often found dreadful conditions.[30]

---

[25] Amon, 416; Pörtner, 85. [26] Pörtner, 87. [27] Ibid., 92–3. [28] Hurter, 2: 184
[29] Amon, 417. [30] Pörtner, 99.

Tensions increased, especially in Graz itself. There in early June 1590, renewed efforts to counter the presence of citizens at Protestant services provoked the outbreak of urban riots. A Protestant mob threatened a St. Bartholomew's Day Massacre of Catholics. Yet the violence was contained.[31] Archduchess Maria experienced the unrest at first hand. Twelve-year-old Ferdinand had already departed for his studies at the Jesuit college in Ingolstadt. The unsettling events confirmed both in their association of Protestantism with violence and rebellion. At the time, Archduke Carl was staying at the Habsburg castle at Laxenburg outside Vienna, where he frequently found respite from attacks of the stone and of gout. He returned to Graz where he died unexpectedly on July 10, 1590, surrounded by his wife and children.[32] His death brought a respite in the campaign to restore Catholicism. In his testament, drawn up in 1584, Carl professed at length his own Catholic faith, called for the exclusion of any of his children from their inheritance should they ever go over to the Protestants, and imposed on his successor the obligation of maintaining his lands in the Catholic faith. Lest there be any doubt about this last point, he reiterated it forcefully in a codicil to the testament, and he declared clearly that his successor was not bound by the concessions made at Bruck.[33]

Meanwhile, young Ferdinand was growing up in Graz. His mother Maria watched carefully over his education and over that of all her children, especially after the death of the archduke. Tradition ascribes piety to Ferdinand from his earliest years. Before he knew prayers by heart, he knelt at Mass and at the Angelus, the prayer recited three times daily commemorating the angel's Annunciation to Mary, and he showed an inner participation in the service. His first tutor, Hans Widmanns, was named when Ferdinand was four, and it is not clear who succeeded him.[34] At eight years of age, he was confirmed and also enrolled as the first student to matriculate at the new University of Graz. At eleven his own household was established and about the same time he was inducted into the Young Students of the Muses *(Alumnae musarum juventutis)* by the rector of the Jesuit college in Graz. This may indicate an early interest in music. As it was, music played a prominent role at the court of Graz under Archduke Carl where Venetian musicians often performed, and Ferdinand himself would maintain this tradition in Graz and later in Vienna.[35] Before he left to study at Ingolstadt, he addressed the assembled members, and afterwards he gave each of them a gold coin with the saying inscribed on it "To Those Who Fight Justly Goes the Crown" *(Legitime certantibus corona)*. Taken from

---

[31] Ibid., 94-5. [32] Keller, 40-1.
[33] Archduke Carl's Testament, June 1, 1584, and Codicil, undated, Hurter 2: 522-35.
[34] Hurter 2: 216. Hurter suggests Carl Weinberger, a Franciscan Minim and well-known preacher, and Andreas Backes, holder of the benefice St. Anna in the castle of Graz.
[35] See Helmut Federhofer, *Musikpfleger und Musiker am Grazer Habsburgerhof der Erherzöge Karl und Ferdinand von Innerösterreich (1564-1619)* (Mainz, 1967).

Boyhood and youth, 1578–1598

Paul's Second Letter to Timothy (2, 5), this was to become his own official motto.[36] The words expressed a firm conviction that remained Ferdinand's throughout his life.

As he approached his twelfth birthday, Ferdinand's parents determined to send him to study at Ingolstadt in Bavaria, where the Jesuits had a college and predominated on the faculty of the university. There seem to have been several reasons for this. Carl and Maria felt that he would be able better to devote himself to his studies there, apart from the distractions of the court, and they also wanted to protect him from any Protestant ideas that he might pick up from the nobility in Graz.[37] Furthermore, Maria consulted with her brother, Duke William of Bavaria, to whom she was very close and with whom she corresponded regularly. They both agreed that he should go to Ingolstadt, where William, nearby, would be able to oversee his education. The duke promised to treat Ferdinand as his own son, a commitment that took on new meaning when Archduke Carl died shortly after Ferdinand's arrival in Ingolstadt. But William did not want the emperor to know that he had proposed Ingolstadt, since he feared that Emperor Rudolf would prefer that Ferdinand study in Vienna or Prague, or Innsbruck, Habsburg lands rather than in Wittelsbach Bavaria. His own son, Maximilian, William added, now studied in Ingolstadt.[38] Notable here is that Ingolstadt was not chosen explicitly because of the Jesuits.

Ferdinand departed for Ingolstadt on January 11, 1590. His entourage counted between thirty and forty. Included in it were: Balthasar von Schrattenbach as tutor, a figure close to the Jesuits and greatly trusted by Ferdinand's parents who was named Ferdinand's *Obristhofmeister* (majordomo) in 1596, to remain in that office until 1615; Johann Wagenring as preceptor, an alumnus of the Jesuits' German College in Rome and archdeacon of Lower Styria, who would be named bishop of Triest in 1592; eight young noble boys along with their teacher, Lorenz Sonnenwender, who served as Ferdinand's court chaplain; and even a court dwarf.[39] With him the new student carried a prayer book given him by his parents. On the inside cover there looked out a miniature of Charlemagne (perhaps anticipating Ferdinand's future), and under it one of the Virgin Mary with the date 1590. The little book counted sixty-nine pages. On the first page Archduke Carl inscribed his name along with the year once again and the motto, "W.G.W." *(Wie Gott Will)*, and beneath Maria added her name along with the words, "I trust, I ask, Maria" *(ich draue, biet, Maria)*. On the reverse side of this first page, there was written, with the much later date, 1622, inscribed by Ferdinand's second wife Eleonore of Mantua, the motto *"Legitime certantibus corona."* The following pages carried the

---

[36] Hurter 2: 235
[37] Ibid., 230–1; Helmut Dotterweich, *Der junge Maximilian. Jugend und Erziehung des bayerischen Herzogs und späteren Kurfürsten Maximilian I. Von 1573 bis 1593* (Munich, 1962), 96.
[38] Hurter 2: 230–1.   [39] Ibid., 2: 236–7; Dotterweich, 92.

signatures of other members of Ferdinand's family, added at times indicated in the text, followed by those of Maximilian of Bavaria and two of Maximilian's brothers, Philip and Ferdinand. Maximilian's motto pointed to a spirituality similar to Ferdinand's, "The Lord of Hosts is with us" *(Dominus virtutum nobiscum)*. Various prayers for the different days of the week filled up the next forty-four pages, and the remaining pages remained blank.[40] Ferdinand obviously treasured this little prayer book. It reveals fundamental attitudes that characterized him for much of his life: attachment to God's will, confidence that God was with him, devotion to the Virgin Mary, and affection for his family including here his Wittelsbach cousins.

Ferdinand's party arrived in Ingolstadt in early February, passing through Munich on the way, where he had the opportunity to meet his uncle, Duke William. On February 5, Maria wrote her brother, "Since you with such desire await Ferdinand, I hope that he has now arrived and behaves in every way in a manner pleasing to you. If he does not act this way, do not, for God's sake, overlook it. He is fearful; once he sees that you're serious, he'll follow [your directives]. Let me know how he pleases you and how you feel toward him. But write me the pure truth, nothing out of love. I command you, speak with the members of his party and the servants periodically." Archduke Carl thanked his brother-in-law, Maria wrote, for the friendly reception of Ferdinand and his kindness towards him. Ferdinand has been instructed, she continued, to obey him in all respects, and should he not do so, he should be punished.[41] Schrattenbach was instructed to keep in touch with Duke William and to follow his instructions. The old castle *(alter Schluss)* in Ingolstadt, then functioning as a storehouse for grain, was fixed up to serve as Ferdinand's residence. Seventeen-year-old Maximilian and his other Wittelsbach cousins gave him a friendly reception; they all visited one another regularly and enjoyed common excursions together, especially hunting expeditions. Ferdinand had a penchant for bear hunting, and at one point recounted all the details of a bear hunt for his mother.[42] All his life Ferdinand remained devoted to the hunt.

For his first three years in Ingolstadt, Ferdinand studied in the college, and only in his fourth year did he pass on to the university proper. The university had undergone a crisis after the death in 1543 of its premier theologian, the well-known opponent of Luther, Johann Eck, whose tomb still adorns the former university church. The number of its students dropped from nearly 300 in 1542 to about 100 in 1546. Duke William IV summoned three Jesuits to the university, including Peter Canisius, in 1549. Eventually they founded a college and secured control of the arts faculty by 1588. But it was not a strictly Jesuit university. Many secular clergy and laymen taught in the schools of law and theology. In the winter semester of 1587, seventy-one

---

[40] Hurter 2: 246–7, n. 48; *Graz als Residenz*, 93.
[41] Feb. 5, 1590, cited in Hurter 2: 248.   [42] Dotterweich, 96, Hurter, ibid. 2: 226.

Boyhood and youth, 1578–1598

students heard lectures at the university, only thirteen of them nobles; most students came from Catholic Germany, but there was one Protestant from Augsburg. The Jesuits brought revived Aristotelian-Thomistic Scholasticism to Ingolstadt, and Thomas Aquinas's *Compendium of Theology* replaced Peter Lombard's *Sentences* as the standard text in theology in the 1560s. The Spanish Jesuit Gregory of Valencia shone as the academic star during Ferdinand's time in the Bavarian town. From 1591 to 1597 he published his *Commentarii Theologici* in four volumes which were to go through twelve editions in the next twenty years. Gregory stood out as perhaps the most vigorous theological supporter of the primacy of the pope in the sixteenth century. Maximilian of Bavaria found in him a confessor and friend, and his theological tomes were later found in Ferdinand's library.[43]

An incident took place early during Ferdinand's first year in Ingolstadt that threatened to disturb his relationship with Maximilian but that, fortunately, had no serious consequences. It had to do with precedence. One Sunday morning Ferdinand came to Mass and claimed a seat in front of Maximilian. The Wittelsbach yielded, and then wrote home immediately about the course he should take in the future. Schrattenbach did not even consider the matter important enough to report to Maria, and Graz only learned about Ferdinand's action through Duke William. Both Ferdinand and Maximilian were reminded by their parents that they were still students, not ruling princes, and they should act as brothers to each other. No permanent animosity towards Ferdinand seems to have taken hold of Maximilian, as some writers have suggested. Maximilian manifested genuine concern for his Austrian cousin when he took ill, and Ferdinand was said to be sad at Maximilian's departure in April 1591.[44]

Archduke Carl died on July 10, 1590, about six months after Ferdinand left home. This must have been a terrible blow to the twelve-year-old. He wrote his mother on July 22, only twelve days after the death, that Schrattenbach the tutor and Wagenring the preceptor had given him the sad news. "The Almighty God had summoned his own dear Herr Father out of this passing valley of tears, in his will, without a doubt to eternal peace and happiness. His death came all too early for Your Highness, for me, and for my dear brothers and sisters. And although I ought to grieve much more than I feel now, I cannot resist God's will. Then I entrust and commit it all to his divine pleasure. May he continue to give me his divine grace and be praised in all his works, and may he give my dear Herr Father and all of us a blessed resurrection on the last day. Amen." And he went on, as an obedient son, to pray that he and his brothers and sisters would continue to find their source of support, after God, in their dear mother.[45] One cannot write this deeply felt letter off as mere formalized

---

[43] Dotterweich, 108–12.   [44] Hurter 2: 254–60; Dotterweich, 96–7.
[45] Ferdinand to Maria, Jul. 22, 1590, Hurter 2: 555–6.

piety. It expresses a deep faith and acceptance of God's will that characterized Ferdinand all his life. Duke William assured Maria that he would care for both her and Ferdinand. Ferdinand started to journey home, perhaps permanently or more likely, for the funeral service for his father, but Maria had him intercepted at Landshut and told to return to Ingolstadt. She instructed Ferdinand that he was now to consider Duke William his father and to obey him in all things, and she encouraged him in his studies.[46]

In his testament Archduke Carl had named four guardians for Ferdinand and his other children: his nephew Emperor Rudolf, the head of the family; his brother Archduke Ferdinand who governed the Tyrol and Anterior Austria from Innsbruck; his brother-in-law Duke William of Bavaria; and his wife Maria. Also stipulated was that Ferdinand would gain his majority at eighteen and only then assume the rule of Inner Austria. To Maria the testament assigned a residence in Judenburg along with a generous income and other privileges.[47] But she was not about to be pushed into an isolated retirement, however comfortable it might be. Her last child, Archduke Carl, was born on August 7, about a month after her husband's death. She refused to move to Judenburg, determined to remain in Graz, and she poured out her heart to God using words from the Scriptures, "O Lord my God, help me as the judge [in the Gospel] helped the poor widow who would not cease to cry out and beseech [him] until he came and helped her out of her need. O Lord, I cry out for your help as the deer [yearns] for running waters, praise your divine name through me, let me see that you have not forgotten me."[48]

Both she and Duke William aimed to secure the regency for her, but the emperor appointed Archduke Ernst, his own brother, instead. The estates took the offensive, urging the return of Ferdinand to Graz from under the Jesuits in Ingolstadt, and they sought to have Maria shipped out to Judenburg. She wrote to the emperor to counter the efforts of the delegation sent to him by the estates.[49] She aimed to keep Ferdinand at Ingolstadt until he completed his studies, and to achieve this goal she had not only to oppose the estates but also to convince the emperor and Archduke Ferdinand, at this point and again in 1593 when Ferdinand completed his studies in the college and started at the university. Both the emperor and the archduke thought that Ferdinand's continuance in Ingolstadt would make it more difficult for him to rule subsequently because of the suspicion of the Jesuit influence on him, and that an apprenticeship, as it were, in Innsbruck with Archduke Ferdinand would teach him more about the art of rule as well as the manner of life of a prince. Even the pope, when consulted, shared this view. Archduke Ernst did too, but he emphasized that Maria would never permit it, and she seems to have eventually

---

[46] Maria to Ferdinand, Oct. 22, 1590, Hurter 2: 557–8.
[47] Testament of Archduke Carl, Hurter 2: 529–30.
[48] Prayer of Archduchess Maria in her own hand, *Graz als Residenz*, 94; Hurter 2: 387.
[49] Hurter 2: 366, 371, 396–7; Keller, 113–23.

convinced him. In 1593 she traveled to Munich herself to talk the matter over with Ferdinand himself, with Duke William, and with members of Ferdinand's entourage. Ferdinand himself definitely wanted to remain in Ingolstadt for the time being. Maria then continued to Innsbruck to convey her position to Archduke Ferdinand in person. There she explained that she wanted to keep her son from mixing with Protestants. In Ingolstadt also, she explained, he could study law, so important for a ruler, and also practice riding and fencing as befitted a prince. Moreover, his father had wanted him to remain in Ingolstadt for four years.[50] Maria won the day. Throughout Ferdinand's years in Ingolstadt she corresponded regularly with him, with Schrattenbach, his tutor, Wagenring, his preceptor, and with Duke William.

Meanwhile, in 1592 Maria accompanied her eldest daughter, Anna Maria, via Vienna to Cracow for her marriage on June 1 with Sigismund III, King of Poland and Grand Duke of Lithuania, who also possessed a strong claim to the kingdom of Sweden which he never succeeded in making good. So Anna Maria became queen of Poland, a development that aimed to advance Habsburg interests in that land and especially the effort to enlist Poland in the war with the Turks, which was about to erupt into a new stage. The union was a happy one. But Anna Maria died in 1598, however, not before giving birth to a son, Wladyslaw, who would ascend to the Polish throne in 1632. Another daughter, Constance, subsequently married Sigismund in Cracow in December 1605, and once again Maria journeyed to the wedding. This match also turned out to be a happy one; Constance died in 1631, a year before her husband. Negotiations for the marriage of another daughter, Maria Christierna, with Sigismund Báthory, the prince of Transylvania, had been initiated in 1593, at the emperor's initiative, with the goal of securing his support in the contest with the Turks. Maria, not completely happy with the arrangements, set out in mid-June 1595 through territory infested with Turks for Alba Julia (Karlsburg) in Transylvania with her daughter for the wedding, where it took place on August 6. Sigismund contracted an aversion to his wife from the start, and the marriage was never consummated. Eventually an annulment was arranged, and Maria Christierna returned to Graz, entered a convent in Hall in the Tirol in 1607, and died there as prioress in 1621.[51]

Young Ferdinand ended up spending five years in Ingolstadt, three in the college and two in the university. His form of education distinguished him clearly from contemporary rulers, apart from his cousin Maximilian. Neither his fellow Habsburg Philip IV of Spain, nor Louis XIII of France, nor Charles I of England, nor Gustav Adolph of Sweden studied at a college or university. Generally, they were educated by tutors. After paying a visit to Ingolstadt in 1594, Aeneas Gonzaga, ambassador of Mantua to the emperor, noted

---

[50] Hurter 2, 406–12. [51] Keller, 178–82.

Ferdinand's middling size, well-proportioned body, and attractive appearance. Yet delicate health characterized him, and interruptions of his carefully planned schedule could influence the state of his health. Sickness compelled him to take to his bed a number of times, and once Maximilian, looking out for him, convinced him of the need to take a bitter medicine.[52] Ferdinand both attended classes and received private tutoring, and he participated in the academic and religious life of the university. Generally, he socialized with the Wittelsbach princes and with the noble youths who accompanied him to Ingolstadt, making excursions into the countryside and hunting. He was not to be found carousing in the town as students often did also in those days. At a Christmas celebration in his first year, he publicly recited from memory a long poem on the Nativity of Christ, and in his first years he also declaimed publicly on the feasts of the Ascension and Pentecost. At one point toward the end of his second year, in a public disputation he served as the objector to theses proposed by a fellow student. A prize was awarded him that same year for his performance in an hour-long public examination in rhetoric. His religious observance edified his fellow students. He regularly attended Mass in the college chapel on Sundays and feast days, a practice he continued at the local parish church, St. Maurice, after he advanced to the university. University pilgrimages found him participating, for example to the shrine of Our Lady on nearby Mount Allerstorff near Biburg for the feast of the Annunciation on March 25, 1593. The following year, during Lent when the Turks were threatening, Ferdinand, along with the Bavarian princes clothed in ecclesiastical garb, opened and closed the Forty Hours Devotion, a period of continual prayer before the Holy Eucharist, conducted with a view to petition God for deliverance from the enemy.[53]

During his years at Ingolstadt, Ferdinand came into personal contact with a number of Jesuits. He attended the lectures of Reiner Fabricius on political rhetoric, and Christopher Silberhorn gave him private lessons in mathematics. The young Adam Tanner, later to become Catholic Germany's leading dogmatic theologian, reviewed with him material from philosophy courses and exercised him in the art of disputation. After he graduated to the university, he periodically invited Jesuit professors to dinner for conversation. Among these were Richard Haller, who later journeyed to Spain as confessor to his sister Margaret, who married Philip III and who fostered the interests of the Austrian Habsburgs in Madrid,[54] the theologian Gregory of Valencia, and the polymath and prolific author and polemicist, Jakob Gretser. On Sunday

---

[52] Hurter 3: 210–11.
[53] Diarium of an Ingolstadt Jesuit, in C.M. Freiherr von Aretin, *Geschichte des bayerischen Herzogs und Kurfürsten Maximilian des Ersten* (Passau, 1842) 1: 477–87; Hurter 3: 201–2, 239–43.
[54] Magdelena Sanchez, *The Empress, the Queen, and the Nun: Women and Power at the Court of Philip III of Spain* (Baltimore, 1998), 17, 50–1, 72–3, 143–4, 183.

Boyhood and youth, 1578–1598

and feast day evenings, then, Gretser often came to the college after Vespers for a concert and then for conversation.[55]

Trips were undertaken from Ingolstadt to Innsbruck, Eichstätt, and of course many times, to Munich to see Duke William. Both the duke of Wurttemberg and the archbishop elector of Mainz visited the young archduke in Ingolstadt. Most importantly, toward the end of his days in Ingolstadt, in late summer 1594, he journeyed to Regensburg to meet for the first time the head of the family, Emperor Rudolf, who had come there from Prague for the diet. Maria wanted to assure that he made a favorable impression on his imperial cousin, and so she summoned Wagenring, now bishop of Triest, to accompany her son. Rudolf graciously received him in his own quarters upon Ferdinand's arrival, and the two conversed several times, about Ferdinand's studies, especially about mathematics, which particularly interested Rudolf, and about the time for Ferdinand to conclude his studies in Ingolstadt. Three times they attended Mass together. There was an opportunity to meet the ambassadors there, Ferdinand talking twice with the Spanish ambassador. Both an imperial privy councillor, Rudolph Corraduz, and Schrattenbach reported all in detail to Maria, who was assured that the visit had gone well.[56]

As the year 1594 approached its end, the time arrived for Ferdinand to wind up his studies in Ingolstadt after nearly five years there; he was now sixteen and was himself eager to return home. Maria and Duke William wanted him to return to Graz, where he could come to know his people. Emperor Rudolf and Archduke Ferdinand of Tyrol, his other two guardians, hesitated, thinking that a year in Innsbruck at the court of the latter would benefit the young ruler. Maria and William prevailed.[57] On December 21, 1594, the university gave Ferdinand a grand send-off in the great hall of the college. There he was presented with a "new type of farewell" in the form of a small volume commemorating his five years at Ingolstadt filled with emblems, illustrations, and poems, including one in "heroic verses" composed by Jakob Gretser, to serve as a reminder for him of his days there. He then traveled to Munich to say his farewells. But the formal permission for him to leave Ingolstadt from the emperor did not arrive until mid-February.[58] The Jesuits then staged another farewell at which Father Anthony Welser praised his merits and thanked him for the gift toward a new high altar for the main chapel which Ferdinand had made, and then entrusted the Society of Jesus to him, for its advance and its defense. Ferdinand, in a moving ex tempore address, declared that he would always care for and have at heart the interests of the college at Ingolstadt as well as the whole Society.[59]

---

[55] Hurter 3: 239.   [56] Ibid., 206–7, 212–15.   [57] Ibid., 229–32.   [58] Ibid., 235–6.
[59] Diarium of an Ingolstadt Jesuit, 484–7.

As he departed Ingolstadt, Ferdinand carried with him a compact "mirror of princes" which Duke William composed for him, his "illustrious prince, dear friend, cousin, and son," out of a "staunch, well-intentioned, paternal love and care." So Duke William responded to Ferdinand's request that his uncle put to writing the advice that he had given him during his Ingolstadt years. First, as one might expect, William counseled him to look to the care of religion, for himself and his subjects. He should "aim, so far as this is humanly possible, and work intensely, so that the same [his subjects] if not all together at least the majority be brought back as soon as possible to the true sheepfold; and since this is not to be achieved soon and all at once, Your Highness [ought to aim] at least not to consent in the meantime to any further new measure to the prejudice of the Church and the Catholic religion, but to exert yourself to the utmost, as I said, to recover once again all that has up to now been neglected or lost," as your father would have surely done had God allowed him to live. Ferdinand should select intelligent, zealous Catholics as his officials and especially as privy councillors, have a theologian [confessor] always near him, to whom he ought to listen and follow, and also have near him fathers of the Society of Jesus, who sought only the salvation of lost souls. He should govern personally himself since he bore the ultimate responsibility for his people, and not commit everything to a minister-favorite. With this advice William warned him against a development that was emerging at some courts at the time, namely the appointment of a favorite or first minister who effectively conducted the government. William's own son, Maximilian, always avoided assiduously such a practice.[60]

William urged Ferdinand always to honor and respect his mother, and to seek her counsel, and also to care for and provide for the education of his many brothers and sisters. He should show concern for the members and servants in his household, all of whom should be Catholic and, in order to forestall deception, be required to make the Catholic profession of faith. Care for the poor and the provision of justice was an obligation for the young prince. Though he needed recreation and entertainment, his personal pleasures such as hunting, dancing, and the theater should be clearly subordinated to his princely obligations. He should pay attention to his military; soldiers too should be Catholic. It was wise to draw up an order of procedure *(Hofordnung)* for the court, and then stick to it. Officials ought to be appointed and promoted on the basis of merit, and not as favors to courtiers. As a prince, he ought to be friendly and genial but not familiar, not act precipitously but "cautiously and circumspectly," and slow to trust others. Festivities such as carnival ought not to get out of hand, since this led to mortal sin, nor should he permit buffoonery or the like at court. Finally, obedience was owed to church commands, and Ferdinand was to give good example to his people by this and by his

---

[60] Bireley 1, 17

Boyhood and youth, 1578–1598

participation in processions, pilgrimages, and other good works.[61] Duke William's mirror of princes laid out a program that Ferdinand was going to follow; it helps explain his manner of government. The defense and advance of Catholicism, allegiance to the Jesuits, and openness to the advice of his mother stood at the top of his list of priorities.

Following the death of Archduke Carl, the emperor's brothers, first Archduke Ernst and then in 1593 Archduke Maximilian, served as regents. Maria and William had wanted the regency for her, but they were unable to obtain it. During the five years of the two archdukes' government, the program for the restoration of Catholicism stalled, but neither did the Protestant estates make any advances. A certain deadlock was reached. The first meeting of the Styrian estates under Ernst, from January to March 1591, was dissolved without any result.[62] At their second meeting a year later, the estates did render formal homage to Ernst without his having to make any concessions to them on the religious issue.[63] A renewed threat from the Turks loomed to the east. Border raids in Croatia by the pasha of Bosnia grew in size and intensity in 1591 and 1592, until the Austrians soundly defeated the Turks at Sissek (Sisak) in Central Croatia on June 22, 1593, a victory that the Austrians were not able to capitalize on because of faulty organization and lack of supplies.[64] The pasha then declared war on the emperor, and there began the Long Turkish War, which continued until 1606. The Turks soon retook the fortress of Sissek. Meanwhile Ernst was called to head the government in the Netherlands, and Archduke Maximilian was named to replace him on September 6, 1593, but he arrived only in Graz early the next year. A minister in Graz, Hans Kobenzl, reported to Cardinal Pietro Aldobrandini in Rome, the papal nephew, that Maria would like to have been appointed regent, but that this would have incited *"gran disgusto."*[65] The new regent was overwhelmed by the situation, facing the danger in the east and having to deal with Protestant estates who did, in the perilous situation, pay homage to him. But they attacked the Catholic Church relentlessly. Emperor Rudolf had to convince him not to resign and to stay in the office until Ferdinand arrived from Ingolstadt.[66] Pope Clement VIII, responding to a letter from Maria, wrote to console and to strengthen her.[67]

---

[61] Duke William's Fürstenspiegel for Archduke Ferdinand, 1595, Hurter 3: 555–60.
[62] The estates of Carinthia and Carniola usually followed the lead of the Styrian estates.
[63] Hurter 2: 419; 3: 53–60.   [64] Rothenberg, 57–8.
[65] Hanns Kobenzl to Cardinal Pietro Aldobrandini (papal nephew), Sept. 4, 1593, *Nuntiaturberichte. Grazer Nuntiatur 3: Nuntiatur des Girolamo Portia und Korrespondenz des Hanns Kobenzl*, ed. Johannes Rainer (Vienna, 2001): 159 (p. 212).
[66] Hurter 3: 169–70, 174–5, 179, 199; Evelyne Webernig, "Der 'Dreizehnjährige Türkenkriege' (1593–1606) und seine Auswirkungen auf Kärnten," in *Katholische Reform und Gegenreformation in Innerösterreich*, ed. Franz M. Dolinar et al (Klagenfurt, 1994), 452.
[67] Clement VIII to Archduchess Maria, Aug. 27, 1594, *Grazer Nuntiatur 3*: #290, (p. 369).

Now seventeen years old, Ferdinand returned to Graz in late February 1595. The Styrian estates went out to meet him and accompanied him to his residence, as was the custom. Emperor Rudolf advised him not to attempt any changes until he reached his majority. But two position papers submitted to him urged rapid action to continue the restoration of Catholicism undertaken by his father.[68] Ferdinand followed the emperor's counsel. His mother had made trips to Bavaria and Innsbruck in 1593, probably to secure support for a petition that Rudolf move up the date for her son's majority, but her efforts met with no success.[69] Archduke Maximilian, who eagerly wanted to remove himself from the affairs of Graz, suggested that Ferdinand be named regent, for himself as it were, and this is what came to pass. On May 3, 1595, Ferdinand was installed as regent by Rudolf acting through commissioners dispatched to Graz for the purpose, on condition that he consult Archduke Maximilian on all significant decisions. Duke William wrote from Munich that now that Ferdinand was to assume the government, Ferdinand should no longer address him as his "subordinate" (*Untergebener*).[70]

Emperor Rudolf also named two figures to Ferdinand's privy council in Graz. Maximilian Schrattenbach, a relative of Balthasar, enjoyed the special favor of Archduchess Maria, holding the position of *Obristhofmeister* for her from 1596 to 1609 after serving briefly as *Landeshauptmann* (captain) of Styria from 1591 to 1593. Both he and his relative Balthasar stood firmly with the Catholic party at court. The second person appointed to the privy council by Rudolf, Siegmund Friedrich von Herberstein, also a Catholic from a family that supplied a number of its members to the service of the Habsburgs, held the post of captain of Styria from 1595 until his death in 1621. Bernhard von Herberstein took up the post of *Oberststallmeister* (Master of the Horse), also in 1595.[71]

Soon to enter Ferdinand's service, in 1597, was a figure quickly to become the minister on whom Ferdinand came most to rely until the minister's death in 1634, the twenty-nine-year-old Hans Ulrich von Eggenberg, a citizen of Graz whose father had held the post of mayor. He rapidly garnered the favor of Maria and of Ferdinand, who raised him and his cousins to the status of baron in 1598. *Obristhofmeister* of Ferdinand's wife, Maria Anna, from 1602, he also entered Ferdinand's privy council that year. Eggenberg had been born a Lutheran but converted some time during his youth. We know little about his early life except that he spent a year at the University of Tübingen in 1583, a university where Lutherans from Inner Austria frequently studied. Perhaps we can see in him, as in two of Ferdinand's Jesuit confessors, Bartholonew Viller and William Lamormaini, father figures for the young prince who lost his father at the age of twelve. Eggenberg undertook two diplomatic journeys to

---

[68] Hurter 3: 252–63.
[69] Hans Kobenzl to Cardinal Aldobrandini, Feb. 22, 1593, *Grazer Nuntiatur* 3: 93, (p. 139).
[70] Hurter 3: 290–2.   [71] Andritsch, 86–7.

Spain. In 1598–1599 he accompanied Archduchess Maria and her daughter Margaret to Madrid for the marriage of the latter to Philip III of Spain, and in 1605 he returned to Madrid apparently on a mission for Emperor Rudolf. Eggenberg acquired a taste for things Spanish, and copies of the first edition of Cervantes's *Don Quixote* and of the complete plays of Lope de Vega, annotated in Eggenberg's own hand, were found in the inventory of his library after his death. He subsequently built a magnificent Renaissance palace outside Graz that bears a clear resemblance to the Escorial and remains one of the showpieces of Graz up to the present day.[72] Spanish influence on Ferdinand's policies often was channeled through Eggenberg, who received many gifts from the King of Spain and in 1621 was received into the prestigious Order of the Golden Fleece.[73] But he was by no means a tool of the Spaniards.

Of the ecclesiastics at court, two bishops, Stobäus of Lavant and Brenner of Seckau, continued to wield considerable influence. In addition, unusually close to Ferdinand for a papal diplomat, stood the nuncio accredited to Graz from 1592 until 1607, Girolamo Count Portia. His role in the restoration of Catholicism, starting in 1598, may have been substantial even though he represented the cautious policy of Pope Clement. The pope assigned more weight to the Turkish threat and to the attacks on shipping in the upper Adriatic by the often rogue Uskoks from their port at Senj (Zengg) and recognized already in Ferdinand's zeal a tendency to the infringement of ecclesiastical jurisdiction.[74] Like Eggenberg and Ferdinand's confessor, the Jesuit Bartholomew Viller, Portia accompanied Ferdinand on his Italian journey in 1598. Of all his advisors, Viller probably exercised the greatest influence on the development of the prince's character and in his manner of rule. A native of Belgian Luxembourg born about 1541, he entered the Jesuits at Cologne in 1558, studied in Vienna from 1562 to 1566, and then was appointed rector of the college at Olmütz (Olomouc) in Moravia. From 1589 to 1596, he led the Austrian Province of the Jesuits as provincial and then the new university in Graz as rector for only two years, 1596 to 1597. He quickly won the heart of both Maria and Ferdinand, and he served as confessor to Ferdinand until he went to Vienna as emperor in 1619. Viller had a sense for the difficulties the prince faced as a ruler in an unusually complex situation, and Ferdinand hung on his advice. Already in

---

[72] Bireley 2, 17–18.
[73] Pavel Marek, "La diplomacis española y la papal en la corte imperial de Fernando II," *Studia Historica, Historia Moderna* 30 (2008): 121.
[74] *Nuntiaturberichte. Grazer Nuntiatur*, vol. 5: *Nuntiatur des Girolamo Portia (1599–1602)*, ed. Elisabeth Zingerle (Vienna, 2012), xi–xii, xxxviii–xxxix. For letters of Pope Clement to Ferdinand urging him to cease violations of church law, see *Epistolae ad Principes*, 3: *Sixtus V. Clemens V. (1585–1605)*, ed. Luigi Nanni and Tomislav Mrkonjiĉ (Vatican City, 1997), Clement to Ferdinand, Jul. 11,1602, and Feb. 15, and May 9, 1603, and Jan. 10, 1604, ##14451, 14602, 14709, and 14848.

a letter of January 27, 1597, to the superior general of the Jesuits in Rome, Claudio Acquaviva, Ferdinand referred to Viller as "my most valuable confessor."[75] Yet some Jesuits in Graz thought that Viller was too close to the court and too sympathetic to Habsburg interests. When it appeared that the Austrian provincial intended to move Viller from Graz, Archduchess Maria wept and Ferdinand made his displeasure very clear to Acquaviva. Viller remained.[76] He facilitated Ferdinand's marriage with his Bavarian cousin Maria Anna, a bond opposed by some at the Habsburg court but desired by his mother and Ferdinand himself, and he became her confessor as well. He also recommended the marriage of Ferdinand's sister, Margaret, to Philip III of Spain.[77]

By the end of the following year, 1596, the time approached for Ferdinand officially to be installed in his own right as the ruler of Inner Austria. As his guardians, Emperor Rudolf, Archduke Ferdinand, and Duke William of Bavaria summoned the Styrian estates. They all sent commissioners to represent them at the formal ceremony of Ferdinand's investiture. This took place first for Styria in Graz in December 1596, and it set the tone for the estates of Carinthia and Carniola. All parties recognized the significance of this first meeting of the Styrian estates with the new ruler. Emperor Rudolf instructed his commissioners to keep the religious issue off the table and to agree to nothing that might prejudice the rights of Ferdinand.[78] In the negotiations leading up to the act of homage or oath of allegiance *(Huldigung)* to be rendered by the estates, the young prince firmly and successfully resisted any discussion of religious matters until after the estates performed their act of allegiance. Afterwards he continued to refuse to take up the religious issues raised by the estates. So, in effect, he dismissed a Protestant interpretation of the Pacification of Bruck as part of the traditional rights and privileges of the estates, and implicitly he followed his father's position that Carl had not bound his successor by the Pacification.[79] Yet neither he nor the estates were ready for a confrontation at this time. For the moment, in practice Ferdinand still respected the concessions made to the Inner Austrian nobility in the Pacification. The estates for their part may have hopefully anticipated that this respect would continue; this may be one reason for their apparent satisfaction with his installation. Ferdinand's spokesman seems also to have implied that there would be an opportunity for discussion of religious matters after the oath of allegiance had been rendered.[80] Other reasons for the surprisingly easy submission of the estates may have been their awareness of the need for unity in the face of the Turkish threat, their fear of social upheaval heightened by peasant uprisings in Upper Austria from 1594 to 1597, and the aforementioned theology of suffering obedience[81]

---

[75] Cited in Andritsch, 104.   [76] Duhr, 38–43.   [77] Andritsch, 104–6.
[78] AKGGI, 1: xxxiii.   [79] Ibid., xxx–xlii.
[80] Verordneten von Steiermark an die von Kärnten und Krain, Dec. 13, 1596, AKGGI, 1: #303, (pp. 222–3); ibid., xl–xliii.
[81] Pörtner, 111–13.

Ferdinand certainly intended to restore Catholicism and believed that he acted well within his rights as ruler to do so. Had not the Peace of Augsburg conceded to princes the right to regulate religion in their territories? In doing so, it had greatly enhanced princely government, and Ferdinand in Inner Austria soon took advantage of this. Most German princes, Catholic or Protestant, at the time understood the religious welfare of their subjects to be a leading responsibility of a ruler; nor can this be written off as a mere subterfuge for the advancement of the prince's own power. Furthermore, many contemporary political thinkers like the widely read Giovanni Botero or Justus Lipsius – to be discussed later – took it as axiomatic that religious dissidence generated political unrest and upheaval, a view that experience had already confirmed for Ferdinand.[82]

The formal oath of allegiance took place on December 12. About eight in the morning, the representatives of the estates escorted the archduke to the castle church in Graz. After the service the archduke and the commissioners of the emperor and of the estates moved to the great hall across from the church. Ferdinand sat in a decorated and cushioned chair upon a stage, with his two younger brothers Maximilian Ernst and Leopold next to him, taking it all in. The various commissioners stood. The ceremony began with a formal exchange between the imperial commissioner and the estates' representatives in which the imperial commissioner referred to the event as a *conjugio* or marriage. Ferdinand then repeated the oath read to him that he would graciously not only acknowledge the "rights, liberties, and praiseworthy customs" of the estates but also protect them, and so at all times be "their gracious lord and ruler." A further oath was then administered to Ferdinand of similar content. He stood, and with bared head and upraised right hand, swore once again to uphold all the rights, liberties, and customs of the estates, "so God help us, and all his saints." A statement of allegiance was then read to the representatives of the estates, after which they together in a loud voice and with upraised right hand responded affirmatively. They thereby formally accepted Ferdinand as their ruler. The trumpet and drums sounded, and Ferdinand made his way among the estates representatives, shaking the hand of each individually.

All then returned to the church for a solemn Te Deum. Upon leaving the church, they proceeded to a formal breakfast banquet to which the prince invited all representatives of the estates. On Ferdinand's right sat his mother, Archduchess Maria, and to his left several of his brothers and sisters, including Archduke Leopold. Count Portia, the nuncio, was seated prominently. The festivities broke off for the Christmas holidays but then resumed with a dance on December 30 after which Ferdinand joined the estates for a meal in the Landhaus.[83] This concluded the meeting of the estates.

---

[82] See Robert Bireley, *The Counter-Reformation Prince: Anti-Machiavellianism or Catholic Statecraft in Early Modern Europe* (Chapel Hill, 1990), for Botero on religion, pp. 61–3, 70–1, 99, and for Lipsius, 88–91, 99, 231.
[83] *AF* 4: 1497–1551.

Similar ceremonies followed with the estates in Klagenfurt for Carinthia, where the estates swore allegiance on January 28, and in Ljubljana for Carniola on February 13, 1597. Ferdinand did not travel personally to the smaller units of Inner Austria to receive their oaths of allegiance, sending commissioners in his place. On February 28, Archduchess Maria wrote her brother Duke William in Munich that the acts of homage of the estates proceeded much more smoothly than anyone had expected.[84] Ferdinand had secured a major victory over the estates.

After his formal installation, Ferdinand became a sovereign ruler with only a moral obligation to the emperor as head of the house.[85] On June 1, an Instruction for [the Conduct of] Government was issued in his name. It followed largely that of his father, as well as similar instructions drawn up in Vienna in 1545 and in Innsbruck in 1551. The government *(Regierung)* was composed of the governor *(Statthalter)*, the chancellor, and eight councillors from the nobility and three with degrees in law. They served as the highest administrative and judicial body of Inner Austria. Ferdinand reserved all major decisions to himself. Here the first task of the government was to maintain and preserve all the rights and privileges of the House of Austria, a provision that manifested Ferdinand's devotion to the dynasty. Two significant changes from earlier instructions dealt with religion and with judicial procedure. With regard to religion, members of the government were to be Catholic, and their task of proceeding against heretics was emphasized more fully than in earlier instructions. As far as judicial procedure was concerned, cases involving the poor, widows, orphans, and prisoners were to be given precedence over other suits. Ferdinand wanted to make special provision for the marginalized.

Rules were also laid down for conflicts of interest. Councillors were not allowed to hear cases involving family members or others known to be their friends. A new Instruction for Government was drawn up in 1609 that modified the earlier one in some respects. The provision calling for the protection of the Catholic faith and the prosecution of heretics was considerably expanded and placed at the top of the Instruction, before the admonition that the government was to look to the protection of the rights and privileges of the House of Habsburg. This may represent a development in Ferdinand's thinking or perhaps more likely, an intent to impress his own thinking more emphatically on a document that had largely been received from his Habsburg predecessors.[86]

Meanwhile, Ferdinand along with Maria and her other children traveled to Prague. There they thanked Emperor Rudolf for his guardianship, and they reported on the woeful religious situation in Inner Austria. Only Ferdinand, his

---

[84] Archduchess Maria to Duke William, Feb. 28, 1596, *AKGGI*. 1: #313, (p. 228), and xlii.
[85] Thiel, 16.   [86] Ibid., 65–70; both Instructions are published in Thiel, 100–50.

family, and assorted courtiers had received Holy Communion the previous Easter in Graz. Subjects seemed to be taking the Dutch and the Swiss for their models. Ferdinand explained his plans for a religious reformation. Imperial councillors conceded that he possessed the right to carry this out, he reported, but they warned him not to provoke the Protestants. Another topic at the visit was marriages, first Ferdinand's prospective union with Maria Anna – his Bavarian cousin, daughter of Duke William and sister of Maximilian – a marriage that would confirm the ties between Graz and Munich. Secondly, there was the anticipated marriage of one of Ferdinand's sisters with the future Philip III of Spain, a project that had been under discussion since a recent visit to Graz of a Spanish representative with a painter in tow, with the purpose of gauging the attractiveness of three of Maria's daughters. This marriage, obviously, would connect Graz with the head of the Spanish branch of the Habsburg family. Rudolf entrusted Ferdinand, as he had his father, the late Archduke Carl, with the defense of the Croatian and Slovenian border areas, and that summer Ferdinand visited Kanisza (Nagykanisza) and other fortified towns and took measures to strengthen them. Ferdinand's representatives at the Diet of Regensburg in 1598 clashed with the representatives of the emperor over the distribution of imperial funds for defense against the Turks, the latter arguing that the greater threat was to Hungary rather than Croatia or Slavonia.[87]

In the months following the installation of Ferdinand, the government did undertake measures to place Catholic pastors in some towns, but they met stiff resistance in the Styrian towns of Aussee, Mitterndorf, and Radkersberg.[88] Only after Ferdinand's return from his journey to Italy the following year did the program of restoration pick up steam.

Apparently, a trip to Italy had long attracted Ferdinand. His journey south from April 22 to June 20, 1598, took on the character of both a pilgrimage and an informative sightseeing tour. The diary of the journey kept by his secretary, Peter Casal, constitutes the principal source for the trip. Casal noted at the start that nowadays even ordinary people – one thinks of the tours increasingly popular with the nobility – undertook tours of foreign countries; so much the more was it appropriate for princes to visit other lands, since this could greatly benefit them in the government of their own territory. Furthermore, the recent agreement between Pope Clement VIII and Cesare d'Este ceding the principality of Ferrara to the Papal States indicated that Italy would not be upset by war. But the trip also became a pilgrimage for which the archduke prepared by fasting; he visited churches and other holy sites, in particular the Holy House of Loreto, along the way, and Mass was celebrated daily. The present was the most suitable time to travel south, Ferdinand reasoned, before he became fully

---

[87] AF 4: 1552, 1717–18; Hurter 3: 385–7, 391–2.   [88] AF 4: 1552; Hurter 3: 399–403.

involved with the affairs of government and his status would require him to journey in the grand style of a prince. Initially, Ferdinand envisioned keeping the journey a secret and he himself traveling incognito. This proved to be impossible. Yet for the most part, he was able to keep a low profile and to avoid state receptions and other such occasions.

Altogether the traveling party consisted of about forty. Prominent among them, at least until they reached Ferrara, was the nuncio Count Portia, who was made to appear as the chief figure of the party for a time, in order to distract attention from Ferdinand. Balthasar von Schrattenbach, the *Obrishoftmeister*, and Bernhard von Herberstein, the *Oberststallmeister*, accompanied Ferdinand as did of course, the secretary Casal. Joining Ferdinand's entourage was also Giovanni Pietro de Pomis, a native of Lodi near Milan who after the death of his patron, Archduke Ferdinand in Innsbruck, was recruited by Archduchess Maria for Ferdinand's service as court painter, medalist, and architect, a position that he held until his death in 1633.[89] Among the five chamberlains (*Kammerherren*) who made the journey was Eggenberg, and the prince's confessor, Father Viller, came along as well. Altogether, they departed from Graz about midday on April 22. Ferdinand left the reins of government in the hands of his mother as regent.

The traveling party moved along in coaches and on horseback. Streams and rivers peaked at this time of year, and only by a near miracle did one of the group escape death when his horse was caught up by the current of the Sän river and swept downstream.[90] Late in the afternoon of April 28 the party arrived in Venice, a state with which Ferdinand was at odds over the regulation of trade in the Adriatic and over the jurisdiction of the Patriarchate of Aquileia, as we shall see. Casal does not tell us where they actually stayed. Ferdinand did not want to lose any time, according to Casal, and that first evening he and three others, including Schrattenbach and Herberstein, took a gondola to the piazza of San Marco and then to the Rialto Bridge, along the way admiring the magnificent *palazzi*. The next morning Ferdinand went to the Jesuit college for Mass, and then his entourage split into three groups for sightseeing. Ferdinand took in the Doge's Palace and St. Mark's Cathedral and then inspected the gold work and jewelry laid out for sale in the piazza.

The next three days were spent visiting the sights of Venice. An attempt was made, to some extent successful, to conceal Ferdinand's identity. The Venetian government, having heard that he was coming to Venice, had sent out a formal party to greet him before he entered the city; but it had returned without finding him. Eventually, Ferdinand was compelled to reveal himself, but the Venetians generally respected his desire for anonymity as he strolled about the city. They offered him a magnificent *palazzo* in which to stay, but the offer was declined.

---

[89] Gerard Marauschek, "Leben und Zeit," in *Der innerösterreische Hofkünstler Giovanni Pietro de Pomis*, ed. Kurt Woisetschlager (Graz, 1974), 15–18.
[90] Casal, 25–7.

He visited the glass works at Murano, where he made several purchases. Two senators subsequently took charge of shepherding him about the city. He attended a session of the Grand Council, where he was not clearly identified for the councillors, and he made a tour of the Arsenal and even walked about one of the ships. Normally, visitors were prohibited from entering either the Council or the Arsenal. Interested in music as he was and familiar with the Venetian tradition, Ferdinand also had an opportunity to hear Giovanni Gabrieli play the organ for him.[91] Another visit to Saint Mark's, this time with the senators, enabled him to see the cathedral treasures. At the evening meal, singers came to serenade him, keeping him up well beyond his bedtime, as Casal noted.

Nor did Ferdinand overlook the churches and convents. And he even had an opportunity to witness the annual ceremony, on Ascension Thursday, when the Doge threw a ring into the sea signifying the marriage between Venice and the Adriatic. All in all, Ferdinand took advantage of the opportunity to enjoy the sights of Venice and the hospitality of the Venetians despite political differences with them.[92]

On May 3, the party left Venice and traveled to Ferrara via Padua, where Ferdinand made a special point of visiting the tomb of St. Anthony. They arrived in Ferrara on May 9, the day after Pope Clement VIII formally entered the city in triumph after having won it back for incorporation into the Papal States. It was a time of great festivity in the city, twenty-seven cardinals having joined the pope for his entry into the city. That very evening Ferdinand dined with the pope in his palace, where he also lodged. Pope Clement told Ferdinand to keep his head covered during their meeting, a high honor. Ferdinand remained six days in Ferrara, until May 15. The second night a fire broke out in a section of the papal palace, apparently set off on the roof by fireworks celebrating the return of Ferrara to papal control; nearly forty people died in the tragedy. Altogether Ferdinand dined with Pope Clement at least four times and assisted several times at his Mass, and he even attended a consistory of the cardinals. In a letter to his mother, whom he wrote regularly during his tour, Ferdinand reported on the topics of his conversations with the pope: assistance for the campaign against the Turks; navigation in the Adriatic, an issue in which the pope shared the concerns of Ferdinand, and most importantly, the appointment of his twelve-year-old brother Leopold to the bishopric of Passau. This extensive ecclesiastical territory enjoyed jurisdiction over large areas of both eastern Bavaria and Lower Austria, and both the Wittelsbachs and the Habsburgs sought to control it. The death in 1598 of the incumbent, Urban von Trennbach, an active Catholic reformer, led to a conflict between the two houses that seriously threatened to cloud their relationship. Ferdinand and his mother were determined that it should be given, with a papal dispensation, to Leopold, and he did eventually obtain it that

---

[91] Federhofer, 54.   [92] Casal, 30–6.

September. But Ferdinand was impatient with the manner in which the pope spoke of the concern in Ferrara. Melchior Klesl, bishop of Wiener-Neustadt and a major figure at the court of Emperor Rudolf, had already lobbied with the pope in Rome for the appointment of the Habsburg candidate.[93] Pope Clement now kept reassuring Ferdinand that all would eventually go well for him while at the same time showing a reluctance to make a clear commitment in the matter. But overall, Ferdinand wrote, he could not adequately describe "the friendly and even confidential manner in which His Holiness spoke with me." He also told of rewarding conversations with the two Aldobrandini papal nephews and with Cardinal Cesare Baronius, the church historian and close adviser of Clement. Interestingly, he seems to have discussed with the pope only briefly his plans to expel Protestants from Inner Austria and to restore Catholicism there. Two years later, the pope reminded him that during their conversations in Ferrara he had lauded his zeal but also discouraged him from undertaking an unduly ambitious program at this time.[94] This initiative had been decided long ago and certainly did not stem from the pope. At their parting Clement declared to Ferdinand, "I wish that Your Highness may become the most prominent prince in the world," to which Ferdinand responded, "That I do not desire, Holy Father; I wish only to arrive at the point, that I can in many ways be of service to Your Holiness and the Roman See."[95]

The entourage continued through the Papal States via Rimini to Loreto whither the Holy House, which the Holy Family had inhabited, had allegedly been transported by angels during the Middle Ages. Only Rome surpassed it in Italy as a goal of pilgrimage. Ferdinand lodged here with the papal governor, carried out his devotions – the chapel was cleared in order to give him privacy – and seems to have witnessed an exorcism. Casal does not mention it in his diary nor is there other evidence for an event recounted by Lamormaini, Ferdinand's later confessor, in his *Virtues of Emperor Ferdinand II* published in 1638, the year after Ferdinand's death. According to Lamormaini, while in Loreto Ferdinand vowed to God, under the patronage of the Blessed Virgin Mary, to drive the Protestants out of Inner Austria and to restore Catholicism there.[96] This vow became a part of the legend surrounding Ferdinand as is evident, for example, from a representation of the event in an illustrated manuscript dating from the 1670s.[97]

---

[93] JohannRainer, "Der Prozess gegen Cardinal Klesl," *Römische Historische Mitteilungen* 5 (1962): 45.

[94] Ferdinand to Maria, Ferrara, May 14, 1598, Hurter 3: 579–81; Cardinal San Giorgio (Cinzio Aldobrandini) to Portia, Rome, Oct. 7, 1600, *Nuntiatur des Girolamo Portia (1599–1602)*, ed. Zingerle, #164.1 (pp.397–8). The two nephews of Pope Clement, Cinzio and Pietro Aldobrandini, conducted the affairs of the secretariat of state during his pontificate.

[95] Casal, 44–52, quote on p. 52.   [96] *Virtutes*, 4.

[97] An incomplete, beautifully illustrated manuscript in the Newberry Library, Chicago, Wing Ms, fzw 1.696, supposedly a copy of Ms. 12800 in the Nationalbibliothek, Vienna, entitled "Theatrum Austriacum seu Virtutum Austriacorum principum Compendium concinnatum" (1696?) attributed to the Jesuit Andreas Paur, tutor of the future Emperor Charles VI, contains

One is inclined to accept Lamormaini's claim, given the vigor with which Ferdinand took up this project after his return to Graz. But the vow only confirmed a resolution that Ferdinand had already taken to continue the work of his father.

Rome was finally reached on the evening of May 24. Ferdinand and several of the entourage rode ahead of the rest, arriving in the city between eight and nine in the evening and taking up residence in the Jesuit novitiate San Andrea near the papal palace of the Quirinal; they sought out the Jesuit house in order to avoid the ceremonies and formalities that a sojourn in the papal residence would have demanded, especially a formal exchange of visits with many cardinals. Ferdinand and his party spent the following days visiting the various churches in Rome, including St. Paul's, St. Mary Major, and the new St Peter's, which was then still under construction, and viewing relics. Crowds often followed them because they could then view objects which were generally closed to the public but were now made available to Ferdinand. A tour of the papal apartments was also on the agenda; Pope Clement had not yet returned to Rome. Ferdinand also paid a visit to the Jesuit superior general Claudio Acquaviva, to express his firm desire to retain Father Viller as his confessor and a readiness to appeal to the pope should Acquaviva decide otherwise.[98] Both the German College, where priests were educated and prepared for work in Germany, and the Roman College, the Jesuit university in Rome, merited visits from Ferdinand; nor did he pass up a tour of the magnificent new church of the Jesuits, il Gesù, constructed for them by Cardinal Alessandro Farnese. On their way out of the city on May 30, after a stay of only five days, they stopped briefly at the city gate to see Santa Maria del Popolo.[99] To his mother Ferdinand related from Rome that Bavarian agents continued actively to work to secure Passau, but he had confidence in the word of the pope and Cardinal Aldobrandini in Ferrara. "If they deceive me, then I'll never trust any priest in the world." He hoped to return home as scheduled, but he might be a few days late, he alerted his mother. Certainly she would not be angry at this. "I have seen so many beautiful things here, especially holy shrines and churches, the like of which I'll not see the rest of my life. It is all worth the expense."[100] Apart from the Capitol and its museums as well as the Coliseum, the classical remains in Rome apparently did not much attract the young prince.

---

an illustration of Ferdinand's vow to extirpate heresy in the Austrian lands allegedly made at Loreto in 1598 along with an extensive citation from Lamormaini's *Virtutes*. I am grateful to Professor Howard Louthan of the University of Florida for calling my attention to this manuscript.

[98] Andritsch, 106   [99] Casal, 61–7.
[100] Ferdinand to Maria, Rome, May 29, 1598, Hurter 3: 581–5; on Ferdinand's visit to Rome see also Elisabeth Garms-Cornides, "Assenza e non presenza. Gli Asburgo a Roma tra Cinque e Seicento," *Gli archivi della Santa Sede e il mondo asburgico nella prima età moderna*, ed. Matteo Sanfilippo, Alexander Koller, and Giovanni Pizzorusso (Viterbo, 2004), 125–8.

Shortly before the departure from Rome on May 30, a courier arrived with an invitation from the Grand Duke of Tuscany to visit Florence, and so the party next headed there, passing through Siena en route and often taking their meals at hostels along the way. In Siena, two fellow students from Ingolstadt came to pay Ferdinand their respects. The Grand Duke respected Ferdinand's desire to travel incognito as much as this was possible. Upon his arrival on June 4, when the Grand Duke came out to meet him, he entered the city not by a main gate but by an auxiliary gate that opened on to a path that led directly to the Palazzo Pitti, where the archduke's party was lodged. The next four days Ferdinand was treated to secular entertainments of various sorts in a way that he had not been elsewhere on his tour: concerts, comedies, dances, and acrobatics, a highlight of which was a performance of Giovan Battista Guarini's recently composed pastorale, "Il Pastor Fido." We do not know directly how Ferdinand appreciated these but as we shall see, he was always fond of music. Casal's enthusiasm for the performances as well as for the tours of the Medici treasures, paintings, precious stones, tapestries, and books perhaps echoed Ferdinand's own. But the religious sights of the city were not overlooked. Ferdinand visited the churches, including Saint Lawrence, where his aunt, the archduchess Johanna, youngest daughter of Ferdinand I and wife of Grand Duke Francesco was buried, as well as the Jesuit college, and he stood as godfather for the grand duke's recently born son at his solemn baptism.[101]

The last days of the tour featured stops in the papal city of Bologna as well as in the Mantua of the Gonzagas, and then as the party continued north it passed through Trent, Bozen, and Brixen. Finally, they arrived back in Graz on June 28, having been gone slightly more than two months. Ferdinand had satisfied his desire to see something of the world of Italy and to visit the holy sites there. Now it was time to direct his full attention to the task of government. First to be dealt with were the Protestants in Inner Austria. Johannes Kepler, the astronomer then teaching at the Protestant school in Graz, expressed in a letter to a friend the fearful anticipation of Ferdinand's return among the Protestants in the city.[102]

---

[101] Casal, 71–9. [102] Franzl, 57.

Chapter 2

Early Years in Inner Austria, 1598–1608

Kepler's foreboding did not deceive him. Ferdinand returned from Italy in late June 1598 more determined than ever to proceed with his program to restore Catholicism in Inner Austria. As we have noted, he probably took a vow to this effect during his visit to the shrine of Our Lady of Loreto. Ferdinand had tended in this direction since his early years. Archduke Carl, regretful of his agreement to the Pacification of Bruck, had in his testament of 1584 urged his son to take measures to restore the faith, and Archduchess Maria regularly pushed him to take action against the Protestants. His confrontation with the Inner Austrian estates over the religious issue – especially between September, 1598, and April, 1599 – crucially affected his political development. As was generally the case during the early modern period, religious and constitutional issues were inextricably intertwined. But other matters also called for his attention during the first years of his government, his marriage to Maria Anna of Bavaria and events on the frontier with the Turks. They seized the Croatian fortress of Kanisza on October 20, 1600, after a long siege which brought them within 125 miles of Graz. Hostilities along the border with the Turks continually threatened Inner Austria.

In the first year of Ferdinand's reign, Protestants had resisted his efforts to introduce religious changes and they had harassed Catholics. Religious tensions ran high. When in 1596 Ferdinand attempted to impose a Catholic pastor on the Upper Styrian parish of Mitterndorf, a parish of which he was the patron, the government's commissioners found their way into the church blocked by a large mob come together from the whole region who had sworn to withstand them even with their lives. The commissioners were compelled to retreat amidst a hail of insults, and a couple of soldiers accompanying them were wounded.[1]

---

[1] *AF* 4: 1552.

Later a government party encountered similar resistance in the Styrian city of Radkersburg. At the pilgrimage shrine of Maria Saal in Carinthia, Lutherans mixed in with the pious Catholics and during services started to whistle and shout. They even raised the skirts of the devout girls and young women. The papal nuncio in Graz, Girolamo Portia, did not escape. On a journey to Bavaria, he stopped, unknowingly, overnight in an inn in Eisenerz, a Styrian mining town valuable to Ferdinand as a source of revenue but also firmly committed to its evangelical pastor. Once the rumor spread that a papist was spending a night in the inn, a crowd gathered and began to grow nasty. The innkeeper's assurance that his guest was only "a gentleman from Italy" did not calm them, and he had to distract them with healthy drafts of drink. The next day the nuncio slipped out of town at the first light of dawn. But it was not only the Protestants who stirred up trouble. Students at the Jesuit college in Graz pitched stones at the Protestant pastor and in their way disrupted his services.[2]

The incident that paved the way for Ferdinand's decisive action started with Lorenz Sonnabenter, a former Jesuit student who had served as a tutor to the archduke's brothers. Whether the course of events had been planned ahead of time is impossible to say. In early 1598, Ferdinand saw to the appointment of Sonnabenter as pastor of the parish in Graz. Shortly thereafter, on August 13, Sonnabenter complained to the Protestant superintendent in Graz that the Protestant ministers there encroached on his ministry as pastor.[3] Strictly speaking, he did have the Pacification of Bruck, as Catholics understood it, on his side. When the superintendent's response did not satisfy him, Sonnabenter directed a letter on August 22 to the committee representing the estates that the Protestant ministers in Graz be dismissed and their ministry ended.[4]

Ferdinand now felt compelled to take action. Archduchess Maria, his confessor Father Viller, and possibly nuncio Portia all advocated vigorous measures against the Protestants, whereas his other councillors urged caution in the face of a possible rebellion at a time when the situation was so tense. But the two bishops, Stobäus and Brenner, probably exerted the greatest influence on him at this time, more so than the Jesuits.[5] And it was to Stobäus to whom Ferdinand now turned for a written assessment of the measures to be taken.

Stobäus then in a long position paper came down on the side of the same gradualism that had emerged from the Munich Conference back in 1579. Rejected were the views of the "politicians" who argued that the struggle with the Turks meant that one could not also move against the Protestants. They exaggerated the strength of the Protestants, and was it not possible that the advance of the Turks came as God's punishment for failure to check the Protestants? Vigorous measures such as imprisonment or torture showed zeal

---

[2] Franzl, 58–60.   [3] Pörtner, 118
[4] Ibid. The committee representing the estates were the Verordneten; they remained in Graz when the estates were not in session.
[5] Hugo Hantsch, *Die Geschichte Österreichs* 1, 4 ed. (Graz, 1959), 297.

but little understanding, and would only stir determined opposition. On the other hand, mildness and religious conferences, experience showed, produced little in the way of positive results. First of all, Ferdinand ought to allow only Catholics in the administrative positions of the territory and the cities, and he then should not accept any new Protestants into the Inner Austrian nobility who dominated the estates. He should endeavor to provide his people with good government, such as justice in the courts and measures against inflation; this would render them more amenable to religious change. One ought not challenge all elements of the population at once: nobles, burgers, peasants, preachers; that too would stimulate resistance. Better to start with the preachers, especially those in Graz, the "disturbers of the peace," who, Stobäus predicted correctly, would yield without much of a fight; they were cowards. The burgers and peasants would come to their senses once the preachers were driven out. But as a precaution, Ferdinand should see to it that soldiers were stationed in Graz.[6]

Ferdinand, then, in a decree dated September 13, closed the Protestant schools and churches in Graz, Judenberg, and all the other cities and towns of Styria, Carinthia, and Carniola, and he ordered all the Protestant preachers and school teachers to leave the territories within fourteen days. He took this measure, he claimed, on his own initiative (*ex proprio motu*), so not as a response to Sonnabenter's protest. His own conscience[7] prompted him to take action. As "archduke of Austria and as hereditary prince in Styria, as overseer (*Vogt*) and feudal lord of this parish [Graz], and as general overseer of all ecclesiastical foundations in his hereditary lands," he had no other choice. A special privilege granted to the house of Austria as well as the Religious Peace of Augsburg also empowered him to take this measure.[8] He appealed to both. The decree stated clearly that Ferdinand was taking action out of religious considerations, namely, to satisfy his own conscience. At the same time, he claimed as ruler in Inner Austria extensive rights over the Church in his territories. A meeting of the full estates scheduled for early November was postponed by the government until after the Epiphany. To the protest of the committee of the estates and their threat of resistance in the matter, Ferdinand responded forcefully on September 23 that they had no effective say in the matter, and that he intended to stand by what he owed "to the Almighty God, the whole of Christendom, and his own conscience." He took ill their implication that he had acted not on his own initiative but at the seductive urging of unreasonable people, presumably his mother, the papal nuncio, the bishops, and the Jesuits and their application of the phrase "the only [church] leading to salvation" to

---

[6] Stobäus to Ferdinand, Lavant, Sept. 13, 1598, Georg Stobaeus von Palmburg, *Epistolae ad Diversos* (Venice, 1749), 16–20 (accessed through the Münchener Digitalisierungs-Zentrum of the Bayerische Staatsbibliothek). This letter is summarized in AKGGI 1: #434 (p. 297), where it is more accurately dated Aug. 21 according to Pörtner, p. 119, n.32, and in Franzl, 61–2.

[7] "zu salvierung ihres Gewissens"   [8] AKGGI 1: #450 (pp. 309–10).

their own confession in opposition to the "old, true, Christian, Catholic religion," in which all their forefathers had lived and died. The committee would be considered rebels and enemies of the fatherland should they attempt to hold up the payment of taxes and so the provision of the soldiers fighting on the front against the Turks. Nor did they have any right to summon the full estates on their own.[9] There followed that same day another decree commanding the Protestant preachers and teachers in Graz to cease their activities immediately and to leave Ferdinand's territories within eight days.[10]

Further protests of the committee of the estates proved fruitless. The government had in the meantime summoned soldiers, many of them Italians or Spaniards, to protect the archduke's residence and to guard the city gates; others were stationed in the city. According to his own account, the vice-chancellor notified the *Landeshauptmann* of Styria early on September 25 that Ferdinand would stand firm and that it would not be wise for the preachers to continue their ministry. That day Ferdinand issued a statement that he could not take responsibility for any concessions "before Almighty God, his strict judgment seat, and all the saints."[11] When the preachers and teachers hesitated to leave and seemed to organize resistance, on September 28 Ferdinand ordered them to depart Graz that same day before sundown and the rest of his territories within eight days, and at the same time he directed a long defense of his actions to an expanded committee of the estates who had assembled in Graz. Some points he repeated, for example, that he acted on his own initiative and not at the urging of Jesuits or other foreigners. Though he was still young, he could make decisions. He recalled for them that at their recognition of him as ruler, he had made no concessions on religion. Nor was he burdening their conscience. To be sure, he was prohibiting the exercise of their faith in many ways. But he was not compelling them to worship or believe in any particular way. They still possessed freedom of conscience to believe what they wanted to believe. So, presumably, he distinguished his measures from those of the Inquisition. In the terms of the day, he still permitted the nobility freedom of conscience if not of worship. Furthermore, their own ministers claimed that in emergencies laymen could preach and administer the sacraments as well as bury the dead. He reminded them of all that the House of Austria had done on their behalf, especially with regard to protection from the Turks. It was for the honor of God and their own temporal and eternal welfare that he issued the decrees that he did. They would, he hoped, be faithful to their obligations both to their ruler and to the fatherland.[12]

The next day the nineteen Protestant preachers and teachers departed from Graz. This struck a powerful blow against Protestant forces throughout Inner

---

[9] Ibid., #457 (pp. 321–4). [10] Ibid., #459 (pp. 324–5).
[11] Wolfgang Jöchlinger an den Landeshauptmann, Graz, Sept. 25, 1598, Ibid., #464 (pp. 330–1); Resolution of Archduke Ferdinand, Sept. 25, 1598, ibid. #465 (pp. 332–3).
[12] Resolution of Archduke Ferdinand, Sept. 28, 1598, ibid. #474 (pp. 346–54).

Early Years in Inner Austria, 1598–1608

Austria as it eliminated their institutional center in the residential city of the archduke. The whole event played out quietly, with no sign of rebellion or unrest.[13] Lamormaini in his *Virtues of Emperor Ferdinand II* called it "a deed worthy of immortal memory" that Ferdinand carried off through his constancy and his confidence in God. When the quiet departure of the ministers was told him, according to Lamormaini, Ferdinand exclaimed in the words of the Psalm, "Not to us, O Lord, not to us but to your name [belongs] the glory," and he immediately returned to his room, knelt down, and humbly gave thanks to God.[14] The outcome exercised a powerful effect on the young ruler.

He had acted against the advice of his councillors, who had warned him of the resistance that his action would provoke, and taken the counsel of those who urged vigorous action and confidence in God. He would not forget this lesson. The next day Archduchess Maria, with a large entourage, left Graz accompanying her daughter Margaret to Madrid, where she was to marry the future Philip III of Spain. Indeed, Philip II had died on September 15. During her long journey to Spain via Italy – she did not return to Graz until mid-August – Maria dispatched a total of forty-six letters to her son. In her first letter from the castle of Leibniz, a day's journey from Graz and the residence of Bishop Brenner of Seckau, she reported a long conversation with the bishop who encouraged them not to yield to fear and who hoped to talk with Ferdinand soon about the coming meeting of the estates.[15] Meanwhile, the Protestant church and school in Judenburg and Ljubljana were closed down on October 8 and 22 respectively, and their preachers and teachers expelled.[16]

For the remainder of the fall, the committee of the estates continued to register protests and Ferdinand to reject them. Attention gradually concentrated on the meeting of the Styrian estates that was scheduled for Graz on January 10, 1599. Ferdinand had prohibited the three estates from holding a joint meeting, so the estates of Carinthia and Carniola also met after the first of the year, but a little later than the Styrian estates. The various estates regularly communicated. The Styrian estates sought relief from Emperor Rudolf in Prague and help from the Upper and Lower Austrian estates, but with no measurable success. At one point Ferdinand took exception to a parenthetical phrase in a communication from the committee of the estates requesting that the soldiers stationed in Graz be removed; the threat of a tumult among the common folk did not justify their presence. The committee referred to a distinctive "*absolutum imperium*" enjoyed by the Styrian estates.[17] In his negative response, Ferdinand requested an explanation of their use of the term

---

[13] Franzl, 63; Pörtner, 122.   [14] *Virtues*. 48–9.
[15] Maria to Ferdinand, Leibniz, Sept. 30, 1598, in Friedrich von Hurter, *Bild einer christlichen Fürstin. Maria, Erzherzogin zu Österreich, Herzogin von Bayern* (Schaffhausen, 1860), 178.
[16] AKGGI 1: lix
[17] Committee of the estates to Ferdinand, Oct. 26, 1598, AKGGI 1: #515 (pp. 386–7.)

absolutum imperium.[18] Archduchess Maria wrote Ferdinand in this context that he ask the estates how they understand the phrase the *plenum imperium* that was normally attributed to princes.[19] So the constitutional issue came clearly to the fore. Maria regularly asked for information about the preachers, and on the eve of the convocation of the estates in Graz, she encouraged her son "not to be intimidated and to show them your teeth."[20]

The long-awaited meeting of the Styrian estates convened in Graz on January 10. Delegates from the estates of Carinthia and Carniola arrived shortly thereafter. Ferdinand, in the proposition that he laid before them, did not touch upon religious or constitutional issues; he restricted himself to military and political matters, explaining the necessity that they vote subsidies in order to confront the constant threat from the Turks as the war with them persisted.[21] The resistance of the estates proved determined at first, and Ferdinand turned to Bishop Stobäus for advice. Stobäus, in a vigorous position paper, encouraged Ferdinand to stand firm and to avoid temporizing. As "vicar" and "minister of God" he had been summoned to restore Catholicism in his lands. A major rebellion was not to be expected. Stobäus appealed to the example of Constantine and other early Christian emperors, thus combining his sense of Ferdinand's vocation with the ancient imperial tradition. Ferdinand's authority came from God. Heresy by its very nature generated unrest and rebellion, and experience showed that a plurality of faith usually resulted in political instability. In fact, the threat of the estates to withhold the contributions necessary for defense against the Turks demonstrated this.[22] The bishop had made a strong case.

But Ferdinand proceeded cautiously, and eventually he won, even though he waited until late July to respond formally to the remonstrances of the estates.[23] At first the two parties continued to spar with each other. Emperor Rudolph refused to take any action. Ferdinand continued with further Counter-Reformation measures, such as the requirement that all students attend Jesuit schools and that no one be admitted to citizenship, much less to an office in a town, without first undergoing an examination by the pastor. Finally, in mid-May the Styrian estates granted the subsidies, to be sure with some conditions, and they were followed in the early summer by the other two estates.[24] Several reasons contributed to their surrender. The continued advance of the

---

[18] Ferdinand to the committee of the estates, Oct. 28, 1598, ibid. #520 (p. 392.)
[19] Maria to Ferdinand, Moscholenzo (Italy), Nov. 7, 1598, ibid. #539 (. p. 399–400).
[20] Maria to Ferdinand, Milan, Jan. 25, 1599, Hurter, *Bild einer christlichen Fürstin*, #24, (p. 233)
[21] Government proposition for the Styrian estates, Jan. 11, 1599, AKGGI 1: #614 (p. 444).
[22] Stobäus to Ferdinand, n.d, Stobaeus, *Epistolae ad Diversos*, 75–85. Pörtner, 122–3, summarizes this communication and dates it between March 12 and April 30, 1599.
[23] Ferdinand's response was dated April 30 but probably was not made public until July 21; see AKGGI 1: #731 (pp. 559–60).
[24] AKGGI 1: lxix–lxx; Styrian estates to Ferdinand, May 15, 1599, summarized, ibid. #746 (p. 573). According to the long position paper submitted by the combined estates on Feb. 24, 1600, they agreed to a grant of 190,000 gulden; see Ibid., #946 (p. 737).

Turks rendered the military situation more and more threatening. Moreover, should they continue their resistance, the Inner Austrian nobility would lose their positions in the imperial army, and Italian and Spanish troops would be brought in to fight the Turks as well as to hold the Protestants in check. So events had unfolded in Upper and Lower Austria in the 1590s.[25]

Ferdinand only made public his answer to the response of the Styrian estates on July 21, after the estates had returned home, even though it was dated April 30. His unbending and eloquent statement of his position has been called the "magna carta" of the Counter Reformation in Inner Austria.[26] He began with the accusation that they sinned when they addressed him, their ruler, in hot, immoderate, sharp, and irritating words. They benefitted the Turks, and that other enemy, the Venetians, when they refused to vote subsidies for the government. Nor did this group speak for all the estates since they excluded from their number the prelates, who traditionally made up the first estate, and most Catholics. Ferdinand made a revealing statement when he claimed that he had undertaken his reformation of religion at the inspiration of the Holy Spirit. This was clearly his belief, and it brought into the discussion Ferdinand's belief in a divine mission. Moreover, he possessed an *absolutum et merum imperium* in his territory, not an *imperium modificatum* as they had implied. His father, Archduke Carl, had wanted to reverse the Pacification of Bruck, and he had left this commission to his son. Ferdinand had made no commitment to them when they recognized him as their ruler. The Protestants had violated the Pacification in many ways by their vilification of the pope and the Catholic clergy, their attacks on Catholic churches, and their pressure on Catholic peasants to worship in Protestant churches. Ferdinand was required by virtue of his office to protect the church, the clergy, and church property. As did King David, to whom Ferdinand compared himself, he trusted in God to defend him from all his enemies, the first of whom were the Turks. All human help had failed. Furthermore, he was confident that all would stand together, Catholic and Protestant, when their country and Empire were endangered, putting the common good before all other considerations.[27]

Exchanges continued in the following weeks between Ferdinand and the committee of the Styrian estates, especially regarding the conditions stipulated by the estates. In response to a sharp protest of the estates against his declaration of July 21, Ferdinand stated clearly once again that he had undertaken the reform of religion out of "the inspiration of God the Holy Spirit, to the honor of the Most Holy, and out of an upright, burning zeal, for the consolation and temporal and eternal welfare of the non-Catholics, his seduced countrymen and subjects, as they will be required to stand before God's judgment seat.

---

[25] Pörtner, 123–4.
[26] Hans Sturmberger, *Kaiser Ferdinand II und das Problem des Absolutismus*, (Vienna, 1957), 18. Österreich Archiv
[27] Hurter 4: 496–522; summarized in AKGGI 1: #731 (pp. 559–60).

He would not allow himself to be diverted from this intention by any human being, and he intended to persevere in it into his grave." He ordered the committee to desist from its protests and conditions,[28] and he continued to press forward with implementation of his decrees. On August 18, 1599, a fine of 5,000 ducats was imposed on Achaz Count Thurn for harboring a preacher in his castle of Kreuz and allowing him to preach, and the preacher himself was to be imprisoned.[29] Nobles were permitted to practice their Protestant faith but not to maintain preachers for that purpose. Two months later, government soldiers seized the Protestant Stiftskirche in Graz when the committee of the estates refused to hand it over.[30] By mid-October the new reformation commissions began to operate in Styria, as we shall see. The Styrian Protestant estates meeting in Graz in January 1600 drew up a detailed protest against the advance of the Counter Reformation, but with little effect.[31]

Only on February 24, 1600, did the combined estates of Styria, Carinthia, and Carniola meeting in Graz respond formally to Ferdinand's declaration of the previous July 21. Their tone was restrained, even obsequious, as they appealed to the traditional mildness of Habsburg rule. The Augsburg Confession was now a "Christian confession that led to salvation," not the "only confession that led to salvation." They rejected many of the charges against them such as the accusation that their refusal to cooperate with the prince aided the Turks and the Venetians. They denied that they had ever called Ferdinand a *modificatum principem*, a term completely unfamiliar to them; they acknowledged him as their "natural hereditary prince... an absolute prince." But they argued that both he, at the time of their formal acceptance of him as prince, and his father, Archduke Carl in the Pacification of Bruck, had conceded to the Protestant nobility the privilege of worshiping on their own lands and in the four cities of Graz, Judenburg, Klagenfurt, and Ljubljana. Furthermore, their grant of subsidies two years before had been conditioned on the prince's respect for these privileges. The activity of the reformation commissions now underway could only be construed as forcing consciences. At the end of their long declaration, they appealed humbly to the prince's fatherly care that he act so as to maintain the desired harmony between the ruler and the estates.[32] But it was all to no avail. That summer, at the end of July, all 150 non-Catholic male inhabitants of Graz were compelled to leave the city. Kepler was one of them.[33]

Ferdinand had now established himself as an absolute prince in Inner Austria, but not in the sense that he eliminated the estates. That was never the case in the Habsburg lands. He would still have to negotiate with them

---

[28] Ferdinand to the Styrian committee of the estates, Jul. 25, 1599, AKGGI, 1: #787 (p. 593-4)
[29] Ferdinand to Achaz Count Thurn, Eisenerz, Aug. 18, 1599, ibid., #799 (pp. 597-8).
[30] Ibid., #821 (pp. 605-6).
[31] Protestant estates to Ferdinand, Jan. 19, 1600, ibid. #908 (pp. 678-89).
[32] Protestant estates to Ferdinand, Feb. 24, 1600, ibid., #946 (pp. 721-51).   [33] Franzl, 69.

especially over taxes which they collected, he would depend upon them for administration of their lands, and he would respect what he considered their legitimate privileges. But he had shown once and for all that he clearly held the upper hand.

Meanwhile, in mid-October of 1599 Ferdinand had inaugurated a new series of reformation commissions that continued through 1600. The reformation commission developed out of the age-old practice of the ecclesiastical visitation with more participation of the government; it was already in use in other territories. Usually a prelate led the commission, accompanied by a privy councillor, perhaps a treasury councillor, a secretary, and a military captain with two to three hundred soldiers to be called upon if necessary to intimidate the populace or defend the commissioners. Upon arriving in a town or village, the commission first dismissed the Protestant preacher if he still remained. The parish community was then summoned, and the bishop undertook a series of instructions on the benefits of the Catholic faith, the evils of Lutheranism, and the advantages of conversion. Non-Catholics were then granted a period of time, usually a month, to decide whether to convert. If they chose not to do so, they were liable to exile, a choice not usually granted peasants, however. The commission then installed a Catholic pastor, and entrusted the village school to him. It checked on the state of the church building and parish finances, and it laid down regulations for services and for conduct, for example, the observance of Sundays and holy days. In a few cases, soldiers destroyed Protestant churches and desecrated their cemeteries.[34]

The first commission, under the leadership of the abbot of Admont, targeted the mining town of Eisenerz, which had previously defied the government's efforts. This time, however, the presence of nearly 500 soldiers accompanying the commission convinced the locals to abandon their plans for armed resistance. The keys to the church were handed over and a Catholic service was held there. The commissioners recommended leniency toward those who had planned to resist, lest harshness stir up a rebellion.[35] The next commission, led by Bishop Brenner of Seckau, took aim at another town that had successfully resisted the reformation of religion, Radkersburg. Here a force of nearly 200 marched on the town in the night of December 16–17, 1599; they needed to summon 500 more troops in order to keep the towns-people in check. A force of 150 troops was left in the town to keep order after the bishop completed his instruction of the people. The lack of competent

---

[34] Leopold Schuster, *Fürstbischof Martin Brenner: Ein Charakterbild aus dem steierischen Reformations-Geschichte* (Graz, 1898), 198, 422–56; Rudolf K. Höfer, "Bischof Martin Brenner als Gegenreformator und katholischer Reformer," *Katholische Reform und Gegenreformation in Innerösterreich 1564–1628*, ed. France Dolinar, Maximilian Liebmann, Helmut Rumpler, and Luigi Tavano (Graz, 1994), 27–35.

[35] Pörtner, 159–60.

priests to take over the parishes returned to the church, among other things, limited the effectiveness of the commissions.[36]

The reformation of religion in Inner Austria undertaken anew by Ferdinand in 1598 would continue in the coming decades. First, Lutheran educational and ecclesiastical institutions had been suppressed and the Protestant elite expelled. External conformity was imposed, and manifestations of heresy severely punished. It is estimated that about 11,000 people left the territory, willingly or unwillingly, between 1598 and 1605.[37] At the same time there began an extensive, determined effort at the Catholic evangelization of the population, a process that in the long run bore considerable fruit, and in which the Jesuits and Capuchins played a major role. The Jesuit university in Graz enrolled 1,200 students in 1619, with several new structures added to accommodate them.[38] Ferdinand founded three Jesuit colleges in Inner Austria, in Ljubljana, Klagenfurt, and Gorizia (Görz). These and other colleges that he helped to support were primarily for the education of youth, but they also served, with their churches, as centers of pastoral activity. On August 8, 1600, 10,000 Lutheran books went up in smoke in a fire in Graz that could be seen from miles away.[39] On the spot of the blaze, the foundation stone for the first of two dozen Capuchin convents in Inner Austria was laid; for the attached Antoniuskirche dedicated two years later, de Pomis created the dominant painting over the high altar, later called "the Apotheosis of the Counter Reformation," celebrating Ferdinand's victory over the Protestants. The Capuchins proved to be highly effective with a broad range of the population.[40] But there long remained pockets of resistance in the form of underground Protestantism (*Geheimprotestantismus*).[41]

During these first years of his rule, a personal matter called for Ferdinand's attention – his marriage – and this was, of course, in the days of dynastic alliances, when marriages were also very much a political matter. During his visits to Munich while a student at Ingolstadt, he had come to know his cousin, Maria Anna, daughter of Duke William and sister of Maximilian, who by 1596 was gradually assuming the responsibility for government in Munich. Though

---

[36] Ibid., 165–6, 188.
[37] Othmar Pickl, "Glaubenskampf und Türkenkriege in ihren Auswirkungen auf das Siedlungswesen und die Bevölkerungsstruktur des österreichischen Länder," *Siedlungs-und Bevölkerungsgeschichte Österreichs* (Vienna, 1974), 98. Institut für Österreichkunde.
[38] Bernhard Duhr, *Geschichte der Jesuiten in den Ländern deutscher Zunge* 2: 1 (Freiburg, 1913): 333–4.
[39] Franz Popelka, *Geschichte der Stadt Graz* 1 (Graz, 1959): 109.
[40] Karl Ammon, "Innerösterreich," in *Die Territorien des Reiches im Zeitalter der Reformation und Konfessionalisierung*, 1: *Der Südosten*, ed. Anton Schindling and Walter Ziegler (Münster, 1989), 114.
[41] Cf. Gustv Reingrabner, *Protestanten in Österreich. Geschichte und Dokumentation* (Vienna, 1981).

Maria had been born three and one-half years before him, displayed a weak constitution, and seemed to be unattractive physically, Ferdinand developed an inclination toward her, an inclination that his mother Maria encouraged also because it would further the bond between the Habsburgs and the Wittelsbachs. In July, 1597, Ferdinand promised Duke William that he would marry Maria Anna. Later that year he traveled to Prague to request permission of Emperor Rudolf for the marriage, which was not forthcoming until October 25, 1598, and in December, 1597, he had dispatched his confessor, Viller, to Rome to secure the necessary dispensation from Pope Clement VIII.[42] Viller, for his part, initially had some reservations about the marriage, for which he incurred the severe displeasure of Duke William. These were based on the delicate health and the alleged unattractiveness of the bride. Of the five sons of Emperor Maximilian, three never married: Emperor Rudolf, Archduke Ernst, and Archduke Maximilian, who assumed rule in Innsbruck of Anterior Austria and the Tyrol after the death of Archduke Ferdinand in 1595 and who also held the position of Grand Master of the Teutonic Knights. The other two, Matthias and Albert, co-ruler of the Spanish Netherlands since 1598 with his wife Isabella, married only later in life and never produced any children. For the future of the dynasty, Maria Anna had to be able to bear children. Furthermore, a lack of physical beauty could in the long run lead to alienation of the two spouses, as one saw often enough in princely marriages.[43]

There then erupted a conflict between the two houses that briefly muddied their relationship. It had to do with the appointment to the rich, extensive prince-bishopric of Passau, which lay between Bavaria and Habsburg Upper Austria and whose ecclesiastical jurisdiction stretched all the way to the outskirts of Vienna. Both Duke William and his sister Archduchess Maria wished to provide adequately for their children. William planned to secure Passau for his son, Philip William, now twenty-one, who had been entrusted with the bishopric of Regensburg when he was three years old; Archduchess Maria looked to Passau for her twelve-year-old Leopold, who already had been named prince-bishop of Strasbourg. Both parties pursued their goals zealously, and at the end of 1597, the cathedral chapter divided evenly between the two candidates for the coadjutorship of Bishop Urban von Trennbach. This left the decision up to Pope Clement VIII. As we have seen, Ferdinand raised the issue with the pope during his visit to Ferrara in May, 1598, and received assurances from Clement. The pope then did deliver for the Habsburgs. But the Wittelsbachs in Munich took his decision hard. William got over it more readily than did Maximilian who, after the death of his agent in Rome that same year,

---

[42] Hurter, *Bild einer christlichen Fürstin*, 338–40; Albrecht 2, 153–4. Whether Viller made a special trip to Rome in late 1597 to obtain this dispensation or whether he secured it when he accompanied Ferdinand on his Italian trip the following spring is not clear.

[43] Bernhard Duhr, *Die Jesuiten an den deutschen Fürstenhöfen des 16. Jahrhunderts* (Freiburg, 1901), 47–50.

did not replace him until 1605 as a sign of his disapproval of the pope's action.[44] In 1602, Ferdinand, for his part, once he learned that Maximilian was pursuing a benefice in Magdeburg for the duke's brother, the elector of Cologne, informed his cousin that he would give up his plan to seek it for his brother, Archduke Carl.[45]

Gradually the waters calmed. Archduchess Maria stayed two weeks in Munich in August 1599, and in October, Maximilian von Schrattenbach and Bishop Brenner journeyed to Munich to conduct the negotiations that led up to the formal marriage agreement. The wedding was scheduled for the following April 23. Maximilian accompanied Maria to Graz with his wife Elisabeth, his brother Albrecht and sister Magdelena, and an entourage of 698 persons.[46] Great efforts went into the preparation for the wedding. An architect was brought from Mantua to oversee the decorations in the city where an arch was constructed for the bride. The court church was richly decorated. Musicians came from Milan. The municipal guard were outfitted in new uniforms. Ferdinand and his three brothers, Maximilian Ernst, Leopold, and Carl – along with members of the estates – rode out a half mile to receive Archduke Matthias, who arrived as representative of his brother, Emperor Rudolf. The king of Poland, the duke of Mantua, the prince-bishop of Bamberg, and the Republic of Venice all sent representatives. Stobäus, bishop of Lavant, preached, emphasizing the benefits for the common good of all Christendom of this union of the Catholic Houses of Habsburg and Wittelsbach. Unfortunately, a dispute over precedence at the wedding banquet between Cardinal Franz von Dietrichstein, bishop of Olmütz, the papal legate who presided at the Mass, and Archduke Matthias delayed the start of the service until after noon, so that the party did not sit down to breakfast until after two in the afternoon and the evening meal had to be cancelled. Dancing continued until after midnight, and the festivities lasted through the following week, concluded by a drama performed by the students of the Jesuit college.[47] The marriage turned out to be a happy one. The two developed an affectionate bond. Maria Anna resembled her aunt and mother-in-law Archduchess Maria in her piety but not in her activity, preferring to stay out of politics and to remain in the background. She bore Ferdinand seven children, including the future Ferdinand III, before her early death in 1616.

Even during periods of formal peace, raids by Turkish troops and skirmishes continued along the borders with the Ottoman Empire in Croatia and

---

[44] Albrecht 2, 136–8.
[45] Ferdinand to Maximilian, May 11, 1602, *Wittelsbacher Briefe aus den Jahren 1590–1610* 5, ed. Felix Stieve (Munich, 1891): #244,(p. 101). Abhandlungen der Phil.- Hist. Klasse der Bayerischen Akademie der Wissenschaften.
[46] Albrecht 2, 154.
[47] Franzl, 76–82; Hurter, *Bild einer christlichen Fürstin*, 339–43; AF 5: 2197–2205.

Early Years in Inner Austria, 1598–1608

Hungary. Defenses along the border were often allowed to deteriorate. In April 1592, Hasan Pascha of Bosnia mounted an invasion of Croatia that surpassed the scale of the normal raid. Encountering minimal opposition, he occupied large swaths of territory. Hasan fell the next year in an unsuccessful siege of the Croatian fortress of Sissek. But shortly afterwards, on August 13, 1593, the Turks declared war on the Empire, setting off the Long Turkish War that would last until 1606. The Turks then took Sissek as they moved forward, and the following year they seized the fortress of Györ (Raab) in Hungary, to the north. To the west, Styria and Carinthia were in danger. After he assumed his regency in Inner Austria, Ferdinand succeeded in raising troops that enjoyed modest success along the borders, and in 1597 Emperor Rudolf charged him with the defense of the Croatian-Slavonian border as he had his father, Archduke Carl. Pleas for assistance from the emperor and the diet met with little success, so that the Inner Austrian lands bore most of the expenses for defense precisely at the time when Ferdinand vied with the estates over his religious program and taxation. On October 20, 1600, the crucial fortress of Kanisza in Lower Hungary fell to the Turks after a siege of forty-four days. The fortress had been poorly supplied, and eventually the Hungarian troops went over to the Turks. Subsequently, the imperial commander was executed in Prague. The loss of this fortress left "a pistol pointed at the heart of Styria." The youthful Ferdinand burned to take the field himself as commander of the army that was to retake Kanisza.[48] It was the one time that he ventured to lead troops personally into battle, and it was to prove a tragedy. As soon as he received news of the fall of the fortress, he began to seek assistance, money, and troops from Philip III of Spain and Pope Clement VIII as well as from the Inner Austrian estates. On August 23, 1601, after a solemn Mass in St. Ægidius in Graz, the nuncio presented Ferdinand with a banner, and prayers were ordered to be said in all the churches of Inner Austria throughout the campaign. Before his departure, Ferdinand drew up a testament. He named his brother Maximilian Ernst regent in case of his death, and he explicitly instructed him to continue the reform of religion. Six weeks later when in camp, after he learned that his wife Maria Anna was pregnant, he named as guardians of an anticipated son, Maximilian Ernst, his mother Maria, and his wife Maria Anna, all to be subject to directives of Emperor Rudolf. In a further codicil added at the same time, he instructed the guardians to protect the fathers of the Society of Jesus and to allow them to keep all that he had given them.[49]

Ferdinand's army then assembled at Radkersburg, 23,000 infantry and 4,000 cavalry, with Vincenzo Gonzaga of Mantua as general under Ferdinand. Delays in funding from the estates held up the operation. The war council advised

---

[48] Rill, 102–3.
[49] Hurter 4: 372–3. In fact, Ferdinand's first child, Christine, was born on May 25, 1601 and died the following June 12. So if Maria Anna had been pregnant, she would have been very early in her pregnancy. Ferdinand's second child, Johann Carl, was not born until 1605.

waiting for troops coming down from up near Győr and from Transylvania to join with Ferdinand's forces. But the papal nephew, Gian Francesco Aldobrandini, commander of the papal troops, insisted that they march immediately for Kanisza, and Ferdinand was unwilling to oppose him. Indeed, he trusted unduly in his general. By September 9, the advance troops of the expedition appeared before Kanisza. But the swampy terrain and the early onset of winter weather greatly hindered operations. By the end of September, 500 men had died from hunger and exposure, and the soldiers did not receive adequate payment to enable them to purchase food. On October 18, Ferdinand's troops stormed the fortress, in vain when the bridge that they had constructed over the swamp land collapsed. In mid-November, further troops arrived from Győr, but the night of November 15, it was later reported, was so cold and the wind so sharp, that the following morning 1,500 soldiers and 500 horses lay dead. Snow buried the field and winds knocked over the sentries. Retreat was the only possible course. The army withdrew, abandoning its artillery, siege material, and 14,000 muskets. Six thousand wounded and sick were left on the battlefield, to be subsequently beheaded by the Turks, and the returning soldiers brought the plague with them. Ferdinand remained crestfallen and silent for a long time, until a table companion told him that it was the weather, not the enemy, that had defeated him.[50] Bishop Stobäus, for his part, who had opposed the assault on Kanisza, saw the hand of providence at work. He congratulated Ferdinand on bearing his misfortune with "Austrian magnanimity." "The outcome of a war and victory lies not in the power of man but in the judgment of the divine spirit that assigns victory to whom and when he will," he consoled him. Ferdinand had demonstrated to the whole world his commitment to the *Respublica Christiana* even to the point of risking his life.[51] Gradually, the archduke recovered his good spirits. But he never again took to the battlefield himself, and he learned to select more competent generals.

Shortness of funds and their inadequate management certainly contributed to the disaster at Kanisza. Ferdinand seems never to have learned the importance of finances for successful government. This was in contrast to his cousin Maximilian of Bavaria, who early on grasped their importance, kept track of every penny, and maintained a substantial *aerarium* or secret fund that enabled him to avoid financial disaster throughout the long Thirty Years War. Later Maximilian would regularly complain about the loose, careless management of funds and the enrichment of courtiers in Vienna. Lamormaini in his *Virtues of Emperor Ferdinand II* admitted the emperor's lack of a sense for money and recognized the complaints about his excessive largesse to the church, the military, and his councillors. Yet he reminded his readers that

---

[50] Ibid., 380–1; Rill, 102–4.
[51] Stobäus to Ferdinand, undated, Stobaeus, *Epistolæ Diversae*, 108–9; Stobäus to Joannes Kesselius, undated, 101–2; see also Stobäus to Bartholomew Viller, Graz, Nov. 7, 1601, Ibid., 106–7.

the retention of competent councillors and generals required money.[52] For a prince, Ferdinand always maintained a modest life style personally.

Fortunately for Ferdinand, the Turks did not follow up their success at Kanisza, and the principal scene of the war shifted north to Székesfehérvár (Stuhlweissenberg) in Hungary, where the emperor's troops gained a significant victory at nearly the same time as the failed siege at Kanisza, only to lose the city to the Turks the following year. In 1603, a major offensive of the Shah of Persia against the Ottomans at the other end of their empire relieved the pressure on the imperial forces in Croatia and Hungary, and as a result of the Persian War the Turks lost interest in the contest for a few fortresses in Hungary.[53] That same year a thirteen-year-old came to the throne in Istanbul, thus weakening the government.

The center of conflict now shifted to the principality of Transylvania. The rule of the unstable Catholic Sigismund Báthory, briefly the husband of Ferdinand's sister, Maria Christierna, had come to an end in 1602. Four religions were represented there: Catholics, Lutherans, Calvinists, Orthodox, plus a handful of Anti-Trinitarians. Emperor Rudolf now sought to subject Transylvania to his control and to implement a rigorous policy of Counter Reformation. His general, Giorgio Basta, behaved ruthlessly with the population and plundered lands of Protestant magnates, including those of the Calvinist István Bocskay, up to that point a supporter of the Habsburgs. Bocskay himself journeyed to Prague in order to seek redress, but he was not able to secure an audience with either Rudolf or one of his ministers. Upon his return home, Bocskay was acclaimed prince of Transylvania on February 22, 1605 and two months later as ruler of Hungary by the nobles of Upper Hungary; he refused to take the title of king. Shortly thereafter the sultan entrusted him with Transylvania and Hungary as fiefs of the Turks. Both were in revolt against the Habsburgs. That summer hostilities spilled over into the eastern portion of Styria. Once again in 1605, Ferdinand's efforts at defense were slowed by reluctant estates. He asked for help from his cousin Maximilian in Munich, but the Bavarian responded that he could do no more and that he needed to protect Bavaria while expressing his displeasure with Rudolf's campaign against the Protestants in Hungary, which only served to stir up the German Protestants.[54] But the imperial general, the Belgian Johann Count Tilly, defeated the enemy forces decisively in December. Already a veteran of the wars in the Netherlands, he was to figure prominently in the Thirty Years War.[55]

---

[52] Robert Bireley, "The Image of Ferdinand II (1619–1637) in William Lamormaini, S.J.'s *Ferdinandi II Imperatoris Romanorum Virtutes* (1638)," *Archivum Historicum Societatis Jesu* 78 (2009), 128–9.
[53] Rill, 106.   [54] *Wittelsbacher Briefe* 6 (1892):17–20.
[55] Evelyne Webernig, "Der 'Dreizehnjährige Türkenkriege' (1593–1606) und seine Auswirkungen auf Kärnten," in *Katholische Reform und Gegenreformation in Kärnten*, ed. Franz M. Dolinar et al (Klagenfurt, 1994), 457.

The situation in Hungary alarmed Rudolf's brothers, Archdukes Matthias, Maximilian, and Albert, as well as Ferdinand, all of whom had begun to question Rudolf's ability to govern. In April 1605, Matthias, Maximilian, and Ferdinand – along with Maximilian Ernest, Ferdinand's next oldest brother – had convened at Linz and then journeyed to Prague. There, on May 28, they finally persuaded a reluctant Rudolf to name his brother Matthias commander of imperial troops in Hungary and to empower him to negotiate with Bocskay. Later that year, on October 22, Rudolf authorized Matthias to enter into talks with the Turks. So began the negotiations that would lead to the important treaties of Vienna and Zsitvatorok the following year. But the Turks and Bocskay continued to advance. Archduke Matthias had few cards to play. Bocskay's representatives arrived in Vienna in 1606 to begin negotiations with the archduke. From the start they made it clear that they would require that the emperor also make peace with Istanbul. Without the concession of religious freedom to the Hungarians, Matthias realized that no agreement would be possible so he yielded on this point even though both Emperor Rudolf and his own councillor, Melchior Klesl, bishop of Vienna, warned him that by doing so he endangered his salvation, and both the new Pope Paul V and Philip III of Spain opposed the concessions. The Hungarian magnates, the free and royal cities, as well as the soldiers in the military, all received religious freedom. But Catholic churches and clergy were not to be seized or persecuted. The Hungarians offered Matthias the crown but when Rudolf objected, he agreed to become only the emperor's representative in the kingdom but with full royal power. Only Hungarians were to serve as royal officials, and they were also to occupy all the fortresses of the kingdom without respect for religion. Bocskay was recognized as prince of Transylvania. The Treaty of Vienna was then concluded on June 23, 1606. Negotiations between the emperor and the Turks began in Buda in December, 1605, when it was agreed that the sultan would give up his claim to superiority and recognize the emperor as an equal. The talks were then moved to Zsitvatorok on the Danube and concluded on November 11, 1606. The possession of territory was to be restored to its status at the start of the war, in 1593, and whether the emperor or the sultan possessed suzerainty over Hungary was left undecided. The peace was to last for twenty years. The Treaty of Zsitvatorok, which would be subsequently regularly renewed, provided more or less for peace and stability to his southeast for Ferdinand, so he could focus his attention and energy on the Protestants in Germany during the looming Thirty Years War.[56] Yet the Turks remained a persistent threat and the southeast an area of serious concern.

Intertwined with the Long Turkish War at its end was the conflict known as the *Brüderzwist* (Brothers' Quarrel) between Emperor Rudolf and his brother

---

[56] Rill, 117–20.

Archduke Matthias, younger by five years and at the time governor of Upper and Lower Austria. Rudolf's other surviving brothers – Archduke Ernst had died in 1595 – Archduke Maximilian, Governor of the Tyrol and Anterior Austria since 1595, and Archduke Albert all had a part in the affair, as did Ferdinand. Albert for a time envisioned for himself the position of king of the Romans and then the imperial succession, and he enjoyed the support of the ecclesiastical electors and periodically that of Rudolf, but he did not promote himself aggressively.[57] Only Ferdinand had by this time produced a legitimate male heir, and this fact had major implications for the succession in the Habsburg lands as well as in the Empire. Intelligent but politically inept and notoriously indecisive, Rudolf had begun to show signs of melancholy and mental illness early on. Famous as a Maecenas, he assembled at his court in Prague a large coterie of painters, philosophers, scientists, writers, magicians, and charlatans.[58] Most of his time and energy he devoted to their activities; he himself never produced anything. For long periods of time he would withdraw from political business, but he resented any action that seemed to diminish his authority. For years he dabbled with various proposals for marriage but he never took a wife, and he refused to discuss any plans for the succession. His situation had deteriorated significantly starting in 1600. At that time the astronomer and astrologer Tycho Brahe predicted his death at the hand of a monk, and he became more of a recluse. That summer Matthias visited him in Prague, to urge Rudolf to propose him for election as king of the Romans, and so recognize him as his successor to the imperial title. Rudolf rejected this proposal and peremptorily dismissed two of his chief ministers because they had supported this move.[59] The succession was at stake.

In October Matthias met with Ferdinand and Maximilian in the small town of Schottwein about half way between Graz and Vienna, thus avoiding the curious eyes of Prague, to discuss the situation.[60] Should Rudolf die without a clear successor in the Empire, the Lutheran elector of Saxony and the Calvinist elector of the Palatinate, according to the imperial constitution, would serve as imperial vicars until an election could be held, and it was not a far reach that a Protestant emperor would be chosen. Philip III of Spain instructed his ambassador in Prague to take every possible measure to secure the election of a king of the Romans. The king realized that in order to maintain Spain's position in Europe, and especially in the Netherlands

---

[57] Luc Duerloo, *Dynasty and Piety: Archduke Albert (1598–1621) and Habsburg Political Culture in an Age of Religious War* (Farnham, 2012), 210, 237, 248–51, 255–6, 259–61. Often but not always election to the kingship of the Romans during the tenure of the current emperor preceded subsequent election to the imperial office.

[58] See R.J.W. Evans, *Rudolf II and His World: A Study in Intellectual History, 1576–1612* (Oxford, 1973).

[59] Rill, 122–3.

[60] Joseph Hirn, *Erzherzog Maximilian. Der Deutschmeister, Regent von Tirol*, ed. Heinrich Notflatscher (Bozen, 1981) 2: 371–2; Hurter 5:77.

and in Italy, Spain needed firm Habsburg leadership in Bohemia and in the Empire. On November 22, 1601, Pope Clement VIII wrote a letter in his own hand to Rudolf imploring him to propose a candidate for king of the Romans. The emperor responded by refusing to receive papal or Spanish emissaries in audience. Matthias and Archduke Maximilian journeyed once again, separately, to Prague but without any success. Rudolf then unpredictably initiated the Counter- Reformation measures in Hungary that incited the Bocskay rebellion.[61]

Archdukes Maximilian and Ferdinand met with Matthias in Linz in April, 1605, as we have seen. They hoped to take joint action to resolve the impasse. Together they journeyed to Prague, despite Rudolf's prohibition of the trip, with the intent of convincing Rudolf to marry and to appoint Matthias governor in Hungary. On their arrival May 5, Rudolf received them in a gracious manner but then declined to speak with them for a week. He did agree at this point to appoint Matthias governor in Hungary and to allow him to negotiate with Bocskay. But Ferdinand could not secure a private audience to discuss his own interests. Another trip to Prague in December 1605 by the three archdukes brought no significant progress on the succession. They also encouraged the imperial electors to take action. By this time the negotiations with the Hungarians and the Turks towards the Treaties of Vienna and Zsitvatorok of 1606 were under way. Rudolf, to be sure, confirmed these, as have we seen, but reluctantly and with secret reservations.

Matthias now seized an initiative. He summoned Archdukes Maximilian, Ferdinand, and Ferdinand's brother Maximilian Ernst to Vienna in order to follow up on the meeting at Linz the previous year. There at Matthias's behest, they came to a secret agreement on April 25, 1606, that after declaring Rudolf incompetent to govern named Matthias head of the family as well as Rudolf's successor in Upper and Lower Austria and in Hungary and Bohemia, and called for his election as king of the Romans. Rudolf would remain emperor and could reside either in Prague or Linz. If Rudolf refused, they would resort to force. Matthias would confirm the two treaties of Vienna and Zsitvatorok then being negotiated about which Rudolf still hesitated, and he would marry, without Rudolf's permission. The archdukes determined to seek the support of the pope and the king of Spain as well as the Catholic electors and princes of the Empire for this arrangement. Archduke Albert, in the Netherlands, reluctantly signed on to the agreement on November 11.[62]

Ferdinand had signed this agreement without enthusiasm, claiming that he wanted to prevent any rumors that he now pursued the succession for himself, and he insisted upon its being kept secret. He told neither his confessor nor

---

[61] Rill, 124–5.
[62] BA 5: 847–54; the text of this agreement is in Joseph Hammer-Purgstall, *Khlesl's, des Cardinals, Directors des geheimen Cabinetes Kaisers Matthias, Leben* 1 (Vienna, 1847): #177 (pp. 427–8); Duerloo, 210–11, 262–3.

Duke William about it.[63] When he returned to Graz, his mother had severe reservations regarding it, fearing that the attachment to Matthias might prejudice Ferdinand's further advancement. She convinced Ferdinand not to send an emissary to Spain, as Matthias had requested, to notify Philip III of the agreement of Vienna. Archduke Maximilian also wavered in his commitment to the agreement. Rudolf now became active in his own defense, inviting the electors of Mainz and Cologne to send delegates to Prague for talks. He even intimated that he would prefer Archduke Leopold, Ferdinand's brother, as his successor. Matthias would have had greater support from the estates of the Habsburg territories had he made concessions on religion more quickly, concessions which his minister Klesl still opposed.[64]

Rudolf then on August 6, 1606, summoned a diet for Regensburg that did not actually convene until January, 1608. This diet would introduce Ferdinand to the broader stage of the Empire when Rudolf subsequently named him his commissioner for the meeting of the estates. Rudolf intended in the first place that the diet provide further funding for defense against the Turks; he remained determined to campaign against them and to bolster defenses even after the Treaty of Zsitvatorok. But a diet meant that all the controversial issues between Catholics and Protestants regarding the interpretation of the Peace of Augsburg of 1555 would once again come up for debate. This settlement had brought peace to an Empire tired of conflict after the upheaval of the Reformation and then the War of the League of Schmalkeld. It legalized two confessions within the Empire, the Catholic and the Lutheran, as laid out in the Confession of Augsburg of 1530. Princes were henceforth to have the right to determine which of the two confessions was to prevail in their territories. The confessional situation was frozen in the imperial cities as it existed in 1552, that is, with either Catholicism or Lutheranism or both permitted. Territorial church lands – those subject to the authority of a prince or city – that had been seized by the Protestants up to that time were surrendered on condition that no more be seized. With regard to imperial church lands – the ecclesiastical states subject directly to the Empire – it was agreed, according to the Ecclesiastical Reservation, that should a prelate go over to Protestantism, he would have to forfeit his territory and all the privileges that went with it. This provision was meant to protect especially the widespread ecclesiastical church lands in west and northwest Germany, in particular the three electorates Mainz, Trier, and Cologne.

Negotiators of the Peace of Augsburg, despairing of complete agreement, had left some provisions vague, and each confession soon developed its own norm of interpretation of the Peace. The Protestant party understood the Peace to establish parity between the two confessions. The Catholics, on the other

[63] Hurter 5: 95.   [64] BA 5: 853–73.

hand, considered the concessions to the Protestants to be exceptions to the general law of the Empire that in no way established equality between the two parties. To their mind, any differences were to be settled according to traditional canon and imperial law. Three points of difference stood out. The Catholics had ceded territorial church lands secularized prior to the Peace. But could not a Protestant prince on the basis of his right to determine the religion of his territory confiscate church lands subject to his jurisdiction and located within his territory? Invoking this argument, the Protestants had seized many territorial church lands after the Peace. They also contended that they had not agreed to the Ecclesiastical Reservation, and even if they had, what was to be done when a cathedral chapter elected a Protestant prince-archbishop or prince-bishop? Thirdly, who was to interpret the Confession of Augsburg? A number of German territories had gone over to Calvinism but still claimed not to have overstepped the bounds of the Peace.

Out of the ambiguities of the Peace of Augsburg, there gradually emerged conflicts that helped to produce the Thirty Years War. In the 1580s, after the generation that concluded the Peace had passed from the scene, divergent interpretations of the Peace provoked first prolonged litigation, then political conflict, and finally military confrontation. Both sides became more militant. The Palatinate, after going Calvinist in 1559, took the lead of an aggressive party that often split from a more conservative Lutheran party led by Electoral Saxony. In 1583, when the Archbishop-Elector of Cologne announced that he intended to convert to Protestantism and to retain his territory, Duke William of Bavaria, encouraged by Rome and with the help of Spanish troops from the Netherlands, intervened decisively and so prevented the electorate from going Protestant with the result that the Protestants would obtain a four-to-three majority in the electoral college and then probably elect a Protestant emperor. The militant Protestant party refused to accept the authority of the two imperial courts, the Imperial Court Council (*Reichshofrat*) in Vienna and the Imperial Cameral Council (*Reichskammergericht*) in Speyer, so that the legal system was brought to a state of paralysis. The diet became more contentious and threatened to become paralyzed too, with the Palatinate party refusing to recognize the majority principle in religious matters. The Diet of 1603 voted generous funds for the war against the Turks but it failed to make progress on the religious issues.

Then in the course of 1607, the affair of the small imperial city of Donauworth greatly increased tensions. There a minority of Catholics had begun to revive processions in 1605 and 1606. Protestants, illegally, disrupted them without city authorities intervening. The Catholics took their case to the Imperial Court Council, whose jurisdiction over the case was contested in any event. The court imposed the unusual penalty of the imperial ban on the city, and instead of entrusting the execution of the penalty to the Swabian Circle or administrative district as should have been the case, it called upon Maximilian of Bavaria to carry it out. His forces marched into the city on December 17, 1607. In lieu of payment for the expenses of the military operation, Maximilian then occupied the city and eventually incorporated it into Bavaria. This alleged grab of Donauworth in late 1607 greatly upset the Protestants on the eve of the diet.

Why did Rudolf elect Ferdinand to be his commissioner at the Diet of Regensburg of 1608 instead of his brother, Matthias, who had filled this role at earlier diets? Because he resented Matthias's efforts to compel him to take steps to arrange the succession and had come to hate his brother. He may also have realized that Ferdinand, who by now had fathered several children, represented the future of the dynasty rather than any of his childless brothers. Rumors circulated that Rudolf's selection of Ferdinand signaled that he intended to propose him rather than Matthias as king of Romans and so to exclude Matthias from the succession.[65] The Protestants were not happy with the choice of Ferdinand, whose implementation of the Counter Reformation in Inner Austria scared them, but Rudolf may have settled on him because the emperor now considered Ferdinand's firm stance on religious issues to be more congenial. Electoral Saxony at first opposed the appointment, and he was supported by Johann Schweikard von Kronberg, as of 1606 the new archbishop-elector of Mainz who tended towards composition or an understanding with the Protestants. Cologne remained noncommittal. But once the appointment had become public, it would have been difficult to reverse it. Saxony did eventually come around to accepting Ferdinand, promising to have his commissioner work with him in Regensburg.[66] The nuncio in Prague, Antonio Caetano, reported from sources at court that the emperor had required Ferdinand to promise not to raise the issue of the succession at the diet and that he had assigned Ferdinand several associates without whose agreement he could do nothing.[67] Because the emperor did not attend himself, neither did most of the princes, who instead sent commissioners to represent them.

Ferdinand himself appears at first to have been reluctant to serve as Rudolf's commissioner.[68] He took his task seriously. As imperial commissioner, he knew that he had to appear in style and entertain lavishly. More than 400 persons accompanied him to Regensburg, among them Balthasar von Schrattenbach and Father Viller. Eleven hundred and thirty-seven barrels of wine were brought from Austria, as well as tuna fish and oysters from the seacoast.

---

[65] Franzl, 111; according to the nuncio in Prague, a secret deal was rumored between the imperial councillor, Andreas Hannewald, and Archduchess Maria. Hannewald's wife, in a visit to Graz on an alleged pilgrimage, offered on behalf of her husband a firm hope of Rudolf's making Ferdinand king of the Romans in exchange for a proper reward. Maria suggested as her reward a castle worth 150,000 talers as soon as Ferdinand was elected, Antonio Caetano to Cardinal Scipione Borghese, secretary of state, Prague, Jan. 7, 1608, *Antonii Caetani, Nuntii Apostolici apud Imperatorem Epistolae et Acta 1607–1611*, ed. Milena Linhartová 2 (Prague, 1937): #11 (pp. 16–17).

[66] Caetano to Borghese, Prague, Sept. 17, 1606, ibid. 1 (Prague, 1932): #135 (pp. 178–9).

[67] Caetano to Borghese, Sept. 24 and Oct. 15, 1607, ibid, #152 (p. 194) and #187 (p. 232).

[68] Borghese to Caetano, Rome, Aug. 4, 1607, ibid., #64b (p. 94).

The entourage with its accouterments needed eight hundred 800 horses and twenty-eight heavy wagons for transport. The party left Graz on November 13, 1607, and after a stop in Passau to visit Archduke Leopold, arrived in Regensburg on November 28. There several imperial councillors awaited Ferdinand, including Andreas von Hannewald, a confident of Rudolf, and Leopold von Stralendorf, both of whom had had a hand in the Donauworth affair. Rudolf had sent them to assist Ferdinand at Regensburg.[69] Ferdinand communicated regularly throughout the diet with the court in Prague. At the request of the emperor, Pope Paul V did not send an official representative to the diet as was normally the case, neither a legate nor the nuncio in Prague, Antonio Caetano. Rudolf and many Catholic princes feared that a papal representative would only raise the hackles of the Protestants and render it more difficult still to obtain funds for defense against the Turks. The pope instead dispatched to Regensburg as a papal agent Felice Milensio, a former superior general of the Order of the Hermits of St. Augustine. His instructions called for him to keep a low profile, maintain contact with Catholic princes, and report all the information that he could gather to Cardinal Scipione Borghese, the papal nephew in Rome.[70] A second papal agent at the diet, Johannes de Riccio – Caetano's auditor, who brought to Ferdinand a papal brief encouraging him to stand firm in the cause of religion – reported from Regensburg early in the diet that matters were going well. Ferdinand had received him most courteously shortly after the agent's arrival.[71] The German humanist Caspar Schoppe, who after converting from Protestantism, had made a name for himself in Rome as a Counter-Reformation polemicist, offered to serve as a papal agent in Regensburg, but Paul V, who had little use for him, would not hear of it.[72] But he did travel to the diet.

Ferdinand faced a daunting task in Regensburg, apart from his unpopularity with the Protestants from the start. Rudolf wanted above all to secure funds from the estates to support 24,000 troops for the campaign in the east. Ferdinand presented the main points of the imperial proposition, "with great feeling" according to Milensio,[73] at the opening of the convention on January 12 and came down strongly on this note. The same day, Ferdinand wrote Maximilian of Bavaria asking for his support in the matter.[74] But the Protestant party led by the Palatinate would not approve these funds unless the Catholics made concessions on the interpretation of the Religious Peace. The Palatinate delegates later insisted that they would not submit to majority decisions in the

---

[69] Ritter 2: 225; Franzl, 112–3.
[70] Caetano to Borghese, Dec. 31, 1607, *Epistolae et Acta*, #293 (p. 381).
[71] Caetano to Borghese, Jan. 21, 1608, ibid., 2 (Prague, 1937): ##28, 29 (pp. 44–6, 46).
[72] Borghese to Caetano, Dec. 22, 1607, ibid., 1: # 279 (p. 363).
[73] Milensio to Borghese, Regensburg, Jan. 23, 1608, ibid., 2: #3 (appendix) (p. 387).
[74] Ritter 2: 224; BA 6: #27 (p. 164, n.1); Ferdinand to Maximilian, Jan. 14, 1608, *Wittelsbacher Briefe* 7 (1893): #314 (p. 61).

matter of the Peace. The situation in the east was also deteriorating for Rudolf. The emperor's position regarding the Treaty of Zsitvatorok remained unclear. Some accused him of not accepting it, whereas he called attention to Turkish violations of the treaty. Delegates from Mainz in Regensburg later reported that the imperial proposition seemed to call for continual war.[75]

Matthias now summoned representatives of the Hungarian and Upper and Lower Austrian estates to Pressburg (Bratislava) where in early February they formed an alliance to keep the peace with the Turks, and they began to raise an army against Rudolf. The Spanish ambassador now switched his support to Matthias, who enjoyed Protestant and some Catholic backing.[76] The allies at Pressburg then dispatched a delegation to Rudolf in Prague, where the emperor accused them of open rebellion. Ferdinand remained staunchly loyal to Emperor Rudolf. He wrote to his mother on February 8, "I would never believe Archduke Matthias's good sense would be so dulled, that he would want to make decisions so contrary to God and to international law, so evil and worthy of punishment. But if he does, God cannot and will not let it go unpunished."[77] To justify his actions, Matthias made public the secret agreement of Vienna of 1606 with Ferdinand and Archduke Maximilian and later with Albert, to the great embarrassment of Ferdinand. Ferdinand had had misgivings about the agreement almost as soon as it was signed. Now he sent Sigismund von Trautmannsdorf to Prague to explain the situation at the time, to seek the forgiveness of Rudolf as did Archduke Maximilian, and to maintain the trust that Rudolf had placed in him. If Eggenberg had been with him at the time, he later remarked, he never would have gone along with the alliance. Ferdinand also intercepted a courier in Regensburg whom Matthias had sent to the electors seeking their support. This greatly angered Matthias, who considered it a breach of international law, and he now began to threaten Ferdinand with an invasion of Styria and to incite the Styrian estates against him.[78] Ferdinand found himself caught between the two brothers; his mother urged him to try to maintain neutrality between them.[79]

Meanwhile, he sought to reach out to the Protestant party. He hoped to meet with Christian of Anhalt, the leading minister of the Palatinate, and for this purpose he sent the humanist Schoppe to Amberg to arrange a conference,[80] and he asked the elector of Trier, whom he thought close to the Elector Palatine, to try to persuade him to alter his views. He sought contact with the delegation from Wurttemberg. But an early optimism about the possibility of agreement

---

[75] Delegates of Mainz to Archbishop-Elector Johann Schweikard, Mar. 15, 1608, BA 6. #97.
[76] Rill, 137; Hurter 5: 140–4, 150–2.
[77] Ferdinand to Maria, Feb. 8, 1608, Hurter 5: #4 (pp. 425–9),
[78] Hurter 5: 249, 256; Rill, 138; Ferdinand to Maria, Mar. 1, 1608, Hurter 5: #10 (pp. 447–8).
[79] Hurter 5: 213.
[80] Mario D'Addio, *Il pensiero politico di Gaspare Scioppio e il Machiavellismo del Seicento* (Milan, 1962), 72.

with the Protestants soon gave way to the realization of their obstinacy on the Religious Peace, an obstinacy that was matched by his and that of Maximilian of Bavaria. The Protestants wanted the diet to confirm the Religious Peace; the Catholics would agree to this only on the condition that the Protestants return all the church lands that they had confiscated, illegally to the mind of the Catholics, since 1555. As he wrote later to Maria, "better to allow the diet to collapse than that anything dangerous or harmful to religion be admitted."[81]

At the instruction of Rudolf, Ferdinand now sought a meeting with Maximilian and Duke William, neither of whom had come to Regensburg in person.[82] He was to seek advice from his Bavarian cousin and his uncle, whom he called his "father" in his correspondence with Maria. Father Viller was sent to Munich, to arrange a meeting. Both Rudolf and Ferdinand wanted to obtain the support of the Bavarians in the *Brüderzwist*. But Maximilian, though he obviously favored Rudolf, meant to keep his distance from the conflict. Ferdinand and the imperial councillor Hannewald met with William alone then at Bruhl outside Regensburg, on March 11. According to William in his report to Maximilian, Ferdinand asserted that "matters were in the worst state, and worse was yet to fear unless God took extraordinary measures."[83] They discussed the impact that Matthias's rebellion would have on the negotiations in Regensburg, and Ferdinand expressed the regret that he now felt for the agreement with Matthias. Ferdinand remarked incidentally, William noted, that he needed to forge an alliance with Maximilian, to which William responded with silence, not wanting to commit his son. Precisely at that time talks were beginning between Maximilian and other Catholic princes about the formation of an alliance of Catholic states. Hannewald asserted clearly that Rudolf depended on the Bavarians, and he recalled the testament of Emperor Ferdinand I that stated that should there be a dispute among the Habsburgs, they should seek help from the Bavarians. Ferdinand wanted William to accompany him back to Regensburg, but William thought that this might raise suspicions and so he declined.[84] Two days later William reported to Maximilian that Rudolf wanted to flee to Bavaria with his valuable objects; he did not trust his own people.[85] On the other hand, he wanted Maximilian to come to see him in Prague, a trip that Maximilian always tactfully avoided.

---

[81] Ferdinand to Maria, undated (probably about Mar. 15), Hurter 5: #14 (p. 460).
[82] William had made a quick visit to Regensburg shortly after the opening of the diet, from January 23–29, staying at the Carthusian monastery and conferring with the bishop of Regensburg. But it is not clear that he conferred with his nephew at this time. See Milensio to Borghese, Jan. 29, 1608, *Epistolae et Acta* 2: #5 (p. 391).
[83] William to Maximilian, Mar. 11, 1608, BA 6, #92 (p. 253).
[84] Franziska Neuer-Landfried, *Die katholische Liga. Gründung, Neugründung, und Organisation eines Sonderbundes, 1608–1620* (Kallmünz, 1968), 26–9.
[85] William to Maximilian, Mar. 13, 1608, *Wittelsbacher Briefe* 7, #323 (pp. 69–70); Rudolf to Ferdinand, Mar. 14, 1608, BA 6, #95 (p. 257).

On March 16, in a speech to the plenum of the diet given at the instruction of Rudolf, Ferdinand once again called for recognition of the Religious Peace by all parties. But this pleased neither side. Catholics thought that he had yielded points but Protestants realized, correctly, that he understood the Catholic interpretation of the Peace.[86] Yet the proposal did not fail completely; it won over the Saxons, who were more open to compromise. The Palatinate party now split from them, and the two would remain divided until 1631 at the time of the Edict of Restitution. Two days later, Ferdinand and Hannewald met with William and Maximilian himself in Straubing, where Ferdinand requested Maximilian's advice and assistance. It had become clear that the Protestant delegates would contribute nothing to the war, which many of them saw as being waged against their brothers in Hungary. Both the Bavarians strongly supported Rudolf. By now Ferdinand had learned from Trautmannsdorf that Rudolf had accepted his request for pardon, a gesture that, Ferdinand reported to his mother on March 20, greatly consoled him.[87] Maximilian counseled Ferdinand to explain the situation in Hungary more clearly than he had; if the problems of the Religious Peace were not resolved, then the Catholics should proceed toward the formation of an alliance.[88] Ferdinand and Archduke Maximilian then called upon Matthias to come to Prague for a conference with all the members of the house as well as the electors; they wanted reconciliation of the two brothers and they did not want the diet to fail. But Matthias's anger toward Ferdinand grew after the incident with the courier, and he attempted to incite members of the Inner Austrian estates against Ferdinand. Ferdinand wondered why the Hungarians were so angry with him since he had taken no action against them, and whether Matthias now aimed at seizing the government of Inner and Anterior Austria with the Tyrol, too. He recognized that Rudolf had wronged Matthias, but Matthias should put aside thoughts of revenge.[89] Maria was now raising troops in Inner Austria, an initiative with which her son agreed reluctantly and with the caution that no occasion be given others to cause trouble. Eggenberg in Graz sought the aid of Spanish troops.[90] But Ferdinand still held out hope for reconciliation with Matthias and the Hungarians.[91]

Throughout April Ferdinand kept Maximilian and William informed of events and regularly asked for their advice. Both he and the Bavarians now stood behind Rudolf and a hard line with the Protestants on the Religious

---

[86] Address (*Interpositionsschrift*) of Ferdinand to the diet, Mar. 16, 1608, BA 6, #100, p. 261.

[87] Ferdinand to Maria, Mar. 20, 1608, Hurter 5:, #15, (p. 468)

[88] Minutes of the Meeting at Straubing between Ferdinand and Hannewald, and William and Maximilian, Mar. 18-20, 1608, BA 6, #103 (pp. 267-71).

[89] Ferdinand to Maria, Apr. 5 and 10, Hurter 5: ##19, 20 (pp. 484-96).

[90] Ferdinand to Maria, Apr. 5, 1608, Hurter 5: #19 (pp. 484-9); Maria to Ferdinand, Apr. 13, 1608, Hurter 5: 553-9; Eggenberg to Ferdinand, Apr. 12, 1608, Ibid., 563-6.

[91] Ferdinand to Maria, Apr. 5, 1608, Hurter 5: #19 (p. 488).

Peace. Their correspondence focused more on the conflict between Rudolf and Matthias than on the diet. Ferdinand reminded Maximilian that as a Christian he had an obligation to assist in reconciliation. By April 12, a conciliatory answer had arrived from Matthias. Matthias's secretaries, Ferdinand wrote his mother, deflecting responsibility from the archduke himself, had used sharp words and stated untruths; he thought it better not to contradict Matthias directly and to use a moderate tone in his response.[92] The Bohemians now seemed to be on the point of rebellion, he wrote Maximilian on April 16, and the Protestants were becoming more "impertinent" at Regensburg.[93] The nuncio, the Spanish ambassador, and Bohemian officials had set out to negotiate with Matthias as he marched toward Bohemia.

The situation was worsening, Ferdinand informed Maximilian,"but God will not abandon the authority established by him to be exposed to the ridicule of the world but will certainly stand by [this authority] with his rich blessings." Most Protestant delegates had informed him that they were departing, and he had recommended that Rudolf prorogue the diet.[94] On April 19, the Moravian estates joined the alliance of Hungary and Upper and Lower Austria, and Matthias began to head toward Bohemia with an army of 35,000 made up of Hungarians and Austrians.[95] By this time, in late April, the delegates of the Palatinate had departed from Regensburg. Rudolf made a final effort to save the diet. In two propositions dated April 21, he made it clear that he accepted the Treaty of Vienna with the Hungarians and would recognize their estates, and he would implement the Treaty of Zsitvatorok. But there was no movement on the Religious Peace. The Saxons refused to go so far as to vote funds for the emperor under the circumstances, and Catholic delegates opposed the suggestion of obtaining funds from the Catholic states alone, a move promoted by Ferdinand, because this would only deepen the division with the Protestants.[96] Ferdinand departed Regensburg on May 6, and the next day the emperor formally closed the diet.

The day before the dissolution, delegates of the Catholic states discussed the formation of a Catholic alliance once again. Schoppe subsequently wrote a vigorous paper insisting that the Catholics needed an alliance to defend the Church, as well as the structure of the Empire. Ferdinand had brought the matter up to Maximilian at their meeting in mid-March. But Maximilian tended to keep the Austrians out because he wanted to avoid involvement in the *Brüderzwist*. On May 12, Protestant states led by the Palatinate formed

---

[92] Ferdinand to Maria, Apr. 12, 1608, ibid., #20 (p. 496).
[93] Ferdinand to Maximilian, Apr. 12 and 16, 1608, *Wittelsbacher Briefe* 7: ##333-4, (pp. 81-3).
[94] Ferdinand to Maximilian, Apr.25 and 27, 1608, ibid. ##336, 337 (pp. 83-4).
[95] Rill, 140; Hurter 5: 249-56. The lands of the Bohemian crown included Bohemia proper, Moravia, Silesia, and Upper and Lower Lusatia, each with its own estates.
[96] Two Imperial Propositions, Apr. 21, 1608, BA 6: #147 (pp. 314-26); Ferdinand to Rudolf, Apr. 28, 1608, BA 6, #158 (pp. 340-2).

the Protestant Union at Ahausen in Lower Saxony. Wurttemberg, Hesse-Kassel, Brandenburg and a number of other Protestant territories and imperial cities soon joined; Saxony and many imperial cities remained apart.

Meanwhile Matthias continued his progress toward Bohemia. Rudolf wanted to flee but Bohemian officials would not permit him to do so. Officials of the Bohemian estates then met outside Prague with Matthias and Rudolf, where the Spanish ambassador, the nuncio, and a representative of Archduke Albert assisted in the negotiations. By the Treaty of Lieben (Lebeň), a suburb of Prague, on June 25 agreement was reached that Rudolf would continue to govern Bohemia but Matthias was assured of the succession there. Matthias was recognized as ruler in Hungary, Upper and Lower Austria, and Moravia, and the Treaty of Zsitvatorok was once again confirmed. So armed hostilities were avoided. Nothing was said about the imperial succession. But shortly thereafter, the Austrians and Moravians, ominously, concluded a secret agreement that they would press Matthias for religious concessions similar to those granted the Hungarians.[97]

The Diet of Regensburg failed in every respect. It represented the continuing breakdown of imperial institutions confronted with the religious division in the Empire. No progress was made toward composition of religious differences, nor were funds voted to support the war in the east. Pope Paul dispatched a brief dated March 8 to Ferdinand through Milensio lamenting the failure of the diet up to that point but recognizing Ferdinand's efforts on behalf of the Church. Ferdinand responded to the papal agent that "he would risk his state, his blood, and his life rather than permit that the Catholic faith or the Church suffer the least damage."[98] Over the diet hovered the *Brüderzwist,* and the Donauworth affair intensified suspicions on both sides only a few weeks before it opened. Ferdinand had been dealt a weak hand in his first major venture into imperial politics. Despite a few half-hearted gestures, he did not make progress in bringing the religious parties closer together. Nor was this to have been expected from him, given his record in Inner Austria. In the dispute between Matthias and Rudolf, having become convinced of the inability of Rudolf to govern, he had at first tended to support Matthias's efforts to secure the succession. So he had entered the agreement at Vienna that he later so regretted. He wavered for a time, attempting to remain neutral. He then decisively shifted to Rudolf, for two reasons. He came to see Matthias increasingly as a rebel against legitimate, God-given authority as the archduke organized forces to march on Rudolf, and he also became wary of Matthias's concessions to the Hungarians, especially on the religious issue. On both the conflict between Rudolf and Matthias and the religious issue, he looked to Maximilian of Bavaria as well as Duke William for advice and assistance, and he was evidently influenced by the Bavarians.

---

[97] Rill, 143–4.   [98] Milensio to Borghese, Apr. 2, 1608, *Epistolae et Acta* 2, #21 (pp. 416–8).

Ferdinand communicated regularly with his mother Maria during his stay in Regensburg, and the twenty-two letters that he sent her between February 3 and April 18 tell us much about him and his relationship to his mother. Many of these long communications stretch to five or six tightly printed pages today, and they frequently jumped from topic to topic and then back again. A deep affection along with respect for her position and her judgment bound Ferdinand to his mother, who often stood in for him as regent during his absences from Graz. He regularly addressed her as "Your Highness, the Archduchess, my most gracious and most loving mother," and signed himself her "most subordinate and most obedient son to the death."[99] Initially, he wrote also to his wife, Maria Anna, but in a note addressed to her and added to a letter to his mother of March 4, he excused himself from further letters to "my golden treasure" because he simply did not have time.[100] Maria Anna carried a child at the time, and Ferdinand regularly asked his mother to care for her and expressed his hope to be with her as the time of her delivery neared. His correspondence with his mother dealt with all the significant matters of state as well as of the family, and it manifested an interest and affection for his family and household. Copies or originals of all his political correspondence were sent to Maria in Graz, and Ferdinand often assured her that he would not make a decision until he had heard from her (and often from the councillors in Graz), which does not mean that he always followed her advice. He consulted her on policy at the diet as well as in the dispute between Rudolf and Matthias.

Another matter that frequently surfaced in their exchanges was arrangements for the marriage of his sister, Maria Magdelana, to Cosimo II, the Grand Duke of Tuscany. A letter from Maria Magdelena to her brother in Regensburg reveals a familiar relationship between the two. Maria Magdelena relates for Ferdinand all her dance partners at the recent Fasching celebrations.[101] For her marriage the Graz branch of the family required the consent of the emperor, the head of the Habsburg family, as did all members of the family for their marriages, and the dilatory Rudolf stalled on this for a long time. Maria Magdelena did eventually wed Cosimo, in Graz on September 14, 1608. The occasionally erratic behavior of Ferdinand's brother Leopold, now bishop of Strasbourg as well as bishop of Passau, caused concern for both Ferdinand and Maria. At one time they feared that he was becoming too French, and then Ferdinand suspected that Leopold aspired to be governor of Upper Austria in place of Matthias, a development of which they both disapproved.[102] Ferdinand

---

[99] "Duerchleichtigste Erherzogin, genedigste mein herzallerliebste Frau Mutter;" "E (Eure). Fl. (Fürstliche) Dt. (Durchlauchts) unndterthenigster und gehorsamster Sun bis in den Dott."
[100] Ferdinand to Maria, March 4, 1608, Hurter 5: #10 (p. 450).
[101] Maria Magdelena to Ferdinand, Graz, Feb. 20/22, 1608, *Graz als Residenz: Innerösterreich 1564–1619*, ed. Berthold Sutter (Graz, 1964), 371–5.
[102] Ferdinand to Maria, Apr. 10, 1608, Hurter 5, #20, (p. 494–5).

occasionally commented on his leisure activities, especially his hunting excursions and the modest celebration of Carnival in Regensburg. After hearing a young Italian singer perform, he remarked to his mother that they probably could bring him to Graz if they found him a good wife.[103]

Maria's health deteriorated notably during Ferdinand's absence, and she would die before his return to Graz. She regularly complained of headaches, and he sympathized with her. "Should God will it that I could suffer in place of Your Princely Highness, I would want from the bottom of my heart to do so," he wrote touchingly.[104] To her complaint that she was no longer useful to anybody, he responded, with proper deference to her as her son, that she was unfair to her children when she began to talk this way. All her obedient children would feel it deeply should they lose her. "We all see you in no other way than as a consoling sign of God's blessing. So I beseech Your Princely Highness, for God's sake, take good care of your health and think how much we all depend on Your Princely Highness."[105]

Around early March, Ferdinand grew increasingly impatient with developments in Regensburg and began to express his desire to be back in Graz, with his mother and his wife, his brothers and sisters, and his children. He wanted to be home with his wife during her pregnancy. "Had I known that this matins [?] or diet would last so long," he wrote on March 1, "no one would have been able to get me to leave home,"[106] and twelve days later he wished that he could just "get up and ride home with the mail... My time here is so long, and I wish so often that I were home that I cannot adequately express it to Your Princely Highness; it is truly patience under duress, a bitter herb."[107] "If only there were a way to be found by which I could travel away from here [towards home] with my honor and profit to Christendom."[108] Only his honor and his sense of responsibility kept him in Regensburg. Similar expressions filled his letters until his departure from Regensburg on May 6. But in the meantime, Maria's situation grew worse, and she died on April 29, at the age of fifty-seven. Rudolf had summoned Ferdinand to Prague after the conclusion of the diet but upon learning of Maria's death, the emperor readily realized that Ferdinand had to return to Graz. Maria had arranged for her funeral and burial in the convent of the Poor Clares in Graz, a convent that she herself had founded in 1603 and to which she had frequently retreated, often with one of her daughters.[109] Because the grave was not ready at the time of her death, her body lay in state in the choir of the convent church until September 4, when it was finally laid to rest with all the solemnity of the church's rites. Ten days

---

[103] Ferdinand to Maria, Feb. 25, 1608, ibid.: #7 (p. 435).
[104] Ferdinand to Maria, Mar. 1, 1608, ibid.: #9 (p. 442).
[105] Ferdinand to Maria, ibid., 444–5.   [106] Ferdinand to Maria, ibid, 446.
[107] Ferdinand to Maria, Mar. 12, 1608, ibid., #12 (p. 453).
[108] Ferdinand to Maria, Mar. 29, 1608, ibid.,: #17 (pp. 477–82).
[109] Rochus Kohlbach, *Die Barocken Kirchen von Graz* (Graz, 1951), 12.

later Maria Magdelena married Duke Cosimo of Tuscany in Graz, but all the participants wore black as they remained in mourning for Maria.

Maria had first drawn up her will in 1591, the year after the death of her husband, Archduke Carl. Ferdinand, her first-born son, was designated her universal heir. This did not mean, she stated explicitly, that her love for her other children was any less. Rather he, along with his other burdens, presumably of government, bore the responsibility for their welfare. She hoped that they would be satisfied with their portion. In a codicil added shortly thereafter, Maria assured her son that the Pacification of Bruck, which had been the nail in Carl's coffin, did not bind him. He should never allow himself to be cajoled by anyone into burdening his conscience as Carl had. He should take mild and proper means to lead his subjects back to the Catholic faith so as not to endanger the salvation of his own soul. Rather than endanger his own soul, he should flee into an uninhabited forest, there to serve God with a pure conscience. Maria entrusted to him the college of the Jesuits, which he should protect as his father had, especially because the fathers had so many enemies. One can only imagine the impression that this testament made on Ferdinand upon his return to Graz.[110]

Ferdinand had lost the most important person in his life, the one who more than any other had formed his character and his outlook.

---

[110] Hurter 5: 321–5.

Chapter 3

Toward the Succession, 1608–1618

In the decade following the Diet of Regensburg of 1608 and the death of his mother, the issue of the succession predominated for Ferdinand, first the succession of Matthias in the Habsburg lands and in the Empire, and then his own. Ferdinand considered the succession to be closely associated with the preservation of Catholicism in the Empire. Despite the Treaty of Zsitvatorok of 1606, the situation on the frontier with the Turks still remained a cause for concern, and the politics of the Empire increasingly drew Ferdinand into its orbit. For the rest of his life, the emphasis of his policy and his attention shifted back and forth between the Habsburg Austrian lands and the kingdoms of Bohemia and Hungary, which together constituted the territory of the developing Habsburg Monarchy, on the one hand, and the Empire on the other. His capacity to implement a policy in the Empire depended to a degree on the strength of his position in his own lands, and his later role as emperor enhanced his status in those lands. As the decade progressed, Ferdinand also had to deal with conflicts to the south over borders and over control of trade in the Adriatic Sea with Venice and with the fractious Uskok pirates, refugees from lands occupied by the Turks.

Protestant states, mostly Calvinist and led by the Palatinate, had concluded a Union at Ahausen near Nördlingen on May 12, 1608, shortly after the end of the Diet of Regensburg. Their articles of confederation stressed its defensive character. The formation of a Catholic League did not merely respond to this Protestant initiative. The three ecclesiastical electors of Mainz, Trier, and Cologne had earlier held discussions about an alliance, vulnerable as they were to attack because of their nearness to the Palatinate.[1] At his meeting with Duke

---

[1] Albrecht 2, 407–8.

William in the course of the Diet of Regensburg, Ferdinand had raised the issue of an alliance with Bavaria, but William had remained noncommittal. Maximilian wanted to keep the Habsburg territories out of a prospective league because he did not want it to become involved in the family dispute over the succession in the Habsburg lands and because he aimed to serve as its leader. The three ecclesiastical electors agreed with Bavaria on the formation of a league at a meeting at Andernach on the Rhine on July 7, 1608, and after several conferences, it came into existence at a meeting in Wurzburg from February 10 to 19, 1610. The new Catholic League was composed of two sections, an Upper German section headed by Maximilian that included a number of ecclesiastical states from the south, and a Rhenish section also composed of church territories including the three ecclesiastical electorates. It was headed by Johann Schweikard von Kronberg, the new archbishop-elector of Mainz who tended much more towards an understanding with the Protestants, especially the Lutheran states led by Electoral Saxony, than did Maximilian. Later in August, under pressure from Spain, which agreed to provide subsidies to the League, Archduke Ferdinand was given the title of a director of the League and a vice-protector, but he had to sign over all authority in the League to Maximilian. The Catholic League also understood itself to be defensive in character; its purpose was the defense of the Catholic religion in the Empire and the maintenance of peace, especially the Religious Peace.[2]

Meanwhile Ferdinand had begun himself actively to promote his own version of a Catholic league. In this he was influenced by the peripatetic polemicist Caspar Schoppe, who had become attached to his entourage at the Diet of Regensburg. In April 1609, Schoppe drew up, at Ferdinand's request, a position paper advocating a Catholic league that had a significant impact on the archduke. His visit with Christian von Anhalt at Regensburg the previous year as well as with other Protestant princes had convinced Schoppe of their intentions to fish aggressively in the troubled waters of the Habsburg territories, but his knowledge of Catholic courts persuaded him that Catholic "money and power" equaled that of the Protestants. But the Catholic states needed to unite, first among themselves and then with the Habsburgs. Many Catholic princes pursued their own interests to the neglect of the common good, and they feared that any common venture would be manipulated to serve the augmentation of Habsburg power in the Empire. For this reason, and because of the conflict among the Habsburgs, an Austrian archduke, presumably Ferdinand, ought not to take the initiative in the formation of a league but to leave it up to another Catholic prince. The goal of the league ought to be the maintenance of the Religious Peace of Augsburg, which was also very much in the Habsburg interest and to which the heretics could not really object.

---

[2] Ibid., 411–12, 424.

Schoppe understood the Catholic interpretation of the Peace. So the League would aim at two principal objects, the enforcement of the Ecclesiastical Reservation that prevented the loss of an ecclesiastical principality to the Protestants, and the enforcement of the decisions of the Imperial Court Council which, Schoppe assumed, would restore to the Catholics the church lands that the Protestants had confiscated, illegally from the Catholic perspective, since the Peace of 1555. The recent Diet of Regensburg had shown that the Protestants had no intention of yielding on these points. Among the ecclesiastical territories to be reclaimed were the archbishoprics and bishoprics of Magdeburg, Minden, Halberstadt, Bremen, Verden, Osnabruck, Meissen, Naumburg, and Merseburg. So Schoppe laid out the substance of what would twenty years later be the Edict of Restitution. In that it aimed at the recovery of lost church lands, the goal of the league proposed by Schoppe outstripped the more modest defensive one being actually drawn up by the Catholic League at the same time. His league, Schoppe argued, ought to pursue aid from the pope, the king of Spain, and the Italian princes, indeed to welcome them as members. One might even consider this league to have as its goal the defense of Catholicism throughout Europe, since the enforcement of the Religious Peace in the Empire was crucial to the general state of Catholicism in Europe. And all this would be to the benefit of the House of Habsburg, though one ought to avoid stating this explicitly. Revenues from the reacquired lands would be applied to the financing of the league, and both the pope and the Italian princes would be drawn to support it by the prospect of control of appointments to the recovered lands.

Schoppe wanted the pope, Paul V, to take the lead in the formation of this league, and he proposed that the pope dispatch a legate to Germany for the purpose of organizing it. He even suggested for this task Cardinal Francesco Sforza di Santa Fiora, as much a soldier as an ecclesiastic and well acquainted with the affairs of Germany. But the legate's assignment was to be kept secret, and it was to be given out that he traveled to Germany in order to promote the implementation of the Council of Trent and to attend to other ecclesiastical business.[3]

Ferdinand took this ambitious proposal seriously, and it shows the state of his thinking at this early time. Partly because of the valuable counsel he had provided in Regensburg, Ferdinand selected Schoppe himself as the emissary to be sent to Pope Paul V and to the cardinals in Rome, even though Schoppe had resided at the court of Graz for only a few days.[4] Per orders of Ferdinand, an instruction was drawn up for Schoppe that closely mirrored the polemicist's own position paper and incorporated large portions of it verbatim. It described the lamentable state of the Church in Germany, and it foresaw as likely a military conflict if an attempt to recover church lands was launched.

---

[3] "Relazione dello Scioppio all'Arciduca Ferdinando su la Lega cattolica" (April, 1609), Mario D'Addio, *Il pensiero politico di Gaspare Scioppio e il antimachiavellismo del seicento* (Milan, 1962), 685–92.

[4] Peter Casal, secretary to Ferdinand, to Scioppio, Graz, May 30, 1609, ibid. 738–40.

The pope, Spain, and the Italian princes should all be included in the league, whose purpose extended, as in Schoppe's paper, to the general defense of the Church. Interestingly, the legate to be sent to Germany, Cardinal Sforza it was hoped, was to attempt to persuade the German Catholic states to support the league financially, but nothing was said directly about papal subsidies for the league. Schoppe was to remind the pope of the support that he had promised Ferdinand should the estates in Inner Austria attempt to extort liberty of conscience from Ferdinand.[5]

Schoppe made his way towards Rome, where he was well known, in early June 1609. His presentations to Paul V, summarized in two papers, laid out Ferdinand's position even more aggressively than the instruction for Schoppe. Ferdinand believed, Schoppe wrote, that without a "just war," it would be impossible to resist the seizure of more church lands and even more so, to reclaim those already lost. The Catholics had the resources to do this if they were united. The pope should support the efforts already undertaken by Maximilian. Many Protestant nobles inclined to conversion, which would give them the opportunity to place their sons in ecclesiastical positions. Schoppe sought to convince the pope that the dispatch of a legate to Germany would not further provoke the Protestants, obviously a papal concern, especially if the true nature of his task were not revealed, and he indicated that a further pretext for the legate's mission might be to promote the conversion of select German Protestant princes whom he named, among them the duke of Wurttemberg, by clearing up the misconceptions that many of them had of Catholic doctrine.[6]

Paul V did not accede to Ferdinand's request. Under the date of September 4, 1609, he posted a Breve to Ferdinand informing him that Schoppe would communicate his answer to him.[7] The pope, despite encouraging his efforts on behalf of the league, tactfully turned down Ferdinand's request for funding, for several reasons apart from the shortage of funds at the Vatican. He did not want to offend the emperor; Klesl opposed the formation of a league as undermining his new policy of composition of differences. The pope did not want to promote tensions that would lead to war. Furthermore, out of consideration for King Henry IV of France, he hesitated to support a project now funded in part by the king of Spain. Paul did approve a modest subsidy for the League later after the death of Henry.[8] Ferdinand wrote Schoppe, who

---

[5] "Istruzione dell'Archiduca Ferdinando allo Scioppio per la Legazione a Roma," July 9, 1609, Ibid., 693–9.

[6] "Relazione dello Scioppio a Paolo V su la lega cattolica," and "Relazione dello Scioppio a Paulo V sulla missione in Germania di un Legato pontificio per l'organizzione de la Lega," ibid., 700–14.

[7] Paul V to Archduke Ferdinand, Sept. 4, 1609. Ibid., 741.

[8] Ludwig von Pastor, *Geschichte der Päpste im Zeitalter der katholischen Restauration und des Dreissigjährigen Krieges* 12 (Freiburg, 1927): 524–5; Franziska Neuer-Landfried, *Die katholische Liga: Gründung, Neugründung und Organisation eines Sonderbundes 1608–1620* Kallmünz, 1968): 76, 100–1.

remained in Rome for several months, that he had "not gladly" learned of the pope's decision. He also cautioned Schoppe about his "too free speech" in Rome. Ferdinand's emissary in Rome had apparently bitterly criticized Archduke Matthias. This helped no one, Ferdinand admonished Schoppe. But the polemicist inclined to strong language. The following year he defended Ravaillac, the assassin of Henry IV, as the instrument of divine punishment for the king.[9]

Ferdinand's initiative for the formation of a Catholic league also grew out of further events within the Habsburg lands. On July 24, 1608, not long after the Treaty of Lieben, Matthias met in Schottwein with Archduke Maximilian, Ferdinand, and his two brothers Archdukes Maximilian Ernest and Leopold, where they all agreed to support Matthias as successor to Rudolf. So Ferdinand and Matthias reconciled at this point. But neither Rudolf himself, who refused to recognize his brother, nor the ecclesiastical electors, who contended that Matthias had betrayed the faith by yielding to the Hungarians, went along with this.[10] The Moravian estates paid homage to Matthias after he promised that there would be "no religious persecution." But the Protestant estates of Upper Austria and the Protestant majority of the estates of Lower Austria now refused to pay homage to Matthias unless he made more significant religious concessions. Otherwise, they threatened to return to Rudolf. Ferdinand, for his part, attempted, in vain, to reconcile the two brothers in order to take away this option from them.[11] Meanwhile the Protestant Union led by Christian von Anhalt attempted to exploit the situation in the Austrian territories. Only after long negotiations and considerable soul-searching did Matthias yield to the estates of both territories on March 19, 1609. The following April 29, 1609, he received the homage of the Protestant members of the estates of Lower Austria – the Catholic members had already accepted him – and on May 17 of the Upper Austrian estates. As a result, Pope Paul excommunicated him and Bishop Klesl refused him Holy Communion.[12] Ferdinand also vigorously opposed the concessions that Matthias made to the Austrian Protestant estates, calling them "vexing and scornful for the House and for religion."[13]

The Bohemian estates, not to be outdone, now moved to render secure the promises Rudolf had made to them as Matthias marched on Prague. Here, too, protracted negotiations took place, and armed conflict threatened before Rudolf, on July 9, 1609, agreed to the Letter of Majesty presented to him by the estates. This justly famous document established equality between Catholics and adherents of the *Confessio Bohemica*, which had initially been drawn up in 1575 and approved orally by Emperor Maximilian II. Practically, the Letter

---

[9] D'Addio, 109–10.   [10] Rill, 145–6.   [11] Ibid., 150   [12] Ibid., 151–2.
[13] Ferdinand to Archduke Maximilian, Feb. 19–20, 1609, cited in Joseph Hirn, *Erzherzog Maximilian, Der Deutschmeister und Regent von Tirol*, ed. Heinrich Notflatscher (Bozen, 1981) 2: 548–50.

granted religious freedom to members of all three estates and their subjects who adhered to the *Confessio,* that is, Utraquists, Bohemian Brethren, Lutherans, and even by extension, Calvinists. The Letter recognized their ecclesiastical administration or consistory, so that they could appoint pastors, and their control of the Charles University, to which they could appoint the professors. In addition, they were allowed to name a committee of "Defenders" independent of the king, who were to participate in resolving disputes among the confessions. Another provision allowed them to build churches and schools, even on royal lands; its interpretation would lead to later disputes. The Letter of Majesty bound all future kings of Bohemia to observance of these concessions. A further measure approved by Rudolf empowered the Defenders to summon Protestant officials and councillors as well as six deputies from each administrative district for consultation on religious matters, especially when the rights of Protestants seemed to be violated. The formation of this body seemed to create a center of Protestant power apart from the Habsburg government.[14]

Meanwhile a crisis threatening war and the intervention of both the Protestant Union and Catholic League blew up over the succession in an agglomeration of territories on the Lower Rhine, the duchies of Jülich, Cleves, and Berg, and the counties of Mark and Ravensburg, that together constituted a significant political power in the northwest of the Empire on the border with the Netherlands. Their ruler, the deranged Duke John William, who had supported the Catholic cause in the religiously divided duchies, died in March, 1609, without an heir. The Calvinist elector of Brandenburg, John Sigismund, had a strong claim to the inheritance, but Duke Wolfgang William of Neuburg could also make a case for it. He was to convert to Catholicism in 1613 and marry Maximilian's sister Magdelena the following year. Emperor Rudolf sent Ferdinand's brother, Archduke Leopold, bishop of Passau and after 1608 also of Strasbourg, to administer the territories until he could render a decision. But Leopold could accomplish little against the forces of the two claimants who had occupied the duchies. For a time, it looked as if both the Protestant Union and the Catholic League would intervene. Henry IV of France, fearing that Jülich might fall into Habsburg hands through the intervention of Rudolf and Leopold, planned an invasion of the territories. With English and Dutch backing, he aimed to mount a more general attack on the Habsburgs that also foresaw, in combination with Savoy and Venice, an invasion of Milan. But the assassination of King Henry IV on May 14, 1610, deprived France of its leader.

[14] The Letter of Majesty is printed in *Quellen zur Vorgeschichte und zu den Anfängen des dreissigjährigen Krieges,* ed. Gottfried Lorenz, (Darmstadt, 1991): #10 (pp. 92–10). Under the same date, there was issued an agreement between Catholics and adherents of the *Confessio Bohemica* on ecclesiastical affairs, ibid., #11 (pp. 101–3). See also Karl Richter, "Die böhmischen Länder von 1471–1611," in *Handbuch der Geschichte der böhmischen Länder,* ed. Karl Bosl, 2 (Munich, 1974): 172, 190, and Brockmann, 58–60.

Both the Union and the League then backed off from a confrontation, Maximilian contending that once the Union offered a compromise settlement, the League as a defensive organization could not refuse it. He did not want war.[15] Eventually, after tense negotiations, the territories were divided between the two claimants by the Treaty of Xanten of 1614, and so a major conflict was avoided.

After Rudolf's concession of the Letter of Majesty in Bohemia, Ferdinand and Bishop Klesl, who now functioned as Matthias's principal minister, undertook to reconcile the differences between Matthias and Rudolf. Rudolf continued to avoid a commitment on the succession, and he began to demand the return of the Austrian lands and Moravia that he had surrendered, under duress he claimed, to Matthias. Klesl met with Peter Casal, Ferdinand's secretary at Schottwein in November 1609, and they began to plan a meeting of the archdukes with Rudolf and Matthias in Prague where Maximilian of Bavaria, they hoped in vain, would serve as an arbitrator. At issue now was the retention of the imperial title in the House of Habsburg and the balance of power between the prince and estates in the Habsburg territories. Ferdinand expected the estates to raise their demands.[16]

In a long communication of December 2, 1609, Eggenberg laid out a policy which Ferdinand seems to have followed. The minister urged Ferdinand to remain firmly "in the middle, as you have done thus far, and with considerable glory [for yourself]." It may be true that the Austrian territories now want to return to Rudolf because of the concessions he has made to the Bohemian estates. But if you support them in this, you risk alienating Matthias. If you oppose their alleged desire, then you offend Rudolf. The heretical Austrian estates, you indicate, have made contact with the Hungarians. Eggenberg encouraged Ferdinand to keep in touch with the Spaniards to learn what they thought of Matthias's actions, and he urged him to continue to work towards the meeting in Prague. More than anything else, a reconciliation between Rudolf and Matthias would benefit both religion and the dynasty.[17]

Only on May 1, 1610, did the princes assemble at the Hradschin in Prague, where Rudolf hosted them imperially with food and drink. Among those attending were Archdukes Ferdinand and Maximilian, the Catholic electors of Mainz and Cologne, the Protestant elector of Saxony, Landgrave Ludwig of Hesse-Darmstadt, and the duke of Brunswick, Heinrich-Julius, who was to play a significant mediating role. Despite Rudolf's objections, the princes invited Matthias, whose delegates then arrived on May 31. Maximilian of Bavaria declined to come, in accord with his policy of avoiding involvement in Habsburg affairs. Increasingly as the meeting proceeded there lurked over

---

[15] Neuer-Landfried, 98.   [16] Hurter, 6: 248–50.
[17] Eggenberg to Ferdinand, Dec. 2, 1609, ibid. 6: 641–3.

it the threat of military intervention by Archduke Leopold who initially had raised an army of nearly 15,000 at Rudolf's behest in Passau and Strasbourg, ostensibly to be employed in the contest in the duchies to the northwest but now moving ominously and destructively through Lower Austria towards Bohemia. When the other princes turned initially toward Ferdinand and Maximilian to make a choice between Rudolf and Matthias, they refused to take sides. Matthias had now established contact with the Protestant Union.[18]

Negotiations continued through the summer in Prague, with delegations including Ferdinand journeying intermittently to Vienna to meet with Matthias. Initially, they attempted to convince him to return Upper and Lower Austria and Moravia to Rudolf, but he insisted that he could not do this without the consent of the estates, and they adamantly refused to submit to Rudolf. Eventually an agreement was reached, forged for the most part by the duke of Brunswick, that culminated in a ceremony held in the great council room of the Hradschin, the imperial residence in Prague, on October 9, 1610. Archdukes Ferdinand and Maximilian, representing Matthias who was not present, apologized to Rudolf according to an agreed upon formula for Matthias's actions against his brother, and Rudolf accepted the apology according to a prearranged formula. Rudolf acknowledged the impossibility of the return of the lands in question to him by Matthias. Matthias, for his part, recognized Rudolf as emperor and as head of the house, and he promised to show his gratitude for Rudolf's renunciation of his claims to the territories by an annual payment to his brother in cash and wine. Important for Rudolf's honor was the public ripping into pieces by Ferdinand and Maximilian of the agreement reached at Vienna in April 1606 and the transport of the fragments back to Matthias in Vienna. This understanding directed against him had always stuck in Rudolf's craw. Archduke Albert wrote to Ferdinand from the Netherlands on November 16, 1610, "In this tragic time, you are the one to whom ought to be attributed the vital establishment and recovery of the imperial majesty, the Roman Empire, and the beloved posterity [of the family]."[19]

Yet despite the settlement at the Hradschin, the quarrel between the brothers had not been resolved. The issue of the succession in the Empire remained, and Rudolf now announced that he favored the young Leopold as his successor; he even went to far as to adopt Leopold. The emperor, driven by continuing enmity, was determined to keep Matthias from the succession. Leopold had not participated in the princes' conference in Prague and, more importantly, had not been a party to the fateful agreement of Vienna of 1606, and he now possessed a formidable military force. The electors of Cologne and Mainz favored Leopold because he had never made religious concessions to the Protestants as had Matthias. The nuncio in Prague, on the other hand, urged the election of Matthias; he opposed Leopold as too meteoric and as

[18] Rill, 176–7; Hurter 6, 251–87.   [19] Cited in Hurter 6: 341–2; ibid., 272–342; Rill, 177–80.

unacceptable both to the heretics and to the other Austrian princes.[20] Ferdinand, who had left Prague after the ceremony at the Hradschin, now dispatched Casal back there to remonstrate with his troublesome brother about sowing renewed ill will between Rudolf and Matthias, and he indicated that if Leopold continued to do so, then he, Ferdinand, would have to side with Matthias.[21] Leopold was also considering a marriage with a sister of Maximilian of Bavaria. But the problem for Leopold was that he did not possess a major territory – his bishoprics did not weigh in the scale – that would be necessary to support him in the imperial office.

Leopold and his camarilla, with the support of Rudolf, now sought to seize Bohemia, destroy the Letter of Majesty, and make Leopold ruler. The whole enterprise was ill-considered. His troops plundered and devastated Lower Austria on the way to Bohemia, where they crossed the border on February 13, and were soon in Prague with Leopold. But Leopold's stroke failed; his troops could not take the Altstadt and were eventually pushed back by the troops of the estates. The adventuresome archduke abandoned Prague on the night of March 10–11, and Matthias entered the city on March 24 with 18,000 soldiers; the Bohemian estates had called on him to come. In the ensuing chaos, some Catholics looked with hope to Ferdinand.[22] On May 23, Matthias was crowned king of Bohemia in the Cathedral of St. Veit, but only after he had recognized the Letter of Majesty as well as other limitations on his authority and the alliance of the Bohemian estates with those of Upper and Lower Austria and Hungary that was in the process of formation. To foster this, he promised to summon a general meeting of the estates of the various territories. So the estates further restricted the power of the ruler. Klesl initially recommended the rejection of these stipulations. Rudolf now retained only the imperial title and the right to continue to reside in Prague; yet he still machinated with representatives of the Protestant Union.[23]

The issue of the imperial succession remained. A Habsburg family conference was held in Vienna in late December 1611 and attended by Matthias, the archdukes Ferdinand, Maximilian, Ferdinand's son, Johann Carl, as well as the Spanish ambassador Balthasar de Zúñiga as representative of Philip III and a representative of Archduke Albert. Leopold was not present. Here it was decided to support Matthias for the office of king of the Romans and so eventually as emperor.[24] Both the papacy and the king of Spain now favored him.[25] But he faced opposition. This came above all from the ecclesiastical

---

[20] Final Relation of Antonio Caetani, nuncio to the emperor in Prague, Dec. 10, 1610, *Le istruzioni generali di Paulo V ai diplomatici pontifici 1605–1621*, ed. Silvio Giordano (Tübingen, 2003), 2: 745, 747–8.
[21] Instruction for Casal, Apr. 4, 1611, cited in Hurter 6: 406–8.   [22] Ibid., 501–2.
[23] Rill, 180–6.   [24] Ibid., 191.
[25] Instruction for Antonio Caetani, nuncio in Spain, Oct. 27, 1611, Giordano 2: 793.

electors who considered him all too ready to compromise with the Protestants as his concessions in the Habsburg lands demonstrated, and they at first inclined toward Archduke Albert. The three Protestant electors remained wary of Matthias. At this point, the switch of position on the part of Bishop Klesl proved significant; he now functioned practically as Matthias's first minister and would, after Matthias's election, become his director of the privy council.

Klesl, as we have seen, at first opposed the concessions that Matthias had made to the Austrian and Bohemian estates in order to secure their recognition of him as ruler. But at the time that Matthias recognized the Letter of Majesty in the spring of 1611, Klesl was rethinking his position. Just as he began to approach the courts of Brandenburg and the Palatinate in search of compromise, he received a commendation from Paul V for his defense of the Catholic cause. But Klesl now came to the realization that some form of compromise was vital for the defense of the Empire and in fact, for the good of religion itself in the long run. The continuing Turkish threat greatly influenced Klesl's change of heart. Only with the support of the Protestant states could one hold off the Turks over the long haul. Better to make some relatively minor concessions on religion to the Protestants than to allow the Balkan lands, Hungary, and then the Empire to fall under Turkish dominion. To Klesl's mind the German princes, including Maximilian of Bavaria, underestimated the force of this prospect. Furthermore, the bishop foresaw that only composition between the Catholic and Protestant parties in the Empire, especially between the Catholic League and the Protestant Union, would prevent war and upheaval in the Empire. The bishop acted on the principle of the lesser evil or the greater good.[26] So he assumed the position of a *politique*, that is, one who in the usage of the time would make concessions on religion for the greater good of the state, in this case the Empire, and ultimately for religion itself. Henry IV's policy in France with the Edict of Nantes in 1598 as well as limited toleration in the Netherlands seems to have influenced his thinking.[27] He took this position, he declared in a conversation with a member of the Palatinate privy council, despite the opposition of Archduke Ferdinand and the elector of Cologne.[28] Shortly afterwards, following Matthias' election as emperor, he

---

[26] Johann Rainer, "Der Prozess gegen Cardinal Klesl," *Römische Historische Mitteilungen* 5 (1962): 51–60; Rudolf Neck, "Österreichs Türkenpolitik unter Melchior Khlesl," Dissertation, University of Vienna (1948), 76–7.

[27] Wolf Dietrich von Raitenau, the Archbishop of Salzburg, held a similar position; see Hirn 2: 551. Rona Johnston Gordon, "Melchior Khlesl und der konfessionelle Hintergrund der kaiserlichen Politik im Reich nach 1610," in *Dimensionen der europäischen Aussenpolitik zur Zeit der Wende vom 16. zum 17, Jahrhundert*, ed. Friedrich Biederbeck, Gregor Horstkemper and Winfried Schulze (Berlin, 2003), 199–222, shows the fundamental consistency of Klesl's confessional and foreign policy.

[28] Rainer, 55–6.

initiated protracted negotiations with the Turks that envisioned a revision and clarification of the Treaty of Zsitvatorok to the benefit of the emperor.[29]

Klesl now began actively to gather the support of the Protestant electors for the election of Matthias. He reassured the Calvinist Elector Palatine and the elector of Brandenburg of the moderation of Matthias whom, they realized, was at any event constrained by the estates of his territories. The elector of Saxony already tended toward the candidate of the House of Habsburg with its long imperial tradition. So a majority of four was secured for Matthias. The three ecclesiastical electors eventually came around to make the vote unanimous, but only on the day of the election itself in Frankfurt, June 13, 1612. Rudolf, meanwhile, had died on January 20, at enmity with and plotting against Matthias until the end. So in Frankfurt the electors chose not a king of the Romans but the Holy Roman Emperor himself. Matthias had attained his goal, and with the support of Ferdinand. Ferdinand, for his part, had not sought the imperial title at this time, readily yielding to Matthias even though – as the nuncio in Prague had noted in his final report of December, 1610 – all the hope of the House of Austria rested on him.[30] Nor had he attempted to prevent his brother Leopold's candidacy.

Emperor Matthias relished the pageantry and accouterments of the imperial office. In December 1611, the fifty-nine-year-old emperor had taken to wife the twenty-six-year-old Archduchess Maria Anna, daughter of Archduke Ferdinand who had governed Anterior Austria prior to Archduke Maximilian, in the hope of begetting an heir. Lazy by nature and bored with the details of government, he delegated most of his authority to his director of the privy council, Bishop Klesl.[31] Matthias now summoned, at Klesl's recommendation, a diet initially scheduled to convene in Regensburg on April 24, 1613, but which did not open until August 13; it would be the last diet until 1640. Klesl and the emperor aimed to attain two main goals at the diet. First, they hoped to secure funds for defense against the Turks to the southeast, especially in volatile Transylvania. There both the emperor as king of Hungary and the sultan claimed suzerainty. A new Turkish war was liable to break out.[32] On October 23, 1613, the Transylvanian estates, supported by the Turks, elected as their prince the Protestant Bethlen Gàbor of the Hungarian Bethlen family, who then acknowledged the sultan as overlord. Four days later the pro-Habsburg Sigismund Bathory, who had been married to Ferdinand's sister, Maria Christierna, was assassinated. Border difficulties centered around the recovery of the three cities Esztergom (Gran), Kanisza, and Eger (Erlau)[33] for the emperor and

---

[29] Neck, 77–8; Ritter, 2: 390.
[30] Final Report of Antonio Caetani, Dec. 1610, Giordano 2, 744.   [31] Rill, 212–13.
[32] Adam Haas, *Der Reichstag von 1613* (Würzburg, 1929), 22.
[33] Eger (German Erlau) in northeast Hungary is not to be confused with Eger (German, Chub in Czech) in Bohemia.

for Archduke Ferdinand. Secondly, Klesl hoped to apply his new policy of conciliation with the Protestants in the Habsburg lands to the Empire and in the process to reestablish the authority of the emperor, which he considered a necessary step toward the political, and religious, good of the Empire. He recognized the failure of force to resolve the religious issues in France, the Netherlands, and England, and he admired the achievement of Henry IV in France.[34] Archduke Ferdinand did not attend this diet, serving instead as governor of Upper and Lower Austria and as Matthias's representative in Hungary while the emperor resided first in Linz and then in Regensburg.[35] That January of 1613, Ferdinand – along with his brother Maximilian Ernst and his two older sons, Johann Carl and Ferdinand Ernst – participated enthusiastically in the Carnival in Vienna with its tournaments, animal baiting, mock peasant weddings, and dramatic farces.[36] Ferdinand traveled regularly.

In the winter of 1612–1613, well before the diet convened, Klesl circulated among the Catholic princes a proposed compromise, minimal in itself, with the Protestants. It had to do with the archbishopric of Magdeburg, an ecclesiastical territory which had been confiscated by the elector of Brandenburg and was now held by Christian Friedrich, the elector's brother. Following the Ecclesiastical Reservation, Catholics up to this time had refused to recognize Protestant administrators of ecclesiastical territories, much less seat them in the diet. Klesl proposed that the emperor recognize the secular authority of the administrator in Magdeburg by investing him with the territory for three years, without granting him a seat in the diet and reserving all papal rights. The elector of Mainz initially responded favorably to this proposal on January 21, 1613. But Maximilian of Bavaria rejected it, preferring to keep the peace through the mutual threat of war rather than through reconciliation of differences. In a meeting of the Catholic League along with other sympathetic Catholic states in Frankfurt in early March, the delegates rejected any recognition of Magdeburg. Klesl journeyed to the meeting to argue the volatility of the Turkish front and the need for composition of the religious differences in the Empire, but unsuccessfully.[37] Apart from the determination not to yield illegally seized church property to the heretics, the Catholic states were persuaded that this recognition of Magdeburg would soon result in its seating in the council of princes of the diet. This in turn would set a precedent leading to the seating of other ecclesiastical principalities held by the Protestants and eventually give to the Protestants the majority in the council of princes in the diet, with disastrous results for the Catholics.[38] The activist Protestant Union led by the Palatinate took a similarly rigid position. Splitting off from them and more ready for compromise was the elector of Saxony and other Lutheran states including Hesse-Darmstadt.

---

[34] Ibid., 27, n. 79; Rill, 214–15.   [35] AF 8: 550, 638–9.   [36] AF: 542.
[37] Neck, 82.   [38] Haas, 27–33; Ritter 2: 381–3.

The attitudes toward the issue of Magdeburg set the tone for the diet when it finally convened on August 13. In his opening proposition the emperor did agree to take up the religious issue before his request for contributions for the war effort against the Turks; this was a concession to the Protestants. But there existed little common ground on the interpretation of the Religious Peace and the imperial constitution. The Protestants urged that in the diet, as well as in the courts, the majority principle be abandoned and decisions rendered on the basis of composition between the two parties. It was clear already by August 17 that the Catholics would not abandon this principle since they enjoyed a majority in both the college of electors and the college of princes.[39] Two days later, the states of the Protestant Union and their allies responded negatively to the emperor's opening proposition.[40] Still, Klesl attempted to find some compromise. On September 4, he argued to a select group of Catholic representatives that the Protestants feared that the unbending application of the majority principle and so the Catholic interpretation of the Religious Peace would result in widespread war. News of hostilities on the Turkish front transmitted by a courier from Archduke Ferdinand briefly moved some toward concessions, and the diet voted a minimal grant of thirty Roman months for defense against the Turks, the last grant made for this purpose for forty-two years.[41] But the crisis passed. Many Catholics joined Maximilian of Bavaria in resisting the *politique* Klesl. On September 20, the ecclesiastical electors asserted the uselessness of further negotiations.

The last weeks of the convention were taken up by the Catholics with a plan to reorganize the Catholic League. Klesl had long opposed the existence of a purely confessional alliance, hoping to create a league including some Protestant states that would be political rather than religious and have as its primary aim the defense of imperial authority. In fact, through his agent in Rome in 1612, he had countered the efforts of both Ferdinand and Maximilian to secure papal support on the grounds that a confessional league would enhance the prospects for war.[42] The proposed goal of the league now read "the conservation of imperial authority and the imperial constitution," not the defense of the Catholic religion, and so it lost much of its confessional character. It also now counted three rather than two directorates: a Rhenish directorate headed by Schweikard, the elector of Mainz; a Bavarian directorate under Maximilian; and the third directorate, the Austrian including Swabia as well as Austria and with Archduke Maximilian as its leader. Archduke Ferdinand continued to serve as vice-protector. Furthermore, the new articles of the league required, if time allowed, the approval of the emperor before any defensive action was undertaken. And this action was to be taken in the name of the emperor. So Klesl achieved a goal that he had long pursued, the destruction of the Catholic League. But this new Regensburg defensive alliance never really functioned and

---

[39] Haas, 54–61.   [40] Ritter 2: 385.   [41] Neck, 90.   [42] Haas, 26–7.

was never ratified by Maximilian of Bavaria. He rather consolidated the Bavarian directorate but then resigned his position of director largely because of conflict with Archduke Maximilian over Habsburg influence in Swabia. Shortly afterwards, at the bidding of neighboring ecclesiastical princes, he undertook the formation of a much more restricted defensive alliance. Only after the outbreak of the Thirty Years War would the Catholic League revive.[43]

On October 22 Emperor Matthias prorogued the Diet until May 1, 1614 but it never reconvened.

Shortly after his return from Regensburg, Emperor Matthias sent Ferdinand an extremely pessimistic assessment of the political situation, especially with regard to the continuing efforts of the estates in the various Habsburg territories, Upper and Lower Austria, Bohemia, Moravia, Silesia, and Hungary, to assert their alleged rights and to expand their political power, and with regard to the situation on the border with the Turks. The structure of the Habsburg lands would endure until he died, he lamented, but then it would all collapse.[44] From August 11 to 25, 1614, committees of the estates from the Bohemian lands met with Emperor Matthias in Linz. Ferdinand and Archduke Maximilian were also present. Little was accomplished in the negotiations with the estates except to reach agreement to keep the peace with the Turks.[45] The following year in a treaty reached at Tyrnau (Trnava/Nagyszxombat) on May 6, Matthias recognized Bethlen Gàbor as ruler of Transylvania and agreed to minor territorial adjustments. Then two months later, on July 15, Klesl concluded a renewal of Zsitvatorok with the Turks regulating the Turkish–Hungarian border and leaving open the issue of suzerainty over Transylvania. Ferdinand's hope to regain the fortresses of Esztergom and Kanisza, or at least to construct a second fortress at Kanisza, was not realized.[46] But movement toward stabilization of the border with the Turks was maintained. His success in negotiating this settlement with the Turks won for Klesl a cardinal's hat.[47] Yet issues still remained, and further treaties with the Turks were signed in 1616 and 1617, and the Treaty of Komorn (Komáron) on March 1, 1618, finally resolved many of the issues. But the coming Bohemian rebellion raised grave dangers for the Habsburgs in the east as the rebels reached out for assistance from Bethlen and the Turks. Only in the later years of the coming war could the emperor feel secure in the east, and this followed for the most part from the difficulties and unrest that the Turks faced at home and from Poland and Persia.[48]

---

[43] Albrecht 2, 439–50.   [44] Brockman, 45, n.30.
[45] AF 8: 636, 640, 692; Hugo Altmann, BA 12 (Munich, 1978): 159–60.
[46] Neck, 131–2; Ritter 2: 390–1.   [47] Rainer, "Der Prozess gegen Cardinal Klesl," 64.
[48] Neck, 172, 190, 216, 220–1; R.R. Heinisch, "Habsburg, die Pforte, und der Böhmische Aufstand," Südostforschungen 33 (1974): 128–30.

Toward the Succession, 1608–1618

The succession in both the Habsburg lands and the Empire remained a critical issue. Both Klesl and the Spanish ambassador had brought it up to the fifty-five-year-old emperor on the day of his imperial election.[49] One could not permit an interregnum which would open the door to the control of the imperial office by the two Protestant vicars, the Palatinate and Saxony. Some discussion had taken place at the Diet of Regensburg. Emperor Matthias, Ferdinand, and Archduke Maximilian then returned to the matter at the time of the meeting of the committees of the estates of the Bohemian lands in Linz in August 1614. Archduke Maximilian endorsed Ferdinand, who already had two sons, renouncing though not yet officially the imperial succession for himself and guaranteeing to secure the renunciation of Albert. Both of them were childless.[50] Both soon did renounce their claims in favor of Ferdinand. Ferdinand, in a private conversation with the nuncio who was also present in Linz, professed his allegiance to the pope and his intent to restrict the religious concessions made by Matthias in the Habsburg lands.[51]

But two principal obstacles stood in the way of Ferdinand's succession. One was the firm opposition of Klesl. He still envisioned a composition between the Catholic and Protestant states and so peace in the Empire, which he considered essential for effective defense against the Turks in the long run. The candidacy of Ferdinand, with his reputation for vigorous Counter-Reformation measures, would effectively prevent the desired composition. To attempt to force the election of Ferdinand might well lead to the withdrawal of the Palatinate and Brandenburg from the electoral council, their protest of the election, and further confusion in the Empire with resulting damage to the House of Austria, the Empire, and the Catholic religion.[52]

The second obstacle came from Spain and was indeed welcomed by Klesl. The Spanish ambassador in Central Europe, Balthasar de Zuñiga, had reminded Philip III in 1611 of a remark that his predecessor had made several years previously, that the king had a valid claim to the thrones of Bohemia and Hungary. In late June and early July, 1613, Matthias, Ferdinand, and Zuñiga met in Linz to discuss the Spanish position.[53] Philip's mother Anna, the eldest daughter of Emperor Maximilian II and sister of Rudolf, Matthias, Maximilian, Ernst, and Albert, had never renounced her claim to the two thrones. Philip's claim through his mother, the Spaniards argued, as grandson of Maximilian outweighed the claim of Ferdinand as his nephew. Both claims, it should

---

[49] Altmann, 159.   [50] Ibid., 160.
[51] Placido De Marra, nuncio at the imperial court, to Cardinal Scipione Borghese, secretary of state, Linz, Nov. 14, 1614, as cited in Alexander Koller, *Imperator und Pontifex. Forschungen zum Verhältnis von Kaisehof und römischer Kurie im Zeitalter der Konfessionalisierung (1555–1648)* (Münster, 2012), 160.
[52] Rill, 242.
[53] Helfried Valentinitsch, "Die Reise Erzherzog Ferdinands von Innerösterreich nach Linz im Jahre 1613," *Festschrift Berthold Sutter*, ed. Gernot Kocher and Gernot D. Hasiba (Graz, 1983): 399–443

be noted, understood the two crowns to be hereditary, which neither estates would readily admit. Zuñiga aimed above all at the acquisition of a firm basis for Spain in Central Europe in the crown of Bohemia. This would also give Spain a vote in the electoral college of the Empire and might well lead, for Philip's son, to the imperial office, and so a return to the days of Charles V.[54] Various other candidates were also proposed for the imperial office from outside the Habsburg circle, including Maximilian of Bavaria and even Louis XIII of France. Right up until the spring of 1618, the young Frederick, Elector Palatine, attempted to convince Maximilian to seek the imperial office, arguing that his election would prevent Habsburg domination in the Empire and forestall the threat of the imperial office becoming hereditary. But Maximilian never seriously considered this possibility. He saw the Palatinate proposal of his candidacy as an attempt to split the Catholics and drive a wedge between himself and the Habsburgs. This in turn might well delay the election of an emperor and so enable the Elector Palatine to function as vicar during an interregnum. In addition, Maximilian realized that Bavaria did not possess the territorial base necessary to support the imperial office.[55]

During the coming years from 1615 to 1617, Klesl with his delaying tactics effectively stymied efforts to proceed toward an election in the hope of an agreement between Catholics and Protestants. Plans for an electoral convention to elect a king of the Romans and for a diet to negotiate came and went. In late 1615, Matthias adopted Ferdinand as his son, indicating in this way his intent for the succession, even though he still hoped for a child himself. Matthias also feared that he might be pressured to abdicate if a king of the Romans were elected.[56] At one time in 1615, when it was rumored that Archduke Ferdinand might be considering yielding to the Protestants on some points, he received a letter from his uncle, Duke William in Munich. "I do not believe this," he wrote, "about one who once declared, 'he would let his land and people go and wander about in a simple shirt rather than agree to this.' He should remain as he is; nothing else would bring good fortune. He should not allow himself to be seduced by Klesl's clever political talk. He ought to consider how well his affairs had prospered despite the concerns of the politicians. Accordingly he had achieved grace before God and the world. It was his own concessions that had brought the emperor so low. If he should allow himself to do the same, so would his subjects demand the same, and all his lands fall into heresy."[57]

Ferdinand assuaged some of Matthias's concerns the following year when he assured him that he would not interfere in the current emperor's government and that he would respect the rights of any children that Matthias might have.[58]

---

[54] Magdelena Sanchez, "A House Divided: Spain, Austria, and the Bohemian and Hungarian Succession," *Sixteenth Century Journal* 25 (1994): 887–92.
[55] Albrecht 2, 472–87.   [56] Hurter, 7: 23–4, 30, 56–8.   [57] N.d., cited in ibid., 29.
[58] Brockman, 46.

In early 1616 Archduke Maximilian, who most persistently urged the election, hatched a plan to settle the election of Ferdinand once and for all militarily. It called for the raising of an army of 24,000 in the Netherlands to be financed by funds from Spain, the pope, and the ecclesiastical princes. The army would serve the purpose of reestablishing imperial authority in the Empire and enabling the emperor to enforce the laws of the Empire and the decisions of the majority in the diet in favor of the Catholic position and in the electoral college in favor of Ferdinand. It would also assist Ferdinand in creating order in the Habsburg territorial lands. Foreseen as general of this army in the likely event that Archduke Albert would decline the position was to be Archduke Ferdinand himself. With some reservations, Ferdinand seems to have gone along with this plan. Archduke Maximilian presented it to Matthias in Prague in mid-February, 1616. He successfully persuaded the emperor to take action to push forward the election of Ferdinand; Matthias agreed to undertake a journey to Dresden to win the vote of the elector of Saxony. But Matthias and his councillors responded ambivalently to the plan for military intervention. It was leaked to a minister of the Palatinate – some suspected by Klesl – and when it became public, it stimulated an enormous stir among the Protestants when they learned of the design to resolve outstanding issues in the Empire by force. Once he became aware of the plan, Maximilian of Bavaria – always wary of Habsburg ambition – also opposed it partly because he saw it as concentrating excessive power in the hands of the Habsburgs and diminishing that of the Catholic League. So the plan died a quiet death.[59] Meanwhile, in a resolution of March 14, 1616, Matthias once again asserted his determination that Ferdinand succeed him.[60]

At the end of June 1616, Archduke Maximilian and Ferdinand first decided to take measures to force Klesl from office as soon as the Spaniards made their position clear if progress had not been made on the succession. Archduke Maximilian then began to press more insistently for the removal of Klesl. In mid-October 1616, he sent an emissary from Innsbruck to Graz to complain of the perverse style of government in Prague that could only be remedied by the dismissal of the cardinal. Ferdinand wanted to know how this was to be done, and he advised that it was necessary to await the outcome of the negotiations with Spain. Maximilian then suggested three ways in which Klesl might be removed. Ferdinand responded following a position paper drawn up in the hand of his secretary dated October 31, 1616. All was kept top secret.

Ferdinand rejected the first method proposed by Maximilian, the dispatch of representatives of all the archdukes and electors or princes directly to confront Matthias with an enumeration of Klesl's actions. Matthias would only inform Klesl himself of this initiative and the situation would be worse than ever.

---

[59] Albrecht 2, 474–6; Altmann, *BA* 12: 160–81; Brockmann, 47–8 and n. 40.
[60] Brockman, 46.

Maximilian's second suggestion called for a resort to the pope to threaten Klesl with excommunication. But according to Ferdinand, Klesl had not committed any ecclesiastical offense, and it would be difficult to excommunicate him for his policy. Furthermore, the whole procedure would become public and then further delay a resolution of the succession. Thirdly, Maximilian proposed approaching a theologian for an opinion on the misdeeds of Klesl that would allow them to resort to assassination, by poison or even hanging. This Ferdinand turned down vigorously, thereby manifesting his attachment to legal process. It would be difficult to find such a theologian. Much worse, this would be to act without any formal charge against the cardinal or opportunity for defense or proper trial. Such a bloody method had never been employed by the House of Austria, and it would have evil consequences. Ferdinand would never stoop to such methods. He recommended rather that Klesl be sent on an important mission or assignment away from the court, and in his absence the emperor be confronted with his misdeeds. While away from the court, the cardinal could be arrested but then given an opportunity to defend himself. If he then agreed to no longer hold up the resolution of the succession, all would be well. A letter would also be sent to the pope explaining why such action was taken against a cardinal of the Church. Ferdinand's response seems to have calmed Maximilian, if only briefly.[61] Emperor Matthias himself wrote to both Philip III and to his own youngest sister, Archduchess Margaret, who intermittently resided at the Madrid convent of the Descalzas Reales and exercised considerable political influence,[62] encouraging them to hurry with the Spanish position on the succession. Soon the results of the negotiations with Spain would arrive.

At his meeting with Emperor Matthias and Ferdinand in Linz in early July 1613, shortly before the opening of the Diet of Regensburg, Zuñiga had informed Ferdinand that Philip III was ready to claim the thrones of Bohemia and Hungary.[63] The issue darkened relations between the Spanish and Austrian branches of the family. One reason that the Spaniards felt justified in urging the claim was that they considered the balance between the two branches of the family to have been upset by the persistent transfer of funds from Madrid to Vienna. Vienna had long been dependent on subsidies from Spain. The Austrians warned Madrid that persistence with its claims held up and endangered the succession in Hungary and especially in Bohemia and thus, the Habsburg position in Central Europe. Not only did it render more likely the death of Matthias without the designation of a king of the Romans as his successor; it also encouraged the Bohemian estates to look elsewhere for their king. Division over the issue also characterized the decision makers in Madrid.

---

[61] Position paper of Leonhard Götz, Oct. 31, 1616, Hurter 7, 585–9; Ferdinand to Archduke Maximilian, Nov. 4, 1616, ibid., 589–92; Hurter, 7: 66–9.
[62] Ibid.   [63] Valentinitsch, ibid.; Ritter 2: 430–1.

The expansionist Zuñiga probably thought of actual Spanish acquisition of the two kingdoms by the future Philip IV. Others like the duke of Lerma, Philip III's favorite, considered that the Spanish reach was already over-extended, and he advocated disengagement in Central Europe. Other policy-makers found themselves in the midst of these two extremes. They realized that a Spaniard would never be acceptable as a king in either of the two kingdoms. But they aimed to secure compensation from Vienna for the surrender of Madrid's claims in terms of lands to be ceded by Ferdinand once he became emperor. Some looked to the Austrian possessions in Alsace and the Tyrol. Acquisition of these territories would strengthen the Spanish hold on the so-called Spanish Road, which Spanish troops took from Genoa up to the Netherlands. Others considered more desirable three fiefs of the Empire in Italy over which the future emperor would be able to dispose. Finale, close to Genoa on the Ligurian Sea, would give the Spaniards an alternative port to Genoa for the transport of their soldiers should they lose the support of the Genoese. Piombino lay on the western coast of Italy across from the island of Elba; Spanish ships traveling to or from the Levant or Naples passed through the straits between the two. It would also serve as an alternative port to Genoa. The Spaniards had already constructed a fort in Corregio in Lombardy, which enhanced control of the road to Flanders.[64]

Archduke Ferdinand contested Philip III's juridical claim to the succession in Bohemia and Hungary. He would not compromise on this. But he recognized the political necessity of compensating his cousin and brother-in-law for the renunciation of his claims. In three stages Ferdinand and Eggenberg negotiated with Zuñiga at the imperial court, in the summer of 1613, the turn of the year 1613–1614, and again in the summer of 1614 in Linz. Ferdinand agreed to a place for Philip's male children ahead of his own female children in the line of succession; but this meant little since he already had two sons. He offered Philip several small ports on the Adriatic Sea but he refused the Spanish desire for the Tyrol and Anterior Austria or Alsace. Talks continued in Vienna into 1615 until Zuñiga was about to be recalled, and they focused more and more on Alsace. Ferdinand hesitated to surrender territory that had long belonged to the Austrian branch of the family, and perhaps more importantly, he feared the uproar this surrender of German territory would provoke if it became public and its interpretation as a concession to the expansion of a feared "universal Spanish monarchy." The Austrians would be seen as the stalking horse for Spain in the Empire, and this would isolate them from German Catholics as well as Protestants.

In late 1615, Iñigo Velez de Guevara y Tasis, Count de Oñate, was designated to succeed Zuñiga as point man for Spain in the negotiations with Ferdinand and as ambassador in Vienna. But he moved slowly to take up his

---

[64] Sanchez, 886–97.

new position at the imperial court and only arrived in Prague in February 1617. In the fall of 1616, just as he and Archduke Maximilian considered the removal of Klesl, Ferdinand persistently urged the Spanish court to conclude negotiations in letters to Philip III and other major figures at the court of Madrid, including Archduchess Margaret who was also Ferdinand's cousin. Meanwhile continuing talks between Ferdinand and Zuñiga led to an agreement dated Graz, January 31, 1617 by which Philip gave up his claim to the thrones of Bohemia and Hungary, and Ferdinand consented to the placement of Philip's male heirs before his own female heirs. More importantly, in a secret document of the same date, Ferdinand promised to cede Finale and Piombino to Philip once he became emperor. The future of Alsace was left open; Ferdinand stated that once he came into the possession of Alsace, if he could not transfer it to Philip, he would provide an adequate substitute.[65]

But this was not the end. Oñate, when he finally arrived in Prague in early February – he had taken his time despite the urgency with which the Austrians viewed the matter – rejected the agreement reached by Ferdinand and Zuñiga, insisting on an unambiguous transfer of Alsace to Spain along with the Tyrol. Intense negotiations followed. Ferdinand faced a difficult choice: either important progress on the succession issue but at a high price in territorial compensation and perhaps a storm in the Empire if the surrender of the two territories to Spain became known, or a further dangerous delay regarding the succession if he refused to surrender the two Habsburg territories. Ferdinand opted for the former, which appeared to be the lesser evil. One could no longer postpone a final agreement on the succession, crucial as it was to both the future of Catholicism and of the Habsburg position in Central Europe. So in a secret agreement of March 20, 1617, Ferdinand agreed to the future cession of Alsace and the two associated territories of Hagenau and Ortenau to Spain. Oñate then dropped his demand for Tyrol. Ferdinand also received in the final settlement a subsidy of nearly one million talers from the Spanish treasury, to assist him in a conflict which had broken out with Venice over trade in the northern Adriatic Sea.[66] Neither the emperor nor Archduke Maximilian nor Ferdinand's brothers were privy to the secret agreements. Their conclusion led then to the final public treaty of June 6, 1617, which was confirmed by the emperor on June 15. Throughout all the agreements, Ferdinand persistently asserted his legal right to the succession.[67] As matters eventually turned out, none of the Alsatian territories ever passed to the Spaniards.

Just as Ferdinand was negotiating the succession, a long-simmering conflict on the border of Inner Austria with the Republic of Venice demanded his attention. It has often been called the War of Gradisca because of the central role in it

---

[65] Brockman, 50–5.   [66] Geoffrey Parker, *The Thirty Years War*, 2 ed. (New York, 1997), 37.
[67] Brockmann, 55–8.

of the Austrian fortress town of Gradisca in Friuli. The Venetians insisted on control of the Adriatic as their "mare clausum," exercising a "mini imperialism" and so they hindered the commerce of the Austrians through the ports of Fiume and Triest, sometimes resorting to blockades. In the long run, the Austrians could not countenance this. The Venetians also feared encirclement by the Habsburgs, Spanish Milan to the west and Spanish Naples to the south, Austrian Inner Austria and Istria to the north and east.[68] The Uskoks or "refugees" from lands seized by the Turks provided the occasion for the conflict. A people of mixed South Slav and Albanian origins, Christians, they for many years had supplied troops to the Austrian government for defense against the Turks in the borderlands of Croatia and Hungary. Subsequently, many Uskoks had settled along the northeastern Adriatic coast and especially in the fortified port city of Senj on the Croatian coast. They came to live principally from piracy. From Senj they raided smaller ports and seized ships on the sea. They attacked Venetian as well as Turkish shipping, claiming that the Venetians underhandedly aided the Turks in the area. They became "the scourge of the Adriatic."[69] As far back as 1548, Venice had complained to Emperor Charles V about the activities of the Uskoks. After the transfer of authority for the Croatian–Slavonic border with the Turks from Vienna to Graz in 1578, different policies toward the Uskoks emerged at the two Habsburg courts. Klesl in Vienna desired peace with Venice; but Graz found the Uskoks useful for defense against the Turks and for limiting Venetian claims in the area.[70]

In the late 1590s, the Venetians undertook vigorous reprisals against the Uskoks, blockading their ports, burning their ships, and inflicting bloody punishments on them. In 1600 Archduke Ferdinand took measures to end the most blatant assaults of the Uskoks, but the commissioner he appointed to oversee his initiative was murdered. Agreements between the Austrians and Venice of 1600 and 1604 failed to resolve the issues as did another of 1613. Violence between the Venetians and Uskoks intensified. At one point Venetians mounted the heads of Uskok pirates around the Piazza San Marco, and Uskoks in a victory banquet ate the heart of a Venetian commander.[71] Ferdinand even sent an expedition to Senj in 1614 to put a stop to Unkok raids; his forces beheaded several Uskok leaders. But the Venetians ignored the measures that he took against the Uskoks. Finally in 1615 open war broke out when Venetian troops crossed the border into Inner Austria and seized territory. As Ferdinand declared to Klesl, "He did not want war; rather he had long exercised patience and suffered

---

[68] Ruth Simon, "The Uskok 'Problem' and Habsburg, Venetian, and Ottoman Relations at the Turn of the Seventeenth Century, *Essays in History* (Charlottesville, 2000), 8, 11, http://etext.lib.virginia.edu/journals/EH/EH42/Simon42.html, accessed Aug. 29, 2006; H. Valentinitsch, "Ferdinand II., die innerosterreichischen Lander und der Gradiskanerkrieg 1615–1618," *Johannes Kepler 1571–1971*. Gedenkschrift der Universitat Graz (Graz, 1975), 501 (quotation), 505, 530.
[69] Heinrich Kretschmayr, *Geschichte von Venedig* 3 (Vienna, 1933; rpt. Aalen, 1964): 275.
[70] Simon, 5.   [71] Frederic C. Lane, *Venice: A Maritime Republic* (Baltimore, 1973), 198–9.

severe damage. But as the outrages regularly continued, his office, his duty, and his honor did not allow him to keep silence any longer and to leave his territory and people miserable... History teaches how you can trust the lords of Venice."[72] Ferdinand who was in the process of assuming the Habsburg inheritance in Central Europe could not afford to be humiliated by the Venetians.

At first the Venetians gained the upper hand as they advanced into Austrian territory. But their efforts to take the fortress of Gradisca failed after a first siege from February 12 to March 30, 1616. Mismanagement characterized the war effort on both sides, and they both looked elsewhere for assistance. The Austrians received help with the arrival of 3,000 Spanish troops under Balthasar Marradas, and the Venetians with 5,000 Dutch and English troops under Count Johann Ernst of Nassau-Siegen. As we have seen, the Spaniards also provided Ferdinand with a handsome subsidy. But it did not help Venice's relationship with Ferdinand when in March 1616 the Venetians took the archduke's confessor, Father Viller, prisoner on his way back from a general congregation of the Jesuits in Rome and then held him for eleven months. At the time Jesuits were prohibited from entering Venetian territory, and Viller had imprudently attempted to journey through it in the guise of a secular priest.[73] In March 1617, another siege of Gradisca by the Venetians began; it lasted into November but again fell short of its goal. Meanwhile, Ferdinand, who faced great difficulty in raising funds from the estates of Inner Austria, succeeded in recruiting several qualified generals, including the Czech nobleman Albrecht von Wallenstein. Wallenstein brought with him at his own expense 180 cavalrymen and eighty musketeers. Too small a number to make a major difference in the war, they did contribute to a daring maneuver that helped relieve the siege on September 22. The general returned to Bohemia in December, having come to the attention of Ferdinand and won his gratitude.[74]

A peace agreement had been reached in Paris on September 26, 1617, with the energetic assistance of Cardinal Klesl, but hostilities continued on the Isonzo River until early January 1618. The Uskok pirates were to be resettled fifty miles inland from Senj, their ships to be destroyed, and an Austrian garrison to be stationed in the port city to make sure that the provisions were carried out. For their part, the Venetians were to withdraw from the towns in Austrian territory that they had occupied. But the fundamental issues of the border and of freedom of the sea in the Adriatic were left unresolved.[75] Ferdinand's attention was now turned to securing the support of the Bohemian estates for his election as king. Had the War of Gradisca not been settled before the Bohemian rebellion,

---

[72] Ferdinand to Klesl, Apr. 3, 1616, cited in Hurter 7: 103–4.
[73] Hurter 7: 101; Bernhard Duhr, *Geschichte der Jesuiten in den Ländern deutscher Zunge*, 2: 2 (Freiburg, 1913): 214 and n. 5
[74] Golo Mann, *Wallenstein* (Frankfurt, 1971), 140–5.   [75] Kretschmayr 3: 275–89.

Ferdinand would have faced a war on two fronts and the Venetians might well have allied with the rebels and the Protestant forces that supported them.

Matthias had moved the court from Prague to Vienna in late 1612, not long after his election as emperor. Before his election as king of Bohemia, he had confirmed the Letter of Majesty and also promised to summon a general meeting of the estates of the lands he governed as territorial ruler: Bohemia and its associated lands Moravia, Silesia, and Upper and Lower Lusatia, Hungary, and Upper and Lower Austria. He intended now to interpret the Letter of Majesty strictly and to favor the Catholics in other ways, leaving in Bohemia a government that was dominated by Catholics even though they made up only ten to fifteen percent of the population. The surge of initiative on the part of the estates which had helped Matthias to power now began to lose its force partly because the estates of the various territories found it difficult to cooperate and partly because Klesl manipulated them cleverly. One could not expect Matthias to summon the estates before the conclusion of the diet of 1613. But the emperor did convoke the estates of the Bohemian crown for Linz, not unruly Prague, in 1614, as we have seen, and again the following year in Prague. In the first instance, the estates of the lesser entities – Moravia, Silesia, and the Lusatias – resented the superiority that the Bohemians claimed for themselves, and this prevented effective cooperation. The next year, the grant of funds for the Turkish front where Bethlen Gàbor was again stirring up trouble in Transylvania stood out as the first item on the agenda. But this meeting ended in a "general confusion;"[76] policies of the different territories toward the Turks conflicted and delegates came without instructions. Klesl realized that the territories had not coordinated their policies, and he exploited their differences. No funds were granted. But the situation on the Turkish front was stabilized to a degree in 1615, as we have seen, by renewals with adjustments of the Treaties of Vienna and Zsitvatorok of 1606. A general meeting of the estates of all Matthias's territories convened in Vienna in June 1614, to discuss confederation and common defense, but the same outcome resulted. Particular interests overrode a common goal. The Upper Austrian estates were split between the nobility and the cities; many members of the Lower Austrian estates favored the Habsburgs. The Hungarians for the most part stood apart and observed. The Bohemians ended up voting the government subsidies for five years, and Matthias could now claim that he had fulfilled his promise to summon a common meeting of all the estates.[77]

So when Klesl, under continued heavy pressure from Archduke Maximilian and after the conclusion of the treaty with Spain, from Count Oñate too, finally called a meeting of the Bohemian estates, for August 1, 1617, to pay homage to or to elect Ferdinand as their king, the position of the estates had declined from what

---

[76] Rill, 261. [77] Ibid., 259–63, 285–8.

it had been ten or even five years earlier.[78] Whether they were convening merely to recognize Ferdinand as king or to elect him remained vague initially. There were precedents for both.[79] If the former prevailed, then the estates implicitly accepted a hereditary right of Ferdinand to the crown, but when they came together to pay him homage, they could insist on conditions for their homage.

Illness overtook Matthias in late April, and briefly it appeared that he might not survive, leaving the succession unregulated. Empress Maria summoned Maximilian and Ferdinand to come to Prague immediately. Klesl discouraged this, and Ferdinand turned back when he heard from the bishop. Then a group of Catholic noblemen led by the *Obristhofmeister*, Count Leonhard Helfried Meggau, burst into Matthias's sick room at a time when Klesl was absent, and secured from him a promise to move up the date for the upcoming meeting of the Bohemian electoral diet to June 5. This change was promulgated on May 1. Maximilian queried Ferdinand by courier whether they ought to arrest Klesl. Ferdinand responded that at this time it would not be beneficial to lay hands on the cardinal's person. "It would be better to treat him leniently, so that there would be no reason [for him] to hinder the matter [that is, the succession] and he would remain devoted to the future ruler." Should the emperor's health improve, then the cardinal would destroy all his papers that he did not want to become public, his arrest would be of little value, could cause us considerable embarrassment, and might drive him to desperate measures. Should Matthias die, however, Ferdinand continued, then other measures would have to be taken including the raising of troops, an endeavor to be committed to the Spanish ambassador.[80]

Ferdinand and Maximilian arrived in Prague on June 1. Matthias's illness turned out not be as serious as anticipated, and the electoral diet opened as scheduled on June 5. It was a "triumph of direction and manipulation."[81] Members of the government party, made up of Ferdinand's supporters led by the Bohemian chancellor Zdenek von Lobkowitz, were in the minority; they wanted to establish hereditary succession in the Habsburg family, and they left nothing to accident. They summoned many of the prominent members of the opposition to a discussion in the Bohemian chancery before the diet opened. There, in the course of the conversation, they intimated that Ferdinand's succession was taken for granted. Some were won over. When others protested that this was up to the diet, it was suggested that if they felt this way, they might need two heads. As a result of this intimidation, some nobles stayed away from the meeting of the diet. Then on the morning of June 5, in another meeting in the chancery with leading nobles, Adam von Sternberg, high burgrave, told them that the succession had already been decided and that it would be wise not to resist. Wenzel von Ruppa, an experienced member of the estates, raised the question of the election of the king. Sternberg countered that the evidence of

---

[78] Richter, "Die böhmischen Länder von 1471–1740," in *Handbuch der Geschichte der böhmischen Länder*, 2: 271–2.
[79] Rill, 287–8   [80] Hurter 7: 200–1.   [81] Rill, 287

tradition did not support election. He argued in a long paper that the events of 1608 and 1611 departed from the custom that dated from Ferdinand I's assumption of the throne in 1526. Some were convinced by his presentation. Recent research seems to have substantially confirmed Sternberg's position.[82]

All the members of the assembly then proceeded into the hall of the diet where Matthias greeted them with Ferdinand and Maximilian at his side. Klesl read his proposition for him. Matthias affirmed that because of his age, he had to see to the succession. His two brothers Maximilian and Albert had renounced their claims because of age, and so he asked the estates to "accept, proclaim, and crown" Ferdinand as king.[83] But the opponents led by Count Matthias von Thurn were not ready to yield. They were determined to defend the principle of election and to postpone a decision. As their speaker, they chose Count Heinrich Schlick. But Ferdinand then summoned Schlick to a private conversation during which he convinced the count to change his position. The next day at the decisive session, the estates were called to vote, not as corporations, that is, as the lords (*Herren*), knights (*Ritter*), and cities, as was usually the case, but each member individually. This put added pressure on each one. Schlick announced his change of view. Few opposed. Sternberg then proclaimed that Ferdinand had been "accepted" by the estates.[84] The next day the estates came together for a final vote. Count Thurn argued that an election was called for. Sternberg contradicted him. All the estates voted to accept Ferdinand except Thurn and one other noble. Sternberg interpreted the vote as the "acceptance" of Ferdinand.[85] So the Bohemian estates committed a fateful error; it would be very difficult to justify their rebellion a year later after they had either accepted or elected Ferdinand.

But the recognition of Ferdinand by the estates of Bohemia did not come without conditions. Matthias's recommendation of Ferdinand to the estates had assumed that he would confirm all the privileges and rights, with no exceptions, granted the estates by previous emperors and kings of Bohemia. Ferdinand had to promise that after the death of Matthias when he was crowned, he would draw up such a confirmation and present it to the high burgrave of Prague. This meant above all that Ferdinand had to swear to uphold the Letter of Majesty granted the Bohemian estates by Rudolf back in 1609 and later confirmed by Matthias. Ferdinand also had to agree that he would not interfere in the government as long as Matthias lived, thus allaying the emperor's fears that he would be forced out of office.

---

[82] Jaroslav Pánek, "Ferdinand I–der Schöpfer des politischen Programms der österreichischen Habsburger?" in *Die Habsburger Monarchie 1620 bis 1740*, ed. Petr Ma' ta and Thomas Winkelbauer (Stuttgart, 2006), 65–6. According to Pánek, Ferdinand I had secured from the estates in 1545 the recognition of hereditary succession.

[83] Cited in Rill, 289.

[84] Anton Gindely, *Geschichte des dreissigjährigen Krieges*, 1: *Gesschichte des böhmischen Aufstandes von 1618* (Prague, 1869): 159–69.

[85] Rill, 289.

Ferdinand found it difficult to guarantee the Letter of Majesty. Catholics divided on the issue. Zdenek von Lobkowitz, chancellor of Bohemia, and Count Jaroslav Martinitz, a government officer, along with Count Vilém Slavata, a convert to Catholicism, member of the hard line Catholic party at the court of Prague, and holder of a number of important government offices, advised Ferdinand to reject it, a move that would perhaps have provoked rebellion at that time. Instead Ferdinand took the advice of Klesl who argued that rejection of the Letter would greatly endanger his chances to be accepted in the other lands of the Bohemian crown and to be elected Holy Roman Emperor. When he secretly consulted the Jesuits of Prague on the matter, they affirmed that he might choose the greater good, that is, the succession to the kingship and all the benefits that it would bring to the Church in the long run, over the lesser good, the rejection of the Letter.[86] As the nuncio at the imperial court, Antonio Caetano, had written ten years previously, "there was no easier way, in short, to preserve the Catholic religion in Germany and in the whole north than this, to maintain Bohemia in the hands of the House of Austria," and so to provide the House with the territorial basis for the imperial title.[87] So on June 28, the eve of his coronation, Ferdinand provided the estates with his formal written commitment to uphold the Letter of Majesty. At the procession into the cathedral for the coronation, Ferdinand remarked to Slavata that he was glad that he had been able to acquire the crown without pangs of conscience.[88] Once he made this commitment, Ferdinand certainly intended to keep it. He was a deeply religious man who took seriously his oaths and his legal obligations. What he might have intended was to interpret the Letter very strictly according to its words and then to have counted on the Protestants, in their zeal and enthusiasm, to themselves violate the Letter and so free him from his obligation to observe its provisions.[89] Subsequently he was to employ such a procedure.

Ferdinand's coronation as king of Bohemia took place, then, on June 29, 1617, in the cathedral of St. Veit atop the Hradschin, the complex of the royal castle in Prague, amidst grand ritual and great festivity. At its conclusion, coins bearing the words of Ferdinand's motto *"Legitime Certantibus"* were distributed to the crowd. On the last of the five days of festivities a drama was performed in the great hall of the Jesuit college about the life of the early Christian Emperor Constantine for which Ferdinand summoned his own

---

[86] A text with their position has not survived. According to Gindely, 372, the Jesuits replied that Ferdinand could not have issued the Letter of Majesty but that he might confirm it if that was the only way that he might acquire the kingship.

[87] Antonio Caetano to Cardinal Scipione Borghese, Prague, Nov. 12, 1607, *Antonii Caetani Nuntii Apostolici apud Imperatorem Epistolae et Acta, 1607–1611*, ed. Milena Linahartová 1 (Prague, 1932): #222 (pp. 276–7).

[88] Gindely, 373. For this statement of Ferdinand, Gindely draws on a letter of Slavata to Martinitz written much later, Sept. 24, 1646.

[89] See Francesco Gui, *I Gesuiti e la rivoluzione boema: alle origini della guerra dei trent'anni* (Milan, 1989): 210–13.

musicians from Graz. The choice of Constantine pointed to the hopes that many Catholics had for Ferdinand.⁹⁰

Shortly after the coronation in Prague, Ferdinand began to prepare for a visit to Elector John George of Saxony in Dresden for discussions about the succession in the Empire. Along with him went Emperor Matthias, Archduke Maximilian, and, reluctantly, Cardinal Klesl. They arrived by ship on the Elbe on August 4. The genial Ferdinand impressed John George who complained to Ferdinand of the tricks of the Calvinists. Amidst the usual hunting expeditions and balls that continued for two weeks, they agreed on the convocation of an electoral convention on February 1, 1618, in Frankfurt which, it was hoped, the electors would attend in person. John George agreed to undertake to convince the two Calvinist electors, the Palatinate and Brandenburg, to support the Habsburg candidate, Ferdinand. While Ferdinand was in Dresden, a fight broke out between the son of the Spanish ambassador and a member of the staff of the Florentine ambassador. The Spaniard stabbed the Italian, killing him. Bohemian authorities wanted to prosecute the Spanish aggressor, but they were called off out of fear of Spanish retaliation that might result in harm to imperial interests.⁹¹ After his return to Prague, Ferdinand received there the homage of the estates of Moravia. He visited his younger brother, Archduke Carl, bishop of Breslau, at his residence in Neisse in Silesia; Carl had been named bishop of Breslau back in 1608 at the age of eighteen and prince-bishop of Brixen in 1613. Ferdinand then proceeded to Breslau itself for acceptance by the estates of Silesia on September 24 and 25, and from there to Upper and Lower Lusatia. So he completed his round of all the estates of the Bohemian crown.⁹² On October 26, he made his solemn entrance back in Graz as king of Bohemia.

But Hungary and the crown of St. Stephen remained, to be approached only after the first of the new year. The political situation in Hungary was still more complicated than that in the Bohemian lands. Here, too, the issue of free election versus homage had to be faced; the Hungarians did not want a hereditary monarchy. But their estates showed relatively little interest in cooperating with the Bohemian and Austrian estates; Hungary and Transylvania confronted the Turks, and relations with them enjoyed a high priority with the Hungarians. Klesl pointed out their minimal devotion to the Habsburgs. Earlier he had written that "he would gladly be their good friend but he did not want to be involved with them in either ecclesiastical or secular business. Neither ten notaries nor one hundred witnesses could keep track of the hourly reformulations of their fickleness." He looked to the negotiations with them with concern.⁹³ Furthermore, Matthias hesitated to move toward making

---

⁹⁰ Hurter 7: 208–9; for a detailed description of the coronation, see the *AF* 8: 1115–42.
⁹¹ *AF* 8: 1148.   ⁹² Ibid., 1146–51.   ⁹³ Hurter 7: 216.

Ferdinand king in Hungary, fearing further diminishment of his own authority. Finally, he summoned a diet to convene on March 23, 1618, in Pressburg.

The two Hungarian nobles who from 1608 to 1616 had held the office of Palatine, the representative of the king with the estates, had been Protestants and stood closer in fact to the estates than to the king. Now the office was vacant. At the opening of the diet, the Hungarian magnates reminded Matthias that he had to appoint a new Palatine before they proceeded to the choice of the king. Emperor Matthias responded that it was not proper to select the servant before the lord and promised to appoint a Palatine right after the selection of the king. The Protestant and anti-Habsburg magnates then, though in the minority, were strong enough to convince the body of the estates to demand from Matthias confirmation of their right to a free election of the king before proceeding to this election. Arguments could be made on both sides of the issue. Ferdinand I had been elected by the estates in 1526, and so had Mathias in 1608. But the Habsburgs had expended much blood and treasure in the defense of Hungary against the Turks. Eventually Klesl worked out a compromise. The magnates declared that they had no intention of abandoning the House of Habsburg. But no explicit statement of a free election was made. Later in the protocol of the diet, it was stated that the estates, at the recommendation of the emperor and according to the manner and freedom that had always been recognized, unanimously elected Archduke Ferdinand to be their king.[94] Negotiations long continued. The Hungarians laid down conditions for their homage to Ferdinand. Some of the estates' complaints related to the alleged abuses of German soldiers in Hungary. Ferdinand yielded on many points, unwilling to prolong the negotiations further. He received considerable support from Peter Pazmany, a former Jesuit renowned for polemical, diplomatic, and pastoral skills who had been named Archbishop of Esztergom (Gran) and so Primate of Hungary in 1616. For him the future of the Catholic Church in Hungary as well as effective defense of Christendom against the Turks required a firm bond between Hungary and the Habsburg dynasty.[95] Finally on May 16, 1618, Ferdinand was proclaimed king, and the following day he appointed Count Sigismund Forgách (Forgács), a Catholic and an ally of the Habsburgs, to the office of Palatine. Only on July 1 was Ferdinand crowned king. In the meantime, on May 27, while he was sitting at table in Pressburg with his ally, Cardinal Pázmany, who had provided him with crucial support, news of the rebellion in Prague arrived.[96]

Lamormaini, who by this time knew Ferdinand well, in his *Virtues of Emperor Ferdinand II*, published shortly after Ferdinand's death, drew two examples

---

[94] Rill, 292–3.
[95] Peter George Schimert, "Péter Pázmany and the Reconstitution of the Catholic Aristocracy in Habsburg Hungary, 1600–1650," Dissertation, University of North Carolina at Chapel Hill, 1990, 240–69.
[96] Ibid., 293–4; Hurter 7: 223–8.

Toward the Succession, 1608–1618

of Ferdinand's desire to conform himself to the will of God from the year 1616. It was reported to Ferdinand in Graz that Archduke Maximilian had stated in Prague that he would not leave the city until Ferdinand had been recognized as the successor in the Habsburg lands and kingdoms. Ferdinand's prayer, in response to this, as he related to Lamormaini, was, "Lord, if it is to your praise and glory and to my salvation, that I become greater than I am, exalt me and I will glorify you. If it is to your praise and honor and my salvation, that I persist in the grade where I now am, preserve me and I will glorify you. If it is to your praise and glory and my salvation, that I am in a humbler grade, humble me, and I will glorify you."[97]

That same year Ferdinand suffered two major personal losses. Within two weeks he lost his oldest brother, Maximilian Ernst, whom he had entrusted with various political responsibilities, and his wife, Maria Anna of Bavaria. In contrast with his mother Maria, Maria Anna had kept her distance from politics. Despite her sickly nature, she had born him seven children, four sons and three daughters. The first son, Johann Carl, died at age fourteen in 1619, and the second, Ferdinand Ernst born in 1608, would eventually succeed him. At the same time that he lost his brother and his wife, Ferdinand also saw the Venetians invade Friuli in an attempt to take Gradisca and also imprison his confessor Father Viller. Lamormaini used the archduke's constancy in this wave of setbacks to illustrate his equanimity, his patience, and his trust in God's Providence.[98] Ferdinand, according to Lamormaini, lived chastely from 1616 to 1622, from his thirty-sixth to his forty-second year, when he took as his second wife Eleonore Gonzaga. In 1617, shortly after the death of Maria Anna and at the time of his visit to the Saxon court at Dresden following his election as king of Bohemia, the Lutheran widow of Elector Christian II and sister of the king of Denmark seems to have caught his eye; it was noted at the court that the two danced together several times and enjoyed their conversation. Cardinal Klesl promoted this attachment as part of his program of composition with the Lutheran princes, and even the king of Spain and some Jesuits seconded the project, according to Lamormaini in annotations that he made in his own author's copy of *The Virtues of Emperor Ferdinand II*. Lamormaini himself opposed any thought of such a union because of the difference of religion, and nothing came of the talk of a possible marriage.[99]

---

[97] *Virtutes*, 30–1.   [98] Ibid, 64–5.   [99] Ibid., 6 (annotations), 30, 54; AF 8:1148.

Chapter 4

The Bohemian Rebellion, 1618–1621

May 23, 1618, proved to be a fateful day for Ferdinand, for the Empire, and for Europe. About nine o'clock that morning Count Thurn, who had led the opposition to Ferdinand's recognition as king of Bohemia, now led members of a Protestant assembly meeting in Prague up the stairs of the Hradschin Castle and into the council room. There they seized two of the regents who had been appointed by Emperor Matthias to govern the kingdom of Bohemia, Counts Vilém Slawata and Jaroslav Martinitz. The assailants considered the two to be instruments of an imperial policy to subvert the Letter of Majesty that had been conceded by Matthias in 1609 and confirmed by Ferdinand the previous year, and so to recatholicize Bohemia and set up an absolute monarchy. Ignoring his pleas for a chance to go to confession, five armed men lay hold of Martinitz, dragged him to a window and pitched him through it, to his certain death, as they thought. Next came Slawata's turn. He managed to cling to the window sill until a blow from a knife handle forced him to lose his grip and fall to the earth about fifty feet below. In the wake of the two there plunged a secretary, Philip Fabricius. So there took place what came to be called the Defenestration of Prague. Yet all three survived the violence. They landed on a pile of dung and were rescued, with only Slawata incurring a significant injury. He later commissioned an ex-voto painting showing angels guiding him gently to earth, and many Catholics attributed the survival of the three to a miracle.[1]

The event had been carefully planned by Protestant plotters in order deliberately to provoke an incident that would cause a break between the assembly and the Habsburg ruler, though it was meant to appear as the assembly's spontaneous action. The method of "defenestration" had been chosen because

---

[1] *Virtutes*, 108; Volker Press, *Kriege und Krisen: Deutschland 1600–1715* (Munich, 1991), 192; Wilson, 3–4.

The Bohemian Rebellion, 1618–1621

of a Bohemian precedent dating from the Hussite Wars. The Letter of Majesty admitted varying understandings. Matthias determined to interpret it according to his sense of the strict letter. Interpretations clashed, for example, over whether Protestant churches could be built on ecclesiastical lands. Protestants contended that these lands were ultimately royal lands and so were open to the construction of churches by the Protestants. The government responded with vigorous action to Protestant attempts to locate churches on lands under ecclesiastical jurisdiction in Braunau (Broumov) and Klostergrab (Hrob), throwing citizens of the former into prison and demolishing the rising structure in the latter. Protestants also resented Matthias's increasingly consistent policy of reserving for Catholic appointees the major positions in the government of Bohemia. It was to protest these measures that the Protestant assembly had gathered in Prague. Thurn and his band then successfully radicalized the situation. On May 25 the Protestant assembly was constituted as the estates, and a provisional government was elected composed of twelve directors, to replace the regents and the Bohemian chancellery. The estates began to raise troops, and by mid-June they had driven an imperial detachment from the town of Krumau (Český Krumlov) and were approaching Budweis (Ceské Budjovice) on the border with Upper Austria. A rebellion was underway.

Ferdinand was just sitting down to dinner in Pressburg on May 27 with Klesl and his host, Peter Pázmány, archbishop of Esztergom and primate of Hungary, when news of the events in Prague reached him. Immediately he remarked to a Saxon diplomat that this trouble had its origins elsewhere.[2] His coronation as king of Hungary did not take place until July 1, and the long delay of this event and then the outbreak of the rebellion postponed indefinitely the electoral convention that had initially been planned for May for Ferdinand's election to the imperial office. The day after the news of the Defenestration arrived in Pressburg, Ferdinand, after consultation with councillors, recommended to Matthias that he dispatch an emissary to Prague to encourage the remaining regents to stand firm and to discuss the measures to be taken. The emissary, after taking in the situation in Prague, recommended a settlement with the estates, and the regents remaining in Prague tended in the same direction. The latter advocated a peaceful resolution of the differences once the insurrectionists disarmed.

Yet the seizure of power by the rebels, the establishment of a provisional government of directors, and the start of raising an army, rendered a quick settlement unlikely. Soon the government in Vienna came to consider the upheaval in Prague as an attempt to establish a republic in the Venetian model and to deprive the Habsburgs of their inheritance. In early June, in a letter to Matthias, Ferdinand now called for a vigorous response to the rebels.

---

[2] Franzl, 182.

The imperial vice-chancellor Hans Ludwig von Ulm supported this position, as did Matthias' emissary who after further assessment of the situation recommended military action. Klesl along with Maximilian von Trautmannsdorf, a young imperial councillor, and others agreed with Ferdinand that an offer to the rebels to negotiate peacefully was inconsistent with the emperor's reputation, and they advocated the recall of troops from the Adriatic front and the pursuit of subsidies from Spain to fund the troops.[3] In a letter to Ferdinand of June 4, Matthias himself inclined at least to attempt negotiations with Thurn, to which Ferdinand responded three days later, "for my part to write to Count Thurn now, since matters have progressed so far, is neither advisable or practicable."[4] The Spanish ambassador, Count Oñate, also advocated a firm policy toward the rebels, and he already was strongly encouraging Madrid to come to Ferdinand's aid. For Ferdinand to lose Bohemia would undermine the Spanish position in Europe and prevent the emperor from aiding the Spaniards either in the Netherlands, where the Twelve Years Truce of 1609 between Spain and the Dutch Republic was soon to run out, or in Italy.[5]

A position paper, most likely drawn up by Klesl probably in June, outlined the policy eventually adopted by Ferdinand toward the rebels. In recent years the Bohemian and Austrian estates led by Protestant members had successfully claimed rights and privileges, it read, that belonged properly to the crown, championing for example the extension of the free exercise of religion for inhabitants of crown lands and asserting their control over taxes. "So they have brought their lords into such a servitude that they can scarcely take action in the lands that they have inherited or exercise their sovereign authority except in so far as their subjects allow it, so that there remains to them [the lords] only the name of sovereign authority, and its exercise remains with the non-Catholic subjects." They envisioned a republic, and they planned a confederation with other Habsburg lands with a view to forming a common front against the ruler. Truly the upheaval stemmed from the devil. Nor did government policy come away without blame. Too long the rulers had shown weakness and timidity in response to the challenge of the estates. But there was a bright side: "God had undoubtedly willed to bring about this troubling, terrible situation, so that the whole world and all reasonable men of whatever religion could recognize how repulsive, unjust, unchristian, unreasonable, unevangelical and worthy of punishment and execution [were the actions of the rebels]. So the fundamental argument of the rebels, to which they everywhere appeal, that this is a matter of religion, collapses and fails to convince.... So ought your Majesty and your whole House ... take advantage of this opportunity to rid yourself and your House of this yoke and servitude, and once again to recover your territorial sovereignty. You have God, your House, and all Christian authorities who are

---

[3] Brockmann, 65–73.   [4] Ferdinand to Matthias, Jun. 7, 1618, cited in ibid., 73.
[5] J.H. Elliott, *The Count-Duke of Olivares: The Statesman in an Age of Decline* (New Haven, 1986), 57.

intent to retain their territory, their people, and their territorial sovereignty on your side. You cannot lose anything. If assaults of the estates as enumerated continue, you will certainly lose eventually with great harm and derision. Should you lose [militarily], since the outcome of war is uncertain, you would lose with honor and not shamefully." The author argued appealing to divine providence. "God had decreed such absurdities so that the government could now once and for all throw off such servitude" and undertake a thorough reform of government in Bohemia. "A resort to arms would be necessary." The government should paint the rebellion as directed against legitimate authority and downplay the religious element. In this way it would more easily secure the support of princes eager to maintain their authority, whether Catholic or Protestant, and make it more difficult for the rebels to obtain outside support. So argued, for example, an emissary sent to Nuremberg and Saxony in July.[6] The rebels for their part, with a view to attracting support from Protestant princes, emphasized that Habsburg actions were directed toward religious repression.

Following his return to Vienna, and apparently after some infighting at court, Ferdinand was charged with the responsibility for the affairs of Bohemia on July 14, with final decisions still left in the hands of Matthias.[7] But Ferdinand then realized that the situation compelled him to adopt a moderate policy; he simply did not have the resources to put down the rebellion. Yet he and Archduke Maximilian did undertake the removal of Cardinal Klesl from court, a move that they had long contemplated. They took this step even though Klesl had, apparently, supported a hard line against the Bohemian rebels, because the two feared his policy of composition with the Protestants in the Empire and his seeming obstruction of Ferdinand's election as king of the Romans. Oñate was in on the plan. On July 19 Ferdinand and Maximilian paid the cardinal a visit in his quarters, and then they invited him to the Hofburg, the imperial residence, for a return visit the following day. Upon his entrance into the Hofburg, he was told that he was under arrest by order of King Ferdinand. After a brief resistance, he exchanged his cardinal's robes for the cassock of a simple priest and then was taken in a waiting coach to the castle of Ambras near Innsbruck where he was held in strict confinement. Matthias, sick in bed, after a brief protest yielded to the removal of his close adviser and friend.[8] Pope Paul V had long opposed the moderate policy of Klesl and attempted to persuade the cardinal to change it, and the nuncio in Vienna, Ascanio Gesualdo, seems to have been alerted ahead of time to the arrest of Klesl.

---

[6] Position paper of Klesl regarding the unrest in Bohemia, Pressburg, mid-June 1618, in Lorenz, #34 (pp. 253–6); Brockmann, 76–8, 81–2. A number of authors have been suggested for this position paper including Oñate, Eggenberg, and Ferdinand himself, but Brockmann favors Klesl, p. 76, n.51, despite the hard line taken in it. On the mission to Nuremberg and Saxony, see Brockmann, p. 81, n.76.
[7] Brockmann, 74, esp. n. 47.   [8] Franzl, 186–8.

But the pope could not allow to go unpunished the attack on a cardinal of the Church, which automatically brought excommunication on the perpetrators, namely, Ferdinand and Maximilian, even if they had acted in good conscience. On the other hand, he did not want unduly to provoke Ferdinand whose policy he supported and whom he saw as the future hope for the Church in the Empire. On August 6, the matter was discussed at a secret consistory of the cardinals in Rome. The nuncio was instructed to inform Ferdinand and Maximilian that they needed to seek absolution at least conditionally (*ad cautelam*) from the excommunication that they had incurred and to provide a list of the charges against Klesl. When no adequate response was forthcoming from Vienna, in February the pope dispatched to Vienna an extraordinary nuncio, Fabrizio Verospi, to clear up the matter. Ferdinand – Archduke Maximilian had died in the meantime – at first refused to seek absolution; he claimed that he had acted in good faith and in the interest of both the church and the state, a position with which Cardinal Robert Bellarmine, one of the most influential cardinals in the curia, seemed to concur.[9] Verospi was to explain to Ferdinand that his explanation might be valid in the area of conscience, but despite the opinion of the theologians in Vienna, to satisfy the requirements of church law and to avoid scandal he had to request absolution from the pope for his actions.[10] Ferdinand did then yield to the pope's demand and submitted a petition for absolution which was then readily accepted.[11] He also agreed to the transfer of Klesl to Verospi's care, who then brought him to the monastery of Sankt Georgenberg near Schwaz in the Tirol where he remained in papal detention. In 1622 after he was allowed to move to Rome, the Holy Office freed him from prison and annulled the case against him for lack of evidence, a verdict that did not sit well with Ferdinand.[12]

Realizing the weakness of their position, both Matthias and Ferdinand now agreed to negotiate with the rebels with the help of Saxon mediation, but on condition that the rebels dismissed the troops they had recruited and dissolved the government that they had formed. Ferdinand courted Saxony also because he needed its vote for his election as emperor. As its position further deteriorated Vienna gradually backed off from these conditions. By October 1618, the Silesians, the Upper and Lower Lusatians, and the Upper Austrians had joined the Bohemians, and mercenary troops under Count Ernst Mansfeld financed

---

[9] Johannes Rainer, "Cardinal Melchior Klesl (1552–1630). Von 'Generalreformator' zum Ausgleichspolitiker," *Römische Quartalschrift* 59 (1964): 31–3.
[10] First Instruction for Fabrizio Verospi, extraordinary nuncio to the emperor, February 1619, *Le istruzioni generali di Paulo V ai I diplomatici pontifici (1605–1621)* ed. Silvano Giordano (Tübingen, 2003): 2: #93 (pp. 1137–44).
[11] Paul V to King Ferdinand, Oct. 25, 1619, *Bullarium diplomatum et privilegiorum sanctorum Romanorum pontificum Taurenensis editio* 12 (Turin, 1867): #cccxxiii (pp. 455–6).
[12] Johannes Rainer, "Der Prozess gegen Cardinal Klesl," *Römische Historische Mitteilungen* 5 (1962): 131–7.

The Bohemian Rebellion, 1618–1621

for the Bohemians by the duke of Savoy had seized the city of Pilsen (Plzen), a Catholic stronghold in Bohemia. Rebel forces invaded Lower Austria Emperor Matthias's death on March 20, 1619, produced no significant change in policy. The next day Ferdinand notified the regents, who remained powerless in Prague, of Matthias's death with the order to communicate the news to his Bohemian subjects. Ferdinand took for granted that he now succeeded to the throne of Bohemia, and he continued to refuse to recognize the government of the directors.

For the estates in Prague, to be distinguished from the directors, he confirmed the Letter of Majesty as he had prior to his acceptance as king the previous year, a step he was careful to publicize among the Protestant states of the Empire. According to the report of the Saxon representative in Vienna, before issuing this confirmation Ferdinand consulted with his confessor, Father Viller, who approved it as necessary under the circumstances in order to avoid greater evils.[13] Toward the end of April Ferdinand informed the estates that he had ordered his general, Count Charles Bucquoy, a veteran of the campaigns in the Netherlands, to suspend hostilities so long as the forces of the rebels did not provoke him, and he invited the estates to send a delegation to Vienna for negotiations. He then confirmed the privileges of the Silesian and Upper Lusatian estates, and continued to support Saxon efforts at mediation.[14] A settlement with the Bohemian estates had not been ruled out. Policy was in flux. Yet Ferdinand's letter to Eggenberg of April 3, 1619, showed that he hoped that forceful military action might still resolve the impasse in his favor, especially after the directors refused his confirmation of the privileges of the Bohemian estates. Similarly to Klesl's paper immediately following the Defenestration, he thought that in the end with God's help Habsburg authority would be fully restored in the hereditary lands and kingdoms and the position of the Catholic religion be stabilized there and in the Empire.[15] There were limits to the concessions he was willing to make. He would "rather die and perish," he reassured Maximilian of Bavaria's envoy, than go beyond what he had, under duress, confirmed in the Letter of Majesty.[16] Maximilian had advocated a hard line from the start.

Meanwhile, from the outset of the rebellion, Vienna pursued foreign support. Already in July 1618, Matthias approached Pope Paul V for subsidies to face the danger, and Philip III endorsed the emperor's plea. Initially Paul did not expect the trouble in Germany to last long, but in September 1618 the papacy began to pay out, if irregularly, a monthly grant of 10,000 gulden. This was doubled as a result of an urgent request from Ferdinand in December 1619 when Vienna was threatened, yet the amounts fell well behind what Vienna

---

[13] Brockmann, 91, n. 118.   [14] Ibid., 73–83. 82–92.   [15] Ibid, 95–6.
[16] Ibid, 90, citing the final report of the Bavarian envoy, Mar. 8, 1619.

hoped to obtain.[17] The Spanish ambassador Oñate had taken it upon himself to retain in imperial service 3,000 Spanish troops scheduled to be released after the war with Venice, and he urged Madrid to send funds for their upkeep. Letters flew from Vienna to Archduchess Margaret, Ferdinand's aunt in the Descalzas convent in Madrid, and to the imperial ambassador Franz Christoph von Khevenhüller.[18] This uncorked a lively debate in Madrid that was won by the newly dominant figure at the court of Madrid, the former ambassador in Vienna, Zúñiga, who favored the reassertion of Spanish power in Central Europe. By May 1619, a Spanish army of 7,000 was marching from Flanders to Vienna, and by early 1621 Ferdinand could call on 40,000 Spanish troops. Funding flowed generously from Madrid to Vienna, 3.9 million talers by early 1621 and six million by the end of 1624.[19]

Maximilian of Bavaria recognized from the start the potential European significance of the rebellion in Bohemia. But initially he hesitated to come to Matthias's assistance. He feared that his active intervention in the conflict might encourage the Protestant Union to come to the aid of the Bohemians, and he needed to look to the defense of his own lands. On the other hand, he refused to serve as a mediator between the parties lest he be compromised by unacceptable religious concessions. Some in Vienna laid the responsibility for the expansion of the conflict at Maximilian's door for his failure to provide ready assistance to the embattled emperor.[20] Only after the death of Matthias did Maximilian's position gradually change.[21]

Meanwhile negotiations with heads of the Upper Austrian estates, who openly expressed their readiness to confederate with the Bohemians, broke down as they claimed the right to administer the government after the death of Matthias until their recognition of his successor. Through much of the spring of 1619 Ferdinand carried on talks in Vienna with the Protestant members of the estates of Lower Austria, who constituted a large majority of the body, about their recognition of him as their ruler. In early June, then, there took place an event that was to become incorporated into Habsburg lore as the "Stormy Petition" (*Sturmpetition*). An army of 15,000 under Count Thurn, after invading Moravia and forcing the Moravians to join the anti-Habsburg coalition, approached Vienna. They counted on allies within the city walls. Folks streamed into the city from the suburbs; all the city gates but one were closed on June 3. Initially, Ferdinand had only 300 soldiers to defend the city. He called for

---

[17] Albrecht 1, 37–8.
[18] Magdelena S. Sánchez, *The Empress, the Queen, and the Nun: Women and Power at the Court of Philip III of Spain* (Baltimore, 1998), 178, 183.
[19] Geoffrey Parker, ed., *The Thirty Years War*, 2 ed. (London, 1997): 43–5.
[20] Final Report of the Bavarian envoy to Vienna, early November 1618, BANF 1: 1 #46 (p. 88, n.5).
[21] Albrecht 2, 490–3.

troops from nearby Krems under Count Henri Dampierre. Tension ran high. The morning of June 5, Thurn's troops crossed the Danube and began to lay siege to the city. That morning between ten and twelve o'clock, Ferdinand met in the Hofburg with the Protestant members of the estates who remained reluctant to recognize him unless he agreed to their religious and constitutional demands. In the midst of their meeting, there suddenly arrived in Vienna by boat a unit of Dampierre's cavalry. They made their way to the Hofburg where they intimidated and dispersed the members of the Protestant estates. Ferdinand had not foreseen this development; indeed, he seems to have apologized to the estates for the irruption of the troops. But he did exploit the situation. Shortly afterwards about 2,800 Hungarian troops also arrived to assist Ferdinand, and the Jesuits mobilized many of their students. Thurn did not possess adequate siege material, and his lines of supply could not hold up. In addition, the Bohemians had suffered a major defeat at the hands of General Bucquoy near Záblati in southern Bohemia, and they needed assistance to defend Prague. So on June 12, Thurn began to withdraw. Ferdinand survived the crisis.[22]

Without vouching for the account, Lamormaini described in his *The Virtues of Emperor Ferdinand II* how Ferdinand allegedly reacted at the height of this crisis. He retired to his room to pray. There Father Viller came upon him kneeling before the crucifix. Ferdinand told his confessor that the Lord had reassured him from the crucifix, "Ferdinand, I will not desert you," and from this experience he had drawn hope and strength.[23] Eventually this story spread in Vienna. It is pictured in the multi-volume *Annales Ferdinandei* of Franz Christoph von Khevenhüller,[24] and the crucifix from which Christ allegedly spoke was preserved and given to members of the family for veneration at the time of their death. Whether one accepts this story or not, it illustrates a popular belief about Ferdinand's confidence in God. He had escaped, perhaps miraculously, from a seemingly hopeless situation.

Shortly before Thurn's appearance before Vienna, Ferdinand could have benefited a second time from a bold deed of the Bohemian nobleman Wallenstein. Wallenstein, now a commander in the Moravian militia but known as an arch-papist, hoped to retain a portion of the Moravian infantry for Ferdinand. Late in the evening of April 30, he stopped with them in the town of Olmütz where the treasury of the Moravian estates was located. He forced the treasurer with the threat of death to hand over the key to the treasury. There 96,000 talers were found. Wallenstein and his accomplices loaded them on to eight wagons and headed for the Austrian border and Vienna. Learning of this bold stroke, Thurn sent a detachment in pursuit but they were unable catch up with Wallenstein before he reached the border on the night of May 5. The next day

---

[22] Helmut Kretschmer, *Sturmpetition und Blockade Wiens im Jahre 1619* (Vienna, 1978). Militärhistorische Schriftenreihe 38.
[23] *Virtutes* 10–11.   [24] 12: 2387.

he presented the sum to Ferdinand in an audience. Ferdinand had perhaps never seen such a sum assembled in one place, and he desperately needed funds. But he questioned the legality of Wallenstein's action. Ferdinand was not yet strictly at war with the Moravians. After deliberating with his councillors, he determined that the funds should be returned, and so they were, secretly. Ferdinand's sense of legality won out over his desire for advantage. He also may have wanted to bolster the forces in Moravia who remained loyal to him.[25] Following the withdrawal of Thurn's forces, the soldiers that had come to Ferdinand's aid, especially the Hungarians, badly misbehaved in the city. The situation remained tense. Negotiations with the estates stalled, and at the end of June many of the Protestant members of the estates moved to the small town of Horn about one hundred miles to the east, out of reach of the influence of the Catholic members.

Immediately following the death of Emperor Matthias, Schweikard, the archbishop-elector of Mainz and chancellor of the Empire, had summoned the meeting of the imperial electors, which had originally been planned for the previous spring, for Frankfurt on July 20, 1619. Ferdinand had already lined up the votes of the three ecclesiastical electors, and he seemed reasonably certain of John George of Saxony's vote. The Bohemians, who were about to depose Ferdinand, dispatched a delegation to Frankfurt to contest his right to vote in the election, but they did not even receive a hearing. Frederick, the Elector Palatine, had for several years encouraged Maximilian of Bavaria to stand for the imperial title, arguing that this would prevent the gradual evolution toward a Habsburg hereditary claim to the imperial title and a Habsburg monarchy in the Empire. Maximilian, aware of the limitations of Bavaria's position, would have none of the proposal. He also recognized that should he challenge Ferdinand, he would drive a wedge between himself and his cousin that would drastically weaken the Catholic forces in the Empire.

Leaving his brother Archduke Leopold in charge in the city, Ferdinand departed Vienna on July 10 with a modest party of forty that included Eggenberg and the Bohemian chancellor Lobkowitz. They avoided the direct route through hostile Upper Austria, traveling south through the mountains then up to Salzburg and on to Munich on July 19. The death of Archduke Maximilian had now removed an obstacle to cooperation with Bavaria. In Munich, Duke Maximilian offered Ferdinand encouragement and a promise of support from the Catholic League that he was now reviving but not one as open-ended as Ferdinand had wanted.[26] Ferdinand and his entourage, which had swelled to nearly one thousand, entered Frankfurt the evening of July 28. Citizens of Frankfurt feared that the Catholics might attempt to seize the city. Rumors

---

[25] Golo Mann, *Wallenstein* (Frankfurt, 1971), 168–73; Wilson, 279.   [26] Albrecht 2, 498.

The Bohemian Rebellion, 1618–1621

spread that Frederick of the Palatinate planned to kidnap Ferdinand; troops of the Protestant Union nearly encircled the city. Schweikard trembled at the thought that the Protestants intended to carry out a Saint Bartholomew's Massacre of the Catholics. His confessor later reported that in a vision the Virgin Mary had reassured the archbishop and told him to proceed with the election of Ferdinand; "there is no counsel against the Lord," he asserted.[27] Ferdinand himself for the most part did not participate in the discussions of the electors but calmly spent much of his time in the area around Frankfurt indulging his passion for the hunt. Schweikard even reproached him for absenting himself from their deliberations.

Finally, on August 28, the three ecclesiastical electors, the representatives of the three Protestant electors, and Ferdinand assembled in the electoral chapel of the cathedral of St. Bartholomew for the election. The archbishop-elector of Trier cast the opening vote for Ferdinand. Maximilian of Bavaria's brother, Ferdinand, archbishop-elector of Cologne, after noting that his brother would not accept election, followed with a vote for Ferdinand. The delegate of the Palatinate then came out for Maximilian in a last effort to promote his candidacy. Ferdinand himself asked to postpone his own vote. The Saxon representative spoke out for Ferdinand, and in his wake the representative of Brandenburg followed. Schweikard himself then voted for Ferdinand, and Ferdinand, not wanting to do an injustice to himself as he said, voted for himself. Seeing the way things were going, the representative of Frederick changed his vote to one for Ferdinand, and thus the decision was unanimous. So Ferdinand was elected Holy Roman Emperor.[28]

The same day as Ferdinand's election there arrived in Frankfurt the foreboding news that the Bohemians had deposed him as king of Bohemia. Ferdinand received it with equanimity, indicating that he would deal with the Bohemians later. The ceremony for his coronation was set for September 9 in the cathedral of St. Bartholomew. Archbishop Schweikard presided at the Solemn High Mass with the ancient coronation ritual. In the course of the ritual, the archbishop put to Ferdinand a series of questions to which he responded with an oath. He took them very seriously, we can be sure. "Do you intend through works of justice to preserve the holy faith handed down by Catholic men?," the archbishop asked. "I do," responded Ferdinand. "Do you intend to be the faithful protector and defender of the churches and the ministers of the churches?" "I do," answered Ferdinand once again. So the new emperor took up the task of Protector of the Church (*Advocatus Ecclesiæ*) that was customarily attached to the imperial office. His responses to subsequent queries committed him to rule according to the traditional law and constitution of the Empire. So he guaranteed the rights of the princes. His respect for law and tradition tempered any inclination toward absolute

---

[27] *Virtutes*, 105.   [28] Franzl, 202–4; Ritter, 3: 41–3.

rule in the Empire as well as in his territories. A final question asked "whether he intended reverently to exhibit due subjection and loyalty to his father and lord in Christ, the Lord Roman Pope and the Holy Roman Church." Again, he responded with a vigorous affirmative. After an acclamation by the princes, bishops, and other dignitaries, the archbishop proceeded to the actual coronation.[29] So Ferdinand became the most exalted prince in Christendom. If the office no longer carried with it the power that it had once held, it still exercised a certain mystical authority and influence especially when held by a prince who knew how to exploit it.

After the ceremony in the cathedral, Ferdinand and the dignitaries crossed the Römerplatz to the town hall for a banquet. As called for by his new dignity, Ferdinand ate at a table elevated above the others and was served by the representatives of the secular electors. The people celebrated on the town square where coins were distributed with Ferdinand's motto, *Legitime certantibus corona*.

While the electoral convention was meeting in Frankfurt, the Bohemians undertook further initiatives. On July 31, 1619, the five territories of the Bohemian crown – Bohemia proper, Moravia, Silesia, and Upper and Lower Lusatia – formed the Bohemian Confederation, which the Upper Austrians and the radical segment of the Lower Austrian estates at Horn joined as allies, not full participants, on August 16.[30] Together they envisioned an aristocratic republic on the model of Venice or perhaps of the Polish–Lithuanian Commonwealth. The Bohemians formally deposed Ferdinand on August 19, contending that he had not been elected constitutionally. They then looked about for a new monarch, but their initial choices – John George, the elector of Saxony, and Bethlen Gàbor, the prince of Transylvania – declined the honor. They then turned to the Calvinist Elector Palatine, Frederick V, whom they elected on August 26, two days before Ferdinand's imperial election. Indecision held Frederick for a time as his councillors argued the pros and cons of acceptance. His mother warned him of the war that would inevitably spread should he accept the Bohemian crown. Prince Christian of Anhalt, his principal councillor and architect of the Protestant Union, encouraged him to take up the challenge. A sense of religious obligation to respond to a call from divine providence, much as Ferdinand felt, as well as a desire to advance the fortunes of his dynasty probably most influenced his eventual decision to accept the crown

---

[29] Hans Sturmberger, *Kaiser Ferdinand II und das Problem des Absolutismus* (Munich, 1957), 40–2. Sturmberger draws these questions from the coronation of Emperor Ferdinand III in 1637 noting that the ceremony had long remained the same.

[30] On the Bohemian Confederation, see Joachim Bahlcke, "Landtagsakten (unter besonderer Berücksichtigung der Verhältnisse in der frühneuzeitlichen Habsburgermonarchie," *Quellenkunde der Habsburgermonarchie (16.–18. Jahrhundert). Ein Exemplarisches Handbuch*, ed. Josef Pauser, Martin Scheutz, and Thomas Winkelbauer (Munich, 2004), 360–2, and the literature indicated there.

The Bohemian Rebellion, 1618–1621

offered him by the Bohemians. He also relied, unrealistically, on vague commitments of support from his father-in-law, James I of England, from the Dutch, and from the Protestant Union. He set out from Heidelberg on October 7, with a party of officials and 153 wagons. By the end of the month, he arrived in Prague where a cheering crowd welcomed him. Their enthusiasm would soon cool as Frederick and his Calvinist associates displayed little respect for the sensibilities of the citizens of Prague.[31]

After his coronation as emperor, Ferdinand remained for a time in Frankfurt conferring with the ecclesiastical electors and with Oñate. He then set out for Munich for negotiations with Maximilian. Along the way news reached him that Bethlen Gàbor, the prince of Transylvania, had invaded Hungary and was on his way to assist the Bohemians. So his situation deteriorated further. In Munich from October 2 to 5, Eggenberg served as the principal imperial negotiator of the Treaty of Munich of October 8, 1619, which was to have far-reaching significance for the rest of the war. The preamble of the treaty spoke of the "pressing and extreme danger in which the aforementioned imperial majesty and House of Austria and beyond this all the Catholic states of the Empire and the Catholic religion itself found themselves."[32] The treaty aimed to preserve the constitutional and religious order in the Empire. The success of the Bohemian rebellion would lead to a four-to-three Protestant majority in the college of electors and the immediate danger of a Protestant emperor, and the feared intervention of the Protestant Union in support of the Bohemians would further weaken the Catholic position in the Empire. According to the terms of the treaty, Maximilian at the behest of Ferdinand and the Catholic electors agreed to assume the "absolute and unlimited directorship" of a Catholic defensive alliance, or the revived Catholic League. Here Ferdinand, in his close association with the Catholic League, seemed to compromise his new position as emperor who was expected to stand as a neutral judge above the parties in the Empire;[33] of course, he understood that he took this step for the benefit of the Church and for the Empire. For the maintenance of the League, the necessary funds were to be provided in a manner not yet clarified. In fact, in the years ahead Maximilian himself would supply most of the League's funding.

Ferdinand and Maximilian agreed that neither of them would enter separate negotiations or individually make a settlement with the enemy. Ferdinand then promised to reimburse Maximilian for his war costs beyond the duke's contributions to the League and to assign to Maximilian Austrian lands as a pledge of future payment. Moreover, should Bavaria lose territory in a future peace treaty, Ferdinand committed himself to compensate the loss with Austrian lands. Ferdinand, on his own initiative as he admitted, but perhaps suggested

---

[31] Wilson, 282–5. [32] Cited in Albrecht 2, 505. [33] Brockmann, 155–60.

by Oñate and certainly intimated by Maximilian, promised orally to transfer the electoral title from Frederick of the Palatinate to Maximilian. This corresponded to a long-standing goal of the Bavarian Wittelsbachs and especially of Maximilian, who contended that back in 1356 at the time of the issuance of the Golden Bull, which fixed the constitutional structure of the Empire, they had been improperly deprived of an alternation in the electoral dignity with their Palatine cousins. The legality of such a transfer by Ferdinand was certain to be contested. In a second verbal commitment, Ferdinand agreed to allow Maximilian to hold on to any territory in the Empire that he might occupy in the anticipated hostilities. Maximilian had in mind the Upper Palatinate as well as the Palatinate lands along the Rhine. So the Bavarian duke figured to gain from his support of Ferdinand in the moment of the emperor's distress.[34]

The desperateness of his situation inclined Ferdinand to make concessions to those Protestant members of the Lower Austrian estates who had not departed for Horn, to keep them from joining the alliance against him. But he could not reconcile this with his conscience. Three days before the Treaty of Munich was concluded, Ferdinand sent Maximulian von Trautmannsdorf over to the Jesuit college in Munich to secure the opinion of the fathers there. Three of them signed the opinion that was drawn up: Jakob Keller, then the rector of the college and author of many polemical writings; Jakob Gretser, the theologian and polemicist; and Casper Torrentinus, a confessor at court. Father Viller, after Ferdinand's coronation as emperor, had asked to be released from his office because of his age and increasing feebleness. The three Jesuits agreed that under the extreme circumstances in which he found himself, Ferdinand could confirm for the Protestant nobility the privileges that Matthias had granted them back in 1609 if they in turn would render him homage and reject the offer of alliance from the rebels. So a lesser evil could be tolerated for a greater good, the preservation of religion and of Habsburg rule in the Empire.[35] Normally, according to the three Jesuits, the emperor would have to obtain the approval of the pope for such a concession. But there was not time for this in the present situation. However, for the greater security of his conscience, Ferdinand ought to have recourse to the Holy See as soon as possible.

Accordingly, two days later Trautmannsdorf was dispatched to Rome to lay the matter before Pope Paul V. Once he had described the disastrous situation to the pope in detail, Trautmannsdorf was to make four requests. Was it not possible, Ferdinand asked on the first, most important issue, to retreat a little from the strict position on toleration of heretics, for which Ferdinand would otherwise be ready to shed his blood, rather than to lose the whole territory of

---

[34] Albrecht 2, 502–9.
[35] Position paper, Oct. 5, 1619, in Thomas Brockmann, "Gegenreformation und Habsburgische Bündnispolitik," *Landes- und Reichsgeschichte. Festschrift für Hansgeorg Molitor zum 65. Geburtstag*, ed. Jörg Engelbrecht and Stephan Laux (Bielefeld, 2004) appendix #2, (pp. 189–90). Studien zur Regionalgeschichte 18.

Lower Austria once and for all, destroy a flourishing church, and cause the loss of thousands of souls? Ferdinand, after all, had not himself first made these concessions. Secondly, Ferdinand urged Pope Paul to increase his monthly subsidy from 10, 000 to 100,000 florins, and to dip into the emergency funds held in the Castel Sant'Angelo for a one-time loan of one million crowns. Thirdly, Trautmannsdorf should convince the pope to use his influence to keep other Italian states, that is, Venice and Savoy, from aiding the rebels. In the last place, then Ferdinand took up an idea which Schoppe had suggested back in 1609 and which he and other princes would return to regularly in the coming years. The pope ought to assume the initiative for the formation of an alliance of the leading Catholic rulers for the preservation of peace and the defense of the Catholic religion in Europe. In this respect Ferdinand may have been influenced by *A Trumpet Call to Holy War*, a booklet published in early 1619 by Schoppe, then living in Milan.[36] If Trautmannsdorf found the pope to be closed to his message, then he was, with the assistance of the cardinal protector of the Spanish nation, Gaspare Borgia, to seek an audience with the consistory of cardinals, in order to persuade them to encourage the pope to action.[37]

Pope Paul's response to Trautmannsdorf's mission, which did not reach Vienna until late November, was to have a major impact on Ferdinand. Trautmannsdorf was admitted to a personal audience with the pope as soon as he arrived in Rome, and he found the pope well-informed about the situation in the Empire. When the issue of concessions to the Protestants arose, the pope responded that even in this dire situation, "I say, that because the confirmation [of the concessions] would be a mortal sin, I am not able to consent to them; I say consent, for the rest ..." There the pope left off. Trautmannsdorf took this to mean that as pope he could not give his consent but would let the matter pass. The next day Ferdinand's emissary sought out the cardinal-nephew, Scipione Borghese, for further clarification. "From the pope's response," the cardinal stated, "you can readily conclude that His Holiness wants to close his eyes when the emperor confirms these concessions but he cannot previously consent to the concessions by reason of his office. And so he leaves the matter to the prudence of the princes as to what is more expedient to do to preserve the state and religion. This is what the pope said clearly enough with the words, 'for the rest.'" If we had known this six months ago, Trautmannsdorf commented, Austria would not find itself in such a desperate situation.[38] Never again would Ferdinand appeal to Rome about the permissibility of

---

[36] Sturmberger, 21–2. Schoppe himself had been influenced by the enigmatic Dominican, Tommaso Campanella, then sitting in a Neapolitan prison. Schoppe's booklet was entitled *Classicum Belli Sacri, A Trumpet Call to a Holy War*.
[37] Instruction for Trautmannsdorf, Munich, Oct. 7, 1619, Brockmann, "Gegenreformation und Habsburgische Bundnispolitik," appendix, #3 (pp. 190–6).
[38] Trautmannsdorf to Ferdinand II, Rome, Oct. 24, 1619, Brockmann, "Gegenreformation und Habsburgische Bundnispolitik," appendix #4 (pp. 197–8).

religious concessions to the Protestants. Trautmannsdorf did not succeed at this time in securing more funds from the pope, but after the first of the year and another threat to Vienna, the pope agreed to double the monthly subsidy to the emperor and to initiate efforts, to be kept secret, at a Catholic alliance.[39]

Once again avoiding travel through Upper Austria, Ferdinand journeyed from Munich to Graz. There the citizens prepared a magnificent entry for the newly crowned emperor who passed under a triumphal arch designed by de Pomis, and they bestowed on him a golden cup along with a gift of 150,000 gulden. They were now proud of him. Graz prospered during his reign. New buildings arose including two monumental structures, the Mausoleum designed by de Pomis to house Ferdinand's remains along with the Katherinenkirche begun in 1614 but not completed until much later, and the new building of the Jesuit university completed only in 1627. Residences of citizens and palazzi of the nobility were renovated. Despite the departure of Protestants, Graz's population continued to increase and would do so during the coming war.[40] Many folks immigrated from Bavaria and southern Germany, and many had long come from northern Italy as musicians, painters, architects, cooks, pharmacists, falconers, and members of religious orders; indeed, the Italians had their own quarter in the city close to the archducal residence, and they gave an Italianate touch to the city's life.[41] They certainly contributed to the dances, concerts, and entertainments at the lively Habsburg court. Now Ferdinand departed from Graz, never to return, and the city gradually declined to provincial status after its years as an archducal residence. While in Graz for this last time, Ferdinand sat at the bedside of his oldest son, Johann Carl, who died at fourteen years of age on the following December 19.

When Ferdinand reentered Vienna on November 24, 1619, he found the city in chaos, on the brink of an urban uprising, and under siege by Bohemian forces and by an Hungarian army under Bethlen Gàbor. Nearly 75,000 people crowded within the walls, practically doubling the normal population. Housing was short. Soldiers, many of them Hungarians, mistreated the citizens. Food and wood for fuel were hard to find. Further away, troops raised by the Upper Austrian estates invaded Lower Austria, and forces raised by the Protestant estates of Lower Austria threatened Krems up the Danube. Then "a great miracle" took place, worked by divine providence, as the Venetian ambassador later reported.[42] Bethlen had left Transylvania inadequately

---

[39] Ludwig von Pastor, *Geschichte der Päpste seit dem Ausgang des Mittelalters 12: Leo XI. und Paul V. (1605–1621)* (Freiburg, 1927): 573–4.
[40] Fritz Popelka, *Geschichte der Stadt Graz* 1 (Graz, 1959): 115–17; 2: (Graz, 1960): 311, 315.
[41] Ibid., 2: 315, 317.
[42] Report from Germany of Polo Minio, Oct. 16, 1620, *Die Relationen der Botschafter Venedigs über Deutschland und Österreich im siebzehnten Jahrhundert*, ed. Joseph Fiedler, 1 (Vienna, 1860): 87–8. Fontes Rerum Austricarum.

The Bohemian Rebellion, 1618–1621

protected, and his enemies took advantage of this. Ferdinand had for a time sought support from King Sigismund III of Poland who was married to his sister Constance, going so far as to offer him the bishopric of Breslau. But Sigismund's interests lay in the Baltic where he maintained his claim to the crown of Sweden. Yet he permitted Cossacks from his kingdom to join Cossacks raised by an Hungarian magnate, who had long opposed Bethlen, and on November 22, these troops routed the small army left in Transylvania by Bethlen. Bethlen then, perhaps overreacting to the threat to his rear, began to lift the siege of Vienna, and on January 23, 1620, he concluded a provisional truce with Ferdinand. The Bohemian forces did not have the resources to continue the siege, so they too started to retreat. Yet Ferdinand was to enjoy only a brief respite in the east.

Gradually preparations were being made to take military action against the rebels in Bohemia. From late 1619 until late July 1620, Ferdinand worked hard to secure from the estates of Lower and Upper Austria formal recognition of himself as their ruler. He succeeded to a degree with the first, but he failed with the second. Ferdinand consulted his new Jesuit confessor, Martin Becan, on the issue of limited toleration for the Lower Austrian estates. Father Viller had asked to retire, and Ferdinand and the Jesuit superior general in Rome, Vitelleschi, had mutually agreed on Becan as his replacement. A Dutch Jesuit born in 1563, Becan had taught theology at Cologne, Würzburg, and Mainz before coming to the University of Vienna in 1614, and along the way he had earned a reputation as the most distinguished controversial theologian in Germany.[43] In 1621 he dedicated to Ferdinand his popular *Handbook of the Controversies of our Time*.[44] Reasons of health had compelled him to return to Mainz in 1619, but now he was summoned back to Vienna. Once he had been named to the position of confessor, the emperor urged him, in letters of December 18 and January 1, 1620, to come as soon as possible.[45] He arrived in early February 1620, and he would remain an important figure in Vienna until his death in early 1624.

Even after hearing from the Munich theologians and from Trautmannsdorf's mission to Rome, Ferdinand remained undecided about the permissibility of confirming the religious privileges conceded to the Lower Austrian estates by his predecessors Maxmilian and Matthias. So he now sent Eggenberg to Graz to secure the opinion of the Jesuit theologians there. Of these, William Lamormaini stood out as the author of their response. As professor of philosophy and theology and then as rector of the university in Graz since 1613, he had come to know Ferdinand well, and he would

---

[43] A controversial theologian was one who specialized in the areas of controversy with the Protestants.
[44] *Manuale controversiarum hujus temporis* (Würzburg, 1621).   [45] Dudik, 258–9.

eventually come to Vienna and serve as Becan's successor as imperial confessor after the latter's death in 1624.

Lamormaini elaborated a vision of history that was to have a great influence on Ferdinand. He started his long and detailed response by challenging the juridical validity of the concessions made by Matthias. So the question became simply whether Ferdinand could in good conscience concede the practice of the Confession of Augsburg to the Protestants in Lower and Upper Austria and promise it for the future. Lamormaini responded that the emperor could not make this concession "unless there would be an insuperable necessity and clearly evident danger, that, unless this was conceded and promised, the Catholic religion would either perish [in these territories] or suffer much greater harm." The Christian prince was required to lead his people to salvation, and for him to promise to permit heresy was to go directly against this obligation. At the most the Christian prince could permit the exercise of heresy as long as the state of necessity persisted; he could not promise it beyond that, and he would have to say that he did not intend to bind his successors. Lamormaini then made it extremely difficult to admit that a state of necessity actually existed. The emperor needed to secure the agreement of both the Catholic League and other Habsburg princes including the King of Spain. Lamormaini probably knew that Maximilian opposed concessions as we shall see. More importantly, Lamormaini continued, "the forces that the rulers of the House of Austria had at hand to secure their patrimony and to recover Bohemia were not to be evaluated in a merely human manner as unbelieving princes or those waging unjust war do. But [they should consider] that they are subject to the assistance and direction of the just God, whose minister and vicar the Christian prince is and whose cause he ex officio advances." We must not foolishly expect miracles, Lamormaini admitted, "yet more trust is to be placed in God's help than in human resources. It is known that God is accustomed to aid, not with miracles but miraculously [with his providence] those princes who champion his cause and who seek the honor of God rather than their private advantage." Of this there were many examples including contemporary ones.

Lamormaini argued that Saxony would not object to a hard line in Lower Austria. The Protestant estates supported the Calvinist Elector Palatine in Prague, and they threatened to rebel against Ferdinand's legitimate authority. Both these policies would alienate the Lutheran John George who, in addition, had voted for Ferdinand as emperor and whose House had always tended to support the Habsburg emperor. To yield to the demands of the estates would only result in more extensive demands as developments in the other Habsburg lands demonstrated. Furthermore, Ferdinand would need to consult with other members of the House, presumably the King of Spain and Archduke Albert, before making concessions. If after this consultation, Lamormaini acknowledged, agreement was reached that an insuperable necessity did exist, then concessions might be made in vague terms and with the understanding that once the state of necessity ended, so did the concessions.[46] Lamormaini had set the bar very high, especially when one allows for divine intervention.

Ferdinand now turned to Becan for another theological opinion. The emperor probably knew that Becan had allowed for a less rigid position in his *On Keeping Faith with Heretics* of 1608,[47] and may have favored him as confessor for this reason. Becan argued that Ferdinand simply did not have the resources to impose a settlement on the Protestants in Lower Austria, and he went on to cite Thomas Aquinas to the effect that in such a situation one had to accept the lesser evil. For Becan the adherence of the Lower Austrian estates to the Bohemian Confederation along with the continued exercise of their religion, which Ferdinand could not prevent in any event, constituted the greater evil. No reference to divine intervention appeared in Becan's paper. Moreover to Becan's mind, toleration of the Austrian Protestants would facilitate good relations with Saxony. The confessor made a rhetorical point when he claimed that Ferdinand had greater justification to tolerate Protestants than the pope did to allow Jews in Rome.[48]

Fortified by Becan's opinion and following further negotiations, on July 8 Ferdinand granted to the Lower Austrian nobility the practice of the Confession of Augsburg as had been conceded earlier by Emperor Matthias. Most of his councillors including Cardinal Dietrichstein voted in favor of this decision. Even the nuncio seems to have tacitly acquiesced in it. Oñate supported it but then reversed his position and Spain subsequently criticized it. Maximilian of Bavaria did not approve of it. One who opposed it in Vienna was the president of the Imperial Court Council, Johann Georg von Hohenzollern, who in a later letter to his brother, an official at the court of Maximilian, explained the reasons for Ferdinand's decision. The emperor wanted to bring over to his side a significant number of the moderate Protestant nobility in Lower Austria and so consolidate his authority there. Secondly, he wanted to convince both them and John George of Saxony, along with other moderate Protestant states, that the conflict was over his legitimate authority and not directly over religion. The recalcitrant nobles had rebelled by joining the Bohemian Confederation.[49] In the course of the later negotiations Ferdinand assured the nobles, "Believe my words," he told them, promising as archduke and as emperor to treat them "as a father does his children."[50] So a significant number of the Lower Austrian Protestant nobility, along with the Catholic nobles, formally recognized

---

[46] Apr. 20, 1620, ARSJ, Boh. 94, ff. 65–6. A notation indicates that this was read to the emperor on May 10, 1620.
[47] *De fide hereticis servanda* (Mainz, 1608); see also his *Manuale Controversiarum* (Würzburg, 1623), #16 (pp. 479–80).
[48] ARSJ, Boh. 94, ff. 80–89a; see Alois Kroess, "Gutachten der Jesuiten am Beginn der katholischen Generalreformation in Böhmen," *Historisches Jahrbuch* 34 (1913): 9–10.
[49] Brockmann, "Gegenreformation und Habsburgische Bundnispolitik," 173–4
[50] Cited in Arno Strohmayer, *Konfessionskonflikt und Herrschaftsordnung; Widerstandsrecht bei den österreichischen Ständen 1550–1650* (Mainz, 2006). 269.

Ferdinand as ruler on July 13, 1620. The agreement did not extend to the towns. So Ferdinand was able to avoid losing all the Protestant nobility of Lower Austria to the Bohemian Confederation.[51] In line with his attachment to legal obligations, Ferdinand subsequently remained faithful to this agreement though he did tend to interpret it narrowly, as we shall see. Pope Paul as well as Cardinal Bellarmine in Rome were displeased with Becan's approval of the limited toleration, but once Becan explained the whole situation to Vitelleschi, the superior general defended him. The following year Ferdinand made similar concessions to the Silesian and Hungarian estates, again with Becan's approval.[52] So at this time he came again to accept to a degree the argument of toleration as "the lesser evil." Lamormaini's call to trust in more than human means was rejected. Ferdinand drew back from the risk involved. But in each case involving toleration in the period 1617–1620, it should be noted, it was not a question of conceding new religious privileges or rights to the Protestants but rather of confirming those that his predecessors had granted. This lessened Ferdinand's responsibility.[53]

The situation on the Hungarian front remained volatile in the first half of 1620 as the Turks along with Bethlen increasingly became a factor there despite the Treaty of Zsitvatorok and its subsequent modifications. Vienna quickly recognized after the Defenestration that the Turks might well seek to exploit the differences among the Christians.[54] By the end of 1619, Bethlen and the Bohemians were seeking support in Constantinople where a war and a peace party clashed and where Ferdinand's and the Confederation's representatives vied for influence. Turkish affairs colored every aspect of policy in Vienna during 1620. On January 23, Ferdinand had concluded an armistice with Bethlen, as we have seen. It called for the withdrawal of the Polish troops that had defeated Bethlen and the recognition of his rule in the areas of Hungary that he controlled. Bethlen then promised to cease to support the Bohemian rebels and to assist in the pacification of Hungary. The agreement faced considerable opposition in Vienna, especially from Ferdinand's Hungarian councillors who rightly suspected Bethlen's sincerity. In a letter of February 12 to the three archdukes (Albert, Leopold, and Carl), the three ecclesiastical electors, and Maximilian, Ferdinand provided an explanation of his action that brought out his concern for the Turks. Bethlen already controlled most of Hungary. The agreement preserved for Ferdinand the royal title and a remnant of the kingdom. This in turn contributed to the strengthening of

---

[51] Brockmann, "Gegenreformation und Habsburgische Bundnispolitik," 169–73.
[52] Robert Bireley, *The Jesuits and the Thirty Years War: Kings, Courts. and Confessors* (Cambridge, 2003), 40–1.
[53] Brockmann, 134–5.
[54] Reinhard Rudolf Heinisch, "Habsburg, die Pforte, und der Böhmische Aufstand," Part 1 *Südostforschungen* 33 (1974): 125–6.

The Bohemian Rebellion, 1618–1621

Hungary in its traditional role as the defensive bastion of Europe against the advance of the Turks. Ferdinand feared the invasion of Styria by Bethlen and the Turks. The truce would also stabilize the Hungarian front, it was hoped, and so free Ferdinand to cope with the Bohemians and their allies.[55]

But the arrangement did not work out as Ferdinand had anticipated. Despite the armistice, Bethlen formally joined the Bohemian Confederation on April 25, and in mid-May the Confederation – now composed of Frederick, the estates of the Bohemian crown, Upper Austria, and Hungary, a large Protestant faction of the Lower Austrian estates, and Bethlen – determined to send a delegation to Constantinople. At nearly the same time, Bethlen himself made a specific offer of an alliance to the Turks. At the Hungarian diet at Neusohl (Banská Bystrica) in June, plans were discussed for an invasion of Styria, and on August 23, exactly one year after the Bohemians' deposition of Ferdinand, the Hungarian estates deposed him as king and elected Bethlen in his place, without however crowning him.[56]

The long-planned great embassy of the confederates did not depart until August 27. It represented a desperate move to secure help from the Turks after Frederick had failed to obtain significant support from any European power. Specifically, they wanted 10,000 Turkish and 6,000 Tartar troops. But the delegation only arrived in Constantinople on November 14, after the decisive battle of the White Mountain.[57]

During the first half of 1620, Ferdinand worked to secure the assistance of Maximilian and of John George of Saxony for the defeat of Frederick in Bohemia. He also continued to carry on negotiations with the Upper Austrian estates in the hope that they might show signs of a compromise. The Treaty of Munich with Maximilian the previous October had left many questions open regarding the Bavarian's support of Ferdinand. In December 1619, the Catholic League had been reconstituted in a meeting at Würzburg, with an Upper German and a Rhenish directorate, both comprised nearly completely of ecclesiastical states apart from Bavaria. Maximilian was named director for Upper Germany and shortly afterwards assumed in practice the same roll for the Rhenish electorate. At Würzburg it was also decided to raise an army of 25,000 troops. Shortly before that Spain had granted Archduke Albert in the Netherlands the freedom to invade the Palatinate from the north. On January 19, 1620, Ferdinand declared Frederick's election as king of Bohemia invalid.

The electors of Mainz, Trier and Cologne, John George of Saxony and his associate Ludwig of Hesse-Darmstadt, and a representative of Maximilian held an important meeting at Mühlhausen in Thuringia in late March that was

---

[55] Brockmann, 138–44.
[56] Heinisch, "Habsburg, die Pforte, und der Böhmische Aufstand," Part 2, *Südostforschungen* 34 (1975): 94, 99–103.
[57] Ibid., 110–13.

intended to bring John George clearly into Ferdinand's camp for the campaign against Frederick. An aversion to Calvinism and allegiance to the emperor had long characterized the policy of the Lutheran electorate, and this applied to the current elector. But he also looked to his own religious interests. Contact was maintained with the court in Vienna during the meeting. All of the princes including Saxony agreed that Frederick and the Bohemians were guilty of rebellion and that they would cooperate to defeat them. One question to be dealt with was whether the imperial ban should now be issued against Frederick as a notorious rebel. This amounted to the most severe punishment available to imperial authorities, a measure that would provide the juridical basis to deprive Frederick of the Palatine electorate as well as territory. The issue was both legal and political, and councillors in Vienna were divided on how to proceed. Did his election capitulation require Ferdinand to obtain the consent of the electors or was it sufficient simply to consult them before banning Frederick? Maximilian's chief legal adviser, unsurprisingly, declared neither consent nor consultation to be necessary. But the emperor was not to be pressured by Maximilian. Eventually, both he and the electors in Mühlhausen decided that consultation sufficed. This was a valid position that still lay within the bounds of legality.[58]

Once again Ferdinand displayed his attachment to the law as well as a readiness to push it close to its limits. For political reasons, the electors at Mühlhausen advised him not to declare Frederick under the ban at this time, and Ferdinand followed their counsel. Both Ferdinand and the electors feared that proclamation of the ban would stir German Protestant princes and especially James I of England to come to the defense of Frederick. Again, in accord with the advice of the princes at Mühlhausen, on April 30 Ferdinand formally warned Frederick that if he did not vacate all Habsburg territories by June 1, he was liable to the ban. As it turned out, Ferdinand did not formally declare Frederick to be under the ban until after the battle of the White Mountain.

The Catholic electors at Mühlhausen then made further major concessions to John George in order to bring him over to their side. These came to be called the Mühlhausen guarantee (*Mühlhausener Assekuration*). John George was assured that the Catholics would make no effort to repossess by force the ecclesiastical territories that Saxony and other Protestant states of the Lower and Upper Saxon Circles had confiscated after the Peace of Augsburg of 1555, illegally in Catholic eyes, so long as these states supported the emperor. The Catholics retained the right to pursue the recovery of the territories by judicial means, and they did not concede to the Protestant administrators the right to sit in the imperial diet. Ferdinand approved this concession on April 21. This compromise on the Ecclesiastical Reservation marked a retreat from a position

[58] Brockmann, 167–9.

that both he and Maximilian had long defended and approached the position advocated by Klesl earlier. So Ferdinand displayed a further flexibility in his policy.[59] Yet the emperor always inclined more to toleration when it involved states of the Empire than when it involved the territories that he governed directly and for which he bore greater responsibility.

Ferdinand had been in additional negotiations with Saxony over the previous months and as the princes met at Mühlhausen, he informed the Saxon elector that he agreed to the conditions that John George had laid out for his participation in the campaign against Frederick. They were similar to those that Ferdinand had made to Maximilian in the Treaty of Munich. As compensation for his role in the defeat of Frederick, John George was to receive Upper and Lower Lusatia as well as another as yet unnamed principality to be recovered from the rebels.

Ferdinand's success in bringing John George to his side represented a significant triumph. Vienna could now much more convincingly portray the whole Bohemian rebellion as principally a political rather than a religious matter. The Bohemians revolted against legitimate authority. Furthermore, with John George on his side, Ferdinand successfully hindered the formation of a united Protestant front. Elector George William of Brandenburg, even though personally a Calvinist, would generally follow the lead of John George. Both Protestant electors remained aligned with Ferdinand until the fateful Edict of Restitution ten years later.

Until late May, Ferdinand still hoped that further negotiations might bring Upper Austria back to recognition of his authority. Nor did he want to allow Bavarian troops to invade the territory. Only on May 19 did the delegates of the Upper Austrian estates depart from Vienna, thus ending any hope for an agreement with Ferdinand. Ten days later the emperor dispatched to Maximilian a commission to invade Upper Austria with the League army.[60] But one further matter had yet to be cleared up, the role of the Protestant Union. That would take place with the help of France.

The army of the Protestant Union had nearly surrounded Frankfurt at the time of Ferdinand's election. One would have expected them to come to the assistance of Frederick either in Bohemia or in the area of the Palatinate. But the army of the revived Catholic League had grown substantially while the army of the Union declined. In May 1620, about 9500 Union troops near Ulm were confronted by nearly 30,000 League troops in the area of Gunzburg. The long state of preparedness had weakened the Union forces, and contributions from member states, especially cities, had fallen off substantially. Their allies in Lower Saxony suffered from the recent agreement between John George and the emperor. Some financial support came from the Dutch but James I was now engaged in negotiations with Spain regarding the "Spanish

---

[59] Ibid., 175–7; Ritter, 3: 83.   [60] Brockmann, ibid., 176–7.

Match" between his son, Charles, and the Infanta of Spain, and he faced a recalcitrant parliament unwilling to grant him funds.[61] Yet Maximilian hesitated to dispatch the League army to Bohemia with a Union army poised to attack Bavaria or the ecclesiastical states to the west.

In the late fall of 1619, Ferdinand had also sought the support of France against the Bohemian rebels, sending Count Wratislaw von Fürstenberg to Paris to plead his cause. Fürstenberg emphasized Catholic solidarity and the threat to monarchical rule represented by the rebels in his audiences with Louis XIII. The king did in fact authorize the dispatch of troops to assist Ferdinand, and an army began to assemble. But they never crossed the border. Opposition at court to direct aid to the traditional Habsburg enemy won out, and instead the king decided to attempt to mediate the conflict in the Empire and so to assert the French claim to be the arbiter in Europe[62]

In late June Maximilian initiated negotiations with the Protestant Union, to determine its intentions. At this point a French delegation led by the Duke of Angoulême turned up in Ulm with a view to mediating the dispute in Germany. Their efforts resulted in the Treaty of Ulm of July 3 between the Catholic League and the Protestant Union. The two parties agreed to maintain neutrality in the west but they left the opportunity open for both parties to intervene in the conflict in Bohemia to the east. So Maximilian and the League no longer needed to worry about an attack along the Rhine and could intervene actively to the east in the Habsburg lands. The Protestant Union decided not to come to the aid of Frederick and the Bohemians. Archduke Albert did not participate in the negotiations in Ulm, so that he could freely send an army down the Rhine from the Netherlands. In September Spanish troops accordingly occupied the Palatinate lands on the left bank of the Rhine, territory that Spain would hold until the Peace of Westphalia. The Protestant Union offered little resistance and indeed went out of existence the following year. Meanwhile, the French delegation traveled on to Vienna where they hoped to mediate the conflict between Ferdinand, and Frederick and the Bohemians. But they were rebuffed in Vienna. In a final audience, Angoulême was told by the Bohemian chancellor Lobkowitz that "there being nothing more to be gained from treaties since he [Ferdinand] was resolved to secure complete obedience from his subjects, and this could only be assured by the sword."[63] So the French intervention, without intending to do so, worked greatly to the advantage of Ferdinand and Maximilian.[64]

The League army of 21,500 finally crossed the border into Upper Austria on July 24. Tilly held the post of commander but Maximilian, contrary to his general practice, accompanied the invading forces. They faced little organized

---

[61] Albrecht 2, ibid., 521–2.   [62] Bireley 2, 47.
[63] Cited in Georg Pagès, *The Thirty Years War 1618–1648* (New York, 1970), 71.
[64] Albrecht 2, 520–2.

The Bohemian Rebellion, 1618–1621

opposition, taking Linz on August 3 where the Upper Austrian estates surrendered on August 20, recognizing Maximilian as imperial commissioner. The Protestant leaders had fled. Count Charles Bucquoy with an army of similar size – made up of Walloon, Spanish, Neapolitan, and Tuscan infantry along with Polish cavalry – started out from Krems at the same time to drive out the enemy forces that remained in Lower Austria. Ferdinand did not march with the imperial troops. Meanwhile Ambrogio di Spinola, the Italian general in Spanish service, led his army down from the Netherlands into the Palatinate lands on the left bank of the Rhine. John George did not invade Lusatia until early September. Descriptions of the campaigns show that neither Johann von Grimmelshausen in his classic seventeenth-century novel of the war, *The Adventures Simplicius Simplicissimus*, nor the artist from Lorraine Jacques Callot in his series "The Miseries of War" exaggerated. Earlier Ferdinand had complained to his general Bucquoy of

> the crimes of my soldiers who have committed unacceptable excesses, so that they have not even spared little infants, beating them to death, killing them and throwing them into the streets. It is as difficult to prevent such excesses among the soldiers when they are paid irregularly as it is to punish these crimes if one wants to maintain discipline and readiness for war, but when they reach such a degree of atrocity that they are able only to draw down divine punishment, then it is necessary to impose exemplary punishment. One ought to be able completely to prohibit such abominable acts, against nature as well as religion, if one tries to pay the wages regularly.[65]

According to one account, in late September imperial troops slaughtered close to 2,000 men and women after taking the town of Brahatz in Bohemia. Often soldiers' atrocities were responses to harassment of the troops by peasants. Maximilian at one point ordered sixteen soldiers to be hanged for torching villages.[66]

Prague had initially greeted Frederick with enthusiasm amidst festivities and masques, and people received him well in the other lands of the Bohemian crown. His wife Elizabeth gave birth on December 17, 1619, to a crown prince, the future Prince Rupert, the royalist general in the English Civil War. But the glitter quickly wore off. As we have seen, Frederick had not been able to raise funds from foreign sources, and he had little more success in doing so in the Bohemian lands even when his government resorted to confiscating Catholic church lands. He failed to grasp the nature of Bohemian Protestantism with its mix of Lutherans, Calvinists, Utraquists, and Bohemian Brethren.

---

[65] Letter of March 22, 1620, cited in Olivier Chaline, *La bataille de la montagne blanche: un mystique chez les guerriers* (Paris, 1999), 66, n.40.
[66] Sigmund Riezler, ed., "Kriegstagebücher aus dem ligistischen Hauptquartier 1620," *Abhandlungen der Phil.-Hist. Klasse der Bayerischen Akademie der Wissenschaften München* 23, 1 (Munich, 1906), 93, 135.

At Christmas 1619, his radical Calvinist court preacher Abraham Scultetus incited an iconoclastic attack on the magnificent medieval art of St. Veit's Cathedral in Prague that defaced paintings and statuary and shattered stained glass windows. Only popular opposition halted his attempt to topple into the Moldau below the famous statutes on the Charles Bridge. Such actions alienated Protestant as well as Catholic Bohemians, who saw their cultural as well as religious heritage assaulted. Nor did Queen Elizabeth's penchant for French fashions find favor in Prague. Frederick's ministers found it nearly impossible to coordinate government and to overcome the tensions among the lands of the Bohemian crown as they attempted to raise an army. About 25,000 troops stood at his disposal in the summer of 1619, but they were poorly disciplined and at least twice mutinied when the government was unable to pay them. Already in the summer of 1620, Frederick was being called the "Winter King."[67]

After the forces under Maximilian and Tilly had conquered Upper Austria they marched eastwards, where they joined the army of Bucquoy at Zwettl in Lower Austria not far from the Austro–Bohemian border. Up until this point there had been no agreement on an overall strategy. Tension now developed between the two commanders. Bucquoy hesitated to submit to the authority of Maximilian, and he now wanted to move northeastwards into Moravia, whereas Maximilian and Tilly advocated a march directly northward toward Prague in order to provoke a decisive battle with the enemy army and to avoid a long period in winter quarters which would weaken the army. Maximilian also wanted to defeat the rebels before the Turks were liable to intervene.[68] When confronted with the issue of command, Ferdinand made it clear that the Blessed Virgin was his *Generalissima*, and then ordered the cautious Bucquoy to follow the Bavarian plan.[69] By November 7, the Catholic army reached the outskirts of Prague. The army of Christian of Anhalt had raced back to defend the city. So the stage was set for the Battle of the White Mountain, a brief encounter but the most decisive battle of the Thirty Years War.

The Catholic forces of about 30,000 outnumbered the Protestant army of about 21,000 defending the city. The latter, hardly a Bohemian army, composed of German mercenaries, troops from Moravia and Silesia, and Hungarian Protestants, was ensconced at the summit of the steep White Mountain that rose up west of the city of Prague. They were exhausted from forced marches back to defend the city and upset by lack of pay. Early on the morning of November 8, Polish and Walloon horsemen seized a village at the base of the mountain and slaughtered the unsuspecting Hungarian soldiers, a harbinger of the violence to come.

---

[67] Wilson, 286–8; Ritter 3: 79–81.   [68] Heinisch, 2:111.   [69] Franzl, 224–5

At this point the charismatic figure, the Carmelite Domenico à Jesu Maria, assumed a role that was to give to the battle an intensely religious character. Maximilian had requested of Pope Paul that he send the Spaniard Domenico, then superior general of the Carmelites, to accompany the Bavarian army on its campaign against the heretics and to assist it with his prayer and counsel. The Catholics needed God's help to prevail over the heretics. On their march through Bohemia, the Bavarians had found in an abandoned farm house an image of the Nativity that had been defaced with the eyes of all the figures torn out, except that of the Infant but including the Blessed Mother. Domenico seized upon this image as an example of the iconoclastic outrages of the Protestants who had previously run amuck in Prague. With the preaching of Domenico, the campaign became one of vengeance fought with the help of the Blessed Virgin Mary and the saints to defend their honor against the destructive iconoclasts. Scapulars with Mary's image were distributed to the soldiers.

After the initial skirmish at the base of the mountain on November 8, the octave day of the feast of All Saints, a council of war was held by the Catholic leaders, Maximilian, Tilly, and Bucquoy. The first two favored a direct assault up the mountain; their troops outnumbered the enemy by 10,000. Bucquoy wanted to wait and then to dispatch troops around the mountain to attack the Protestants from its other side. The enemy occupied a strong position, he argued, and a defeat before the gates of Prague would undermine the morale of the troops. Then into the council of war carrying the defaced image of the Virgin there burst, apparently uninvited, Padre Domenico. Repeated visions, he assured the others, had guaranteed victory, with the help of the angels, over the enemies of God. His intervention settled the matter. The troops received with enthusiasm the orders to attack. The Irish Jesuit confessor of Bucquoy, Thomas Fitzsimmons, prayed aloud the Salve Regina as the Catholic troops began their push up the mountain. The left flank of the estates' army fled, but then their troops counterattacked and seemed to repulse the Catholic charge. At this point Tilly committed the Italian cavalry and the Polish Cossacks. Domenico on horseback led them on holding up the defaced image of the Virgin and his crucifix as they annihilated the enemy shouting their battle cry, "Maria." The battle was over in less than two hours, the roughly 1,000 fatalities testifying to the intensity of the violence. Frederick, who had emerged to join his troops just at the moment of the victorious Catholic surge, fled the city with his wife and entourage, never to return.[70]

The next morning, at the behest of Maximilian and Bucquoy, Padre Domenico led a triumphant Te Deum in the Capuchin church in Prague. Afterwards

---

[70] Olivier Chaline, "The Battle of the White Mountain (8 November 1620)," in *1648: War and Peace in Europe*, 1: *Politics, Religion, Law and Society*, ed. Klaus Bussmann and Heinz Schilling (Münster, 1999): 95–102; Bireley, *Jesuits and the Thirty Years War*, 42–3. For a thorough study of Padre Domenico and the Battle of the White Mountain, see Chaline, *La bataille de la montagne blanche*.

Maximilian met with the members of the Bohemian estates in the refectory of the Capuchins. They hoped to return to the situation of 1618 prior to the rebellion, thus retaining all the rights and privileges they had then enjoyed. This was not to be. Ferdinand demanded their complete submission, Maximilian informed them while promising to intercede for them with the emperor. This they rendered on November 16, renewing the homage they had made to Ferdinand at the time of his coronation in 1617. The following day the Bavarian duke left for Munich, leaving the Moravian Prince Karl von Liechtenstein in charge as Ferdinand's commissioner. Maximilian and Bucquoy had hoped to prevent a sack of Prague but they were unable to do so. Imperial and Bavarian troops ravaged the city for several weeks sparing neither Catholics nor Protestants. Only the Jews avoided harm. Ferdinand had ordered that the ghetto be protected because of the loyalty that the Jews had shown to him throughout the whole crisis. With the arrival on December 3 of the Bohemian chancellor, Lobkowitz, order was gradually restored.[71]

Back in Vienna, Ferdinand had remained confident of victory even as his ministers feared the worst. Rumors of the victory reached Vienna in mid-November but only on November 23 did he learn of the full extent of the victory. Immediately he wrote Bucquoy asking for the names of those who had distinguished themselves, so that he might reward them. At the emperor's direction a great victory procession was held from the Augustinerkirche to the cathedral where Cardinal Dietrichstein preached the sermon, and a golden crown worth 10,000 gulden was made for the statue of Our Lady at the pilgrimage church of Mariazell.[72] Padre Domenico notified Pope Paul of the victory within two days, and he dispatched a fuller account on November 13. To Padre Domenico the victory was "miraculous,"[73] to be attributed to Jesus and Mary, and eventually many throughout the Catholic world thought the same. Lamormaini later wrote in his *The Virtues of Ferdinand* II that the divine presence was "evident" at the White Mountain when the Catholic troops charged upwards against the well-fortified enemy.[74] A great celebration was held in Rome on December 3. Paul V presided at a service of thanksgiving at St. Mary Major, then walked, accompanied by cardinals and ambassadors, from Santa Maria sopra Minerva to the German church of Santa Maria dell' Anima where he celebrated a solemn Mass with a Te Deum. Subsequently, a small Roman basilica of the Carmelites originally dedicated to St. Paul was renovated under the direction of Carlo Maderno with financing from Cardinal Scipione Borghese, the papal nephew, and dedicated to Santa Maria della Vittoria. There the image of the Nativity borne by Padre Domenico during the battle was enshrined above the altar.[75] Meanwhile, between 1622 and 1624

---

[71] Chaline, *Bataille de la montagne blanche*, 387–98.
[72] Franzl, 229.   [73] Chaline, *Bataille de la montagne blanche*, 403.   [74] *Virtutes*, 107–8.
[75] Chaline, *Bataille de la montagne blanche*, 403–4, 416, 420, 416, 420, 454, 511, 515, 521.

a church was constructed on the battlefield of the White Mountain, Our Lady of Victory, where a replica of the image was venerated.

The rivalry between Ferdinand's general, Bucquoy, and Maximilian and Tilly remained alive and indeed heated up after the battle; it pointed to the tension between the two courts. Bucquoy, in a report to Ferdinand that was intended to be passed on to Philip III of Spain, devoted as much space to criticism of Tilly as he did to his account of the engagement with the enemy.[76] Maximilian had been feted upon his triumphant return to Munich in a ceremony featuring a panegyric delivered by Father Keller that later appeared in print. Shortly afterwards a pamphlet published pseudonymously by Bucquoy's confessor, the Jesuit Fitzsimmons, *On the Battle of Prague and the City's Surrender*, attributed the victory chiefly to the imperial general, without criticism of Tilly or Maximilian; a second edition appeared at Vienna the next year under the pseudonym Constantius Peregrinus.[77] Maximilian was incensed, and Keller replied from Munich with a vitriolic, anonymous attack, *Constantius Peregrinus Punished*, in which he assigned the principal credit to the Bavarian duke for the success of the campaign and the victory at Prague. The exchange probably would have continued and further affected relations between Vienna and Munich had not Bucquoy died and the Jesuit superior general intervened to discipline his two charges.[78]

News of the outcome of the battle of the White Mountain only reached Constantinople in early January, and at first it encountered considerable skepticism. A detailed treaty had been signed by the delegates of the Bohemian Confederation and the Turks in late November which did not, however, include specific military or financial assistance to be supplied to the Bohemians by the Turks. But it was all too late. The Treaty of Zsitvatorok with its modifications remained in force. The Turks now gradually turned their attention to war with Poland and with Persia. Bethlen and the Hungarian dissidents remained alone in the field. He was finally forced to accept the Treaty of Nikolsburg (Mikulov) on December 31, 1621. This required him to surrender the Hungarian royal title as well as territory in Hungary but he did hold on to two principalities in Silesia, Ratibor and Oppeln. We have not heard the last of him. Count Thurn continued to incite him to take up arms against Ferdinand. How different

---

[76] Ibid., 404–5.
[77] *De Praelio Pragense Pragaequo Ditione*. The pseudonym was Candido Eblano. (Eblana is Dublin.) A second, expanded edition appeared in Vienna in 1621, under the pseudonym Constantius Peregrinus. Large extracts from this brief book have been published under the title "Diary of the Bohemian War 1620" in Henry Fitzsimmons, *Words of Comfort to Persecuted Catholics*, ed. Edward Hogan, S.J. (Dublin, 1881).
[78] Bireley 2, 43–4.

history might have turned out had the confederates succeeded in securing earlier, effective aid from the Turks.[79]

Now that the rebels had been defeated, Ferdinand had to decide how to deal with those who had attempted to unseat him and whom he considered guilty of lèse majesté. When delegates of the Bohemian estates and the citizens of Prague approached the victorious Maximilian, he had refused to give them any guarantees and required of them unconditional submission. He urged a hard line toward the conspirators and their allies. "The iron is hot," he wrote Ferdinand, do not lose the opportunity to deal with their constitutional and religious privileges. There was to be no return to the pre-1618 situation as the members of the estates hoped.[80] Liechtenstein hesitated to start aggressively rounding up rebels partly because hostilities still continued in Silesia and Lusatia and against Bethlen as well as in western Bohemia. He did not want to provide a stimulus to the enemy to resist further.[81] On February 6, Ferdinand instructed him to begin arresting members of the Bohemian directorate as well as other rebels who remained in Prague and to pursue those who had left the city. Liechtenstein had already sent him a long list of those he considered guilty.[82] Though in the past the king of Bohemia had normally presided in person in cases of lèse majesté, Ferdinand took the advice of his councillors not to do so. To be present at the meting out of punishments would harm his image among his subjects. The councillors also feared for his security.[83] Ferdinand then appointed Liechtenstein himself to preside over the trial and a team of commissioners to assist him. Both Slavata and Martinitz, the victims of the Defenestration, declined to serve on the commission, and in general inclined to lenience.[84] The commissioners arrived in Prague on March 13, with instructions that the trial was to be held in the council room of the Prague castle from which the imperial ministers had been hurled. It was not to be a normal process in that the guilt of the defendants was considered notorious.[85] So there came into existence what came to be known as the Prague Blood Court (Das Prager Blutgericht).

Initially, only seventeen defendants stood before the court on March 27. A long list of charges was read to them in German and in Czech, and they were allowed to answer only "yes" or "no" as to their guilt. Then each defendant was examined individually by the commissioners, and more defendants

---

[79] Heinisch, 2: 118–21.   [80] Albecht 2, 532–3.
[81] Karl von Liechtenstein to Ferdinand II, Jan. 21, 1621, Christian Ritter d'Elvert, *Die Bestrafung der Böhmischen Rebellion: Die Korrespondenz Ferdinand II. mit dem Fürsten Liechenstein* (Brünn, 1868): #12, p. 11. Another reason that Liechtenstein hesitated to move against the rebels was that Maximilian, on his first arrival in Prague, had apparently assured all those in the city of "protection of their life and even their security," a promise that he probably made with a view to establish initial order in the city.
[82] Ferdinand to Liechtenstein, Feb. 6, 1621, d'Elvert, #15, p.21.
[83] Position paper of the councillors, undated (early March), ibid. #35, pp. 46–7.
[84] Franzl, 232   [85] Liechtenstein to Ferdinand, Apr. 7, 1621, d'Elvert #36, pp. 49–54.

The Bohemian Rebellion, 1618–1621

were added. In the course of these examinations new evidence came to light of the Directors' contacts with Bethlen Gàbor and the Turks as well as with the Upper and Lower Austrians. They were also seen to have attempted to incite Ferdinand's subjects in Inner Austria against him.[86] Ferdinand followed the process as closely as he could from Vienna, and he awaited the news with eagerness. Finally, on May 17, the commissioners sent on the list of those to be sentenced to death and the mode of execution. They did recommend leniency for some defendants including Directors because of extenuating circumstances. One of these was William Popel von Lobkowitz whom they characterized as "a simple idiot (ein Pur lauter Idiot)" who had been misled by others to side with the rebels. He had been among the first to surrender to Maximilian, and he then discouraged further resistance and encouraged the estates to submit to the Bavarian duke. Moreover, the service of his family to the monarchy deserved consideration. The commissioners left up to the emperor the decision whether to allow a Protestant preacher to accompany the condemned to the place of execution; this would be an issue in the following weeks.[87]

Now it was up to Ferdinand to make the final decision on the fate of those condemned. He did modify some sentences as recommended by the commissioners to show "his grace and goodness." But he still hesitated to order the executions, and he instructed Liechtenstein not to carry any out until he received a further resolution from Vienna. He did inquire about many other figures, including Count Schlick, whose names did not appear on the list sent him by the commissioners. They were to be further examined, under torture if necessary, to uncover the extent of the plots against him and his House. Catholic chaplains were to be sent to those condemned; Ferdinand wanted to do all that he could for the salvation of the rebels. Lutheran but not Calvinist ministers might be permitted to visit the defendants in prison but not to accompany them publicly to their death.[88]

At this point a position paper drawn up almost certainly by Ferdinand's confessor, Becan, helps us to understand the emperor's mind as he approached his decision on the defendants.[89] One finds in Becan's paper an elaboration of the same attitude as that later attributed to Ferdinand by Lamormaini in his chapter "Justice with Mercy" in the *The Virtues of Emperor Ferdinand II*. "As often as he saw that no harm came to either the public or a private good,

---

[86] Liechtenstein to Ferdinand, Apr. 29, 1621, ibid., #39, pp. 55–8.
[87] Liechtenstein to Ferdinand, May 17, 1621, ibid., #42, pp. 59–68, citation, p. 61.
[88] Ferdinand to Liechtenstein, May 26, 1621, ibid., #43, pp. 68–70, #45, pp. 70–1.
[89] ARSJ, Boh.94, ff. 120–22.; see Veronica Pokorny, "Clementia Austriaca: Studien zur Bedeutung der Clementia Principis für die Habsburger im 16. und17. Jahrhundert," *Mitteilungen des Instituts für österreichische Geschichtsforschung* 86 (1978): 311–63, here 350–6, and Alois Kroess, "Gutachten der Jesuiten am Beginn der katholischen Gegenreformation in Böhmen," *Historisches Jahrbuch* 34 (1913): 257–94.

he tempered the rigor of justice with the mildness of mercy," Lamormaini wrote of Ferdinand.[90] Justice in the service of the public and private good came first, then mercy. Becan in his consultation presented three opinions, one attributed to a Bohemian, the second to an Austrian, and the third to a German. The Bohemian asserted in a manner anticipative of Lamormaini's later view that "an opportunity was now offered the emperor" of eliminating heresy as well as punishing rebellion, and there was no excuse for not seizing it. He appealed to instances in the Old Testament where God had ordered the punishment and even death of apostates, as in the case of Moses who ordered that 3,000 Israelites be put to death for worshiping the golden calf. The Austrian called for widespread amnesty. He argued that only such a policy would win over the support of the population. Harshness was bound to incite further unrest. To support his position, he cited passages from the Gospel where Jesus displayed mercy and forgiveness, and he appealed to the tradition of "Austrian clemency." Becan, in the person of the German, called for the proper admixture of justice and mercy. "There is no true justice where mercy is lacking, and no true justice without mercy," he wrote. The Bohemian position considered all heretics to be rebels, he declared. But this was not the case; many heretics supported the emperor. Nor was this, he insisted, a war of religion. On the practical level, to take harsh measures against all heretics would only unite them against the emperor, Lutherans, Calvinists, and Anabaptists. Ferdinand needed to keep Saxony on his side. The Austrian's position, according to Becan, would result in even greater harm by eliminating justice. Justice required the punishment of evildoers. To allow the rebels off without punishment would only encourage later rebellions, both in Ferdinand's territories and elsewhere. His subjects would murmur that Ferdinand treated loyal and disloyal subjects in the same way. This violated all sense of fairness. Moreover, someone had to pay for the expenses of the war and the devastation wrecked by it. Ferdinand should deprive the defendants of life, privileges, and property, Becan wrote, according to the degree of their guilt, always keeping the law and the public good in mind. There Becan left the matter, leaving decisions on individuals up to Ferdinand. At the end, he made clear that the Scripture passages cited by the Austrian which dealt with forgiveness applied to private persons, not to ruling princes with responsibility for the public good.

On June 2, then, Ferdinand authorized Liechtenstein to proceed with the executions. He also acceded to Liechtenstein's renewed request to permit a Protestant preacher to attend at the death scene of those to be executed. Changes in the number of those to be executed and the method of execution continued to be made until the last minute.[91]

---

[90] pp. 84–7.
[91] Ferdinand to Liechtenstein, Jun. 2 and 16, 1621, d'Elvert #46, pp. 72–3, and #49, p. 88.

The Bohemian Rebellion, 1618–1621

On June 21, 1621, "the most celebrated execution in Czech History" took place in the packed Old Town Square of Prague.[92] Seven hundred Saxon soldiers had been brought in to help secure the site, thus involving Saxony in the executions. At five in the morning, twenty-eight prisoners were led under heavy guard to the platform, draped in black, on which the scaffold stood. They included some of the most prominent members of Czech society, many in their sixties and seventies. Twenty-four were beheaded, three were hanged. One, Jan Theodor Sixt of Ottersdorf, was pardoned at the last moment as he approached the scaffold, thus intensifying the drama of the situation by raising the expectation of further pardons. Johannes Jessenius, rector of the University of Prague, who had long polemicized and machinated against Ferdinand even advocating an alliance with the Turks, had his tongue cut out before having his head cut off and his body quartered and displayed. The whole grisly event lasted about four hours, and the executioner used four swords to accomplish his task. Twelve of the heads were displayed on the tower of the Charles Bridge where passers-by could readily view them; there they remained for ten years.[93] The morning of the execution Ferdinand prayed for the condemned before the image of the Blessed Mother at his favorite pilgrimage destination, Mariazell in Styria. There, as he remarked to the abbot of the monastery, he came to pray for the souls of those whose lives he could not spare and so imitate his Lord by interceding for his enemies.[94]

Ferdinand, in responding to Liechtenstein's brief report of the executions, commended the governor for the good order that he had maintained and the care with which he had carried out his task. He went on to note that there remained many more, also in the towns, at least as guilty of complicity in the rebellion as those who had been executed, and he ordered the commissioners to continue their investigations. It would not be fair to allow the other guilty ones to remain unpunished.[95] Liechtenstein urged Ferdinand to hold back. Mansfeld remained in the field in western Bohemia and Bethlen to the east. The imperial forces did not effectively control Bohemian territory and would have great difficulty in suppressing likely popular uprisings. People might well flee, and into the hands of the enemy. Better to wait until a more propitious time to carry out punishments and, as Ferdinand also intended, to expel Calvinist preachers.[96] Acting on this advice Ferdinand issued what he called a general pardon – that is, no more executions, bodily punishments, imprisonments, or deprivations of status – except for those already condemned in absentia and those persisting in rebellion. So he exercised his "mercy and goodness" as he put it. But fines and loss of property were still to be imposed.

---

[92] Howard Louthan, *Converting Bohemia: Force and Persuasion in the Catholic Reformation* (Cambridge, 2009), 22
[93] Ibid., 22–31.   [94] Franzl, 236–7.
[95] Ferdinand to Liechtenstein, Jul. 2, 1621, d'Elvert #52, pp. 94–5.
[96] Liechtenstein to Ferdinand, Jul. 14, 1621, ibid. #53, pp. 95–9.

In these cases the commissioners were to make their judgment on the basis of justice; Ferdinand reserved to himself the exercise of mercy, and he often showed consideration for the situation of widows and children of the rebels. Calvinist preachers as fomenters of rebellion were to be expelled, and this for political not religious reasons.[97] A second tribunal was set up in Brno (Brünn) for Moravia, headed by Slavata and Cardinal Dietrichstein. Twelve Moravians were sentenced to death, but no executions were carried out. Ferdinand commuted their sentences to life imprisonment, and all went free within ten years.[98]

As grisly as it was, the number who suffered at the hands of the Blood Court was small in comparison to Henry VIII's suppression of the Pilgrimage of Grace or Alba's Council of Troubles in the Netherlands. Ferdinand clearly thought that justice required it. He was particularly incensed with the rebels who aimed to bring the Turks into the conflict. No similar event would take place in his reign.

---

[97] Ferdinand to Liechtenstein, Jul. 26, 1621 and Jan. 18, 1622, ibid. ##55, 62, pp. 106–7, 110–13.
[98] Wilson, 352.

Chapter 5

Consolidation and Expansion, 1621–1628

At the time of the executions in Prague on June 21, 1621, Ferdinand had nearly completed his forty-third year. Military operations continued against Bethlen in the east, and Maximilian's forces began to occupy the Palatinate lands of Frederick to the west. Ferdinand turned his attention to the consolidation of his position in the Austrian and Bohemian lands as well as in Hungary. According to Robert Evans, the Habsburg Monarchy, which would continue to exist until the end of the First World War, was based essentially on an alliance of the Habsburg dynasty, the aristocracy, and the Catholic Church.[1] It can be considered a "composite monarchy," that is, one in which a sovereign ruled usually over several territorial units each with its own constitution and traditions.[2] Ferdinand's form of moderate absolutism was exercised through the church and through the aristocracy or *Herren* who held high office and dominated in the estates of the various territories. Ferdinand consolidated the alliance of the three, and so more than any other individual he must be considered the founder of the Habsburg Monarchy, which would emerge from the Thirty Years War, despite its many setbacks, as a major European power. In 1621 and the following years, Ferdinand was drawn increasingly into the politics of the Holy Roman Empire, initially by the support that he gave to Maximilian's claim to the Palatinate electoral dignity and lands in accordance with the promise that he had made in the Treaty of Munich of 1619. Throughout the remainder of his reign, there would exist an increasing tension between his goal of consolidation of the Habsburg territories and the effort to project his power

---

[1] Robert J. W. Evans, *The Making of the Habsburg Monarchy: An Interpretation* (Oxford, 1979).
[2] The classic article on "composite monarchies" is John H. Elliott, "A Europe of Composite Monarchies," *Past and Present*, #137 (Nov., 1992): 48–71, rpt. in John H. Elliott, *Spain, Europe, and the Wider World 1500–1800* (New Haven, 2009), but he has little to say about the Habsburg Monarchy.

into the Empire, chiefly for religious reasons as we shall see. His ability to act decisively in the Empire depended on a solid base in the Habsburg lands, and his position in his Habsburg lands drew strength from his status as emperor. The claims of the Habsburg lands and the claims of the Empire both had their supporters in his inner circle.

Ferdinand's last will and testament signed on May 10, 1621, thus before the executions in Prague, provides a key to his thinking at this time.[3] In it he alluded to a testament that he had drawn up dated June 20, 1616, which has been lost, and he noted that much had changed since then. His testament shows clearly his intent to unify all his lands in a single line through primogeniture and through the Catholic religion. Successful defense against the constant threat from the Turks as well as the upheaval in his own lands and in the Empire required this unity. Ferdinand began with a statement that should not be dismissed as a mere commonplace. He expressed his awareness that he too would die and like every other human being he would have to render an account to God for his life, and so much the more because of the high station and responsibility to which he has been called, "to govern with peaceful rule, similar justice, paternal care, love, and grace as well as resolute defense." To this end he would bend all his efforts, as well as to the maintenance of the necessary unity within the House of Habsburg which was crucial for the future of all Christendom. To the "ancient, universal, Catholic, Apostolic, Roman faith" he committed himself and "to the extent that this was humanly possible," all the lands and subjects entrusted to him by God. His soul he commended with heartfelt feeling to the mercy of his Redeemer and to the intercession of the Blessed Mother and his favorite saints including Blessed Ignatius Loyola, founder of the Society of Jesus, who had not yet been canonized.

All his lands Ferdinand bequeathed to his "beloved son" Ferdinand Ernst, and he vigorously affirmed that this law of strict primogeniture should be observed by all his descendants in the future. Ferdinand's brothers, Archduke Leopold and Carl, were urged to accept this arrangement. Ferdinand's insistence on primogeniture departed notably from the action of his grandfather, Ferdinand I, who had divided his inheritance among his three sons, Emperor Maximilian II and the Archdukes Carl, Ferdinand's father, and Ferdinand, ruler of the Tyrol and Anterior Austria, and his call for unity in the family certainly grew out of his observation of the enmity between Rudolf and Matthias. In the event that he should die before his son reached his majority, Ferdinand determined that a committee made up of King Philip IV of Spain, his cousin Archduke Albert in the Netherlands, his two brothers

---

[3] "Testament Kaiser Ferdinands II. Wien 10 Mai 1621," in Gustav Turba, *Die Grundlagen der pragmatischen Sanktion*, vol. 2: *Die Hausgesetze* (Vienna, 1913) #5, pp. 335–51.

Leopold and Carl, and interestingly, the Wittelsbach Duke Maximilian of Bavaria, his brother in law, should exercise the regency.

Ferdinand firmly ordered his son to maintain his lands in the Catholic faith, and so to continue the tradition established by Emperor Ferdinand I and Archduke Carl, Ferdinand Ernst's grandfather. Above all, he was to keep out all sects and heresies which only generated disobedience and all sorts of difficulties and led eventually to the decline of all spiritual and temporal government. Religious unity was essential for effective government, he asserted, and so was in tune with many contemporary political writers from Machiavelli to the Anti-Machiavellians Giovanni Botero in his *On Reason of State* (1589) and Justus Lipsius's in *Six Books of Politics* (1590), two copies of each of which could be found in Ferdinand's personal library.[4] Towards the end of the testament he returned to a similar theme, urging his heir to keep before his eyes always the Almighty God and his commandments and to remember that his territory and people were not given to him by God for his private use and worldly prestige but for the glory of his name and for their spiritual and temporal benefit.

Much less is said in the testament about the role of the aristocracy in the estates, but it is not completely overlooked. Ferdinand's instruction that his heir was to respect all the legitimate rights and freedoms of his subjects indicated his intent to recognize the position of the estates. He always considered himself to act within the law in his dealings with them, and he recognized the need to incorporate them into his government. Signing his testament as witnesses along with Ferdinand himself were his close associates representing his various lands: Peter Pazmany, Archbishop of Esztergom for Hungary; Eggenberg and Trautmannsdorf for Inner Austria; Carl von Harrach and Sdenko von Lobkovitz for the Bohemian lands; Johann Baptista Werda von Werdenberg for Lower Austria; and Leonhard Helfriedt von Meggau for Upper Austria.

In a lengthy codicil to this testament dated the same day, the emperor first recounted all that he had accomplished in Inner Austria for the restoration of the Catholic religion. Then he vigorously instructed his son and all his heirs to continue this work, to not allow themselves to be daunted by obstacles; "they should keep in mind that this was God's work and not doubt his assistance, help, and blessing, just as we with the same divine assistance have carried out and brought to a successful conclusion this reformation despite the dangerous times and situations ..." To this end he ought always to defend the clergy and to foster their work and especially that of the Society of Jesus, which had

---

[4] Giovanni Botero, *Della ragion di stato*, ed. Luigi Firpo (Turin, 1948) 2: 15–16 (pp. 135–41), 5: 3–9 (pp. 179–202); Justus Lipsius, *Politicorum sive civilis doctrinae libri sex* (Frankfurt, 1590): 4: 2–4 (pp. 89–94); *Ad libros politicorum Breves Notae* (printed and paginated continuously with this edition of the *Politicorum*), 3 (p. 255). For Ferdinand's personal library, see the Österreichische Nationalbibliothek, Vienna, Handschriften 13,531; it is not clear when this list of books was drawn up, perhaps about 1616.

accomplished so much to advance the work of the Church not only in the Austrian lands but throughout Christendom. The pope was not mentioned. As with the body of the testament, the codicil was signed by Ferdinand in his own hand as well as by the aforementioned councillors.[5]

Ferdinand did not have a "favorite" who dispatched much of the business of government for him as did his contemporaries Philip IV of Spain in the Count-Duke Olivares and Louis XIII of France in Cardinal Richelieu.[6] In the *Essential Prince* (*Princeps in Compendio*), a brief mirror of princes of uncertain authorship but originating at the court of Vienna in 1632, the author recommended that the prince have a leading minister but that he never allow him to make decisions and that he carefully restrict his powers so that the impression never arose that the minister controlled the prince.[7] Ferdinand governed with the assistance chiefly of four councils: the privy council (*Geheimrat*), the Imperial Court or Aulic council (*Reichshofrat*); the treasury council (*Hofkammer*), and the court war council (*Hofkriegsrat*). Of these the chief was the privy council, and the others reported to it. The privy council convened nearly every work day in the council room (*Ratsstube*) of the Hofburg, and Ferdinand rarely missed a session. The privy council did not make decisions on its own but made recommendations to Ferdinand for decision. Lamormaini cites Ferdinand as saying that "it was more secure to follow the advice of the councillors, even though occasionally the matter did not turn out well, than to be governed by the judgment of one man," presumably himself. The emperor encouraged free discussion among the councillors and carefully listened to those in the minority, too. In matters of religion Ferdinand first turned to the theologians, and in important affairs sought the opinion, according to Lamormaini, of others.[8]

Many of the councillors also held positions in the imperial household. In 1628 there numbered approximately twenty privy councillors. But one was not entitled to participate in a meeting of the council by virtue of the title of privy councillor. Privy councillors were invited to each meeting, so that normally at a meeting from five to eight were present.[9] Some did not reside regularly in Vienna like Cardinal Franz von Dietrichstein, bishop of Olmütz and governor

---

[5] Turba, 351–5.
[6] On the favorite, see J.H. Elliott and L.W.B. Brockliss, ed., *The World of the Favorite* (New Haven, 1999) and Michael Kaiser and A. Pečár, *Der zweite Mann im Staate. Oberste Amtsträger und Favoriten im Umkreis der Reichsfürsten im 17. und 18. Jahrhundert* (Berlin 2003). Zeitschrift für historische Forschung, Beiheft 32.
[7] "Princeps in Compendio," ed. Franz Bosbach, *Das Herrscherbild im 17. Jahrhundert*, ed. Konrad Repgen (Münster, 1991), 100–1. Schriftenreihe der Vereinigung zur Erforschung der Neueren Geschichte, 19.
[8] *Virtutes*. 74.
[9] Mark Hengerer, *Kaiserhof und Adel in der Mitte des 17. Jahrhunderts: Eine Kommunikationsgeschichte der Macht in der Vormoderne* (Constance, 2004), 72, 120, 290. Historische Kulturwissenschaft 3.

Consolidation and Expansion, 1621–1628

of Moravia who remained in his see, and Gundacker von Liechtenstein, brother of Karl. Though a member of the council from 1620 to 1638, after 1626 he resided for the most part on his lands in Bohemia. Some were off on diplomatic missions. Others were called in for their expertise in a particular area.

The most regular participants in the privy council meetings during the 1620s and 1630s were four. First there was Eggenberg who held the title of director of the privy council from 1619 until his death in 1634, and for a brief time served also as *Obristhofmeister*, an office that was responsible for the management of the whole imperial household. Nuncio Carafa called him in 1628 "the absolute master of the will of the Emperor." When his periodical illnesses prevented him from attending an important council meeting, the meeting was often held at his bedside in his residence. When after being named governor of Inner Austria in 1625 he was frequently absent in Graz, Ferdinand regularly sent a courier to solicit his opinion on important matters.[10] Anton Wolfradt, the son of a tailor, after study at the German College in Rome, entered the Cistercian Order but then in 1613, at the nomination of Emperor Matthias, was named Abbot of the Benedictine Monastery of Kremsmünster in Upper Austria. Having been entrusted with several diplomatic missions by Ferdinand, perhaps at the suggestion of Eggenberg to whom he was close, he was named president of the court treasury in 1623 and so took over the unwelcome task of managing Ferdinand's finances. The next year he was introduced into the privy council where he remained until his death in 1637. Anton Wolfradt held his position in the treasury until 1631; at that time Cardinal Dietrichstein consecrated him the first prince-bishop of the see of Vienna. Persistent efforts in Vienna in the 1630s to have him promoted to the cardinalate never succeeded. In the 1630s, the nuncio Malatesta Baglioni characterized him as concerned above all with his own personal interest and easily influenced by gifts or bribes. Also according to Baglioni, he and Eggenberg participated in a scheme in the 1630s to double the taxes on peasants in Inner Austria beyond which the government had imposed and then to skim off the excessive revenue for themselves.[11]

Maximilian von Trautmannsdorf would accomplish his most significant achievement with the conclusion of the Peace of Westphalia in 1648. But he was long a trusted adviser of Ferdinand II. Like Eggenberg a native of Graz and a convert, he does not seem to have been a client of the former. At the age of

---

[10] Carlo Carafa, "Relatione dello stato dell'imperio e della Germania, 1628," ed. J.G. Müller, *Archiv für Kunde österreichischer Geschichtsquellen* 22/23 (1860), 296–7. In his report of 1630, the Venetian ambassador, Sebastian Venier, attributed to Eggenberg the same influence over Ferdinand as did Carafa; see *Die Relationen der Botschafter Venedigs über Deutschland und Österreich im 17. Jahrhundert*, 1: *Matthias bis Ferdinand III*, ed. Josef Fiedler (Vienna, 1866), 157–8. Fontes Rerum Austriacorum, Section 2, vol. 26.

[11] Baglioni to Barberini, Oct. 6, 1635, *NBD* 7: *Nuntiaturen des Ciriaco Rocci, des Malatesta Baglioni, und des Mario Filonardi. Sendung des P. Alessandro d'Ales*, ed. Rotraut Becker (Tübingen, 2004) #94.5 (pp. 539–40); ibid., Baglioni to Barberini, May 19, 1635, #54.5 (p. 329).

twenty-five he came to Vienna to a post on the Imperial Court Council where he remained until he entered the privy council in 1618. He was admired for his integrity and his negotiating skills. The year 1633 saw him named *Obristhofmeister* of the future Ferdinand III, an appointment that presaged his importance in the succeeding reign. In his report of 1630, the Venetian ambassador named as the three most important councillors Eggenberg, the abbot of Kremsmünster, and Trautmannsdorf.[12]

But one cannot overlook Peter Heinrich von Stralendorf. Born in Vienna in 1580, he was the son of Leopold von Stralendorf, who had risen in the service of the elector of Mainz to become vice-chancellor of the Holy Roman Empire from 1607 to 1612. Peter Heinrich succeeded his father in this position in 1627, and remained there until his death in 1637. He had become vice-president of the Imperial Court Council in 1620, a position that he also held until his death. This appointment led to his entrance into the privy council in the early 1620s where he then became the principal liaison with the Imperial Court Council. As vice-chancellor of the Empire – the archbishop of Mainz was the chancellor – Stralendorf directed the imperial chancery through which passed the affairs of the Imperial Court Council as well as much of the political correspondence with other states of the Empire. Strongly Catholic, Stralendorf generally inclined to the interests of Maximilian of Bavaria. Other privy councillors frequently in attendance at least for a time were Slavata, Cardinal Pazmany, Meggau, who served as *Obristhofmeister* from 1621 to 1622 and again from 1626 to 1637, and Ramboldo Collalto, a native of Venice who rose up through the ranks of the military eventually to serve as president of the imperial war council from 1624 until his death in 1630.

Ferdinand's usual procedure was to assign a matter to a committee or "deputation" of privy councillors or even to an individual. The makeup of the committee or the choice of the individual might indicate the direction that the emperor wanted the discussion to take. A report would then be made to the whole council, and discussion leading to their recommendation would ensue. The emperor would make the decision then or subsequently. In grave matters, for example where life and death were involved, Ferdinand would always pray before starting the process toward a decision, and he would bring in others from outside the council. In still other cases, he would also turn to the Imperial Court Council or the war council for their views. In some delicate cases or in cases where secrecy was of the highest order, instead of working with the council as a whole, he would solicit a paper directly for himself from each councillor. Lamormaini suggests that this procedure had a twofold advantage: that the emperor learned the opinion of each individual councillor and that the one consulted would think himself the only one consulted and so would be much more careful about preserving the necessary secrecy lest he incur the

---

[12] *Relationen der Botschafter Venedigs.* 157–8.

blame for the matter becoming public.¹³ Sometimes the emperor would depute a small group of councillors to negotiate with an ambassador or with representatives of the various estates,

The Imperial Court Council served as the ultimate judicial instance for the Empire and became much more prominent with the paralysis of the Imperial Cameral Council (*Reichskammergericht*) in Speyer because of confessional conflict. But it also dealt with more general legal and political matters usually regarding the Empire. Though there were as many as thirty court councillors, divided fairly evenly between nobles and lawyers, usually from twelve to fourteen were on hand to deal with the matters brought to the council at a particular time. The Imperial Court Council drew many members from the Empire beyond Ferdinand's lands. The court treasury council counted around seven members and the war council about the same.¹⁴

In the period of political consolidation following the victory at the White Mountain, Ferdinand's thoughts turned to a second marriage. His first wife, Maria Anna, had died in 1616, and he had now remained a widower for nearly six years. There had been some talk of marriage to the widow of the elector of Saxony back in 1617, but this had not proceeded very far. Marriage attracted Ferdinand at this time for two reasons. First, concern for the succession in his many territories moved him, a concern that also was evident in his testament. This he communicated to Philip IV of Spain through his ambassador, Count Khevenhüller. To be sure, he now had two sons, Ferdinand Ernst and Leopold William, born in 1614. But he had already lost his first-born son, and in this age of high mortality, one could not be sure that the others would survive, especially given their fragile health. Conscience urged him to provide further for the succession as well as Habsburg candidates for bishoprics. But he also longed for female companionship once again which would drive away the melancholy that often shortened one's life.¹⁵

Initial inquiries pointed towards Italy and turned up as the most suitable candidate the twenty-three-year-old Eleonore Gonzaga, daughter of Duke Vincenzo I of Mantua and Eleonore Medici. Her renowned beauty, her intelligence, her good nature, and her piety made her attractive as a spouse. Her mother died when she was ten. She was then placed in the care of her aunt, the widowed Duchess of Ferrara, the sister of Duke Vincenzo, and after her death Eleonore resided in the Poor Clare Convent of St. Ursula in Mantua where she remained until her marriage to Ferdinand.¹⁶ Ferdinand's trusted Eggenberg was dispatched in September to Mantua to seek the hand of Eleonore for the

---

[13] *Virtutes*, 74–6.   [14] Hengerer, 63–70, 120 (n. 450), 290–2.

[15] Franzl, 249–50; Otto G. Schindler, "Von Mantua nach Ödenburg: Die Ungarische Krönung Eleonoras I. Gonzaga (1622) und die erste Oper am Kaiserhof," *Biblos* 46 (1997): 271–2.

[16] After her death, the Jesuit Hermann Horst authored an idealized portrait of Eleonore, *Virtutes Annae Eleonorae Mantuanae Imperatricis, Ferdinandi II Austriaci Romanorum Imperatori*

emperor. Eleonore gave her consent, and the wedding took place among only family and friends in Mantua on November 21, 1621, with Eggenberg serving as Ferdinand's proxy. To the disappointment of the court of Mantua, which was accustomed to celebrate weddings with great festivity and would liked to have done so in the case of a marriage of a Gonzaga princess to the Holy Roman Emperor, Ferdinand insisted on keeping the marriage quiet until the Peace of Nikolsburg with Bethlen on December 31, 1621. This did allow for a grand celebration in Mantua on January 18, three days before Eleonore departed to meet Ferdinand at Innsbruck, from where Archduke Leopold now governed the Anterior Austrian lands. As reward for his successful mission, Ferdinand bestowed on Eggenberg the duchy of Krumau (Krumlov) in Bohemia and shortly thereafter named him a prince of the Eümpire.[17] The Spaniards were not happy with Ferdinand's Italian marriage or with Eggenberg's role in arranging it, and with good reason as we shall see.[18]

Ferdinand, after stopping for a visit with Archbishop Paris Lodron in Salzburg, arrived in Innsbruck on February 1 and Eleonore made her appearance the following day after a trip over the Alps. Only at this point did the emperor see his new wife for the first time. Because of the continuing war and especially its expense, Ferdinand wanted to keep the celebration in Innsbruck relatively simple. He brought with him the conductor of his court orchestra, the well-known Giovanni Priuli, along with twenty-two singers, fourteen instrumentalists, thirteen trumpeters, and twenty-four choir boys. Still, the festivities did not match those held at Mantua before Eleonore's departure. The new bride was solemnly received in the court church with a "beautiful motet" followed by a Te Deum. Then before the altar with both dressed brilliantly, the marriage was solemnized. There followed the wedding banquet, and the emperor then accompanied Eleonore to her room and he himself retired to his "from where he could, through secret doors, approach her."[19] During the celebrations that continued over the next few days, the students of the Jesuit college presented a program in which Ferdinand was once again addressed as Constantine. The new pair departed for Vienna on February 7 where they arrived on February 26 after making several stops along the way including one again in Salzburg. Ferdinand had prohibited any unusual pomp for their entrance into the city. They were received with a solemn Te Deum in St. Stephan's Cathedral, and the next Sunday there followed a sumptuous banquet with accompanying music.

Eleonore did not bear her husband the expected sons, clearly a disappointment to Ferdinand, but they had a happy, affectionate marriage. Eleonore's biographer later claimed that her care extended his life by three years.[20]

Conjugis (Vienna, 1656); it was obviously modeled after Lamormaini's *Virtutes Ferdinandi* but it has nowhere near the content of Lamormaini's book.

[17] Schindler, ibid. [18] Julius Otto Opel, *Der niedersächisch-dänische Krieg* 2 (Halle, 1880): 156.
[19] Schindler, ibid.; Franzl, 253. The citation is from *AF*, 9 (Leipzig, 1716), 1615. [20] Horst, 10.

In contrast to Ferdinand's first wife, Maria Anna, she was to emerge as a major figure in the cultural and eventually the political life of Vienna. Her cultural influence became evident at the Hungarian diet held at Sopron (Ödenburg) where Ferdinand and Eleonore arrived on May 24. The diet had been called to clear up several matters left open by the Peace of Nikolsburg. In the course of the negotiations, the Hungarians took the initiative themselves to crown Eleonore queen of Hungary. This took place amid great solemnity on July 26 in the Franciscan church with the primate of Hungary, Archbishop Pazmany, celebrating the coronation Mass. After the Mass there came a festive banquet with forty-five tables set throughout the rooms of the town castle. Joined at table with the imperial pair were the papal nuncio Carlo Carafa, the Spanish ambassador Oñate and the Tuscan ambassador, Pazmany, and the new Hungarian Palatine Count Szaniszló Thurzó. That afternoon came a "bello ballo" in the Rathaus where Ferdinand and Eleonore opened the dance together. The next Sunday there was performed a "Comœdia in musica," featuring a well-known Mantuan tenor, Francesco Campagnolo. The music for this performance has been lost but it has recently been hailed as the first Italian opera performed either in the Habsburg lands or Germany. Shortly after the return of the pair to Vienna, Eleonore saw to the performance of another music drama at court and then a ballet.[21] So she initiated her campaign to bring Italian opera and ballet to Vienna.

In a letter of April 29, 1623, Ferdinand proposed to his two brothers, Archdukes Leopold and Carl, that all the Austrian lands be united as a kingdom.[22] The proposition showed again Ferdinand's intent to consolidate his territories; neither Bohemia nor Hungary were included in the proposal, probably because they were already kingdoms. The emperor noted that both Emperor Frederick III and Ferdinand I had taken steps in this direction but then had not been able to proceed further. Neither Archduke Leopold nor Archduke Carl had been pleased with the stipulations regarding the succession in the emperor's testament. Both envisioned themselves as eventual ruling princes, and they looked back favorably on the manner in which Ferdinand I divided his inheritance. Their brother Ferdinand had now excluded them from the succession until his own line died out which was not at all likely. The creation of a kingdom would have made it still more difficult for either Leopold or Carl to secure their own principalities. Leopold while still retaining his bishoprics of Passau and Strasbourg had succeeded the deceased Archduke Maximilian as governor of the Anterior Austrian lands and Tyrol in 1619 with his residence at Innsbruck. At the time of the solemnization of Ferdinand's wedding in Innsbruck in February 1622, Leopold had been absent, holed up in

---

[21] Schindler, 282–9.
[22] Printed in G. Wagner, "Pläne und Versuche der Erhebung Österreichs zum Königreich," in *Osterreich: von der Staatsidee zum Nationalbewusstsein* (Vienna, 1982), 412–13.

the fortress of Zabern in Alsace which was under siege by the troops of Ernest von Mansfeld. Young Carl still held the bishoprics of Breslau and Brixen, and he had succeeded Archduke Maximilian as Grand Master of the Teutonic Order in 1619.

Ferdinand's plan to create a kingdom brought the dissatisfaction of his two brothers to the fore. They both rejected his proposal.[23] The following year Carl was given the position of governor of Portugal by Philip IV of Spain, and he died in Madrid on the way to his new post. So he disappeared from the scene. Leopold had resigned his bishoprics in 1625 in favor of his nephew, Ferdinand's son Leopold William, and having never taken major orders, secured a dispensation from Pope Urban VIII so that he could marry Claudia de Medici the following year. At Innsbruck he set up a magnificent Renaissance court. He then persistently negotiated with Ferdinand until the emperor yielded, for the sake of family harmony, step-by-step. The Jesuit William Lamormaini helped the process along. He replaced Martin Becan, who died in late 1623, as Ferdinand's confessor in early 1624; during his many years in Graz starting in 1598, he had garnered the trust of both Ferdinand and Leopold.[24] By 1630 Ferdinand conceded Leopold practical sovereignty over Anterior Austria and the Tyrol. So Leopold created a collateral Habsburg line in this territory that would continue to exist until 1665. Ferdinand was unable to hold on to the western lands.

Even though he still spent time in Prague, Ferdinand increasingly made Vienna his principal residence and his capital. The city revolved around the court. Ferdinand resided in the Hofburg which was then composed chiefly of what is now known at the Swiss Wing *(Schweizertrakt)* to which he made no significant additions. Some contemporaries suggested that his choice of Vienna as capital was dictated by the attractive hunting grounds that the woods around the city provided and from which he sought to exclude the Lower Austrian nobility.[25] The city and its suburbs grew in population in the course of the war from roughly 35,000 in 1600 to 60,000 in 1637, largely the result of the expansion of government and immigration of nobility with their households, a significant number from North Italy. It was a "winner" in the war; the population of Munich dropped by 60 percent in the course of the conflict.[26] The elevation of the bishopric of Vienna to a prince-bishopric in 1631 further enhanced the city's status. In 1620, an Austrian chancery had been set up

---

[23] Wagner, ibid., 408–32.
[24] Andreas Posch, "Zur Tätigkett und Beurteilung Lamormainis," *Mitteilungen des Instituts für österreichische Geschichtsforschung* 63 (Vienna, 1955): 265–7. Between 1622 and 1632 Leopold addressed fifty-three letters to Lamormaini; Dudik, 249.
[25] Harald Tersch, "Freudenfest und Kurzweil. Wien in Reisetagebücher der Kriegszeit (ca. 1620–1650), "*Wien im Dreissigjährigen Krieg*, ed. Andreas Weigl (Vienna, 2001), 185 and nn. 82–3.
[26] Andreas Weigl, "Residenz-, Bastion-, und Konsumptionsstadt," ibid., 52–7, 94.

Consolidation and Expansion, 1621–1628

distinct from the imperial chancery, to handle the administrative affairs of the Austrian hereditary lands, and in 1624 the Bohemian chancery was moved from Prague to Vienna. Ferdinand undertook a reform of the postal system in his Austrian hereditary lands in 1622 with a view to integrating them further and rendering them separate from the Empire.[27] That same year the president of the treasury council, Gundaker von Liechtenstein, brother of Karl, put forward a program for reform of imperial finances that extended to mercantilist ideas to foster economic development and to criticism of luxury and extravagance at court, perhaps drawn from the contemporary political writers, Giovanni Botero and the Jesuit Adam Contzen.[28] But opposition to the reforms quickly coalesced at court, and Liechtenstein left the office the following year, to be replaced by Anton Wolfradt, Abbot of Kremsmünster, who held the post until 1631 but was also unable to order properly Ferdinand's finances.[29] Ferdinand's economic policy came to aim not at growth but at the preservation of order through the authority left with the noble landowners.[30] Another reform that Ferdinand considered in his early years in Vienna aimed to streamline the procedures of the Imperial Court Council. He commissioned a report on this topic which was read in council on April 4, 1624, and was followed by a decree two years later, but little seems to have resulted from it.[31] Reform did not come easily, especially as the war expanded into the Empire.

Ferdinand came to be known for the loose administration of his finances. Perhaps this showed most clearly in the instance of the Prague Coin Consortium (Prager Münzconsortium) of 1622–1623. This case of deliberate hyperinflation needs to be seen in the context of the "Kipper-und-Wipper"[32] period when some German princes purposely debased the currency coined in their own mints so that they might pay off their excessive debts, especially war debts. The Bohemian rebels undertook this measure in 1619. Ferdinand allowed himself to be caught up in a scheme that turned into what many consider to have been "the western world's first financial crisis" and the high point of the Kipper-und-Wipper period.[33] Shortly after the Peace of Nikolsburg of December 31, 1621 with Bethlen Gàbor, Ferdinand needed funds to pay off the troops to be demobilized as well as to hire others for campaigns foreseen

---

[27] Thomas Winkelbauer, *Ständefreiheit und Fürstenmacht. Länder und Untertanen des Hauses Habsburg im konfessionellen Zeitalter* 1 (Vienna, 2003): 337–8.
[28] Giovanni Botero, *Della ragion di stato* (Venice, 1589), and Adam Contzen, *Libri Decem de Politicis* (Mainz, 1620).
[29] Thomas Winkelbauer, *Fürst und Fürstendiener: Gundaker von Liechtenstein, ein österreichischer Aristokrat des konfessionellen Zeitlalters* (Munich, 1999), 209–18.
[30] Robert D. Chesler, "Crown, Lords, and God: The Establishment of Secular Authority in the Pacification of Lower Austria," (Ph.D. Thesis, Princeton University, 1979), 384.
[31] Hurter 10: 4–5.
[32] Literally, the terms refers to the tipping of scales to identify debased coins.
[33] Wilson, 795–6 (citation); Steffen Leins, *Das Pragermünzkonsortium 1622/1623. Ein Kapitalgeschäft im Dreissigjährigen Krieg am Rand der Katastrophe* (Münster, 2012), 163.

to the west. A secret consortium of mostly Bohemian nobility led by the governor of Bohemia, Karl von Liechtenstein, and with Eggenberg and Wallenstein among the partners, offered to help him meet this financial challenge.[34] In a contract signed on January 18, 1622, in Vienna, Ferdinand agreed to lease all the mints in Bohemia, Moravia, and Lower Austria to the consortium for one year – a period later extended by two months – in exchange for the enormous sum of six million gulden. They raised the funds by forcibly buying up nearly all the silver in the respective territories. They then minted new coins from the silver with an increasing alloy of copper, thus devaluing the currency. This actual operation was overseen by Jakob Bassevi, a wealthy Prague Jew, and the Dutchman Hans de Witte, Wallenstein's financial manager, both of whom were also partners in the consortium. Altogether the consortium issued roughly 29.6 million gulden in bad money. This they used to purchase the silver from the public in the first place, pay the emperor the contracted sum, and then buy up lands confiscated from those who had rebelled against the emperor or settle claims against them.[35] The exact profits of the consortium are hard to determine; they served as the basis, for example, for the fortune of the Liechtenstein family.[36] This manipulated inflation of the currency led especially in Bohemia but also in the Austrian lands and beyond to a widespread breakdown of economic life, genuine hardship, social dislocation, and near famine in some areas. Bakers, for example, would not sell bread for bad money. A miner in one town in Bohemia who in April 1623 received one and one-half gulden wages had to pay twenty-seven gulden for a bushel of rye.[37] None of this had been anticipated by the members of the consortium, much less the emperor.[38] Opposition to the consortium mounted quickly, led by Cardinal Dietrichstein and, it seems, the Jesuits along with Maximilian of Bavaria and other electors at the conference of deputies at Regensburg at the turn of 1622–1623.[39] Ferdinand shut down the consortium in early 1623 and subsequently ordered a devaluation of its coinage by 87 percent.[40] So the financial misadventure gradually came to an end but not without leaving a trail of hardship for many. In 1624, in the wake of the inflation, Ferdinand was determined to be fair, and his councillors wrestled over the rate at which creditors were to be paid.[41]

In 1625 a Bavarian emissary compared conduct at the court of Vienna with that in Munich. "The waste of the lands confiscated [after the rebellion], the boundless concessions to secular and ecclesiastical favorites, the gifts out of all proportion to the church and extravagant expenses for the court – the imperial stables included forty carriages with teams of six horses – do not permit even an

---

[34] Leins, 45, lists sixteen participants in the consortium.   [35] Wilson, 797.
[36] Leins, 107, 112–14.
[37] Arnošt Klima, *Economy, Industry, and Society in Bohemia in the Seventeenth to Nineteenth Centuries* (Prague, 1991), 58.
[38] Leins, 154.   [39] Ibid., 109, 132.   [40] Wilson, 798.   [41] Hurter 8: 312–14.

attempt to introduce an orderly administration," he wrote.[42] Ferdinand overlooked financial manipulations of his painter and architect, de Pomis.[43] In 1630 Lamormaini himself forcefully called Ferdinand's attention to corruption in the government and the obligation to take measures against it lest he incur God's punishment.[44] Nuncio Malatesta Baglione, writing in 1635 after some experience in Vienna, reported simply that "this court is venal, and nothing is obtained without the dint of money."[45] In his *Virtues of Ferdinand II*, the confessor admitted the truth of some charges against Ferdinand of prodigality and lavishness toward the Church, councillors, and the military. His councillors often sought to keep petitioners distant because of the emperor's compassion for hard-luck stories.[46] But while stating that he was not writing an "apology," Lamormaini did attempt to put the charges in context. It was expensive to retain well-qualified councillors and generals, and to keep soldiers from pillage and desertion; they had to be paid well and promptly. His troops never did mutiny. The confessor acknowledged that Ferdinand often put off creditors for a long time but he did point out that in 1628 he paid off debts owed to former officials and servants of Emperors Rudolf and Matthias. In the end it was wiser policy, he claimed, to reward generously ministers and officers as well as clergy who fostered the restoration of Catholicism than to satisfy creditors.[47]

Ferdinand broke the power of the estates in the Habsburg lands, except for Hungary, and he established the clear upper hand of the prince, and in the lands where the hereditary succession of the Habsburg ruler had been challenged, in Bohemia and Upper Austria, he placed it on a firm basis. Only in this sense can his rule be called absolute. According to the Peace of Augsburg, he along with all German princes possessed the right to determine the religion of the territory. Ferdinand never attempted to create – either for individual territories nor for the emerging Habsburg Monarchy as a whole – a bureaucracy of government officials reaching down to the local level as was taking place in other states such as Bavaria, Prussia, and France, despite the advice of Maximilian of Bavaria that he do so in Bohemia.[48] Rather, he sought the cooperation of the estates and their leading group, the lords (*Herren*) or upper aristocracy. His constitutional position varied widely in the different territories. In Inner and Lower Austria, he considered himself bound to observe the traditional rights and privileges of

---

[42] Cited in Opel, 153.
[43] Gerhard Marauschek, "Leben und Zeit," in *Der innerösterreichische Hofkünstler Giovanni Pietro de Pomis, 1569 bis 1633*, ed. Kurt Woisetschlager (Graz, 1974), 40, 52–4, 67.
[44] Lamormaini to the emperor, Sept. 18 and Oct. 14, 1630, Dudik, 337–9.
[45] Baglione to Barberini, May 19, 1635, NBD, ibid.: #54.5 (p. 329).
[46] John P. Spielman, *The City and the Crown: Vienna and the Imperial Court, 1600–1740* (West Lafayette IN,: Purdue Research Foundation, 1993), 58.
[47] *Virtutes*, 88–9.
[48] Eila Hassenpflug-Elzholz, *Böhmen und die böhmischen Stände in der Zeit des beginnenden Zentralismus* (Munich, 1982), 21, 53.

his subjects, even though he tended to interpret them narrowly, and in his testament he had instructed his heir to respect them. In Bohemia and Upper Austria, on the other hand, he took the position that the estates had forfeited their rights and privileges by their rebellion, so that he might start from scratch constrained only by divine and natural law. But here, too, he preserved the estates and intended to govern through them. Hungary, which lay outside the Empire, was a different case. There in the Peace of Vienna of 1624, another agreement was concluded with Bethlen following the renewal of hostilities, and again the next year at the coronation of his son Ferdinand as king of Hungary, he was forced to confirm the freedom of religion and other privileges which Matthias had conceded in 1606 and he had accepted at his coronation in 1617. Even militant supporters of the Counter Reformation realized that he had to proceed cautiously in Hungary where Archbishop Pazmany launched a successful campaign to win Protestant nobility back to the Catholic faith peacefully.

Why did Ferdinand not proceed more aggressively against the estates in his territories? Certainly one reason in the territories that had not rebelled was his respect for law. Even in religious matters, where he may be said to have bent the law, he claimed that he always acted legally. This had been the case early in his rule in Inner Austria when he contended that the Pacification of Brück of 1578 did not bind him. With respect to Lower Austria, Ferdinand in a letter of 1620 to the Elector of Cologne asserted that "he had acted and would act only within the traditional limits 'as this land's indisputable hereditary lord and prince.'"[49] He acted within the limits of the law, interpreted according to his sense of the past, to be sure, which accentuated the role of the prince. Within the Empire he always believed that he acted within the constraints of imperial law; Lamormaini later made this point in his own hand in the margin of his own copy of *The Virtues of Emperor Ferdinand II*.[50]

But why did Ferdinand not eliminate the estates in those territories where he contended that they had forfeited their rights and privileges by virtue of their rebellion, Upper Austria and the lands of the Bohemian crown? In the first place, it was not necessary for him to do so; he had clearly established his sovereignty. More importantly, he needed the estates and he was wise enough to realize this. On the most general level, Ferdinand had come to understand what was an axiom of the practice of rule for both Machiavelli and anti-Machiavellian writers like Lipsius and Botero: a prince could not rule effectively in the long run without the support of the governed and especially the dominant group, in this case, the Herren or aristocracy.[51]

---

[49] Mar. 24, 1620, cited in Chesler, 162.
[50] Vienna, Österreichische Nationalbibliothek, Handschriftensammlung, MS 7378, 61.
[51] Botero, *Della ragion di stato*, 1, 8 (pp. 67–8), and *Aggiunte alla region di stato* 1, 2–4 (pp. 415–24); The *Aggiunte* appeared in 1598 and were usually published with the *Ragion di stato* subsequently; Lipsius, *Politicorum sive civilis doctrinae libri sex*, 4, 8–12 (pp. 103–47). This is a constant theme of Machiavelli's *Prince* and *Discourses on the First Ten Books of Livy*.

More specifically, he realized that the estates had long played a major part in the administration of the Austrian and Bohemian lands, and he was not about to upset this aspect of the *Ständestaat*. His consent to the magnates' widespread control of the peasants on their lands grew not only out of his desire to secure the magnates' support but also out of the need that he perceived to make use of an effective instrument to discipline an unruly peasantry. War consumed more and more funds. Traditionally in his lands most taxes had been collected by the estates, and they had in place an apparatus for this. He needed the magnates for both the payment and collection of taxes. It was no mean achievement for Ferdinand and his successor to raise the funds they needed for a war often fought close to home at the end of which Austria emerged as a major power. From 1631 to 1634, a period when the fortunes of war were least favorable to him, Ferdinand collected nearly two million florins in taxes from the estates of a hard-pressed Lower Austria.[52] Crown and estates or aristocracy cooperated, often at the expense of the peasantry, and this cooperation came to characterize Habsburg rule. Ferdinand followed this policy because he realized that he needed the political and financial support of the estates. His achievement was to secure their participation in government after he had mastered them politically and so to integrate them into his manner of rule. Of the major European states, only the Habsburg Monarchy avoided a major revolution in the course of the 1640s; France, Spain, and England all experienced one. Certainly the policy of Ferdinand continued by his son Ferdinand III contributed to this result.[53]

Ferdinand built upon and expanded a movement that antedated his reign, the creation of a Catholic Habsburg aristocracy of the *Herrenstand* that supported his rule. Its members came to possess lands in various Habsburg territories, to maintain their position in local government and the estates, to attend the emperor at court, and to hold the major posts in the government. Starting in the last decades of the sixteenth century, as a result of a concerted Catholic effort many aristocrats had begun to convert, usually out of a combination of intellectual conviction and a desire for social and political advancement.[54] This aristocracy came chiefly under Ferdinand from Inner and Lower Austria but also from the other Habsburg lands as well as some from Italy, Spain, and even Scotland.[55] Attachment to Catholicism became a practical requirement for

---

[52] Chesler, 363–6, 370, 374.
[53] Ibid., 363. Since the mid-1980s there has been considerable discussion of the use of the term "absolutism" for early modern Europe. For the Habsburg lands, see especially *Die Habsburgermonarchie 1620 bis 1740. Leistungen und Grenzen des Absolutismusoparadigmas*, ed. Peter M'ata and Thomas Winkelbauer (Stuttgart, 2006), where Mark Hengerer, "Die Hofbewilligungen der niederösterreichischen Stände im zweiten Drittel des 17. Jahrhunderts. Zur Frage der Leistungsfähigkeit des Absolutismusbegriffs aus der Perspektive der Hofforschung zur Habsburgermonarchie," 170–7, nicely sums up the state of research.
[54] Winkelbauer, *Fürst und Fürstendiener*, 39–46, 81–4.
[55] Mark Hengerer, "Zum symbolischen Dimension eines sozialen Phänomens: Adelsgräber in der Residenz," in Weigl, ed., 259.

a position at court. Young aristocrats normally first came to court as pages, were promoted to chamberlain *(Kämmerer)* to attend the emperor, and then advanced to higher office. At the same time they maintained a position at home, thus binding the center with the region. Chamberlains rotated in their service at court, often serving for several weeks and then returning to their estates. There were many ways beyond offices at court or in government by which Ferdinand could reward those loyal to him and attach them to himself: the bestowal of lands as after the confiscations following the Bohemian rebellion and the death of Wallenstein, promotion to the nobility and elevation to higher noble status, the grant of imperial titles such as prince or count, nomination to ecclesiastical positions including canonries in the Empire and in the Habsburg lands as well as to the Order of the Golden Fleece and other distinguished orders, appointment to military commands, wedding gifts, and outright money grants.[56] Eggenberg exemplified this aristocracy as did Karl and Gundaker von Liechtenstein. The former, originally from Graz, received many gifts including lands in Bohemia and served as director of the privy council at the same time as he held the post of governor of Inner Austria. The Liechtenstein family owned lands across the Habsburg territories, in Lower Austria, Bohemia, Moravia, and Silesia; Karl served as governor of Bohemia in the years following the rebellion and Gundaker, who long held the title of privy councillor, briefly operated under Ferdinand as president of the court treasury and *Obristhofmeister*.[57] Hans Ludwig von Kufstein, a significant member of the Lower Austrian estates in 1620, after his conversion in 1627 undertook a diplomatic mission to Constantinople, was appointed a privy councillor in 1630, and then named governor of Upper Austria in 1632 where he faced the task of subduing rebellion.[58] Meanwhile, young aristocratic women came to court as ladies-in-waiting where they frequently found their future husbands, thus binding aristocratic families together.[59]

Ferdinand certainly took seriously his obligation to foster Catholicism, but he also realized the temporal advantages to be gained from this. We can already see under him the beginnings of the policy that will later be called Josephinism.[60] One advantage was the bond that a revived Catholic Church provided to hold together the diverse territories and institutions of the Habsburg territories. Under Ferdinand, the growth of a distinctive Habsburg Catholic culture proceeded apace, spreading across the lands of the dynasty especially among the upper levels of the population; it is often known as *Pietas Austriaca*.[61] It was

---

[56] Mark Hengerer, *Kaiserhof und Adel*, 564–85.
[57] Winkelbauer, *Fürst und Fürstendiener*, 189–98.   [58] Schwarz, 171–2, 300–2.
[59] Katrin Keller, *Hofdamen. Amtsträgerinnen in Wiener Hofstaat des 17. Jahrhunderts* (Vienna, 2005).
[60] Theodor Wiedemann, *Geschichte der Reformation und Gegenreformation im Lande unter der Enns* I (Prague, 1879): 629.

characterized, first, by an intense Eucharistic piety that allegedly originated with the founder of the dynasty, Rudolf of Habsburg.

According to the myth, back in the thirteenth century Count Rudolf assisted a priest bearing the Eucharist to a dying peasant in the midst of a terrifying storm. The priest's grateful blessing brought the House its subsequent good fortune. The annual Corpus Christi processions took place in Vienna and throughout the Habsburg lands every spring. Secondly, there came devotion to Mary. Ferdinand actively promoted Mary's feast of the Immaculate Conception and indeed sought to have this privilege of Mary recognized as a dogma of the Church.[62] Mary was for him the *Generalissima* of his armies. Domenico à Jesu Maria had invoked the Virgin at the Battle of the White Mountain. Particular saints whose veneration he fostered were the older ones – Joseph, the Apostles, Francis of Assisi, Anthony of Padua – as well as the newer ones, Theresa of Avila and the two Jesuit saints Ignatius of Loyola and Francis Xavier, all of whom became popular throughout the Habsburg lands.

The second political advantage of the reformation of religion was to bring the power of government to bear on subjects, nobility, burghers, and especially peasants in a new way. "In this way the individual felt for the first time the breath of the modern state."[63] As we have seen, Ferdinand did not attempt to extend the reach of government to the lower levels of society through financial or judicial officers. Rather, it was through the Church and the aristocracy that he aimed to influence the life of the peasants.[64] In Inner Austria, Ferdinand's government already took a much more direct role in Counter-Reformation measures than it had previously under Archduke Carl, when the bishops had taken the lead with the assistance of the prince. Government continued to play a heightened role in the reformation commissions later employed in Bohemia and Lower and Upper Austria. Ferdinand's confessor, the Jesuit William Lamormaini, contended in 1627 in a paper that served as the basis for a Counter-Reformation program in Bohemia that both the ecclesiastical and secular officials of the reformation commissions should appear in the king's name since the heretics would not acknowledge the authority of ecclesiastical authorities.[65] In 1624, Ferdinand extended the jurisdiction of secular courts to disputes over ecclesiastical property in his Austrian lands, and in 1628 he regulated the payment of tithes in Upper Austria.[66] In 1633, at a low point in his fortunes and perhaps with a view

---

[61] See Anna Coreth, *Pietas Austriaca*, trans. William D. Bowman and Anna Maria Leitgeb (West Lafayette, IN, 2004; revised German ed. 1982, first published 1959.

[62] The Immaculate Conception means that Mary was conceived without original sin. It was only recognized by the church as a dogma in 1854.

[63] Inge Gampl, *Staat-Kirche-Individuum in der Rechtsgeschichte Österreichs zwischen Reformation und Revolution* (Vienna, 1984), 6. Wiener Rechtsgeschichtliche Arbeiten 6.

[64] This is a principal thesis of Chesler.

[65] ARSJ, Aust., 23, ff. 1–21. This paper was co-authored by the Jesuit Heinrich Philippi, confessor of the young king of Hungary.

[66] Gampl, 14, 22.

to winning God's favor, Ferdinand issued a lengthy mandate for his Austrian subjects, "A Virtuous Way of Life" (Tugendsame Lebensführung), which provided for checks on Sunday observance and enforcement of the obligation of confession and communion at Easter.[67] Implementation was another matter. Ferdinand remained a staunch patron of the Jesuits, founding at least six colleges and contributing to the endowment of many more, and they returned his generosity with a firm support of his rule.[68] We will soon see how in the contest over control of the University of Prague, Ferdinand and the Jesuits were aligned against Archbishop Harrach and Pope Urban VIII. In the long run, the restoration of parishes was essential to the success of the Counter Reformation, and Ferdinand attempted to use his position as territorial ruler to secure a voice in the appointment of pastors in Lower Austria,[69] and with this came participation in the selection of schoolteachers and sacristans. But progress had to wait here and even under his successor it was slow because of the lack of native priests and the retention of rights of patronage by aristocratic landowners.

The territories that had rebelled against Ferdinand, Upper Austria and the Bohemian lands, underwent the most change after the White Mountain. The estates of Upper Austria paid homage to Maximilian of Bavaria on August 20, 1620, and he appointed Adam von Herberstorff, a native of Styria, as governor of the territory. From the start the Bavarian duke considered Upper Austria not as an occupied territory but as security for the debt Ferdinand owed him according to the Treaty of Munich. John George of Saxony held the two Lusatias as surety, Maximilian asserted, and he clearly had contributed as much to the emperor's success as the Saxon elector. Despite the reluctance of some councillors who contested Maximilian's claim to all the revenues of the territory as long as he held it, Ferdinand agreed to the duke's terms. He had little choice; though he chafed under the terms, he still greatly depended on Maximilian's help. On March 6, 1621, he notified Upper Austrian officials of the arrangement and instructed them to obey the Bavarian authorities. Sovereignty remained with Ferdinand. He hoped soon to recover the territory, but this was not to be the case.[70]

Initially, Herberstorff's measures to pacify the territory met with general acceptance. But differences soon developed with the Upper Austrian estates, who were used to asserting their rights and privileges unlike the estates in Bavaria whom Maximilian had reduced to complete submission. Maximilian

---

[67] Ibid., 4, 18.
[68] The six colleges were at Ljubljana in Carniola, Klagenfurt in Carinthia, Gorizia in Friuli, Kutná Hora (Kuttenberg) and Litoměrice (Leitmeritz) in Bohemia, and Glogau in Silesia.
[69] Ludwig Wahrmund, *Das Kirchenpatronatsrecht und seine Entwicklung in Österreich* (Vienna, 1896) 2: 16–18.
[70] Albrecht 2, 581–3; Hans Sturmberger, *Adam Graf Herberstorff: Herrschaft und Freiheit im konfessionellen Zeitalter* (Munich, 1976), 116–17.

ordered that members of the estates responsible for the rebellion be punished. Though they avoided physical punishment and imprisonment, lands were lost to confiscation, the sale of which went to help pay the costs of the occupation. Demands upon the population for monies to finance the occupation and excesses of the occupying soldiers served to embitter the Upper Austrians. The estates began to yearn for the return of the emperor's government. In the spring of 1625 they issued a formal apology for their part in the rebellion, and Ferdinand pardoned them. They paid a fine of 600,000 gulden, which immediately went toward payment of the expenses of the occupation.[71]

In 1624, rigorous Counter-Reformation measures were introduced in Upper Austria. They resulted in a significant degree from the influence of the new nuncio, Carlo Carafa, who had arrived in Vienna in 1621, and even more so of William Lamormaini, Ferdinand's confessor. The instruction for Carafa, drawn up by the new, more militant Pope Gregory XV and dated April 12, 1621, instructed him to urge Ferdinand to exploit his military advantage in order to restore Catholicism in his hereditary lands as well as in the Empire, even to the point of overthrowing the Peace of Augsburg, which the papacy had never recognized. In Hungary it might be necessary to temporize. "We ought to hope for favorable results from his [the emperor's] victories and from the divine benediction by which he [God] surrounds and protects him," the instruction read.[72]

A native of Belgian Luxembourg and eight years Ferdinand's senior, Lamormaini had entered the Jesuit novitiate at Brno in 1590. Shortly after his ordination to the priesthood in 1598, he was assigned to the Jesuit university in Graz where he taught philosophy and theology and served as the university's rector from 1613 to 1621. During these years he came to know the ruling family well. Notes from the lectures he delivered in Graz show that he defended the right of the Church to compel the obedience of heretics if necessary through the use of the secular arm. As a ruler could force rational men to obey the dictates of the natural law, the Christian prince could compel heretics to follow the Church's laws and punish them if they did not do so.[73] After his term as rector, Lamormaini spent the period from October 1621 to February 1622 in Rome at the behest of the Jesuit superior general, Muzio Vitelleschi. With him he brought for the curia a detailed assessment of the situation of the Church in the Bohemian lands and a plan for the restoration of the Church there that carried the support of Slawata and Martinitz.[74] He met Cardinal Maffeo

---

[71] Albrecht, ibid., 584–5
[72] Instruction for Carlo Carafa, Nuntius am Kaiserhof, Apr. 21, 1621, *Die Hauptinstruktionen Gregors XV für die Nuntien und Gesandten an den europäischen Fürstenhöfen 1621–1623* (Tübingen, 1997), ed. Klaus Jaitner, 1: #6 (pp. 618–25, quote on p. 619).
[73] This did not apply to Jews or non-believers who were not baptized; Universitätsbibliothek Graz, Handschrift #1159, 1, pp. 216–18, 228–34, dated 1608.
[74] *Acta Sacrae Congregationis de Propaganda Fide Res Gestas Bohemicas illustrantia*, ed. Ignaz Kollmann 1: 1622–1623 (Prague, 1923): #4b (pp. 17–41).

Barberini, who would become Pope Urban VIII in 1623, as well as other curial officials, and it seems that he himself was proposed for the cardinalate, a dignity that he always refused.[75] Upon his return to the north, Lamormaini was named rector of the Jesuit college in Vienna, which brought him again into close contact with Ferdinand. When Martin Becan died in late 1623, the choice to replace him naturally fell upon Lamormaini.

Among the goals Lamormaini set for himself as Ferdinand's confessor, besides the emperor's growth in the Christian life, was "that the Catholic religion with the help and authority of this emperor be completely restored in the two Austrias [Upper and Lower], the Kingdoms of Bohemia and Hungary, and in the Roman Empire."[76] On March 25, 1624, the Feast of the Annunciation, in the imperial chapel and with the confessor present, Ferdinand renewed his commitment to the restoration of Catholicism. He vowed "that he would undertake whatever the circumstances seemed to permit" for the good of religion, "not only gladly but with great pleasure and joy." At Ferdinand's request, Eggenberg joined him in the vow. Later in August, Lamormaini informed Cardinal Francesco Barberini, nephew of Pope Urban in whose name the correspondence of the papal secretariat of state was conducted:

It is perhaps necessary that the pope know about this [the vow] so that he realize that great things can be accomplished by this emperor and perhaps even all Germany be led back to the old faith, provided that united in soul and intention and joining all their forces together, having supplicated the benevolent God, these two supreme lights of the world [pope and emperor] take up the matter vigorously and see it through with persistence.[77]

Not surprisingly, then, on October 4, 1624, Ferdinand issued a decree expelling all Protestant preachers and school teachers from Upper Austria. This has been called a *"dies atra"* or black day for Upper Austrian Protestantism.[78] The governor Herberstorff promoted Catholic reform, and he lobbied for stern Counter-Reformation measures in Upper Austria in both Munich and Vienna. He was in touch with Lamormaini.[79] Maximilian had remained cautious, urging Ferdinand to proceed slowly partly out of fear of alienating John George of Saxony.[80] But the emperor pushed ahead; reformation commissions were formed to carry out the decree in the towns and cities. The estates protested,

---

[75] "Vita Lamormaini," ARSJ, Vitae 139, ff. 43, 60–1, 71. This manuscript of 122 folios was sent to Rome in 1649 the year after Lamormaini's death by the author, Eustachius Sthaäl, a Jesuit who lived in community with Lamormaini for many years and clearly admired him. Another copy of the manuscript is found in the archives of the Benedictine monastery of Pannonhalma in Hungary, #37 (118 G30).

[76] Ibid., 44, 54v, 72v.

[77] Lamormaini to Barberini, Aug. 3, 1624, BL 7054, f. 54; see also Vitelleschi to Lamormaini, May 29, 1624, ARSJ, Aust. 3I, ff. 507–8, and *Virtutes*, 4, plus annotation where the dating is confusing.

[78] Sturmberger, *Herberstorff*, 216.   [79] Ibid., 231, 470, n. 81.   [80] Albrecht 2, 585–6.

and opposition began to coalesce. The next October the emperor required all inhabitants to attend Catholic services on Sunday and holy days, and to convert to Catholicism by Easter, 1626. Nobles and townsmen were to be allowed to emigrate if their conscience would not allow them to conform. Further protests of the estates only angered Ferdinand.[81] Finally, the great Austrian Peasants, Rebellion of 1626, which had been planned for some time, erupted prematurely at Lembach in the Mühlviertel on May 17, 1626, and before long a peasant army controlled most of Upper Austria north of the Danube. Added to peasant rejection of the religious measures was resentment of the Bavarian occupation as well as hostility to the noble landowners. A peasant delegation arrived in Vienna in June, but Ferdinand and Eleonore refused to meet with them.[82] Imperial troops began to arrive from Lower Austria in late July joining with the Bavarians, and they soon recovered Linz from the peasants. Members of the estates became wary of the social implications of peasant demands. By the end of November, the peasants had been defeated, and many towns and much of the country devastated. Peasant leaders were executed. Ferdinand confirmed many of the privileges of the estates but he would tend to interpret them narrowly. In Vienna the rebellion was seen principally resulting from hostility to the Bavarian occupation rather than from the religious measures of Ferdinand, and Protestantism was seen as a source of upheaval. On March 26, 1627, Ferdinand informed the estates that the work of the reformation commissions would continue, and two months later peasants were ordered to attend Catholic services.[83] Lamormaini continued to endorse these measures often successfully in the face of opposition of many councillors.[84] The Counter Reformation would continue in Upper Austria with limited success throughout the rest of Ferdinand's reign. Another revolt of peasants erupted in 1632. Altogether about 70,000 emigrés departed from the territory.[85] Upper Austria would remain a center of clandestine Protestantism.

In the 1620s, still more far-reaching measures were introduced in the lands of the Bohemian crown, especially Bohemia proper and Moravia. John George of Saxony held the Lusatian lands provisionally, and eventually they would pass

---

[81] Sturmberger, *Herbersdorff*, 253–4.   [82] Ibid., 274.   [83] Ibid., 327–9.
[84] Jules Cesare Cordara, *Historiae Societatis Jesu Pars Sexta* 2 (Rome, 1859): 184.
[85] This figure is extrapolated from Winkelbauer, *Ständefreiheit und Fürstenmacht* 2: 61. Estimates of this number vary. Othmar Pickl, "Glaubenskampf und Türkenkriege in ihren Auswirkungen auf das Siedlungswesen und die Bevölkersstruktur der österreichischen Länder, *Siedlungs- und Bevölkerungsgeschichte Österreichs* (Vienna, 1974), 97–102, suggests 50,000 for Upper and Lower Austria together, and he notes that many departures took place after 1650 and were prompted by economic opportunities in Germany as much as by religious pressure. For subsequent progress of the Counter Reformation in Upper Austria under Ferdinand see Gunter Khinast, "Beiträge zu einer Geschichte des Landes ob der Enns unter dem Landeshauptmann Hans Ludwig von Kuefstein (1630–1656)," Dissertation, University of Innsbruck, 1967.

fully into his hands, according to the arrangement made with the elector before the suppression of the rebellion. In 1621 Ferdinand confirmed the privileges of the estates of Silesia, which included the free exercise of religion for adherents of the Confession of Augsburg conceded them by Emperor Rudolf in 1609. The desire to placate John George played a role here. The Czechs and the Moravians reached a turning point in their history. The face of the land was altered by the large-scale confiscations and redistribution of rebel property, the introduction of a moderate absolutism, and a vigorous implementation of the Counter Reformation. In Bohemia, after the executions of June 21, 1621, there were to be no physical punishments nor imprisonments for the rebels. But they were to be subject to confiscation of their property and to fines, so that justice would be administered to all those who had defied the emperor, and he would recover the costs of combating the uprising. Some were condemned for slight offenses, like paying taxes to the government of the directors or submitting petitions to them. Karl von Liechtenstein chaired the committee that determined the penalties for the rebels. Altogether there took place an enormous upheaval in the ownership of property as a result of the confiscations. Nearly half of the lords and knights of Bohemia lost all or large amounts of their property. Liechtenstein's commission sentenced 680 persons. Of these, 166 lost all their property, 112 saw their lands changed from allods or lands owned outright to fiefs, and the rest forfeited one-half, one-third, or one-fifth of their property. For the last group, the manner of the transfer of the property meant that they lost more than was strictly required of them. About 300 persons were affected in Moravia.[86]

Of the confiscated lands, a large portion was given to those who had supported Ferdinand, both natives and foreigners; a smaller portion remained with the emperor; and the rest was sold on the market in exchange for a debased coinage produced by the financial manipulation of the consortium that included Liechtenstein and Wallenstein. Besides these two, others who gained notably from the huge transfer of property in Bohemia and Moravia counted Eggenberg, who as we have seen for his role in Ferdinand's second marriage was awarded the duchy of Krumau in southern Bohemia; Cardinal Dietrichstein, the general Balthasar Marradas; and the family of General Bucquoy, who had died. Ferdinand's supporters filled the land and controlled the estates.[87] Of the 417 families that were incorporated into the Bohemian nobility from 1621 to 1656, 281 were foreigners – Germans, Spaniards, Belgians, and Italians – nearly all Catholics and many who held lands in other areas of the monarchy.[88] Nor did the Jesuits come away empty-handed. For their colleges in Prague and Kutná Hora (Kuttenberg) they received eleven estates,

---

[86] Karl Richter, "Die böhmischen Länder von 1471–1740," *Handbuch der böhmischen Länder*, ed. Karl Bosl (Munich, 1974) 2: 284–5.
[87] Ibid., and 290.   [88] Wilson, 354.

lands of the city of Kutná Hora, thirteen houses in Prague, a printing press as well as benefactions for colleges elsewhere.[89]

In late 1621, Ferdinand had already issued Counter-Reformation measures for the city of Prague despite the caution from some ministers to go slowly and above all not to antagonize Elector John George of Saxony. On December 13, all Protestant preachers were expelled from Prague with the exception of two Lutherans who were eventually forced to leave despite the protests of Saxony.[90] One element in Lamormaini's program for Bohemia was the establishment of a Jesuit university in Prague to replace the venerable Charles University, which traced its roots back to 1348. The university had become a center of heresy long before the rebellion, infecting the kingdom with its graduates, and its rector and faculty had enthusiastically given its support to the rebels in 1618. Yet many felt the suppression of the university to be an excessively drastic measure. By the end of 1623, an agreement was reached between the imperial authorities and the Jesuits that combined the enhanced theological and philosophical faculties of the Jesuit college in Prague with the medical and law faculties into a new university, the *Universitas Carolo-Ferdinandea*. The Jesuits would be in charge, appointing both the chancellor and the rector. Concern for orthodoxy, it was thought, required that the Jesuits exercise a monopoly of the theological faculty. Censorship of books for the whole of Bohemia would be the responsibility of the Jesuit rector, and the landed endowment of the old Charles University would pass to the new institution, that is, the Jesuits.[91]

Opposition to this arrangement coalesced quickly. Members of other religious orders resented the Jesuit monopoly of theology. Among these there stood out the gifted, volatile Capuchin, Valeriano Magni, now guardian of the convent on the Hradschin and superior of the Capuchins in Bohemia who saw himself as the champion of the other orders and of the archbishop of Prague, Ernst von Harrach, who himself became a foe of the Jesuits. Harrach, the son of the imperial privy councillor Karl von Harrach and brother-in-law of Wallenstein, had been a brilliant student at the Jesuit German College in Rome. He was appointed early in 1623 to the see of Prague, which comprised all of Bohemia, and was installed in Prague on May 3, 1623.Two years later, at age twenty-eight, he received the red hat on the nomination of Ferdinand. A vigorous personality despite his youth, Harrach took Archbishop Charles Borromeo of Milan as his model and assumed that he as archbishop would take

---

[89] Anton Gindely, *Geschichte der Gegenreformation in Böhmen*, ed. Theodore Tupetz (Leipzig, 1894), 71.
[90] Alesandro Catalano, *La Boemia e la réconquista delle conscienze. Ernesto Adalbert von Harrach e la Controriforma in Europa Centrale (1620–1667)* (Rome, 2005), 62–3. Temi e Testi; see also Hurter 9: 213–24.
[91] Käthe Spiegel, "Die Prager Universitätsunion (1618–1654)," *Mitteilungen des Vereins für die Geschichte der Deutschen in Böhmen* 62 (1924): 13–14, 17–20; Alois Kroess, *Geschichte der böhmischen Provinz der Gesellschaft Jesu* 2:1 (Vienna, 1927): 107–16.

the lead in the restoration of the church in Bohemia.[92] He claimed for himself the chancellorship of the university and ultimate oversight over it according to the papal bulls that had established it. The Council of Trent, he maintained, made him responsible for appointments to the theology faculty as well as for ecclesiastical censorship. Nor was he happy with the transfer of the university's endowment to the Jesuits. Harrach formally presented his objections to the arrangement to Liechtenstein, the Governor of Bohemia, in Prague on March 2, 1624. Negotiations continued but not to his satisfaction, and he threatened the governor and Emperor Ferdinand with excommunication. Eventually, on the basis of a draft drawn up by Lamormaini at the request of Eggenberg, a solution was reached which tilted heavily in favor of the Jesuits. Surprisingly, on November 27, Harrach, now in Vienna and under pressure from the emperor, signed it.[93]

But this was only the start of a long conflict over control of the university, first between the Jesuits and Harrach and then between Emperor Ferdinand, who was determined to have the Jesuits in charge of the university, and Pope Urban, who upheld the claims of Archbishop Harrach. It was to prejudice the relationship between Ferdinand and Urban for the rest of the emperor's reign. The agreement of Vienna still had to be ratified by the papacy; Urban turned the matter over to the newly-created Congregation for the Propagation of the Faith, or Propaganda. Rome hesitated. Feeling there had been building up about the overreach of the Prague Jesuits. Harrach's awareness of this sentiment and pressure from his associates in Prague led him in a letter of June 28, 1625 to the Propaganda to repudiate the agreement. Nuncio Carafa then, increasingly aware of the influence of the Jesuits and especially of Lamormaini, now reversed himself and took the side of the archbishop. Propaganda refused to ratify the agreement. Lamormaini recommended to Ferdinand that he ignore the "little dogs" (cuniculos) who were causing trouble in Rome, and he did.[94]

The matter dragged on. Magni became more involved in the controversy, and he and Harrach were determined that the archbishop would have the last word in the university, and they had support in Rome. The topic appeared regularly in the correspondence of the nuncios. Only in 1654, under Emperor Ferdinand III, did the issue reach a resolution which favored the Jesuits and to which Rome never gave its formal approval.

---

[92] On Harrach see now Catalano.
[93] Lamormaini to Eggenberg, undated before Oct. 14, 1624, *Acta Sacrae Congregationis de Propaganda Fide Res Gestas Bohemicas Illustrantia*, ed. Ignaz Kollmann 2: 1623–1624: #182; the agreement is published in ibid.: #202; Kroess, 2:2: 131–4; Spiegel, 22–4
[94] Lamormaini to the emperor, Jan. 5, 1626, HHStA, Staaten, Romana, Varia, 6; Kollmann, ibid. 295–7; 318–20; Kroess, ibid., 134–6; Spiegel, 15–16; see the minutes of the meetings of the Propaganda Congregation of Aug. 25 and Oct. 29, 1625, *Acta SC de Propaganda Fide Germaniam spectantia, 1622–1649*, Hermann Tüchle, ed., (Paderborn, 1965): ## 101, 107. The pope participated personally in these two meetings,

Consolidation and Expansion, 1621–1628

Meanwhile as the conflict over the university was first erupting in the spring of 1624, Carafa lobbied for more energetic measures to lead the people of Bohemia back to the Catholic Church. But even among those the nuncio estimated to be "good Catholics" as opposed to *i politici*, there was resistance. They feared unrest in Bohemia, and they did not want to lose the support of Elector John George of Saxony. Both Maximilian and the archbishop of Mainz, Schweikard, cautioned a prudent policy. They also still awaited the formal approval of Elector John George to Ferdinand's elevation in 1623 of Maximilian to the electorate formerly held by Frederick of the Palatinate. Carafa sought out Lamormaini, recently appointed Ferdinand's confessor, and found that he, too was urging Ferdinand in the same direction but finding him "a little fearful." Lamormaini then, according to Carafa, suggested to Ferdinand that he seek guidance on the matter in prayer. Four days later Ferdinand told Lamormaini "that after communion God had inspired him to do whatever His Paternity [Lamormaini] said without any question or contradiction." So Carafa reported the event four months later.[95] On May 18, then, about two months after the vow of March 25, Ferdinand issued decrees once again expelling all Protestant preachers from Bohemia and Moravia and prohibiting the exercise of any religion other than the Catholic not only in Prague, other cities, and royal lands but also on baronial lands.[96] Despite these measures, Elector John George sanctioned the acceptance of Maximilian into the electoral college. The event vindicated Carafa and Lamormaini. Trust in God along with bold action paid off.

Yet the implementation of these decrees was poorly organized, too hasty, and stern. Abuses had clearly taken place, such as the expulsion of Protestants for their property. Consultations were held in Vienna starting in spring of 1626 to formulate an effective method of reformation that would not alienate the Protestant states. Among those participating were Eggenberg, Abbot Anton Wolfradt, and Cardinal Dietrichstein, whose program for reform in Moravia had enjoyed considerable success. By the end of the year two proposed plans were under discussion, one prepared by Lamormaini along with another Jesuit, Heinrich Philippi, which enjoyed the approval of the Jesuit faculty of theology at the University of Vienna, and the other, based on a paper by Valeriano Magni, submitted by Harrach.[97] The basic difference between the two programs centered around the role of the emperor in the suppression of heresy in

---

[95] Carafa to the Propaganda, Sept. 25, 1624, Kollmann 2: #165 (esp. pp. 256–68).
[96] Catalano, 70–1.
[97] A copy of the Lamormaini/Philippi plan is found in ARSJ, Aust. 23, ff. 1–21, and it is summarized in Kroess 2:1: 193–8. The sources for Magni's program of reform are an undated "Discorso" of his in Rome, Archivio Congregazione de Propaganda Fide, Scritture originali riferite nelle Congregazioni Generali, 214, ff. 166–75v, and a long report on the negotiations in Vienna sent by Harrach, ibid., ff. 193–243v. These documents were discussed in the May 21, 1627, meeting of the Congregation; see Tüchle, #153.

Bohemia and so the fundamental relationship between state and church. Magni saw the reform of religion as basically the task of the archbishop, whom the emperor should assist when requested to do so. For Lamormaini the Christian prince had the obligation to eliminate heresy in his lands "directly by reason of his office," not only when an ecclesiastical official called on him for help. To be sure, the duty of teaching and leading the faithful fell to the archbishop, but at the same time the chief obligation of the Christian prince was to advance religion. Lamormaini was influenced more by his conception of the Catholic response to the Reformation in Germany than by theoretical considerations of the respective roles of the temporal and spiritual powers. For the most part, according to Lamormaini, the German upper clergy had sat back and watched while the Habsburg and Wittelsbach princes with their allies, the Jesuits, had saved the Church in Germany, and they would continue the work of reform and restoration together. Magni for his part, upheld the tradition of ecclesiastical independence and strict adherence to canon law. This was the way of Carlo Borromeo, Harrach's model.

Lamormaini recommended for the reformation of religion in Bohemia the reformation commissions that had already been employed in the Austrian lands. "Piety can be restored in Bohemia only by a powerful authority," he wrote. Teams of two commissioners, one appointed by the king and the other by the archbishop, would tour the parishes; both would act in the king's name, since the heretics did not recognize the archbishop's authority. A detachment of soldiers would accompany the commissioners in rural areas where hostility might be expected. The commissioners would instruct the people and revive the parishes. A determined time would be given those in the parish to convert after which they would be subject to various pressures and penalties and finally exile. But peasants would not be allowed to emigrate, since they might take the opportunity to secure freedom from their status as serfs. "They were to be brought to the faith by 'penalties moderately and prudently applied.'" Lamormaini generally looked to the long term restoration of Catholicism through the foundation of Jesuit colleges. The education of youth was critical for the future, he realized. But he did not mention schools in this paper apart from the foundation of a seminary for diocesan priests. Protestant nobles could be tolerated provisionally as well as moderate Protestants in the towns, in the hope that they would with time convert. The most dangerous areas existed where both lord and peasants were Protestants; here great prudence was required.

In Magni's plan, the government played a much reduced part. The archbishop would divide the country into four districts, each to be entrusted to an ecclesiastical commissioner whose task would be to revive the parishes. The four districts would eventually become bishoprics subject to the archbishop of Prague. This creation of bishoprics was fundamental to Magni's plan; the Council of Trent entrusted the care for the parishes to bishops. Also in accord with Trent, seminaries would be established in each bishopric for the education of the necessary diocesan priests. A spirit of mildness would prevail. Pressures to convert would generally be avoided since they only produced simmering resentment and false conversions. Lamormaini attempted to accomplish too much too fast, Magni argued. Heretics would be won over better through example and preaching. Moreover, a policy of exile would only depopulate the country.

Finally, on February 5, 1627, new instructions were issued for the reformation commissions favored by Lamormaini. The views of Lamormaini and Philippi generally prevailed, though the role of the archbishop was expanded.[98] So there began a systematic campaign for the conversion of the peasants of Bohemia. It represented "a complicated interplay between force and persuasion."[99] A popular saying in the 1620s asserted that the imperial officer Don Martin de Huerta with the quartering of his dragoons on the population had brought about more conversions more rapidly than had Christ and the Apostles.[100] Progress was slow under Ferdinand II because of the upheaval of the war, the attendant social dislocation, and popular resistance. Only after the war with the General Reformation inaugurated by Ferdinand III in 1650 did the campaign pick up steam as it employed creative methods of evangelization that drew on Bohemian customs and traditions and made use of music and art, pilgrimages, and the veneration of saints without, however, abandoning the use of coercion. Gradually there emerged in Bohemia "a corporate sense of [Catholic] identity" that was to long endure.[101]

Another prickly issue remained. Harrach's predecessor, Johann Lohelius, had called for the return to the Church of all the ecclesiastical lands lost to the Church since the Hussite Wars or equivalent compensation. The Propaganda in Rome supported this claim, and both it and the archbishop hoped to draw the funds necessary for the restoration of the Church from these lands. A commission established to study the issue that included Harrach and Magni recommended as compensation that for the next thirty years one-quarter gulden be assigned to the church for every vat of salt imported into the kingdom.[102] Lamormaini objected to this in his joint paper with Philippi, first on the grounds that the salt tax was already a burden on the poor, but more importantly on principle. As king of Bohemia, Ferdinand was obliged to support the restoration of the Church financially, and he had more than met this obligation. But he was in no way required to honor the claims of ecclesiastics for the return of their lost properties or to compensate them for their losses.

---

[98] Printed in Carlo Carafa, *Commentaria de Germania Sacra Restaurata* (Cologne, 1639), 85–94 (documentary appendix).
[99] Howard Louthan, *Converting Bohemia: Force and Persuasion in the Catholic Reformation* (Cambridge, 2009), 183.
[100] Ibid., 320.   [101] Ibid., 316–24, quote on 24.
[102] Germon Abgottspon von Staldenried, *P. Valeriano Magni: sein Leben im allgemeinen, seine apostolische Tätigkeit im besonderen* (Olten, 1939), 39–42.

To determine now what lands had once belonged to the Church would be impossible. Claims to some lands were void by prescription, other lands had been surrendered with papal approval. Lamormaini then turned to history once again. Ferdinand and his Habsburg predecessors had accomplished much for the Church, and they had generously endowed it. He had sold lands confiscated from the Bohemian rebels to Catholics at greatly reduced prices, in order to strengthen the Church in Bohemia, and he had fought an expensive war, at the urging of the pope, to bring the Palatinate under Catholic control. Lamormaini might well have been motivated in his position by the realization that funds paid as compensation by the emperor for lost Church lands would end up financing Harrach's plan for the restoration in Bohemia and not for the Jesuit colleges that Lamormaini was constructing.

Three years later, on March 8, 1630, an agreement was reached on the compensation for the lost ecclesiastical lands that was accepted by Harrach and by Rome. The salt tax was extended to take in all salt consumed in Bohemia, not only imported salt, and it was to be written into the law of the land that these revenues would accrue to the Church. The Church then surrendered all claims to compensation of confiscated Church lands. Provision was made for the foundation of four new bishoprics but lack of adequate funding prevented its realization.[103]

Carafa had already turned against Lamormaini in late 1625 as a result of the dispute over the university in Prague, and Lamormaini's influence in the discussion of the Counter-Reformation measures pushed him further away from the confessor. Eggenberg also became wary of Lamormaini's position with Ferdinand. In a report of November 26, 1626, Carafa poured out his feelings about the weight carried by the Jesuits and especially Lamormaini at court. The Jesuits used their position to exclude other orders from the emperor's support in favor of their own projects. Even imperial ministers needed Jesuit approval, he asserted. Eggenberg had confided to him, he wrote, that the power the Society enjoyed with Ferdinand would in the long run do it harm. The confessor now, allegedly, aimed to undermine the position of the nuncio with Ferdinand. There had to be a way to deal with the status of Lamormaini and the Jesuits in Vienna.[104]

Ferdinand took decisive if legal measures against the Protestants in his territories but toward the Jews he showed benevolence, partly out of financial considerations but also because of determination to remain faithful to his commitments.[105] As we have seen, Ferdinand extended his protection to the Jews of Prague in the upheaval in the city that followed the victory of the White Mountain. In Vienna he protected them against the regular hostility of

---

[103] ibid., 43–6; Richter, 365–6. [104] Carafa to Barberini, BL 6949, ff. 118–24.
[105] Hans Tietze, *Die Juden Wiens: Geschichte–Wirtschaft–Kultur* (Leipzig, 1933), 50.

Consolidation and Expansion, 1621–1628

the Lower Austrian estates and the citizens of the city who resented their competition. During the early years of the war, the Jews provided him with valuable financial assistance peaking with 20,000 gulden in 1623 but then nothing from 1625 to the tragic year of 1632 when he drew 15,000 from them.[106] In order to ease the tension with the citizenry, in 1625 he assigned the Jews a quarter or ghetto just across the Danube that was conveniently connected to the city by a bridge while allowing them to continue to do business in the center of the city until sundown. Local residents were compelled to move to accommodate them. There they enjoyed more space, and they were able to concentrate their synagogues, school house, and other community buildings, and they benefitted from considerable autonomy. The community grew rapidly from fifteen households in 1625 to thirty-one in 1627, and a new rabbi imported briefly from Prague helped to revive the spirit of the community. For a time Jews were expected to turn out for a German sermon in the church of the Brothers Hospitallers of St. John of God from eight to nine every Sunday morning, and fines were levied should the congregation fall under 200. A prefect was even engaged to awaken those who might lapse into sleep. But since the sermons produced few conversions, they were soon discontinued.[107] The situation of the Jews in Vienna deteriorated under Ferdinand III, and under Emperor Leopold in 1670 they were expelled from the city. On the imperial level Ferdinand insisted that debts be repaid to Jewish creditors by princes who attempted to renounce these after a lapse of time, he confirmed privileges conceded to Jews, and he prohibited military officials from quartering troops on the Jews, and in 1624 from extorting special payments from the Jews of Worms. All in all, his "mildness and love" served the Jews well.[108]

At the same time that in the 1620s Ferdinand started to consolidate his holdings in his hereditary lands and kingdoms, he also was inevitably pulled more and more into the politics of the Empire and indeed of Europe. To this development the future of the Palatinate electoral dignity and the Palatinate lands was central. In the Treaty of Munich, Ferdinand had promised to transfer the electoral title to Maximilian as well as to reimburse the elector for his war costs. Maximilian now held Upper Austria as a pledge of this reimbursement. Ferdinand was determined to recover Upper Austria as soon as possible; it constituted an essential portion of his patrimony. Lands of Frederick of the Palatinate seemed to offer themselves as material for a trade with Maximilian for Upper Austria, but in early 1621 they had not yet been conquered by Ferdinand and Maximilian. Out of consideration for Saxony, Ferdinand had hesitated to banish Frederick of the Palatinate before the White Mountain even though his councillors had assured him that the action would be legal. He now

---

[106] Ibid., 56–7.   [107] Ibid., 58–9.
[108] Gereon Wolf, *Ferdinand II und die Juden. Nach Aktenstücken in den Archiven der k. k. Ministerien des Inneren und des Aüsseren* (Vienna, 1859), 5–26, quote, p. 26.

took this step on January 21, 1621, but acting on the advice of his councillors, he hesitated to take the next step, the bestowal of the electoral title on Maximilian even though his councillors assured him that he could do so legally without the consent of the electors.[109] He realized that he needed the support of Maximilian, both military and financial. Troops of the Catholic League and Spain continued the war to the west as Frederick refused to give up, as did a number of "Protestant Paladins,"[110] Ernst of Mansfeld, Georg Friedrich of Baden-Durlach, and Christian of Halberstadt, a condottiere who had taken the field to defend Frederick.

Yet Maximilian also needed Ferdinand's action as emperor to secure the electoral title. The Bavarian duke pressed Ferdinand to act, and so did the new pope, Gregory XV, who saw the elevation of Maximilian to the electorate of Frederick as the way to assure the election of a Catholic emperor for the foreseeable future, giving the Catholic electors a five-to-two majority in the college and stabilizing the position of the Church in Germany. The papal instruction of April 12, 1621 for the new nuncio Carafa ordered him to work diligently for the transfer of the electorate to Maximilian.[111] In addition, a flood of papal briefs was sent off to princes and important figures in Vienna, Brussels, and Madrid, and the fiery Capuchin diplomat, Hyacinth da Casale, was missioned to make the religious case for Maximilian, first in Vienna and then in Madrid. He arrived in Vienna on July 21, 1621.[112] At the end of June Maximilian had sent Joachim von Donnersberg, his chancellor, to Vienna to promote his cause; Donnersberg visited Martin Becan, Ferdinand's confessor, who then drew up a written opinion in favor of the immediate transfer of the electoral title.[113] In early 1622, when Ferdinand seemed to be dragging his feet on the issue, Pope Gregory dispatched Fabrizio Verospi again to Vienna as an extraordinary nuncio to lobby for the transfer of the electoral title as well as to resolve the issue of Cardinal Klesl.[114]

Ferdinand had every intention to carry out his promise to Maximilian, but he was constrained by the political situation. Though Ferdinand was confident that he could legally transfer the electorate without the consent of the electors, politically he did not want to do so without the agreement of at least a majority. The only one of whose vote he could be sure at this time was Maximilian's brother, Archbishop Ferdinand of Cologne. He badly wanted the support of Lutheran Saxony as a Protestant elector. Archbishop Schweikard, the elector of Mainz, always tended toward a conciliatory position toward the Protestants,

---

[109] Brockmann, 197–201 and n. 31. [110] Wilson, 325.
[111] Instruction for Carafa, *Hauptinstruktionen Gregors XV*, #6 (pp. 613–18).
[112] Brockmann, 210, n. 98.
[113] Robert Bireley, *The Jesuits and the Thirty Years War: Kings, Courts, and Confessors* (New York, 2003), 58.
[114] Two Instructions for Fabrizio Verospi, Jan. 12, 1622, *Hauptinstruktionen Gregors XV.*, ##20, 21 (pp. 826–46, 847–53).

Consolidation and Expansion, 1621–1628

and he hesitated to back Ferdinand unless Saxony did so. Both he, and in his wake the Archbishop-Elector of Trier, inclined to believe that in the long run at least a partial restoration of Frederick would better benefit the cause of peace and the position of the Church. The Calvinist Elector of Brandenburg and also Frederick's brother-in-law could not be expected to cast a vote for the transfer. Spain hesitated on the issue. Madrid feared that the transfer to Maximilian of Frederick's title and lands would generate conflict in the Empire for years, as it did, and would make it difficult for Ferdinand to aid Spain either in the Netherlands, where the Twelve Years Truce of 1609 with the Dutch was about to lapse, or in Italy. Moreover, from 1621 to 1623 Spain was negotiating a marriage of the Infanta with the son of James I, in the hope of lessening the tension between the two countries. James was the father-in-law of Frederick, and Spain did not want to alienate him by supporting measures against Frederick. On the other hand, Spain had a strategic interest in protecting the route of its troops up the Rhine from Milan to the Netherlands along the so-called "Spanish Road," especially as the truce with the Dutch lapsed. So it wanted to hold on to the Palatinate territory on the west bank of the Rhine occupied in 1620 by Spinola and to have the rest of the Palatinate lands held by a sympathetic Catholic prince.[115] In 1621, the Spanish ambassador Oñate vigorously opposed the elevation of Maximilian to the electorate.[116] In mid-August the majority of the privy council – including Karl von Harrach, Liechtenstein, Trautmannsdorf, and Stralendorf – were in opposition. Eggenberg had by this time come over to support the transfer. He and Ferdinand met secretly with Hyacinth before Ferdinand took action.[117]

On August 29, 1621, Ferdinand met Maximilian half way, as it were, by agreeing to bestow the electoral dignity on him and his heirs secretly, and he issued the pertinent document on September 21. Ferdinand explicitly postponed any decision on Frederick's lands. Yet he hoped to secure the good will of Maximilian so that the Bavarian duke would consider a return of Upper Austria to Ferdinand in exchange for the Upper Palatinate, which was soon to be conquered by Bavarian and League troops, a deal that Maximilian rejected. Ferdinand's action was conditioned on the subsequent approval, at least tacit, of Spain and Saxony, and on the continued success of the Catholic armies. It would greatly harm the reputation of both himself and Maximilian, as the emperor explained to Maximilian, if developments forced him to rescind his action. Only Eggenberg, Stralendorf, Hyacinth, and Becan were informed of the secret bestowal of the electoral title, besides Maximilian and several of his councillors.[118]

Hyacinth now traveled to Madrid, commissioned by both Ferdinand and Maximilian, to obtain Spain's consent to the transfer of the electorate. There it

---

[115] Albrecht 1, 50–65, 82–4. [116] Brockmann, 210, n.75.
[117] Ibid., 211–12, 214. [118] Ibid., 213.

took him until May 1622, to secure the consent of Philip IV, a consent which was shortly afterward reversed when James I offered a new proposal to resolve the Palatinate issue. But once the news of Philip IV's approval reached Vienna, Ferdinand, with the consent of the majority of his privy councillors – not all were in agreement – decided for the public bestowal of the electorate on Maximilian at a convention of princes at Regensburg *(Deputationstag)*, which had been scheduled to convene on October 1, 1622; the reversal of the Spanish position did not change his stance. He moved ahead on his own without the approval of Madrid, realizing that he could count on financial and military assistance from his cousin in in any event.[119] He did not see himself as a "junior partner" in the House of Habsburg and in a letter to the Spanish minister Zúñiga, reminded him of the German origins of the House.[120]

Ferdinand steered clearly now toward the convention of princes that had been summoned on July 27, 1622. The ecclesiastical electors and Saxony as well as Maximilian favored a meeting of the German princes to clear up many of the issues facing the Empire and to move toward peace. Ferdinand had made it clear when he informed Maximilian of his decision publicly to elevate him to the electoral dignity that he intended to do this at Regensburg. But he wanted to take this step with the support of as many German princes as possible. On the other hand, he wanted neither a diet nor an electoral convention since in either of these cases he would be dependent upon the assent of the other participants. A convention of princes was a more informal conference, where it would be clear that Ferdinand took this action on his own authority as emperor but with the agreement of the others present.[121]

Ferdinand's military situation had improved with the Peace of Nikolsburg with Bethlen the previous December and major victories of the League army under Tilly combined with Spanish forces over the Protestant Paladins at Wimpfen on the Neckar River near Heilbronn, on May 6 and at Höchst near Frankfurt on June 20, 1622. On September 19, Tilly successfully stormed Heidelberg capital of the Palatinate. The Protestant Union itself had dissolved in May 1621. And of course, Ferdinand now had his new wife. The opening of the convention was delayed, as was usually the case with such meetings. Ferdinand himself arrived in Regensburg with a magnificent entourage on November 24. Two days later came the electors of Mainz and Cologne, followed by the representatives of the elector of Trier, who pleaded illness. Maximilian waited outside the city with an entourage of 400, sending two delegates in the meantime. He would enter personally only after Ferdinand announced his intention to elevate him to the electorate. Ferdinand's hopes for a more general understanding with the moderate Protestant princes were disappointed when Saxony and Brandenburg sent delegates rather than appear

---

[119] Ibid.   [120] Ferdinand to Baltasar de Zúñiga, Oct. 14, 1621, cited in Brockmann, ibid., 220.
[121] Albrecht 1, 76, 83.

personally. The only significant Protestant prince in attendance was Lutheran Ludwig of Hesse-Darmstadt, who was known as a supporter of the emperor. Carafa was there to continue to advocate for the transfer. The Spanish ambassador Oñate was present and continued to oppose the transfer.

After a delay of nearly six weeks during which Ferdinand waited for other Protestant princes to turn up, the convention opened on January 10, 1623, with the formal reading of the imperial proposition which announced Ferdinand's intention to elevate Maximilian to the Palatinate electoral dignity. Maximilian made his formal entrance two days later. Negotiations now began over the electoral dignity and other issues between the Catholic and Protestant princes. Archbishop Schweikard of Mainz proved to be the most significant opponent of the transfer of the electoral title. Since before the outbreak of hostilities, he had pursued a policy of composition with the moderate Protestant princes, especially Saxony. He tried to persuade Ferdinand and Eggenberg of the consequences that would follow from the transfer: the alienation of Saxony and other Protestant princes who would follow him, the deepening of the hostilities between the Catholic and Protestants princes in the Empire, the likelihood that England and other foreign princes would come to the aid of Frederick and so prolong the war. Ferdinand's predecessors, he pointed out, had made religious concessions rather than resort to the sword, probably with a view to Ferdinand I's acceptance of the Peace of Augsburg. Pope Gregory's briefs urged Becan, Ferdinand's confessor, among others, to champion the cause of Maximilian.[122]

Negotiations continued well into February. The expected arrival of the well-known Spanish diplomat, Count Gondomar, an energetic promoter of a Spanish–English alliance, perhaps hurried them on. At one point, according to a Jesuit account, Becan in a dramatic gesture approached Schweikard and "by everything that was holy, beseeched him that he no longer continue to delay what the pope, the emperor, and all good men earnestly desired, and what would be of great advantage to the Catholic religion."[123] Whether moved by such a plea or having recognized the benefits the transfer would be to the Church, Schweikard yielded, but not before he obtained a significant concession. The archbishop succeeded in winning over Ferdinand, the two archbishop-electors Mainz and Trier, and eventually Maximilian himself to a compromise that was reached on February 21. In contrast to Ferdinand's promise of September 22, 1621, the electoral title would be bestowed only on Maximilian personally, not on his heirs, the line of the Munich Wittelsbachs. At the time this meant Maximilian's brothers, since he still remained childless. Upon Maximilian's death, the emperor and the king of England

---

[122] Albrecht 2, Bernhard Duhr, *Geschichte der Jesuiten in den Ländern deutscher Zunge* 2: 2 (Freiburg, 1913): 224.
[123] Giulio Cesare Cordara, *Historiæ Societatis Jesu Pars Sexta, 1616–1633* 1 (Rome, 1750): 487.

would decide whether the electoral title should remain with Maximilian's heirs or be returned to Frederick's son, brother, or another relative.[124]

Maximilian only agreed to this compromise because in a secret understanding reached two days later, Ferdinand guaranteed that the agreement just reached did not prejudice his earlier promise to transfer the electoral title to Maximilian and to his heirs. Even if after the death of Maximilian the electors should decide to return the electoral title to Frederick or his heirs, Ferdinand would see that it remained with the Munich Wittelsbachs, thus adhering to his earlier promise to Maximilian. The details of the conversation between the two cousins are not known. Maximilian undoubtedly knew how to apply pressure on the emperor through his occupation of Upper Austria and the war debts owed him by Ferdinand.[125] Yet one cannot discount the influence on his decision of the advantages for the Church to be gained from a permanent possession of the electoral title by Maximilian and urged insistently by the pope, Carafa, and his own confessor Becan. This guarantee remained secret, though rumors of it did leak out.

The investiture of Maximilian with the electoral title took place in a solemn ceremony held in the palace of the bishop of Regensburg on February 25. Featured was a long oration by the imperial vice-chancellor, Hans von Ulm, that emphasized the crimes of Frederick the Elector Palatine and the merits of Maximilian, which led Ferdinand to undertake the transfer of the electoral title by virtue of his imperial authority. Significantly, the representatives of Saxony and Brandenburg and the Spanish ambassador Oñate boycotted the occasion. Observers noted that Archbishop Schweikard, the imperial chancellor, carried out his duties at the ceremony with little enthusiasm and that Maximilian himself at times appeared to be uneasy. On the day of his investiture, Maximilian wrote to thank the pope for his support.[126]

No decisions were reached on the Palatinate lands at Regensburg; but it would be difficult to separate the lands completely from the electoral title. Spain occupied the lands of the Lower Palatinate on the left side of the Rhine, and Maximilian held those on the right side along with the Upper Palatinate. Ferdinand had hoped, through his bestowal of the electoral title on Maximilian, that his Bavarian cousin would show some flexibility on the issue of war costs and the occupation of Upper Austria. But this was not to be the case yet. According to an agreement reached at Prague in April 1623, Ferdinand recognized that he owed Maximilian twelve million gulden for his expenses in the war. Ferdinand could not possibly pay this sum, so that Maximilian continued to hold both the Upper Palatinate and Upper Austria. Only in 1628 after the Peasants' Revolt in Upper Austria and when he was at the peak of his power would the emperor recover Upper Austria. Meanwhile, both Saxony in 1624, after the confirmation of its concession

---

[124] Albrecht 2, 568–9.   [125] Ibid., 570–1.   [126] Ibid., 572.

Consolidation and Expansion, 1621–1628

of the two Lusatias, and Brandenburg in 1627 acknowledged Maximilian's elevation into the college of electors.

Ferdinand's promise to Maximilian at the Treaty of Munich in 1619 and subsequent developments resulted in the much greater involvement of Ferdinand in the affairs of the Empire. The promise was understandable given the dangerous situation in which Ferdinand then found himself. Perhaps he could have obtained his cousin's assistance with a less generous commitment to him. But Ferdinand had made the promise, and he was one who kept promises. The transfer of the Palatinate electoral title would also benefit the Church as Pope Gregory asserted, he seemed to believe. Frederick refused any concessions on his part, even regarding the crown of Bohemia. But as Spain, Schweikard, and some of his own ministers had recognized, the deprivation of Frederick of his electoral dignity and eventually his lands would cause other princes to come to his aid and give them a pretext to intervene in order to prevent the expansion of Catholic and Habsburg power. England and the Dutch, now at war with Spain after the lapse of the Twelve Years Truce in 1621, would soon move in this direction. Louis XIII of France had supported Maximilian's claim to the electorate and congratulated him on its acquisition.[127] But with the accession of Cardinal Richelieu to the position of first minister in France in 1624, French policy would turn in an anti-Habsburg direction. Frederick had initially expanded the Bohemian rebellion into a European affair by his acceptance of the crown of Bohemia. Ferdinand was now to be pulled more deeply into a European conflict by his support of Maximilian in the Palatinate. But it is hard to see how he might have avoided this.

Meanwhile Tilly's victory over Christian of Halberstadt at Stadtlohn near Münster in the northwest on August 6, 1623, put an end to military opposition to the Catholic forces in the Empire. "The Paladins had been routed and the war in the Empire appeared to be over."[128]

But Bethlen in Upper Hungary had once again raised his head in the hope of working with the now defeated Christian of Halberstadt; once again he sought the aid of the sultan, a reminder that Ferdinand had to remain on alert toward the Turkish front. But partly because of Christian's defeat and the sultan's unwillingness to cooperate, Bethlen was compelled to conclude once again a peace with Ferdinand at Vienna in May 1624, as we have seen, which reaffirmed the terms of Nikolsburg. Ferdinand was able to strengthen his position in Upper Hungary. Assisted by Pazmany, now a cardinal, at the diet of Pressburg in October 1625, Ferdinand succeeded in securing the election of a Catholic, Miklós Esterhazy, as the new palatine, and more importantly, the recognition of his son, the young Ferdinand, as king of Hungary.

---

[127] Ibid. [128] Wilson, 346–7.

Just as the Bohemian rebellion and its immediate aftermath had threatened to destroy the balance in the Empire in favor of the Protestants and to undermine imperial authority, so Ferdinand's victory at the White Mountain and the transfer of the Palatine electorate to Maximilian augured the upper hand for the Catholics and a substantial increase in imperial power. Now three new figures came on the European scene in late 1623 and early 1624 who altered the political landscape. The Count-Duke of Olivares succeeded the deceased Zúñiga as the leading minister in Spain and functioned as the favorite of King Philip IV. He ended the long negotiations with England over a marriage alliance, and he began to campaign vigorously for Ferdinand's aid to Spain against the rebel Dutch. The Twelve Years Truce between Spain and the United Provinces had come to an end in 1621 when neither side showed enthusiasm to renew it. In Rome in August 1623, Cardinal Maffeo Barberini ascended the papal throne. He lacked the militant spirit of his predecessor, the Ludovisi Pope Gregory XV, who had vigorously championed the cause of Maximilian in the Palatinate, and he shared the long standing papal fear of Habsburg dominance in Italy and in Europe and so tended to side with Bourbon France in its rivalry with the Habsburgs.

Lastly, Cardinal Richelieu entered the council of state in France in April 1624 and by August had risen to first minister and favorite of Louis XIII. Shortly thereafter he began to organize an anti-Habsburg front in Italy and in the Empire. Prior to Richelieu's taking office, France had concluded an alliance with Venice and Savoy with a view to expelling the Spaniards from the Valtelline, a crucial Alpine pass in Switzerland that constituted a section of the Spanish Road, the major line of supply for men and equipment from Spanish Milan to the Netherlands. Richelieu continued to prosecute this plan, but the military venture failed and France was forced to conclude the Treaty of Monzon with Spain in March 1626 partly because the government needed to deal with a Huguenot revolt at home. The same trouble with the Huguenots compelled Richelieu to back off for the time being from his efforts in Germany. In June 1624, France negotiated the Treaty of Compiègne that committed it to assist the Dutch against Spain. At the same time the French began to concentrate troops on their eastern border, and Richelieu dispatched emissaries to Copenhagen, Stockholm, and German courts to stir up opposition to the Habsburgs. The following year the sister of Louis XIII, Henrietta Maria, married Charles I who ascended the English throne that year. But the Huguenot rebellion also prevented France from aligning with the Dutch, England, and Denmark in the anti-Habsburg League of the Hague that was formed in 1626 after talks of nearly a year. The cardinal had to attend to business at home for a time.

The new initiative to contain the advance of the Habsburgs now came from King Christian IV of Denmark. Christian had begun his personal rule back in 1596, won a war with his rival Gustav Adolph of Sweden for control of the

Baltic, from 1611–1613, and accumulated a large personal treasure that made him virtually independent of the estates. As Duke of Holstein he was also a prince of the Empire and a member of the Lower Saxon Circle. Though he put himself forward as a defender of Protestantism, religion does not seem to have been his chief motive. He aimed to dominate the Lower Saxon Circle in the north of Germany, to secure control of bishoprics there for his sons, and to halt the advance of imperial forces and authority into the north of Germany. He also probably intended to preempt an intervention of his rival, Gustav Adolf, and in fact after considering such a move, the Swedish king turned his attention back to his war with Poland. Christian began in January 1625 to take part in the talks at the Hague for a Protestant alliance, which he only joined the following year; by this time he had raised an army of 20,000 troops stationed in Holstein along with a fleet of thirty ships. Later that spring he pressured the members of the Lower Saxon Circle to elect him their military leader, and with this he acquired another 7,000 soldiers. A new Protestant union seemed to be forming.[129]

Emperor Ferdinand did not want to continue the war. Maximilian pushed him in this direction in light of the danger emerging from Christian's preparation for conflict. In the spring of 1625, Maximilian strongly encouraged the emperor to raise and to deploy an army in the Empire; he feared the onslaught of a new Protestant alliance which would, one should note, endanger his hold on the Palatinate electoral title and lands. Just at this time the enigmatic Bohemian nobleman Wallenstein came forward with an offer to raise an army for Ferdinand. Twice before he had come to Ferdinand's rescue. He had provided decisive help at a crucial moment during the War of Gradisca and in 1619 he had levied troops for Ferdinand in Moravia and then captured the treasury of the Moravian estates, which Ferdinand had returned. His marriage to a wealthy widow back in 1609 had made him a rich man, and he profited greatly from the land transfers in Bohemia after Ferdinand's victory. During the crisis of the years 1619 to 1623, he loaned Ferdinand, always desperate for funds, 1.6 million florins, and Ferdinand in return elevated his lands in Bohemia to the status of the Duchy of Friedland in 1624. The previous year Wallenstein had offered to raise an army for Ferdinand, but the emperor had declined to accept the offer.[130]

Maximilian's urging and Wallenstein's offer in the spring of 1625 unleashed a series of meetings of the privy council in Vienna with Ferdinand that lasted from April 25 to June 21. Ferdinand hesitated to expand the war. In a letter to Maximilian of April 13, 1625, he had downplayed the threat posed by the Danish king.[131] Among those present at the consultations were Count Ramboldo Collalto, president of the war council, Abbot Anton of Kremsmünster, president of the court treasury council, Gundaker von Liechtenstein,

[129] Ibid., 387–8.   [130] Ibid., 391–3.   [131] Brockmann, 242, n. 193.

brother of the governor of Bohemia, Slawata, Meggau, Stralendorf, and Karl von Harrach. A position paper from which the discussions began emphasized the dangers threatening the emperor from all sides: Italy, Hungary, where Bethlen was in arms again, the Netherlands, and especially in Lower Saxony from Christian and his allies in the Lower Saxon Circle. A solid majority of the council supported a commission to Wallenstein to raise troops so that the emperor could negotiate from a position of strength; they pointed to a preventive war. Eggenberg, who was not in Vienna at the time, then weighed in with a position paper in which he considered the threat from Christian not to be so serious and warned that the emperor's commission to raise a new army would only incite fear in the hearts of his enemies and provoke a disastrous escalation of the conflict. News of Christian's election as general of the Lower Saxon Circle seems to have led to a decision in favor of the commission for Wallenstein. On May 12, Ferdinand notified Maximilian of this. Yet this was not the end of the discussion. The emperor still hesitated. In mid-June the councillors took up the matter once again, having moved to Nikolsburg so that Cardinal Dietrichstein could participate in the talks. On June 23, Ferdinand inquired of Wallenstein about the possibility of releasing officers whom he had already recruited, in light of optimistic reports about movement toward peace. Yet another position paper drawn up for the council on June 30 reemphasized the need for the army in light of new reports about Christian's raising of troops. It raised the possibility of a Danish push into Upper Austria, and once again argued for the need to negotiate from a position of strength, indeed, to take preventive measures.[132] So Wallenstein continued to build up his army.

By the end of 1625, the general had assembled about 50,000 troops. The initial number was chosen at least to equal Tilly's army, and it soon surpassed it. This provided Ferdinand with a military force equal to and then surpassing that of Maximilian's League. By 1627, Wallenstein's army amounted to 100,000, which constituted a vast increase over the size of the armies heretofore employed in the war. Ferdinand's soldiers on the Hungarian front were not under Wallenstein's command. The emperor, assisted by the war council, retained the power to appoint generals and, at least on paper, he kept for himself the ultimate authority to name colonels. Financing his army always remained a problem for Ferdinand, who often teetered on the edge of bankruptcy. Wallenstein developed a system of forced "contributions" or payments imposed on populations in enemy territory. A general or lesser officer would contract with a territory or town for a fixed amount of funds or supplies. Sometimes officers extorted payments from a town in exchange for keeping their troops disciplined. Lands confiscated from enemy princes or landlords were sold or distributed to pay off debts. Land valued at 740,000 florins had

---

[132] Ibid., 238–46; Mann, 363–6; Ferdinand's instruction for Wallenstein, dated Vienna, Jun. 27, 1625, is found in Lorenz, # 10 (pp. 82–94).

been seized from Christian's officers in Lower Saxony and Westphalia by 1630. Ferdinand could also resort to his prerogatives as emperor to bestow titles or other dignities when he did not have land at his disposal. Spanish subsidies helped, and, importantly, in Lower and Inner Austria taxes continued to be regularly collected.[133]

So Wallenstein began to muster his army. But war actually broke out with Maximilian's order of July 15, 1625 to Tilly to invade the Lower Saxon Circle. Back in late April, as the discussions regarding the commission for Wallenstein to raise an army were getting under way in Vienna, Maximilian had requested and obtained from Ferdinand authorization for Tilly to invade the Lower Saxon Circle should that be deemed necessary. Ferdinand then responded with a vaguer permission to pursue the emperor's enemies, and he granted the permission to Maximilian, not to Tilly, thus assigning greater responsibility to the elector himself. In his accompanying letter to Maximilian of May 7, he cautioned Maximilian that neither he nor Tilly should make use of this permission except in an extreme situation. Yet Ferdinand had made a critical concession. He seemed to want to recall it when, still unconvinced of the necessity of war, on July 12 in another letter to the elector he expressed his strong reservations about initiating the conflict when the enemy might still be won over and when this would mean accepting responsibility for the start of hostilities. But Ferdinand's letter arrived too late to forestall the order dispatched to Tilly by Maximilian who "with firm decisiveness" was determined upon military action. There was nothing left for Ferdinand to do but to back up Maximilian's decision.[134] So Maximilian pulled Ferdinand deeper into the Empire.

Neither Ferdinand's commission empowering Wallenstein to raise an army nor his authorization of Maximilian to take the military initiative can be interpreted as an attempt to dominate the Empire, much less to establish a form of absolutism there. He did intend to uphold imperial authority and to defeat those whom he considered to be undermining it. Both Wallenstein's army and the authorization of Maximilian to march into Lower Saxony were fundamentally defensive measures aimed to preserve the integrity of the Empire as he saw it. Nor can one say that with Wallenstein's army he planned to free himself from dependence on the Catholic League as his military arm, though this did result from his possession of his own army.

Even as Wallenstein's army marched north toward Lower Saxony, a peace initiative emerged from the two electors, Mainz and Saxony, an initiative that aimed in the first place to resolve the issue of the Palatinate. Initially the two electors envisioned an electoral convention, but Ferdinand preferred a diet, and eventually a convention of princes, as at Regensburg in 1623, was scheduled for Ulm on August 16, 1625, but then postponed. Ferdinand outlined his position in his response dated August 30 to an emissary sent to Vienna by

---

[133] Wilson, 399–409.   [134] Brockmann, 244–5.

Maximilian.[135] Ferdinand emphasized the urgent necessity for peace in the Empire. For this two conditions were necessary. Imperial authority had to be respected and Frederick had to make a suitable payment to cover the costs of the war. Ferdinand was ready to guarantee a pardon before he formally submitted but the former Elector Palatine would have to make a public submission. The crucial issue was the electoral dignity, Ferdinand declared, asking for Maximilian's view on the issue and reassuring him that he had not forgotten his promises. In his response Maximilian indicated that he would not even discuss his surrender of the electoral title during his lifetime; he refused to take a position on whether he would surrender it for his heirs if this issue proved to be the chief obstacle to peace. He agreed to give up a portion of the Palatinate lands but under conditions that Frederick would never accept. The project then ended when Frederick refused a compromise on either the electoral title or lands. But Ferdinand had shown a readiness to negotiate further toward peace.[136]

The years 1626 and 1627 saw the military fortunes of the emperor and the Catholic League flourish, so that by the end of 1627 they controlled the whole of the Lower Saxon Circle and were pushing up into Denmark. On April 25, 1626 Wallenstein defeated Mansfeld at the battle of the Dessau Bridge, a critical crossing of the Elbe River. After his defeat, Mansfeld reorganized his army and fled toward Upper Hungary in order to join the forces of Bethlen, who had once again taken the offensive, having joined the Hague Alliance thus uniting Ferdinand's enemies in the southeast with those in the north. Wallenstein pursued Mansfeld, whose army gradually disintegrated after Bethlen failed to show up with his army for the planned juncture. Mansfeld fled across the mountains to Venice where he died on December 14. Meanwhile Tilly had crushed the forces of Christian of Denmark at the battle of Lutter am Barenberg on August 27, 1626.

A long position paper drawn up in October 1626 not long after Tilly's victory at Lutter provides insight into the thinking in Vienna at the time. It was not possible to carry on wars in the southeast against Bethlen and then the Turks as well as in the Empire. The councillors, who are not named, favored peace in the Empire and saw the greater danger from the Turks. They feared a religious war in the Empire, reminding Ferdinand that his army contained many Protestant soldiers who might rebel if they thought the war was over religion. Ferdinand had said many times, they recalled, that his only goal was to carry out his imperial obligations and to enforce the Religious Peace. Better to undertake this peacefully, not to attempt to conquer the Lower Saxon Circle. Moreover, and importantly, "in any case, greater advantage is to be expected from peace in the Empire; it is the only way to revitalize the imperial hereditary

---

[135] Response of the emperor to Donnersberg's mission, Aug. 30, 1625, BANF 2: #99.
[136] Bireley 1, 65–70.

lands, to gain the love of the subjects, to develop wealth and obtain authority, to secure the succession in the kingdoms and to improve justice and administration."[137] So these councillors gave a priority to consolidation in the hereditary lands and to defense against the Turks; they looked warily at further advances in Lower Saxony and at the prospect of religious war.

But the military situation soon further improved. Bethlen once again made peace with Ferdinand at Pressburg on December 20, 1626, reaffirming in essence the Peace of Nikolsburg of 1606. This lessened the danger in the southeast, and the Turks showed no intent to take the offensive. Bethlen passed from the scene then in 1629, so ridding Ferdinand of a pesky adversary. In 1627 the emperor had confirmed the position of the settlers in the Military Border area, and three years later with the Vlach Statute (*Statuta Valachorum*) he laid out the rights and obligations of the settlers that stabilized their status for years to come.[138] Wallenstein occupied Holstein in September 1627 and then moved briefly into Denmark. Christian was defeated, even though the war lingered on.

Plans were now afoot for a joint military-commercial venture with Spain that would secure control of the North and Baltic Seas for the two Habsburg powers. This venture had first been proposed by the Spanish minister Olivares back in 1625 and had won the approval of Eggenberg. But the intervention of Christian of Denmark prevented work towards its realization. Now in September 1627, with imperial troops holding most of the north German coast, it was revived and won the support of both Wallenstein and the emperor provided it did not involve Ferdinand directly in war with the Dutch. The ambitious project called for the creation of a naval force to operate in the North and Baltic Seas with the cooperation of Spain, the emperor, the Hansa cities, and even King Sigismund of Poland. The principal goal was to strangle Dutch commerce in the area and so to cut a lifeline crucial for them, and then to develop Habsburg commercial activity there. The project revealed a grand if illusionary vision which pointed toward what was to come. Control of the north would be vital if the coming Edict of Restitution was to be successfully implemented. Crucial to the naval project was the participation of the Hansa cities. Initially they showed interest sending a delegation to the emperor in Prague in May 1628. But they then declined. Wallenstein himself lost enthusiasm once he had been promised the duchy of Mecklenburg in February 1628. Spanish support waned with the loss of their silver fleet in 1628, and the contest over the inheritance of Mantua and Montferrat in Italy that broke out at the end of 1627 summoned the energies of both Spain and the emperor.[139]

---

[137] Position paper of the imperial councillors regarding the continuation of the war, October 1626, BANF 2: 3 #272 (pp. 338–45).

[138] Ekkehard Völkl, "*Militärgrenze und 'Statuta Valachorum*," *Die österreichische Militärgrenze. Geschichte und Auswirkungen*, ed. Gerhard Ernst (Kallmünz, 1982), 16–21.

[139] Anton Gindely, "Die Maritimen Plänen der Habsburger und die Antheilnahme Kaisers Ferdinand II. am Polnisch-Schwedischen Kriege während der Jahre 1627–1629," *Denkschriften der*

At Wallenstein's recommendation, Ferdinand made a generous peace with Christian at Lübeck on July 7, 1629, partly in order to win support from him in case of an anticipated intervention of Gustav Adolph of Sweden.[140]

The period from October 18, 1627, until well into the following spring, Ferdinand spent in Bohemia, mostly in Prague. During this time he took measures to further consolidate his position in Bohemia and also in other lands of the monarchy. Since 1625, a team of councillors had been working out a "Renewed Constitution" *(Verneuerte Landesordnung)* for Bohemia; the team included Ferdinand himself, Eggenberg, Harrach, and Slavata, who were subsequently joined by the Bohemian noblemen Otto von Nostitz and Karl von Liechtenstein, the governor of Bohemia who died in 1626.[141] The new constitution was made public on May 10, 1627, and it went into effect the following November 15 with the meeting of the Bohemian estates. It established a modified form of absolutism that would continue with little change for more than a century. The Renewed Constitution established in Bohemia hereditary succession in the House of Habsburg, thus resolving an issue once and for all that had been contested at the time of Ferdinand's election as king of Bohemia in 1617. Supreme legislative and judicial authority rested with the king. Only the king could summon the estates, and only he could introduce laws. The structure of the estates was reorganized. The clergy, who had been expelled from the estates at the time of the Hussite conflicts, were restored to first place followed by the lords, who dominated the body, then the knights, and lastly the representatives of the cities who collectively had only one vote. The king controlled the introduction of new aristocrats into the body of the estates,[142] but most noble newcomers came to identify with Bohemian interests, and the old Bohemian nobility retained most of the offices.[143] The estates did retain some rights and privileges, above all the right to vote on taxation. Ferdinand realized his need for the estates for his finances, and he summoned them every year from 1629 onwards. In addition, they administered the collection of taxes,

---

kaiserlichen Akademie der Wissenschaften, Philosophisch-Historiche Klasse, 39 (Vienna, 18–91): 2–29; Hans-Christoph Messow, *Die Hansestädte und die Habsburger Ostseepolitik im 30-Jährigen Kriege, 1627–1628* (Berlin, 1935), 11–79. Neue Deutsche Forschungen 3

[140] Wilson, 409–23.   [141] Hengerer, 118, n.442.

[142] The extent to which the Verneuerte Landesordnung established an absolute government is contested. Hans-Wolfgang Bergerhausen, "Die 'Verneuerte Landesordnung' in Böhmen 1627: Ein Grunddokument des habsburgishen Absolutismus," *Historische Zeitschrift* 272 (2001): 327–51," considers it, on the basis principally of a text analysis, absolutist, where Eila Hassenpflug-Elzholz, *Böhmen und die böhmische Stände in der Zeit des beginnenden Zentralismus* (Munich, 1982), Veröffentlichungen des Collegium Carolinums 30, on the basis of practice, sees it as a modified absolutism and certainly not "an instrument of absolutism in the French style" (p. 25), as does R.J.W. Evans, "The Habsburg Monarchy and Bohemia, 1526–1848" *Conquest and Coalescence: The Shaping of the State in Early Modern Europe*, ed. Mark Greengrass (London, 1991), 141–6. I am inclined to the latter view.

[143] Hassenpflug-Elzholz, 61–4, 364.

Consolidation and Expansion, 1621–1628

and at the local level they controlled nearly all the functions of government. Ferdinand wove them into the structure of his rule. In continuity with the Renewed Constitution, a mandate was issued in late June 1627 requiring that all the nobility in Bohemia become Catholic; as a result about one-fourth of Bohemian noble families went into exile.[144] Measures similar to those in Bohemia were taken for Moravia the following year. In Silesia, Ferdinand was kept from such measures by agreements with Saxony, and the two Lusatias had passed to John George.

Ferdinand also consolidated his position in the Austrian territories in 1627 and 1628. In a treaty of February 22, 1628 with Maximilian, he achieved a goal which he had long pursued, the return of Upper Austria, with which the Bavarian had become disenchanted after the Peasants' Revolt of 1626. In return, Ferdinand publicly recognized Maximilian's possession for himself and his heirs of the Palatinate electoral title as well as the Upper Palatinate and the lands of the Lower Palatinate on the right bank of the Rhine. The arrangement strengthened his commitment to the Bavarian ruler. A constitutional and religious settlement similar to the one in Bohemia was introduced in Upper Austria.[145] In Lower Austria, all Protestant preachers and schoolteachers were expelled on September 14, 1627. But Ferdinand kept his promise to the Protestant nobles who had remained faithful to him back in 1620. They were allowed to remain even if their ministers were not. In Inner Austria, non-Catholic nobles were expelled on August 1, 1628. A reasonable estimate suggests that about 100,000 exiles left Upper, Lower, and Inner Austria between 1598 and 1660.[146]

On November 21, 1627, in the Cathedral of St. Veit in Prague, Ferdinand's wife Eleonore was crowned queen of Bohemia, and four days later there took place the coronation of Ferdinand's son, Ferdinand, already king of Hungary, as the hereditary king of Bohemia. Great festivities accompanied both events. Two days later, an opera "La Transformatione di Calisto," was performed in the great Vladislav Hall of the Hradschin Palace, and then on December 6, Jesuit students of the college in Prague performed in the same place a drama "Constantine Victor," attributed to the Italian Jesuit Giulio Solimano, and so they returned to a theme that the Jesuits often associated with Ferdinand. The day of the Jesuit drama, Ferdinand's daughter, Caecilia Renata, wrote her

---

[144] Richter, 289; Thomas Winkelbauer, *Ständefreiheit und Fürstenmacht. Länder und Untertanen des Hauses Habsburgs im konfessionellen Zeitalter* (Vienna, 2003) 2: 28.

[145] Gerhard Putschögl, *Die landständische Behördenorganisation in Österreich ob der Ems vom Anfang des 16. Jahrhunderts bis zur Mitte des 18. Jahrhunderts. Ein Beitrag zur österreichischen Rechtsgeschichte* (Linz, 1976); Gunter Khinast, "Beiträge zu einer Geschichte des Landes ob der Ems unter dem Landeshauptmann Hans Ludwig von Kuefsgtein (1630–1656)," Dissertation U. of Innsbruck, 1967.

[146] Winkelbauer, ibid., 61.

brother, Archduke Leopold William, who had remained in Vienna, that in the evening they would attend a five-hour drama, which she feared would be too long for her.[147]

On December 19, Ferdinand met his triumphant general, Wallenstein, at Brandeis and the general spent several months in Prague. After having deprived the two dukes of Mecklenburg of their territory for having supported Christian of Denmark, on February 1, 1628, Ferdinand conditionally bestowed on his general the duchy as payment for the enormous sums that he owed him and also with a view to boosting the military position of Wallenstein on the Baltic Sea. The following year Wallenstein would be formally invested with the duchy. On April 21, Ferdinand named Wallenstein "General of the Oceanic and Baltic Seas," a title that pointed to the joint initiative being planned with Spain to secure the upper hand over the Dutch in the northern seas, and a week later he was designated "Supreme Captain-General" of the imperial armies with the right to make many appointments normally reserved to the emperor. Some at court, including Wallenstein and Lamormaini, were thought to be considering a campaign against the Turks once German affairs were in order.[148] In the course of the spring, a victory parade was held for the general in the form of a Roman triumph, including captives taken in his campaigns. Another celebration of victory took place at the site of the Battle of the White Mountain where Ferdinand dedicated a church to his patron, Mary.[149] Meanwhile, back in Vienna the new Jesuit church, built under the direction of Lamormaini, was being completed. Under the cornice on the facade one can still read the inscription: "To the triumphant victor, the most good and most powerful God, Emperor Ferdinand II has raised this monument in memory of the Blessed Virgin Mary and Saints Ignatius and Francis Xavier."

Ferdinand reached the peak of his power that winter of 1627–1628. But the electoral convention, eventually held at Mühlhausen from October 18 to November 12, pointed to trouble ahead.

---

[147] Herbert Seifert, "Theateraufführungen der Jesuiten anlässlich kaiserlicher Besuche in Prag," in *Bohemia Jesuitica 1556–2006*, ed. Petronilla Cemus with Richard Cemus, S.J. (Prague, 2010), 965.
[148] Giovannni Battista Pallotto (new nuncio) to Francesco Barberini, May 26, 1628, NBD 1: *Nuntiatur des Pallotto 1628–1630*, ed. Hans Kiewning 1: *1628* (Berlin, 1895, reprint Turin, 1973): #17.
[149] Franzl, 282–3.

ILLUSTRATION 1 Pious Ferdinand born of pious parents
Frontispiece, Franz Christoph von Khevenhüller-Frankenburg, *Annales Ferdinandei* vol. 1 (Leipzig, 1721).
Courtesy of the Newberry Library, Chicago

ILLUSTRATION 2 Archduchess Maria at 26
Cornelis Vermeyen (1577)
Courtesy of the Kunsthistorisches Museum, Vienna

ILLUSTRATION 3 Vow of Archduke Ferdinand at Loreto (1598)
Andreas Paur, "Theatrum Austriacum seu Virtutum Austriacorum Principum Compendium,"
(1696?, manuscript)
Courtesy of the Newberry Library, Chicago

ILLUSTRATION 4 Cardinal Melchior Klesl
Franz Christoph von Khevenhüller-Frankenburg, *Conterfet Kupfferstich*, vol. 2 (Leipzig, 1722)
Courtesy of the Newberry Library, Chicago

ILLUSTRATION 5 Defenestration of Prague (1618)
Courtesy of the Bridgeman Art Gallery International

ILLUSTRATION 6 Dead and wounded on the battlefield
Detail from the Fourth phase of the Battle of the White Mountain on 7–8 November 1620
by Peter Snayers (1592–1667) in the church of Santa Maria della Vittoria in Rome
Courtesy of the Bridgeman Art Library International

ILLUSTRATION 7 Elector Maximilian of Bavaria
Franz Christoph von Khevenhüller-Frankenburg, *Conterfet Kupfferstich*, vol. 1
(Leipzig, 1722)
Courtesy of the Newberry Library, Chicago

ILLUSTRATION 8 Hans Ulrich von Eggenberg
Franz Christoph von Khevenhüller-Frankenburg, *Conterfet Kupfferstich*, vol. 1 (Leipzig, 1722)
Courtesy of the Newberry Library, Chicago

ILLUSTRATION 9 Empress Eleonore as widow
Franz Christoph von Khevenhüller-Frankenburg, *Conterfet Kupfferstich*, vol. 1
(Leipzig, 1722)
Courtesy of the Newberry Library, Chicago

ILLUSTRATION 10 Emperor Ferdinand as model of the Marian Congregation in Vienna
Frontispiece of William Lamormaini, *Ferdinandi II Romanorum Imperatoris Virtutes* (n.l., 1638)
Courtesy of the Bayerische Staatsbibliothek, Munich

ILLUSTRATION 11 Assassination of Wallenstein (1634)
Courtesy of the Bridgeman Art Gallery International

ILLUSTRATION 12 Mausoleum, Graz
Final resting place of Emperor Ferdinand II
Begun by Giovanni Pietro de Pomis (1614) and completed by Johann Fischer von Erlach
Courtesy of Graz Tourismus, (Harry Schiffer)

Chapter 6

Overreach, 1628–1631

Nuncio Carafa, shortly after his recall in mid-1628, drew up a final report on the state of affairs in the Empire, and two years later the Venetian ambassador, Sebastian Venier, delivered a similar report to the Venetian Senate after his return to Venice.[1] Their reports concur to a large degree, and together they help to provide a picture of Ferdinand in his early fifties. The emperor was of middling height, they stated, with a robust constitution and fair complexion. Every type of person he treated affably and with consideration, a point also made by Lamormaini and others. By nature he was a man of peace; he abhorred war of which he had little personal experience; recall the fiasco against the Turks back in 1601. German and Italian he spoke fluently and some Latin. Though he knew both Spanish and French, he never spoke either of the two languages, even Spanish with the Spanish ambassador.[2] Moderation in food and drink characterized him, but according to Venier, he ate unhealthy foods against which the doctors warned him; he preferred to undergo treatments for stomach disorders rather than change his eating habits, an attitude that did not promise a long life, the ambassador noted. For recreation and respite from the burden of government he turned to music and to the hunt, his two passions. The doctors also warned Ferdinand against the exertions of the hunt at his age, but it was impossible to restrain him. He also took

---

[1] Carlo Carafa, "Relatione dello stato dell'imperio e della Germania, fatto dopo il ritorno della sua nuntiatura appresso l'imperatore 1628," ed. Johann G. Müller, *Archiv für Kunde österreichischer Geschichtsquellen* 23 (Vienna, 1860), 101–449; "Relatione de Sebastian Venier Cav.'Proc.'Amb.' estr. in Germania. 1630," *Die Relationen der Botschafter Venedigs über Deutschland und Österreich im 17. Jahrhundert* 4: *Matthias bis Ferdinand III.* (Vienna, 1866): 129–78. Fontes Rerum Austriacarum, Section 2, vol.26.
[2] Carafa, 259, 264; Venier, 144.

great pleasure, Venier added, in conversation with his wife and children in the evening. Usually he retired by 10 p.m., to rise again at 4:30.[3]

Carafa went on at some length about Ferdinand's religious practice. Every morning upon rising Ferdinand attended two Masses in his private chapel, the first for the repose of the soul of his first wife. According to Lamormaini writing ten years later, Ferdinand normally spent one hour in prayer and spiritual reading upon rising before the two Masses as well as half-hours late in the day and before retiring. His reading included the Christian Scriptures, the classic *Imitation of Christ* by Thomas à Kempis, and lives of the saints.[4] Most Sundays and feast days were then taken up for the most part, according to Carafa, with religious devotions. He approached confession and Holy Communion every feast day, especially on the feast days of the Apostles. The early morning Masses were followed by a German sermon by a Jesuit and then a High Mass with "exquisite" music that lasted one and one-half hours. In the late afternoon came another sermon, this one in Italian by a Franciscan, and then Vespers which could continue into the night. On feast days he often attended Mass, sermon, and Vespers in the church of the Jesuits or Capuchins, and he then stayed with them for a meal along with his wife and children. The court accompanied the emperor and the empress when they attended church on feast days.

Further services were in order during Advent prior to Christmas and in Lent prior to Easter. On Maundy Thursday in Holy Week he, his wife, and his family received Communion from the hands of the nuncio, thus giving an example to the whole court of his obedience to the Church's command regarding Easter Communion; he also publicly washed the feet and then served a meal to thirteen poor men, in a traditional act that imitated the actions of Christ at the Last Supper. After this he gave each a shirt and bestowed on each a gold coin which the poor man would continue to receive each month for the rest of his life. The empress did the same for poor women in her private quarters. Regularly Ferdinand and Eleonore participated in the processions on the Feast of Corpus Christi and the Rogation Days four times a year, walking with heads uncovered often through mud and rain, a spectacle that greatly edified the court. Venier added that charity dictated that one assume that a genuine inner piety corresponded to Ferdinand's exterior actions but only God who saw into the heart could know this for sure. Many observers took scandal from the way that the emperor withheld payment from his creditors while spending lavishly on musicians and huntsmen and allowing councillors to divert funds into their own pockets. Nor could they understand how he justified his Italian policy, an issue to which the Venetian Venier was particularly sensitive and which we will soon take up.[5]

---

[3] Venier, 145, 157. [4] *Virtutes*, 21–8. [5] Venier, 147–8.

On normal days, after the two early morning Masses, Ferdinand spent much of the day either participating in council, processing correspondence, giving audiences, or hunting. Venier considered Ferdinand "assiduous and diligent" but "irresolute" in council and dominated by the pro-Spanish Eggenberg,[6] which as we have seen was not always the case. Carafa considered him to be well informed but indecisive. At noon he usually took his meal in the antechamber of his quarters in the Hofburg where twelve chamberlains – six German and six Italian who rotated regularly – waited on him, serving the various dishes and handing him a napkin as appropriate; they also helped dress and undress him. Initially Ferdinand had increased the number of noble chamberlains to several hundred as a reward for service in the wars and as a way of attaching them to his court, but subsequently he reduced their number because of the expense. Many were now only honorary chamberlains. More recently, on feast days and important occasions, he dined publicly with more attendants in the Hofburg's Ritterstuben in the presence of the court and foreign ambassadors. Upon returning from council or from the hunt, Ferdinand held audiences and signed papers, and he always returned from the hunt on Saturdays in time for vespers for Sunday. Evenings found him usually having supper with the Empress in her quarters along with his two sons Ferdinand Ernst, who was the King of Hungary and Bohemia, and Leopold William who at age twenty-four already held the prince-bishoprics of Passau and Strasbourg which his uncle, Archduke Leopold, had previously held, and his daughters Maria Anna, who would become the second wife of Maximilian of Bavaria in 1635, and Caecilia Renata, who would become queen of Poland in 1637. Eleonore's ladies in waiting attended them. The meal was a simple one but with music.[7]

For music and the hunt Ferdinand spared no expense even when the treasury was empty. He sought to have the finest voices and every type of instrument for the court musical ensemble whose principal function was liturgical for the court chapel but whose activity extended to many secular functions as well. Ferdinand had brought with him from Graz the openness of the court there to the new Italian forms, especially the Venetian, and this was intensified by the activity of Empress Eleonore who inclined to the Mantuan tradition. It was under Ferdinand and Eleonore during the war that Vienna began to acquire its reputation as a city of music, both sacred and secular. Ferdinand was "among the rulers of the early seventeenth century most frequently honored with musical dedications."[8] In 1637, even after cutbacks caused by the war, the imperial

---

[6] Venier, 145.
[7] Carafa, 292–300. Another description of Ferdinand's day is found in the *Status particularis regiminis S.C. Majestatis Ferdinandi II.* (Leiden, 1637). It does not differ substantially from Carafa's but it does indicate that he frequently did not retire until after 1 a.m., which would allow for prayer in the late evening.
[8] Steven Saunders, *Cross, Sword, and Lyre: Sacred Music at the Imperial Court of Ferdinand II of Habsburg* (Oxford, 1995), 4–5.

payroll listed by name more than seventy musicians with nearly another eighty, perhaps part-timers, unnamed. Some musicians, notably trumpeters, were rewarded with patents of nobility.[9] According to Lamormaini, Ferdinand found in music refreshment and recreation that then enabled him to attend more diligently to affairs of state and, more importantly, as a most suitable way to enhance divine worship to the glory of God.[10] The emperor showed little interest in the collection of paintings as had Emperor Rudolf or Ferdinand's son, Archduke Leopold William would. Ferdinand undertook little in the way of new buildings for the court, but he did have a dance hall constructed in the Hofburg in 1630 for musical and theatrical performances, and he renovated a summer residence of Emperor Rudolf, now the Amalienburg, to make it suitable for such performances. Music also served as a means of imperial representation and the projection of the magnificence of the imperial office. It served the cause of display not only in the liturgy, public and private, but also in many court spectacles staged for coronations, weddings, funerals, birthdays, and for Christmas and Carnival. Ferdinand delighted in these festivities, which included opera, ballets, and the equestrian ballets often staged on the Burgplatz in front of the Hofburg for which the Habsburgs would become famous.[11]

As for the hunt, Ferdinand claimed to have dogs of every kind and the rarest birds, according to Carafa, and he had in service 150 huntsmen and their assistants. In each kingdom and province, a chief huntsmen oversaw his huntsmen and dogs. Ferdinand loved to fire the arquebus, and he took great pleasure in tracking down and killing deer and wild boar with his own hand and then regaling ambassadors and the nuncio with tales of his success. He kept a careful diary of his prey, noting the exact number of the animals and their type and sometimes the names of those in the hunting party. Empress Eleonore often accompanied him on the hunt where she, too, enjoyed shooting an arquebus. Ambassadors, other foreign visitors, and councillors often participated in hunting parties where business was frequently conducted informally. This gave an individual important access to Ferdinand. Rome instructed one nuncio to be prepared to join Ferdinand on hunting excursions. It was a privilege for a nobleman to secure an invitation to go hunting with the emperor; indeed, the emperor's insistence on the exclusive right to hunt in the areas around Vienna meant that only an invitation from Ferdinand offered the nobleman an opportunity to hunt there at all. Ferdinand made use of the hunting party to garner the allegiance of Austrian noblemen. Hunting was a political event.[12]

---

[9] Carafa, 264; Harald Tersch, "Freudenfest und Kurzweil. Wien im Reisetagebüchern der Kriegszeit (ca. 1620–1650)," in *Wien im Dreisigjährigen Krieg*, ed. Andreas Weigl (Vienna, 2001): 181, 185; Saunders, 22, 25.
[10] *Virtutes*, 70–1.
[11] Saunders, 9–11; The Lipizzaner Stallions of the Spanische Reitschule in Vienna continue the traditions of these performances up to the present day.
[12] Carafa, 267; Tersch, 181–6.

Lamormaini did not hide the fact that Ferdinand's hunting parties damaged peasants' lands. But their complaints were frequently kept from the emperor, he commented, and when he did learn of them, he ordered that the peasants be compensated. When one peasant suffered a personal injury, he was brought to Vienna for treatment and then provided with a new outfit as well as a payment.[13]

Carafa wrote of Ferdinand as a saintly prince *(così santo principe)* with a confidence in God similar to that of King David; no defeat or setback was able to shake it. He had succeeded Matthias at a time of rebellion and war. At one time he retained only the city of Vienna and was on the point of losing it. Despite all the plots of his enemies, he made his way to Frankfurt, there to be elected and crowned emperor. His enemies in the Empire and in Hungary were not able to bring him down because of his confidence in God "as he told me many times." The Divine Majesty wanted to demonstrate that his power far outweighed human judgment. Because he has trusted in the Lord, God had protected, honored, and exalted him. The nuncio testified that he had never seen the emperor commit a grave fault or act against his conscience.[14] Carafa did not mention his own differences with Lamormaini in his report.

The Electoral Convention of Mühlhausen that eventually met from mid-October to mid-November 1627 to resolve the issues facing the Empire called for a resolution of the long-standing dispute of the proper interpretation of the Religious Peace of Augsburg. But two issues now emerged to set back the prospects for cooperation of the emperor with Maximilian and the Catholic electors. The first regarded the electors' fears of the rising power of Wallenstein and the threat that they thought he represented to the imperial constitution. The second resulted from the conflict that emerged over the inheritance of the Gonzaga Duke Vincenzo of Mantua, which included the duchy of Montferrat, who died childless on Christmas night, 1627. The two linked duchies were crucial for control of North Italy, and both France and Spain put forth their own candidates. Ferdinand as emperor and feudal lord of north Italy was inevitably to be drawn into the conflict so important to his Spanish Habsburg cousin.

Maximilian had helped persuade Ferdinand to raise his own army, and the result was the commission given Wallenstein on July 25, 1625. But competition over recruits and resources, along with personality differences and varying strategic conceptions, soon led to misunderstandings and worse between the elector and the general. More fundamental was the shift in political balance gradually brought about by the ascent of the general. Whereas Ferdinand had long been dependent on military assistance from Maximilian and the Catholic League, this now ceased to be the case. With the creation, expansion, and

---

[13] *Virtutes*, 72–3.   [14] Carafa, 260–1.

success of Wallenstein's army, the balance shifted. The military power of Ferdinand grew, and that of Maximilian and the League lessened. The stuff for conflict was present.

Already in 1626 Maximilian and Mainz began to complain that Wallenstein quartered troops on lands belonging to princes of the League, and that the soldiers often treated the inhabitants roughly and even brutally. The general had acquired a virtually independent principality in the duchy of Friedland, and he held court in a magnificent style. His actions pointed to pretensions. His occasional derogatory comments about the electors angered Maximilian and his fellow princes. The Capuchin Valeriano Magni had conceived a hatred for Wallenstein, perhaps because of the initial harmony between the general and Lamormaini and Wallenstein's support of Jesuit colleges. Magni heightened Maximilian's fear of the general when he sent to the elector in late 1626 a report of alleged details of an agreement reached between Wallenstein and Eggenberg at Bruck that November outlining the terms of the general's service and an increase in the size of the army. Though Magni did not say so explicitly, reading between the lines of his report one could infer that the general planned to make Ferdinand an absolute ruler in Germany and so to destroy the German constitution.[15] Whether these charges were true or not, they seemed to fit the pattern of the general's conduct.

Maximilian now summoned a meeting of the states of the Catholic League for Würzburg in February 1627. Prior to the meeting, he circulated among the Catholic electors an abbreviated version of Magni's alarming report. At Würzburg the participants discussed the danger from Wallenstein and the maintenance of the League army, and at the end of their deliberations they dispatched a delegation to Vienna to complain of the misconduct of Wallenstein's soldiers and the general's quartering of troops. Maximilian and the three ecclesiastical electors agreed on the need for an electoral convention to discuss the status of Wallenstein and imperial affairs in general, and Saxony and Brandenburg consented. So a conference of electors was planned for the coming November in Mühlhausen.

When the delegates of the League arrived in Vienna in May, Lamormaini helped to prepare them for their meetings with Eggenberg and Ferdinand, and he encouraged them to be frank in their conversation with the general himself. At this time the confessor and the general maintained a harmonious relationship. Lamormaini sat in on the meeting of the delegates with Wallenstein where the general assured them that he did not want to give the electors cause for complaint. The reception of the delegates in Vienna eased the concerns of the electors.[16] Subsequently, Maximilian and Mainz

---

[15] Ritter, 3: 355–6,
[16] Minutes of the negotiations of the delegates of the League in Vienna, May 10–June 7, 1627, BANF 3: #389; Bernhard Duhr, *Geschichte der Jesuiten in den Ländern deutscher*

agreed to make use of the confessor in order to bring their complaints against Wallenstein to Ferdinand's attention.[17]

As expected, the electors Catholic and Protestant once again took up the issue of Wallenstein at the Electoral Convention of Mühlhausen in October and November. Their fears had escalated once again, and the initial draft of a joint communication for Vienna called for Wallenstein's dismissal and the threat to take up arms against him if something was not done. Word of this draft leaked to Vienna, and drew from Ferdinand a warning not to infringe on his imperial authority.[18] The Catholic electors then, aware that the general restitution of church lands which they called for at Mühlhausen would require a strong military force for its implementation, saw to the elimination of the offensive passages from the communication, and it became just another complaint about the depredations of Wallenstein's army.

During his stay in Prague during the triumphant winter and spring of 1627–1628, Wallenstein saw his status elevated by a grateful Ferdinand with the provisional conferral of the duchy of Mecklenburg and the bestowal of the titles "General of the Oceanic and Baltic Seas" and "Supreme Captain-General" of the imperial armies. The confiscation of Mecklenburg from the two reigning dukes on the grounds of their rebellious support of the king of Denmark and its transfer to Wallenstein represented a vigorous exercise of imperial authority. Before undertaking the confiscation Ferdinand, always concerned to act lawfully, had secured an opinion on its legality from a committee of imperial count councillors that included Stralendorf and Justus Gebhardt, a doctor of law who had converted to Catholicism under Lamormaini's tutelage and who was to play an increasingly important role at the imperial court.[19] They affirmed that Ferdinand could take this measure without any further legal process in light of the notorious character of the duke's offence. The privy council was divided on the wisdom of the measure. One group that probably included Slawata and Trautmannsdorf feared the political ramifications of the transfer of the duchy, especially without any formal process. It would only feed the suspicions already spreading as a result of unwise remarks of Wallenstein that the emperor aimed at a monarchy in Germany similar to that in France and Spain. A heavy monetary penalty should be levied against the dukes and then used to pay off the debts to Wallenstein. The other side – probably including Abbot Anton Wolfradt, president of the court treasury – argued that one could only satisfy the obligations to Wallenstein with the duchy. Otherwise he might resign from

---

Zunge 2:2: (Freiburg, 1913): 706–7; Anton Gindely, *Waldstein während seines ersten Generalats, 1625–1630* (Prague, 1886) 1: 256–9.

[17] Mainz to Maximilian, Aug. 30, 1627, BANF 3: #442, and n. 2.
[18] Carafa to Barberini, Nov. 3, 1627, BL 6218, ff. 253–7.
[19] On Gebhardt, see Bireley 2, 77, 189, 248, n.2.

imperial service with the likely result that the emperor would lose his military advantage and the army might even dissolve.[20]

Wallenstein's advancement convinced Valeriano Magni once again to warn Maximilian of the dangers from the general, this time in the so-called "Capuchin Relations."[21] Though they were clearly exaggerated, his reports were plausible and had some foundation in fact. Wallenstein had no religion, Magni reported, and was possessed by a lust for power. He aimed at an absolute monarchy in Germany for Ferdinand and after the death of the current emperor, the imperial crown for himself. No one dared to oppose him at court. He had won over Lamormaini and the Jesuits by his support of their schools. Only a strong League army could check his growing power.

Maximilian immediately alerted Mainz and Tilly after he read the reports from Prague; they only fed his suspicion of the general. A convention of the League was summoned for Bingen on the Rhine for late June 1628; war might break out between the League and imperial armies. Maximilian again sent his chancellor Joachim von Donnersberg to Vienna to emphasize there the desperation to which the quartering of Wallenstein's troops was bringing some princes. Donnersberg was to seek out Lamomaini and impress upon him how Wallenstein was imperiling the Catholic cause in Germany.[22] As a result Ferdinand did require Wallenstein to reduce the number of troops that he had under arms in Upper Germany.[23]

By the summer of 1628 Wallenstein had begun to retreat from his expansionist policy, and he devoted much of the period between the summers of 1628 and 1629 reorganizing the government of Mecklenburg. He seems to have come to appreciate the limits of imperial power, and he was growing wary of the ambitions of the Swedish king, Gustav Adolph, who had been warring with Poland since 1621. By 1627 the general had already sent a contingent of troops to assist King Sigismund of Poland and to keep Gustav Adolph busy, and in June 1629 he assigned a small army to help out the Polish king. Sweden had assisted the city of Stralsund on the Baltic to weather successfully the siege of the imperials in the winter of 1627–1628, and later that year the Hanseatic cities finally rejected the plans for Habsburg domination in the Baltic. The changing political situation in 1628 convinced Wallenstein of the need for a compromise peace with Christian of Denmark, and as we have seen, peace was concluded at Lübeck in July 1629. The goal was to render Christian friendly in

---

[20] Christoph Kampmann, *Reichsrebellion und kaiserliche Acht: Politische Strafjustiz im Dreissigjährigen Krieg und das Verfahren gegen Wallenstein 1634* (Münster, 1992), 90–8.
[21] The author of the "Capuchin Relations" is disputed. Golo Mann, *Wallenstein* (Frankfurt, 1971), p. 523, for example, assigns them to another Capuchin, Alexander d'Ales, who was sent to Prague secretly by Maximilian in April 1628 to report on Wallenstein's personality and intentions; d'Ales then drew heavily on Valeriano as his source.
[22] Instruction for Donnersberg's mission to Vienna, Jun. 12, 1628, BANF 4: #100.
[23] Ritter 3: 394–5.

the likely case of an attack from Gustav Adolph. Imperial troops left Denmark so that Christian retained his kingdom intact, and no indemnity was demanded of him. He renounced his claims to bishoprics in Lower Saxony and promised to keep his hand out of imperial affairs. This prepared the way for Ferdinand to secure the bishoprics of Halberstadt, Bremen, and Magdeburg for his second son, Leopold William and so to strengthen the imperial presence in the north, much to the consternation of Maximilian.

The dispute over the succession in Mantua and Montferrat soon escalated into a power struggle between Spain and France over the two duchies which were crucial to control of north Italy, and it drew the concentrated attention of the imperial court in Prague in the spring of 1628. Mantua lay to the southeast of Spanish-occupied Milan and Montferrat to the southwest between Milan and Savoy. The imposing fortress of Casale dominated the Upper Po valley from Montferrat. On his deathbed on December 25, 1627, Duke Vincenzo Gonzaga, the brother of Empress Eleonore, designated as his heir Duke Charles of Nevers, a member of the French branch of the family and vassal of the king of France. Spain opposed Nevers, seeing in him a stalking horse for French advance into Italy that would weaken the Spanish position there and throughout Europe, and it proposed its own candidate, Ferrante, the duke of Guastalla, a small Italian principality. His claim was weaker than Nevers's but he argued that Nevers had forfeited his claim by previously taking up arms against the emperor. Nevers, having been alerted to the impending death of Vincenzo, arrived in Mantua on January 17, 1628, and took possession of the territory with a small band of soldiers. Both sides now looked to Emperor Ferdinand as feudal lord of north Italy for a favorable adjudication of the conflict; both territories were fiefs of the Empire. Spain had generously supported Ferdinand in Germany since the Bohemian revolt but had never succeeded in convincing the emperor to come to its assistance against the Dutch. It now made it clear that it expected a decision in its favor. So Ferdinand found himself caught between his obligation as feudal lord to render justice in the case and his Habsburg bond that inclined him towards Spain.

The day after his arrival in Mantua, Nevers sent the bishop of Mantua, Vincenzo Agnelli-Soardi, to represent his case in Prague. Even before his arrival, Ferdinand had assured the permanent Mantuan agent at the imperial court that he would not permit any preemptive strike by the Spaniards against the duchies. Agnelli-Soardi reported that one of the first to visit him in Prague was nuncio Carafa, who guaranteed him papal support, and he found allies in the confessor Lamormaini and in Empress Eleonore. Pope Urban had a profound interest in the issue. His fear of Habsburg domination in Italy, and in Europe, prompted him to favor Nevers's candidacy, and he advocated it secretly. Above all, he wanted to prevent the spread of war into Italy with all its horrors as well as the heresy that would accompany imperial troops. Rome had not forgotten the Sack of Rome in 1527 by the troops of Emperor

Charles V. So papal policy aimed at a peaceful solution of the dispute in favor of Nevers. This was one reason for the assignment of Giovanni Battista Pallotto, first as an extraordinary nuncio to the imperial court in April 1628 and then as the replacement of Carafa. Carafa had by now broken with Lamormaini, and Rome wanted a nuncio who could work with the confessor in the interest of its Italian policy. Lamormaini, for his part, long opposed imperial intervention in Italy because he wanted to maintain harmony between Ferdinand and the pope as urged upon him by Vitelleschi and because he feared it would weaken Ferdinand's position in Germany just as the program of restitution of church property was to get under way. For his part, the Spanish ambassador, now the Marquis of Aytona, pressured Ferdinand to sequester the two duchies until a decision was reached or permit a Spanish force to occupy Montferrat, including the fortress of Casale, to forestall any attempt by Nevers to seize the territory. Eggenberg stood with Spain.

Ferdinand called for a position paper from the Imperial Court Council. In their response dated March 8, 1628, they recognized that Nevers, already in possession of Mantua, clearly had the better legal claim to the two territories, and they found it difficult to justify a sequester. Yet they approved one, for two reasons. First, without a sequester there would certainly be war; Spain simply would not allow the duchies to go to Nevers. But Nevers might be willing to accept a sequester and so avoid the inevitable conflict. Secondly, to forego a sequester would be to surrender the emperor's right to exercise his feudal authority in Italy and so to remain a passive onlooker, whereas a sequester would enable him to exercise his authority in favor of Nevers. The sequester should be administered by a German, not a Spaniard. Ferdinand should make it clear to Madrid that the sequester was not intended as an instrument to foster Spanish interests, that the emperor had "had and knew no greater reason for acting *(rationem status)* than Almighty God, his conscience, and the justice that he was sworn [to uphold] and not to violate." Spain was expected to respect the commissioner sent to oversee the sequester. The council clearly did not incline toward Spain. The privy council – meeting on March 10, 1628, with Ferdinand present – approved the position advocated by the Imperial Court Council. On April 1, he issued an order for his commissioner, Count Johann of Nassau, to take possession of the two duchies. But the opposition of both Nevers and Spain prevented the realization of this measure. Both sides knew that the emperor could back up his order with force only against Nevers. He could not possibly do so with Spain because of his dependence upon Spanish military and financial assistance and because of the dynastic bond. Madrid expected him eventually to come around to its position.[24]

Meanwhile Philip IV, in a letter of February 15, informed Ferdinand that he had authorized his governor in Milan to invade Mantua and Montferrat and to

---

[24] Brockmann, 340–3.

hold them in sequester on behalf of the emperor. On April 2, Spanish troops along with those of its ally, the duke of Savoy, marched into Montferrat and undertook the siege of Casale. Ferdinand on April 19 instructed his ambassador in Madrid, Count Khevenhüller, to lodge a vigorous protest with the king of Spain. Under the pro-Spanish Eggenberg's influence, then, the protest was modified. Initially, it demanded the surrender of the area occupied by Spanish and Savoyen troops to Count Nassau independently of whether Nevers did the same or not. The final version required the transfer of the area to Nassau only after Nevers had first turned over his territory to the imperial commissioner. So there appeared a tilt toward Spain in the emperor's policy. Yet this did not satisfy Philip IV. He had no intention of allowing his and Savoy's conquests in the territories to be handed over to Ferdinand's sequester whether Nevers allowed this or not for the area that he held. Ferdinand continued to hope that both Philip IV and Nevers would submit to the sequester and so war would be avoided.[25]

The Imperial Court Council produced another major position paper on July 30. It recognized the pressure that Ferdinand was under from Count Nassau, who thought that Nevers was only stalling, and from the Spanish ambassador, Aytona. But politically they thought it wiser not to declare the ban on Nevers lest this provoke the intervention of France. More important was justice, and juridically, the council contended, there did not exist sufficient grounds to ban Nevers; he was not formally a notorious rebel nor had he clearly refused to accept the sequester. One could not expect him to yield to the sequester if the Spaniards did not also do so. If he did yield to the sequester, then his territory would best be occupied provisionally by imperial, not Spanish, troops in the name of the emperor. The council then recommended that Ferdinand attempt to secure a pledge from Spain and Savoy that they would accept the sequester. If they did so, and Nevers refused to do so, then he would clearly place himself in the wrong and could be placed under the ban. But, one might ask, was it realistic to think that Spain would concede on the sequester?

Ferdinand acted on the basis of this position paper. He attempted to persuade the Spanish ambassador Aytona to promise that Spain would honor the sequester, and on August 16, 1628, he instructed Khevenhüller in Madrid to explain there that his two goals in the whole matter were the preservation of peace in Italy and a just and fair solution of the issue. Aytona had promised him formally, in the presence of the privy council, that Spanish recognition would follow Nevers's recognition of the sequester. If Philip and his ministers raised difficulties with this promise, then Khevenhüller should clearly state that Ferdinand could not "in justice and with good conscience" *(salva justitia et absque laesione conscientiae)* place Nevers under the ban. Spain ought to seek to come to an agreement in direct negotiations with Nevers that would then be subject

[25] Ibid., 344–6.

to Ferdinand's approval as feudal lord, and not seek to get its way through the immoral use of force. But Spain had no intention of honoring the sequester. Negotiations continued with Nevers through the fall, and Ferdinand, on October 19, proposed that all parties gather in Vienna in early 1629 to settle the issue, and if they could not come to an agreement, he as emperor would make a decision. Ferdinand carefully safeguarded his own imperial authority.[26]

Through 1628 the issue of Mantua stirred passions at the imperial court. On the one side stood Eggenberg, the Spanish ambassador Aytona, and the count of Nassau; on the other were aligned Empress Eleonore, Lamormaini, the nuncios Carafa (until his departure) and Pallotto, and ultimately from Rome, Pope Urban. The position papers of the Imperial Court Council seem to indicate that many of them as well as the privy council sided with the second group. According to a report of the bishop of Mantua, Eleonore threw herself into the battle.

The empress shrieks, exclaims, seeks to persuade the emperor to make some accommodation with the prince [Nevers]. They go together, but she in a way agitated, perspiring and in tears, without success, following the emperor saying that she is not able to reconcile herself to the will of her husband.[27]

Lamormaini encouraged her to imitate the courage of the Jewish heroine, Esther.[28] Pallotto brought a brief from Pope Urban for Lamormaini when he arrived in Prague. The pope beseeched Lamormaini to convince Ferdinand not to bring fire and sword into Italy but to turn his forces against the heretics. "What devotee of the Heavenly Kingdom," he wrote, "would [not] be tormented to see those arms bathed in Italian blood that could quickly be run through the throats of the terrified supporters of impiety? ... What greater glory in the Christian Commonwealth could be compared with that of the Austrian princes than if their triumphant power be decorated by these two titles and they be remembered by history as conquerors of heresy and guardians of the peace?" As his confessor, Lamormaini would share in Ferdinand's glory.[29] Pallotto reported that Lamormaini visited him on May 26, the day after his arrival in Prague, and he assured him that no imperial troops would be sent to Italy.[30]

In his formal response to the pope, Lamormaini promised to do all that he could to prevent imperial troops from moving into Italy.[31] Pope and emperor had to cooperate. But Rome would have to do its part. All the privy councillors

---

[26] Ibid., 346–53.
[27] Cited in Daniela Frigo, "Les deux imperatrices de la maison de Gonzague et la politique 'italienne' de l'Empire (1622–1686)," *Dix-septième siècle*, #243 (2009/2), p. 225.
[28] Pallotto to Barberini, Aug. 19, 1628, NBD 1: *Nuntiatur des Pallotto !628–1630*, ed. Hans Kiewning, 1: *1628* (Berlin, 1895, reprint Turin, 1973), #76.
[29] Urban VIII to Lamormaini, Apr. 15, 1628, BL 2198, ff. 47v-8.
[30] Pallotto to Barberini, May 26 and 28, 1628, NBD 1: *Nuntiatur des Pallotto* 1: #17 (p. 56).
[31] Lamormaini to Urban VIII, Jul. 15, 1628, ARSJ, Aust. 23, f. 40.

wanted peace, Lamormaini wrote, reflecting correctly the view of the councillors. But Nevers had to recognize the sequester and acknowledge the emperor's right to decide the issue. Strongly implied was the pope's obligation to convince Nevers to accept the sequester.[32] For Lamormaini, the issue became principally the need for Nevers to acknowledge the emperor's authority. He later explained for the benefit of the Spanish court through a letter to the imperial ambassador Khevenhüller that Spain's invasion of Montferrat had been unjust because Spain had acted before Ferdinand had made a decision on the matter.[33]

In late July of 1628, the Spanish and Savoyan ambassadors challenged Lamormaini in a stormy session. The Spaniards were well aware that the longer Ferdinand hesitated to intervene, the more likely was French intervention on the side of Nevers. The long siege of the Huguenot fortress La Rochelle on the Atlantic coast of France fully engaged Richelieu and Louis XIII through most of 1628, but one could foresee that it was coming to an end. Lamormaini told the Spanish ambassador, Aytona, outright that Spain's action was unjust. Aytona, shouted in reply, "A cleric is supposed to pray and not to meddle in such matters." Eggenberg, who had now broken with Lamormaini, threatened to resign, but Ferdinand refused to even hear of this and instructed his minister to admonish the confessor. But this hardly deterred Lamormaini. Tension remained. On August 5, Lamormaini informed Pallotto in great confidence that that morning Ferdinand had received Holy Communion with a view to obtaining light on the matter.[34] Lamormaini incurred the enduring enmity of Madrid. Olivares twice accused him through Khevenhüller of mingling improperly in imperial affairs and of working against the king of Spain. The confessor wanted to respond further but Ferdinand refused to sanction this; he wanted to end a fruitless polemic.[35] Olivares would later apply great pressure on the Jesuit superior general, Vitelleschi, in order to have Lamormaini removed from his post in Vienna.

Toward the end of 1628, it became increasingly clear that Nevers would not accept the sequester especially after he had received a promise of French assistance. La Rochelle fell on October 28, 1628, and in a military feat, Richelieu led a French army over the Alps into Italy in the middle of the winter. The French defeated the forces of Savoy at Susa in early March 1629 and then compelled Savoy to abandon Spain and ally with them and soon brought

---

[32] Lamormaini to Francesco Paolucci (Secretary of the Congregation for the Interpretation of the Council of Trent), Jul 14, 1628, ibid., 42–3v; Lamormaini to Barberini, Jul. 15, 1628, ibid., f. 44. Paolucci, whom Lamormaini had apparently come to know during his sojourn in Rome in 1622–1623, counted in Rome as an expert on German affairs.

[33] Lamormaini to Khevenhüller, Jan. 3, 1629, Rome, Archivio Segreto Vaticano, Nuntiatura Germaniae 118, ff. 31v–3v, enclosure with Pallotto to Barberini, Jan. 5, 1629, NBD 2: *Nuntiatur des Pallotto*, 2: 1629, ed. Hans Kiewning (Berlin 1897, reprint Turin, 1973): #6.

[34] Pallotto to Barberini, Jul. 19, 22, 29, and Aug. 5, 1628, NBD 1: *Nuntiatur des Pallotto*, 1: ##51 (citation), 52, 54, 61; Carafa to Barberini, Jul. 22, 1628, BL 6952, ff. 89–94.

[35] Bireley 2, 73–4.

Venice into the alliance. They raised the Spanish siege of Casale and occupied the fortress before the end of March and then waited. April saw the emperor send troops to open the Swiss Alpine passes in preparation for an invasion. Lamormaini and the leading ministers all supported this. Ferdinand could not allow the French to dictate to him in Italy.[36] Ferdinand acted as much if not more to safeguard his authority in north Italy as he did to accommodate his Spanish cousins.

Hope still remained that a military confrontation might be avoided. Maximilian and the other electors wanted to prevent the emperor from engaging in Italy where they saw his intervention as pursuing Habsburg rather than imperial interests. Lamormaini continued to work against escalation of the conflict encouraged by Pallotto and Agnello-Soardi as well as now by Hungarian Cardinal Pazmany, but Agnello-Soardi lamented that "the confessor, formerly all-powerful, no longer has a voice that penetrates to the heart of His Majesty."[37] His enemies argued as Olivares had that other theologians approved the war. Eggenberg and Collalto promoted aggressively imperial military intervention. According to the bishop of Mantua, Eggenberg even advised Empress Eleonore brusquely to stay out of politics.[38] In September Ferdinand approved the mission of 36,000 troops headed by Collalto to occupy Mantua. They reportedly committed many outrages as they passed through Lombardy which greatly troubled Ferdinand. By early December they laid siege to the great fortified city of Mantua but they were forced to retreat on Christmas Day 1629.

Richelieu had not been inactive. In July 1629 a French envoy, Melchior de Sabran, turned up in Vienna, but his mission failed as much by reason of his allegedly haughty manner as of its message, as both Ferdinand and Lamormaini later complained. Richelieu had attempted, unsuccessfully, to derail the peace negotiations between Ferdinand and Christian of Denmark. Now he fostered the Swedish–Polish armistice of September 26, 1629, which was intended by the cardinal to prepare the way for a Swedish invasion of the Empire that would eventually come about. French emissaries paid visits to the courts of Saxony and Brandenburg but with little success. Richelieu did find a receptive ear at the court of Maximilian because of the Bavarian's fear of Wallenstein and now his disapproval of Ferdinand's intervention in Italy. Urban VIII, through his nuncio in Paris, Giovanni Francesco Guidi di Bagno, encouraged these highly secret negotiations between Paris and Munich that would result later in 1631 in a defensive alliance. Maximilian also mediated contacts between Vienna and Paris. In addition, Lamormaini and the Jesuit confessor of Louis XIII, Jean Suffren, with

---

[36] Pallotto to Barberini, Apr. 14, 1629, NBD 2: *Nuntiatur des Pallotto*, 2: 1629 (Berlin, 1897; reprint Turin, 1973): #87.
[37] Bishop of Mantua to Ercole Marliani (Mantuan councillor), Aug. 8, 1629, cited in Romolo Quazza, *La guerra per la successione di Mantova e del Monferrato, 1628–1631* (Mantua, 1926) 1: 395.
[38] Ibid., 1: 378, 387–9.

the consent of Ferdinand and Richelieu respectively, exchanged letters in late 1629 and early 1630, with a view to breaking the impasse, but without success.[39]

At this point the charismatic Carmelite Domenico à Jesu Maria returned to the political stage. After hesitating for a while, in the fall of 1629 Pope Urban determined to send him to Vienna to urge Ferdinand toward peace in Italy. Both Ferdinand and Eleonore were eager to welcome him. He departed from Rome on October 22 with briefs for the imperial pair as well as letters of Cardinal Barberini to them and to Eggenberg and Lamormaini. Exactly a month later he arrived in Vienna. Eleonore visited him in the Carmelite convent on the 24th and Ferdinand on the 27th after his return from a hunting expedition. At the emperor's invitation, he moved into the Hofburg, and in the coming weeks conferred regularly with Ferdinand and Eggenberg, threatening them, it would seem, with divine judgment if they continued the offensive in Italy. Yet despite Ferdinand's great esteem for him and despite Lamormaini's support, Domenico made little progress. Collalto, he reported, represented the principal obstacle to peace.

Domenico's health began to deteriorate, and from January 29 onwards he was confined to bed. Both Ferdinand and Eleonore were present when he received the last rites. His status improved, then, briefly, and he continued to receive visitors and to press his case with Ferdinand. His death finally came on the evening of February 16, with the imperial pair at his side. Ferdinand claimed for himself as relics Domenico's cane as well as his habit. Within a week a miracle was reported due to his intercession, and Ferdinand soon began to press for his beatification, which however has not taken place up to the present day.[40] We can only surmise that Domenico did influence to some degree Ferdinand's gradual agreement to a peace settlement in Italy.

Richelieu led a new French advance into Italy starting in early 1630. The French took over the Savoyan fortress of Pinerolo in late March and by June they had occupied much of Savoy which had turned out to be an unreliable ally. But imperial troops once again besieged Mantua in mid-July, this time seizing the city within a few days and putting it to a vicious sack destroying its great cultural heritage. Once he heard of the plunder, devastation, and rape that the imperial troops had visited upon the city, Ferdinand instructed the commander to punish the evildoers severely, "so that the world will truly and adequately recognize [our] administration of justice and that all these things happened against my gracious will."[41] To the west, the Spaniards occupied

---

[39] Bireley 2, 97–100.
[40] Silvano Giordano, *Domenico di Gesù Maria, Ruzola (1559–1630): Un carmelitano scalzo tra politica e riforma nella chiesa posttridentina* (Rome, 1991), 244–61. Institutum Historicum Teresianum, Studia 6.
[41] Ferdinand to (General) Ramboldo Collalto, Regensburg, Oct. 9, 1630, *Documenta Bohemica Bellum Tricennale Illustrantia*, 5: *Der schwedische Krieg und Wallensteins Ende* (Prague, 1977), #25 (p. 28).

most of Montferrat. So as the Electoral Convention of Regensburg opened on June 3, 1630, the military position in Italy of Ferdinand and the Spaniards had greatly improved.

Ferdinand had always defended the Catholic interpretation of the Religious Peace of Augsburg. Divisions over the understanding of the Peace had characterized the Diet of Regensburg back in 1608 when Ferdinand presided as the representative of Emperor Rudolf. After the defeat of the Bohemian and Austrian rebels and of Frederick of the Palatinate, considerable confiscation and redistribution of lands had taken place. Catholics began to recognize the opportunity to reclaim more secularized church lands and so realize a goal that many had for a long time envisioned. At first, prelates petitioned the Imperial Court Council for restoration in individual cases. But this turned out to be a slow process. So eventually some Catholics took up the idea of a general restitution of all church lands seized, in their eyes illegally, by the Protestants since the Religious Peace of 1555. So there came about the fateful Edict of Restitution of 1629, the measure that most clearly stamped the Thirty Years War as a religious conflict and represented a tragic overreach on the part of Ferdinand and other Catholic princes.

The idea for a general restitution seems to have originated with the archbishop-elector of Mainz, Johann von Schweikard, and his confessor, the Jesuit Reinhard Ziegler. About two months after Tilly's advance into the Lower Saxon Circle, in September 1625, Mainz sent Ziegler off to Munich and Vienna with a proposal. "It almost has the appearance," Schweikard wrote, "that the good God wants to furnish us with a suitable opportunity and circumstances to seek this [the return of church lands] more suitably and to obtain it more easily. This chance we cannot justly pass up; rather we must diligently take advantage of it."[42] So God's Providence was invoked as summoning the Catholic princes to action. The forum for this measure was to be a diet where there would surely be a Catholic majority. Reassurances should be given to Saxony as back at Mühlhausen in 1620 that no measures were aimed at it since it had seized bishoprics prior to 1555.

But neither Maximilian nor Ferdinand showed enthusiasm for the project at this time, both of them less optimistic about the military and political situation. Ziegler had an audience with Ferdinand and Eggenberg between October 2 and 6. Both Ferdinand and Lamormaini were, significantly, uncertain of the legality of the proposed measure, Carafa reported later.[43]

---

[42] Presented in Munich, Sept. 17, 1625, Munich, Bayeriches Hauptstaatsarchiv, Abteilung 2, Geheimes Staatsarchiv, Kasten schwarz 769, ff. 147–50v; see BANF 2: 368, n. 1.
[43] Ziegler to Mainz, Oct. 6, 1625, BANF 2, #117. Imperial response to Ziegler's proposition, Oct. 12, 1625, HHStA, Mainz 120; Carafa to Barberini, Jan. 21, 1626, BL 6949, ff. 6–8.

A policy of widespread restitution of church property still faced substantial opposition in Vienna in March 1627, according to Carafa.[44] The successes of the campaigns that year helped to reduce the reservations. That summer preparations were under way for the Electoral Convention of Mühlhausen to convene in October. Ferdinand selected Stralendorf for his representative at the convention. The procurator of the Bursfeld Benedictine Congregation had now come forward with a request for the restitution of all the Benedictine monasteries in the Lower Saxon Circle that had been confiscated by the Protestants. Ferdinand wrote in his first instruction for Stralendorf dated July 25 that those he had consulted considered the requested restitution to be in line with the imperial constitution, that is, the Religious Peace, but he still hesitated to act because of the guarantees that he had given to Saxony and Brandenburg at Mühlhausen in 1620 and subsequently, and because of the fear of new conflict. Stralendorf should take the matter up with the electors.[45]

Then, in a new instruction from Ferdinand dated October 4, a startling change appeared. Their victories had given the Catholic forces the clear upper hand. The time had come to restore to the Catholics all the lands that had been taken from them illegally since 1555. This was to be "the great gain and fruit of the war." Stralendorf was to elaborate this for the Catholic electors and to seek their advice on the best means to take advantage of the God-given opportunity to secure the Catholics their rights. "Just as up to now we [Ferdinand] have never thought to let pass any chance to gain the restitution of church lands," he added, "neither do we intend now or in the future to have to bear the responsibility before posterity of having neglected or failed to exploit even the least opportunity." There was mention of neither the Religious Peace nor of the Mühlhausen guarantee.[46]

At nearly the same time, a similar shift from caution to militance took place with both Maximilian and Mainz. Nearly the same expressions were used by the two as by Ferdinand. Despite the dangers, Maximilian advised Mainz, "We [see] that the opportunity presented to us by God should be accepted and the course pointed out by him continued." God's Providence showed the way that they should take.[47] Can this convergence of views have been fortuitous? We can speculate, but only that, that the three confessors – Lamormaini in Vienna, Contzen in Munich, and Ziegler in Aschaffenburg – had a hand in it. Lamormaini subsequently claimed for himself an important role in the issuance of the Edict; yet there are no documents supporting his claim this early, and it is doubtful that the idea of the Edict stemmed from him.[48] Contzen boldly urged

---

[44] Carafa to Barberini, Mar. 3, 1627, BL 6950, ff. 13–16v.
[45] Jul. 25, 1627, Rome, Archivio Congregazione de Propaganda Fide, Scritture originali riferite nelle Congregazioni Generali, ff. 144–5 (Latin trans., ff. 143–43v).
[46] Ferdinand to Stralendorf, HHStA, RTA 97b, ff. 206–7.
[47] Maximilian to Mainz, Sept. 7, 1627, Kschw, 773.
[48] See, for example, Duhr, *Geschichte der Jesuiten in den Ländern deutscher Zunge* 2: 1 (Freiburg, 1913): 464.

the restitution of church lands in Munich, as he had done two years previously. The elector of Mainz, then, accompanied by Ziegler, vigorously advocated the restitution of church lands at Mühlhausen.[49]

Before they left Mühlhausen the Catholic electors, riding their victories, obtained the consent of Saxony and Brandenburg for a joint recommendation to the emperor that he render a decision regarding ecclesiastical lands according to the Peace of Augsburg and the imperial constitution. The Protestant electors insisted, however, that there be added to this the vague phrase, "to the extent and inasmuch as submission is made."[50] They were not ready to turn the decision over to the emperor without any further input from a diet or from the interested parties. At Stralendorf's bidding, then, the Catholic electors, in a confidential communication for Ferdinand, advocated the restoration of all church property seized by the Protestants since 1555. They considered the juridical case closed; they wanted action.[51]

Consultations over the restitution of church property urged by the Catholic electors continued in Vienna through 1628. Lamormaini aimed through Carafa to secure support from the pope for Ferdinand's *Imprese cosi gloriose*.[52] Urban responded with a brief to Ferdinand on behalf of the claims of the bishop of Basel, just at the time that the issue of Mantua was heating up. "Not only does the Catholic religion triumph in your victories, but the ecclesiastical order finds in them its firmest support. The churches in Germany hope to regain their former extent and endowment now that the Emperor Ferdinand is victorious. One word from the imperial authority is able to extort from the belly of heretical impiety the sacred riches which it devoured with such rapacity." So the pope wrote on March 25.[53]

That winter of 1627–1628, from the strong position that he occupied, Ferdinand along with his councillors turned to another major issue, the succession in the imperial office. Young Ferdinand Ernst had been crowned King of Hungary in 1625 and King of Bohemia in the fall of 1627. What remained was to insure his succession in the Empire by his election as king of the Romans. Stability in the Empire as well as continued consolidation in the hereditary territories demanded this step. Should Ferdinand die without a designated successor, the ensuing interregnum could result in chaos with France, Denmark, and even Sweden fishing in the troubled waters of the Empire. Even the Protestant electors of Saxony and Brandenburg appreciated this. Assurance of the succession would make possible a much freer exercise of imperial authority in the interest of Church and Empire as Vienna foresaw it. The electors would lose the possibility of exerting pressure on the

---

[49] Bireley 2, 55–6.   [50] Electors to the Emperor, Nov. 4, 1627, BANF 3, # 470 (pp. 738–40).
[51] BANF 3: 697, n.1.   [52] Carafa to Barberini, Feb. 16, 1628, BL ff. 36–8.
[53] Catholic Electors to Nov. 12, 1627, BL 2198, f. 40v.

emperor through the exercise of their votes for the imperial office. Precisely for that reason they opposed an election at this time.

A long memorandum – drawn up by Stralendorf with the help of Trautmannsdorf and Abbot Anton Wolfradt – read before the emperor, the King of Hungary, and Eggenberg, on January 21 and 22, 1628, declared that the emperor's first priority had to be the succession. They agreed in deference to Lamormaini's view that God's power had enabled Ferdinand to obtain victories that they could never have foreseen. But they urged caution in the pursuit of the restoration of church lands which the Catholic electors were now urging. Before initiating an active policy toward the widespread restitution of church lands which might alienate Saxony and Brandenburg, the succession had to be guaranteed. In general, they recommended a policy of caution. They warned against a pursuit of "absolute power" in the Empire, a charge Ferdinand always sought to avoid, they reminded him, and they called for a generous peace with Denmark. More triumphs would only call forth new enemies determined to limit the emperor's power in the Empire.[54]

Ferdinand's councillors recommended a convocation of the electors solely for the purpose of the election of the king of the Romans. Ferdinand then raised the issue with Maximilian and with the new archbishop-elector of Mainz, Georg Friedrich von Greiffenklau, who had succeeded the deceased Schweikard in 1626. Neither found Ferdinand's initiative acceptable. Maximilian wanted a conference that would take up other issues, especially peace with Denmark and the threat that the electors now felt coming from the steady growth and the conduct of Wallenstein's army. Eventually they agreed on an electoral convention, which did not convene until June 1630. The persistent opposition of the electors prevented Ferdinand from obtaining the succession for his son at the electoral convention. The aforementioned paper of the councillors Stralendorf, Trautmannsdorf, and Abbot Anton Wolfradt recommended that the Imperial Court Council review the legal situation surrounding the Religious Peace. This last item probably represented some reservations about the legality of the proposed restitution of church property, which Ferdinand himself seems to have now developed, but it may also have been a pretext to cloak their political doubts.[55] Trautmannsdorf, when he journeyed to Munich to negotiate the return of Upper Austria in early 1628, had recommended caution with regard to the measures regarding church property, but Maximilian wanted to exploit the present opportunity that might not return.[56]

Plans for the restitution of church property now stalled in Vienna, until a joint letter to the emperor in September 1628 from five south German

---

[54] HHStA, Kriegsakten 79, ff. 58–91; see Bireley 2, 58–9, 244, n.52; Brockmann, 290–2, 320–4.
[55] HHStA, Krieg. 79, ff. 58–91; see Bireley 2, 59, and esp. p. 244, n. 52; Emperor to the privy council and to the president of the Imperial Court Council, Jan. 15, 1628, ibid., RTA 98, ff. 1–1v.
[56] Maximilian's response to Trautmannsdorf's proposal, Feb. 21, 1628, BANF 4, #30.

prelates – the bishops of Bamberg, Würzburg, Eichstätt, Constance, and Augsburg – moved them forward. Not privy officially to the recommendations made by the electors at Mühlhausen, they called for the restitution of all church lands seized since 1555. For the Imperial Court Council to deal with individual cases would take forever. Now was the time to act.[57] Ferdinand requested an opinion from the Imperial Court Council and the privy council. The former encouraged action on the bishops' behalf but the latter still hesitated, largely for political reasons. They wanted further assurance of support from the Catholic electors. So a provisional draft was sent to Maximilian and Mainz for comment on October 25. The preamble reaffirmed that the victories given the emperor by God enabled him to restore peace to the Empire and uproot the cause of much strife by a return to the observance of the Religious Peace of Augsburg. The responsibility of his office left the emperor no alternative. The text elaborated the legal case for the Edict and then turned to its main provisions. All territorial and imperial church lands seized since the Peace of Augsburg were subject to restitution.[58] So not even the vote of a cathedral chapter in favor of a Protestant candidate was valid. Also invalid was the controversial Declaration of Ferdinand I, which had apparently allowed freedom of religion in the ecclesiastical territories; so the ecclesiastical princes could enforce uniformity of religion in the same way as other princes. In an accompanying letter then, Ferdinand asked whether the two electors were prepared to assist effectively in the implementation of the Edict.[59] Stralendorf, in a further letter at Ferdinand's behest, asked the two electors whether an attempt should be made to reclaim church property seized before 1552 as some desired – nuncio Pallotto comes to mind – and whether Calvinism should be prohibited, a measure desired by Maximilian as it would make even more difficult any return of Frederick of the Palatinate. Stralendorf seemed to hope for negative response to both queries because of a fear shared by Ferdinand of attempting too much at once.[60]

Meanwhile, Bishop Heinrich von Knöringen of Augsburg took action to defend the legality of the coming Edict when the Imperial Court Council and the privy council seemed to have second thoughts. He commissioned Paul Laymann, Jesuit theologian and canon lawyer at the University of Dillingen, to write a defense of the Catholic interpretation of the Peace of Augsburg. The result was *The Way to Peace* (Compositio Pacis), which was labelled "the Dillingen Book" because of its anonymous publication. Laymann argued forcefully and clearly the case for the Catholic understanding of the Religious

---

[57] Sept. 7, 1628, BANF 4, #134.
[58] It was disputed whether the Religious Peace had prohibited the confiscation of church property from the date of the Peace of Passau in 1552 or the Religious Peace itself three years later.
[59] The draft is in KSchw, 69, ff. 110–28, the letter in ibid., ff. 63–5.
[60] BANF 4, #159; see Brockmann, 363.

Peace.⁶¹ Fascicles of the book started to come off the press in early January 1629 and were immediately shipped to Vienna. *The Way to Peace* received an enthusiastic reception in Vienna, especially by Stralendorf, partly because of its value as a "white book" for the Edict and partly because it enabled Ferdinand honestly to contend that he was merely carrying out the "clear letter" of the Religious Peace. He was not interpreting it. Any remaining hesitation or scruple about the legality of the Edict was removed.⁶² Ferdinand himself remarked in a communication to Collalto in mid-November that "the whole fruit of the victories bestowed on us by God" lay in the recovery of the church lands.⁶³

The Imperial Court Council took up the responses of Maximilian and Mainz as soon as they arrived in Vienna around January 11, 1629. The assurance of support from the two electors should the Edict meet resistance satisfied the council. But it did not favor the suggestion of the electors that a list be drawn up of all the properties subject to restitution. The Edict represented precisely an attempt to bypass the delays that the compilation of such a list as well as detailed attention to individual cases would require. Neither elector considered it wise to attempt to regain church lands confiscated before 1555. The council opposed the prohibition of Calvinism in the Edict but it was inserted anyway in an indirect form by Stralendorf to whom Maximilian had addressed a letter endorsing it; only the Confession of Augsburg was to be permitted. The council decided on both legal and political grounds not to involve the imperial cities in the Edict. The emperor and the privy council made the final decision to promulgate the Edict on March 6, 1629.⁶⁴ The Edict was then published on March 25, precisely the day on which copies of *The Way to Peace* went on sale at the Frankfurt Book Fair. The book was intended to garner popular support for Vienna's argument that with the Edict, Ferdinand was only implementing the clear intent of the Peace of Religion.⁶⁵

The Edict pointed to a massive transfer of church property from the Protestants to the Catholics. It included the imperial prince-archbishoprics and

---

⁶¹ The first edition appeared at Dillingen early in 1629, and later that same year a slightly expanded edition followed. A German translation came the next year.

⁶² Robert Bireley, "The Origins of the *Pacis Compositio*," 1629: A Text of Paul Laymann, S.J.," *Archivum Historicum Societatis Jesu* 42 (1973): 106–37. In HHStA, Religion 33, ff. 129–35v, there is a document entitled "Pronunciata circa Pacification Religionis." Undated, it is found among the documents of late 1628. In my opinion, it is clearly a summary of Laymann's *Pacis Compositio*.

⁶³ Ferdinand to Collalto, Nov. 15, 1628, Peter Ritter von Chlumecky, *Die Regesten der Archive im Marktgrafthume Mähren* 1: *Die Regesten oder die chronologischen Verzeichnisse der Urkunden in den Archiven zur Iglau ... samt den noch ungedrückten Briefens Kaiser Ferdinands des Zweiten, Albrechts von Waldstein und Ramboalds Grafen Collalto* (Brunn, 1856) 2: #xxxvi (pp. 272–4).

⁶⁴ HHStA, Religion 34, 1, f. 36v; Bireley 2, 77–9.

⁶⁵ Bireley, "Origins of the *Pacis Compositio*, 1629," 109, 119; The text of the Edict is found in Michael Casper Londorp, *Der romischen kayserlichen Majestät ... Acta Publica und schriftliche Handlungen* 3 (Frankfurt, 1668): 1048–54.

bishoprics Magdeburg, Bremen, Halberstadt, Minden, Verden, and Ratzeburg, all but Minden in the Lower Saxon or Lower Rhenish-Westphalian Circles, Schwerin already in Wallenstein's hands, and possibly Lübeck and Kamin in the Upper Saxon Circle. The bishoprics held by Saxony and Brandenburg seemed safe for the time being, due to their confiscation before 1552 and to the Mühlhausen guarantee. Beyond this, the Edict looked to the restitution of about 500 territorial institutions, mostly monasteries. In many of these cases the institutions had been incorporated into the territory and their loss would disrupt the territory's integrity. This was especially the case for Württemberg and Brunswick-Wolfenbüttel. But to understand the full impact of the Edict, one must take into consideration the threat that it implied for the Protestants should the Catholics retain the upper hand. Laymann's *The Way to Peace* suggested many further ways in which the Religious Peace might be interpreted to the benefit of the Catholics, for example, in the contention that in all controversial cases, the Catholics were to be favored because the Catholics based their position on ancient and general law, the Protestants on privilege and particular law. By January, 1628, Lamormaini had already alerted Vitelleschi to the need to prepare missionaries for the territory to be recovered from the Protestants, and as a New Year's gift at the start of 1630, he submitted to Ferdinand a plan for a network of Jesuit colleges in the north of Germany, including Saxony and Brandenburg.[66]

Three days after the publication of the Edict, Lamormaini notified Cardinal Barberini of "a deed truly worthy of this Emperor." "No Roman Pontiff since the time of Charlemagne has received such a harvest of joys from Germany," he wrote, "so that we can call Urban VIII blessed since he witnesses such gains for the Catholic religion." Lamormaini was confident that Ferdinand would lead all Germany back to the Catholic faith provided the Lord allowed Ferdinand ten more years of life and, significantly, enabled him to avoid war in Italy.[67]

Little open opposition to the main thrust of the Edict, the recovery of church property, surfaced in Vienna, though only Lamormaini demonstrated enthusiasm for it. The Catholic electors and ecclesiastical princes had supplied the initiative and momentum for the Edict. Stralendorf cautiously supported it, reinforced by Maximilian's urging and Laymann's *The Way to Peace*. Trautmannsdorf had manifested reservations about the policy during his visit to Munich in early 1628. Eggenberg seems to have been unhappy with the Edict but this does not mean that he actively opposed it. In the winter of 1628–1629, he was frequently ill, and he was absent from the session of the privy council on March 6 when Ferdinand formally approved the Edict. He lamented in mid-March to the bishop of Mantua that Ferdinand did not consult him now

---

[66] Vitelleschi to Lamormaini, Jan. 15, 1628, ARSJ, Aust. 3II, f. 954; "Vita Lamormaini," f. 56v–8; Vitellleschi to Lamormaini, Mar. 2, 1630, ARSJ, Aust. 4I, f. 240.
[67] Lamormaini to Barberini, Mar. 28, 1629, BL 7054, f. 72.

as he usually did even when he lay sick in bed, and he indicated that he was thinking of retirement after thirty years of service of the House of Austria in order to look to the care of his soul. He had asked Lamormaini to secure permission from Ferdinand to return to private life, and Ferdinand had granted it.[68] But Eggenberg did not retire. Ferdinand had not yet ordered troops to Italy, so that Lamormaini prevailed over Eggenberg on this issue also. Wallenstein was not happy with the Edict. At this point he saw a need to retrench, as we have seen; he was encouraging the Peace of Lübeck with Denmark and discouraging involvement in Italy. In addition, he feared that to take church lands from Protestant princes who had not opposed the emperor would incite hostility to the emperor at the grass roots and promote religious conflict. But he made no attempt to prevent its issuance, and it is difficult to determine the extent to which his view was known in Vienna.[69] Only Collalto, president of the war council, upon being asked for his view, warned the emperor clearly about the dangers the Edict was likely to provoke. It would stir opposition to Ferdinand in Germany and in the long run incite religious war there, and it would undercut intervention in Italy which Collalto strongly endorsed.[70]

How did Rome react to the Edict? Here one must distinguish between Rome's position and the way it was perceived in Vienna. As we have seen the previous spring, Urban had praised the emperor for his efforts to reclaim church property in a brief supporting the claims of the bishop of Basel. Both Pallotto and Pier Luigi Carafa, the nuncio in Cologne, on the scene in Germany, favored Ferdinand's policy of restitution and were inclined to advocate for more imperial participation in the distribution of recovered lands than was the Curia. So they communicated an impression of greater support from the Curia than was the case, an impression that Lamormaini was only too glad to receive. Shortly after the Edict was published, Pallotto let Barberini know that Ferdinand expected "some notable demonstration of joy" at the event, similar to the Te Deum in the French church in Rome with which Urban had celebrated Louis XIII's victory at La Rochelle.[71] But Barberini was not enthusiastic. The pope would send "an affectionate and laudatory" brief to the emperor and praise his action in consistory. But to celebrate as in the case of La Rochelle would be to do so at the start and not the end of the campaign. A major reason for Rome's response was juridical. The Religious Peace of Augsburg, with its concessions to heretics, had never been recognized by Rome. The pope would not now, Barberini wrote Pallotto, even implicitly acknowledge its validity "either in words or deeds," and he would attend to this in his brief.[72] But in

---

[68] Quazza, 1: 313; Hans von Zwiedeneck-Südenhorst, *Hans Ulrich Fürst von Eggenberg* (Vienna, 1880), 90–1.
[69] Mann, *Wallenstein*, 635–9.   [70] Collalto to the emperor, Dec. 14, 1628, BANF 4, #191.
[71] Pallotto to Barberini, Apr. 7, 1629, NBD 2: *Nuntiature des Pallotto*, 2: #85.
[72] Barberini to Pallotto, Apr. 28, 1629, ibid., #97.

the brief, in which Urban later admitted that an enthusiastic secretary might have exaggerated his feelings, the pope wrote: "Our soul has been filled with a marvelous joy by the recent Edict of Your Majesty which orders the sectaries to return to the priestly estate the ecclesiastical lands they have long held ... Thus heresy will have learned that the gates of hell do not prevail against the church which legions of angels and the arms of powerful Austria so happily defend. How closely you have bound the soul of the pontiff to yourself ... our nuncio will declare to you in a more magnificent fashion."[73] It is hard to see how Ferdinand could have seen anything in this but a hearty endorsement of the Edict. Yet the following February 15, Pallotto was instructed, this time in a communication from the Congregation for the Propagation of the Faith, that while encouraging the emperor's efforts for the return of lands confiscated by the Protestants, he carefully avoid any explicit endorsement of the Edict.[74]

Three issues dominated Ferdinand's political agenda during the months following the issuance of the Edict: Wallenstein, the war in North Italy, and the Edict. Gradually, Ferdinand and the Catholic electors came to consider an electoral convention with the emperor there in person the best means to deal with these and other issues, especially the likelihood of a Swedish invasion in north Germany. Accordingly, in March 1630, the elector of Mainz summoned such a convention for Regensburg, to open on June 3, 1630.

The electoral convention came to resemble a mini-European peace conference. The normal delays held up the opening until July 3. Traveling up the Danube by boat, Ferdinand reached Regensburg on June 19 accompanied in magnificent style by Eleonore, who would be crowned empress in the course of the convention, the king of Hungary, members of the privy and Imperial Court Council, and all together 3,000 persons whom it took ninety-nine tables to feed along the way. Notable among them were the emperor's beloved musicians, seventy-five of them including two female singers with their husbands and children.[75] While in Regensburg Ferdinand kept in touch with events in Vienna through regular correspondence with Seifried Christoph von Breuner, governor of Lower Austria and a privy councillor, occasionally asking him to ship sturgeon, fresh peaches, wine, and later cider to Regensburg.[76] Within the week

---

[73] Urban VIII to the emperor, May 26, 1629, NBD 2: *Nuntiature des Pallotto*, 2: #102.

[74] Propaganda Fide to Pallotto, Feb. 15, 1630, NBD 4, *Nuntiaturen des Giovanni Battista Pallotto e des Ciriaco Rocci (1630–1631)*, ed. Rotraud Becker (Tübingen, 2009): #16.2 (p. 87). The Congregation for the Propagation of the faith was created in 1622 to oversee the missionary activities of the church in Europe as well as across the seas.

[75] Franzl, 302–3; Steven Saunders, *Crown, Sword, and Lyre: Sacred Music at the Imperial Court of Ferdinand II of Habsburg, 1619–1636* (Oxford, 1995), 21 and note 18.

[76] "Aus dem Gräflich Breuner'schen Archive zu Aspern an der Zaya," *Notizenblatt: Beilage zu Archiv für Kunde österreichischer Geschichtsquellen* 2 (1852): 73–5, 89, 90. Seventy-two letters from Ferdinand (and Ferdinand III) to Breuner from 1621 to 1636 are published here over several numbers.

the four Catholic electors arrived: Maximilian; his brother Ferdinand, archbishop-elector of Cologne; the pro-French Philip Christoph von Sötern, archbishop-elector of Trier; and Anselm Casimir vom Wambold, archbishop-elector of Mainz, who had succeeded the deceased Greiffenklau. He was to serve a a prominent voice for the electors and an advocate of understanding with the Protestants.[77] As a protest against the Edict and the burden of Wallenstein's army, Saxony and Brandenburg stayed away in person and sent a delegation. Nearly all the European states sent representatives. Carlos Doria, Duke of Tursi, came as an extraordinary ambassador of Spain with instructions to keep in close touch with Eggenberg. He was to advance the Spanish position on Italy and to argue for imperial support for the Spaniards in the Netherlands.[78] Richelieu's emissaries, the veteran diplomat Charles Brûlart de Léon, and the legendary associate of the cardinal, the Capuchin Father Joseph du Tremblay, only arrived on July 30. Pallotto had been named a cardinal, and his presence at Regensburg threatened to raise sticky problems of precedence, so he was replaced by the nuncio in Lucerne, Ciriaco Rocci who only turned up on August 15. His first task was peace in Italy with the investiture of Nevers. He was instructed to keep in close touch with Maximilian and to follow his lead in all matters touching the electors. Barberini had never told Pallotto of the secret negotiations that Rome was fostering between Paris and Munich, and Rocci was not informed of them either.[79] A minister of the exiled Frederick of the Palatinate was there in company with an English colleague as well as emissaries of many Italian and German states both Catholic and Protestant. According to Reinhard Ziegler, who now served as confessor to the new archbishop-elector of Mainz, thirty-odd Jesuits including Adam Contzen were squeezed into the college in Regensburg. Lamormaini stayed with the imperial party.

The general goal of the convention, according to the initial proposition proposed to the electors by Ferdinand, was to bring about a just peace in the Empire and to settle in the meantime on the necessary measures to defend it against internal and external enemies. Ferdinand came to Regensburg willing to make some compromises. He was ready to listen to the complaints of the electors about the imperial military and Wallenstein. He hoped to obtain the electors' support for his intervention in Italy, which he failed to do, and for defense against the prospective invasion of Gustav Adolph where he

---

[77] On Anselm Casimir, see now Franz Brendle, *Der Erzkanzler im Religionskrieg. Kurfürst Anselm Casimir von Mainz, die geistlichen Fürsten und das Reich 1629–1647* (Münster, 2011).
[78] Philip IV to Tursi, Jul. 15, 1630, Heinrich Günter, *Die Habsburgerliga 1625–1635; Briefe und Akten aus dem General-Archiv zu Simancas* (Berlin, 1908): #32.
[79] Barberini to Rocci, Aug. 10 and 17, 1630, Repgen 1: 2: ##16, 17; see ibid. 1: 1: 201–22; Dieter Albrecht, "Die kurialen Anweisungen für den Nuntius Rocci zu den Regensburger Kurfürstentag 1630," *Quellen und Forschungen aus italienischen Archiven und Bibliotheken* 35 (1955): 282–9.

succeeded. There was no serious attempt to win the electors over to the assistance of the Spaniards in the Netherlands; Ferdinand never showed an interest in this. The Catholic electors had determined they would not proceed with the election of young Ferdinand as king of the Romans until there was general agreement about the issues facing the Empire. Saxony and Brandenburg wanted their grievances remedied regarding the military and the Edict before any election, and none of the electors wanted to surrender at this time their main bargaining point with the emperor. Recognizing the situation, Ferdinand did not push the issue. The Edict was the most important issue at the convention even though it was not on the official agenda. Would Ferdinand and the Catholic electors compromise on it for the sake of internal peace and the assistance of the Protestant princes, especially Saxony and Brandenburg, against the enemies of the Empire, in particular Gustav Adolph who landed on the Baltic coast with an army of 14,000 during the second week of the convention?

Ferdinand was not prepared for the onslaught of the Catholic electors who insisted at the start that the reform of the imperial military and the fate of Wallenstein be moved to first place on the agenda. This shifted the focus of the convention from assistance of the electors to the emperor in defense of the Empire to Wallenstein and the military and ultimately to the role of the emperor in the Empire.[80] Initially, Ferdinand had intended to retain the general and to satisfy the general's critics with minor reforms. But all the electors voted on July 16 to demand the dismissal of Wallenstein as well as a reduction of the number of troops under arms and relief from the burden of supporting the army, this just as Gustav Adolph was landing on German soil, and they communicated this to Ferdinand the next day. This placed Ferdinand on the defensive, threatening to force him to choose between the dismissal of Wallenstein and the diminution of his power on the one hand and a break with the electors on the other.[81] The privy council first committed the matter to a deputation that included Stralendorf. Eggenberg was not included. Ferdinand bound all involved to silence. After a couple exchanges, the four Catholic electors took their complaints to Ferdinand in person on July 30.

Following deliberation, on August 5 the privy council recommended the dismissal of Wallenstein. The general had been neither insubordinate nor disloyal, they recognized, though they were wary of the power he had come to possess and thought that his maintenance in office would confirm the misplaced fear that Ferdinand aimed at an absolute government, a charge they wanted to refute. The only alternative to his release, they emphasized, was a

---

[80] Brockmann, 402,
[81] Minutes of the meeting of the council of electors, BANF 5: 454–5 and n.2. (All the documentation of the Electoral Convention of Regensburg is included under #170, which runs for 315 pages. So I indicate the page rather than the document number.)

clear break with the Catholic electors and this would be disastrous. All the electors would then probably unite against Vienna, and no one know where this might lead especially when one considered the looming threat from Sweden. Furthermore, a break with the electors would certainly obstruct the succession of the king of Hungary. A further week of deliberation followed before Ferdinand informed the electors in an audience on August 13 that he was prepared to dismiss Wallenstein. It was not an easy decision for him. The decision was not made public for close to a month, in order to prepare properly for the notification of the general who submitted meekly but certainly resentful.[82]

Lamormaini recommended the dismissal of the general for the same reason as did the councillors, the need to maintain a united front with the Catholic electors which he, of course, considered necessary for a successful Catholic restoration. Ferdinand sent a handwritten note, dated just "August," to Lamormaini that shows the role that he and Contzen played as go-betweens at the convention. The emperor directed his confessor to try to create with Contzen a positive impression of Eggenberg, whose loyalty he could vouch for after many years of friendship. "For Friedland I do not vouch at all," Ferdinand continued, "and I hope in the Lord that after I have revealed my opinion to the Elector and to him [Contzen], if we have not been able to agree the first and second time, we will at last come to a good conclusion in common agreement."[83] With this note Ferdinand probably wanted to assure Maximilian of his decision on Wallenstein before he informed the other electors. Eggenberg was suspect to the electors because he was close to Wallenstein, yet he made no attempt to save the general as far as we know, perhaps because he, too, realized that there was no realistic alternative to the dismissal.

The struggle for control of the imperial military did not end with the dismissal of Wallenstein. The electors wanted to replace him with Maximilian, and the imperial camp even came to agree with this but under restrictions that were unacceptable to the electors. Precisely at this time Eggenberg broached the issue of the election of young Ferdinand as king of the Romans to the electors. Perhaps if Ferdinand accepted Maximilian as commander of the imperial army, the electors would vote for the succession. But the electors were not inclined to such a deal, partly because it would look as if they had yielded on the issue under pressure.[84] Ferdinand and Eggenberg did raise the succession with the Catholic electors once more at the end of October and in early November

---

[82] The crucial paper of the privy council of Aug. 5 is published in Gindely, *Waldstein wähend seines ersten Generalats* 2: 280–87; Brockmann, 405–11.

[83] Dudik, 273.

[84] Minutes of the conference of the imperial councillors and their position paper, Aug. 15–16, BANF 5: 507–8, 510–13; see also Saxony and Brandenburg to Mainz, Oct. 7, 1630, BANF 5: 691–3, with notes.

but they got nowhere. They now hoped to convene a diet in the coming summer or fall where the election would take place.[85]

On September 3, Saxony, upset about the Edict, informed Ferdinand that he planned to convoke a conference of Protestant states to discuss their common grievances. This stirred fears in the Catholic camp of the revival of the pre-war Protestant Union.[86] About the same time the other Catholic electors seemed ready in the interests of peace to restore some of his territory to Frederick of the Palatinate, a move opposed by Maximilian as communicated to Ferdinand through Lamormaini.[87] This initiative was closed off by Frederick's refusal to make any compromise. But both these developments likely convinced Maximilian to recognize the need to stand firm in a united Catholic front with Ferdinand. So he withdrew his candidacy for the generalship of the imperial army. The Catholic electors were not happy with his withdrawal, and negotiations continued over the form of the imperial military until after the Treaty of Regensburg of October 13 between Ferdinand and France seemed to end the war in Italy.

Both Ferdinand and the Catholic electors then agreed to another compromise regarding the military proposed by Maximilian on October 21 at the same conference of the Catholic electors when he refused to take any responsibility for discussing a compromise on the Edict.[88] Maximilian joined Ferdinand on the Edict and yielded to him on the military. The armies of the League and of the emperor were to remain in their current state until a peace settlement. Regular conferences between the leaders of each army would coordinate strategy, winter quarters, and other issues. Subsequently, Tilly was named commander of both armies in a clumsy arrangement whereby he was responsible to Maximilian for the League forces and to Ferdinand for the imperial army. So Maximilian's initiative provided for a balance between the imperial and League armies, thus strengthening his bond with Ferdinand as he stood with him on the Edict. But the removal of Wallenstein and then the protracted negotiations over the organization of the military weakened the ability of the Catholic forces to meet the advance of Gustav Adolph.

The two French emissaries at Regensburg, Brülart de Léon and Father Joseph, had been instructed to make contact with the electors and cooperate with them, but nothing had been said about talks with the emperor. The presence of the two in Regensburg made it easier for the emperor and the electors to discuss another issue that divided them, the emperor's campaign in Italy. The Catholic

---

[85] Rocci to Barberini, Nov. 4, 1630, NBD 4, *Nuntiaturen des Pallotto und Rocci*, #125.1 (p. 351); Bireley 2, 126.
[86] Saxony to the Emperor, Sept. 3, 1630, BANF 5, p. 678, discussed at the Sept. 16th meeting of the councillors of the Catholic electors, Sept. 16, 1630, ibid., 580–5, 678.
[87] Lamormaini to Ferdinand, Sept. 18, 1630, Dudik, 337–8.
[88] Conference of the councillors of the Catholic electors, Oct. 21, 1630, BANF 5, 643–6.

electors convinced Ferdinand to suggest to the two Frenchmen that the negotiations then under way in Italy be transferred to Regensburg. Indeed, two days after their arrival, Brülart and Father Joseph met with Ferdinand and Lamormaini. The imperial conquest of Mantua in July and the Spanish successes had strengthened Ferdinand's bargaining position. The electors now urged him to withdraw from the Italian theater so as to free troops to confront Gustav Adolph. Talks began on August 11, two days before Ferdinand announced his decision on Wallenstein to the electors. Ferdinand assured him, Rocci wrote on August 19, after his first audience with the emperor, "Monsignore, we will have peace, but not so quickly." The advance of the Swedes persuaded most of the ministers toward a peaceful settlement.[89]

Finally, on October 13, the Treaty of Regensburg was concluded. The peace was beneficial for Ferdinand. It required Nevers to submit to the emperor in proper form, and so it acknowledged his jurisdiction in north Italy. Ferdinand then promised to invest him with Mantua and Montferrat within three months. Richelieu's efforts to form an anti-imperial alliance would have been effectively countered had the critical first article of the treaty been carried out. According to this provision, France promised not to give aid directly or indirectly to the emperor's enemies inside or outside the Empire. Ferdinand promised the equivalent for France. Imperial and French forces were to withdraw from Italy and the Swiss passes in carefully delineated stages. Spain, which was not a party to the treaty, was to abandon Casale to Nevers.[90] Lamormaini had good reason to rejoice; the Spaniards were furious.

Only at the very end of the convention did the news arrive in Regensburg that Richelieu would not ratify the treaty negotiated by his agents; they had exceeded their instructions. The cardinal would not accept the crucial first article and so give up his attempt to form an allied front against Ferdinand, despite the serious illness of Louis XIII and the prospective ascendancy of his enemies including the Queen Mother, Marie de Medici. Just at that time a French envoy was negotiating the terms of France's support of Gustav Adolph's invasion of the Empire.

The chief grievance of Saxony and Brandenburg, as well as of the emissaries of other Protestant states that flocked to Regensburg, was directed against the Edict of Restitution. Neither Maximilian nor Saxony had wanted it on the agenda. The elector of Saxony felt that he had been manipulated by a Catholic majority at Mühlhausen three years before, and he did not want to repeat the experience. Maximilian was firmly behind the Edict, and at Regensburg he opted clearly for solidarity with Ferdinand, regarding it over common cause with his fellow electors Saxony and Brandenburg. But he was intent to keep from the Protestants as much as he could his responsibility for the Edict.

---

[89] Rocci to Barberini, Aug. 19, 1630, Repgen 1: 2: #18.   [90] Albrecht 1, 293–5.

Ferdinand was to bear the onus for it.[91] Had Ferdinand and Maximilian been able to bring themselves to compromise on the Edict, they probably would have been able to keep the allegiance of the two Protestant electors, and so to defend effectively against the Swedish invasion or at least to prevent it from becoming the rout that it became. But that would have been in their eyes to surrender the restoration of Catholicism in the Empire, which was their first priority. The issue of the Edict reveals most clearly the religious dimension of the war.

Many talks and conferences were devoted to the Edict at Regensburg. Saxony persistently pressed the emperor and the Catholic electors for its revocation or at least its suspension. Other Protestant states brought their protests to the convention. Among the Catholics there did exist some sentiment for flexibility on the topic. Some argued that their territories were exhausted and that people could not make any more sacrifices for the sake of the Edict. The Saxon delegate was informed by a Bavarian privy councillor at the start of the convention that the Catholic electors had not yet decided how they would vote on the Edict, and he suggested that Bavaria would be flexible. In mid-July, it was suggested to the delegate from Brandenburg that the two Protestant electors would receive special consideration.[92] Pallotto and Rocci both reported with alarm that consideration was being given to a relaxation of the Edict.[93] In a meeting with deputies of the three Catholics electors, Maximilian, Mainz, and Cologne, and their confessors, the Jesuits Contzen of Maximilian, Ziegler of Mainz, and Georg Schröttel of Cologne, agreed that church lands could be left unchallenged with the Protestants "if we do not have the means to carry out the work." But had this point been reached, as Mainz seemed to think that it had? Concessions might be made, nearly all concluded, in cases of necessity. But when was necessity at hand, that was the question. Lamormaini and Contzen believed that the Catholic princes could expect divine aid in their efforts to restore Catholicism, and so they would have great difficulty in admitting that a state of necessity had been reached. This aid would come from France, Contzen, who knew of Maximilian's secret contacts with Richelieu, and Lamormaini anticipated, once negotiations ended the Mantuan War.[94]

Caspar Schoppe now turned up in Regensburg for the first time since the diet of 1608, and he came, following the defeat of the Calvinists, as a moderate in favor of reconciliation with the Lutherans in Germany. Prior to his arrival, he had composed a short treatise, "The Art of Serving Kings and Princes," which encouraged rulers to greater independence from their religious advisers and

---

[91] Bireley 1, 133
[92] Johannes Gebauer, *Kurbrandenburg und das Restitutionsedikt von 1629* (Halle, 1899), 105. Hallesche Abhandlungen zur neueren Geschichte, 38; Bireley 1, 133.
[93] Pallotto, Vienna, to Barberini, Aug. 3, 1630, Repgen 1: 2: #15; Rocci to Barberini, Sept. 2, 1630, BL 6967, ff. 39–48.
[94] Minutes, Aug. 3, 1630, BANF 5: 473–5; For Contzen's attitude toward France, see Bireley 1, 113, 131, 138, 155–6. 168–70.

was clearly directed against Lamormaini.[95] He secured an audience with Ferdinand on July 23. The emperor referred him to Lamormaini, and the two spent the greater part of a day together, but whether they discussed the Edict or not is not clear. But Schoppe did lobby for flexibility on it at Regensburg.[96] Schoppe's vigorous complaints to Lamormaini about corruption in the imperial government resulted in the confessor's admonitions directed to Ferdinand where he insinuated that the failure to elect the king of the Romans was God's punishment for these abuses.[97]

There was then, at the start of the convention, sentiment for flexibility on the Edict among some Catholics. Yet the Catholic electors backed Ferdinand in his rigid stance. With Lamormaini's encouragement, the emperor refused on July 11 to suspend Counter-Reformation measures in Augsburg.[98] To Saxony's report that Gustav Adolph had seized Stettin (Szczecin) at the mouth of the Oder, Ferdinand replied that he expected the elector's support against the invader. With regard to the Edict, he was, Ferdinand continued, merely administering justice, and he trusted that the Lord, the just God, would help him to deal with any difficulties. Mainz and Maximilian came to his support with letters to John George.[99]

John George's announcement in early September that he planned to convoke a conference of Protestant states upset the Catholics. It encouraged Maximilian to move toward a compromise with Ferdinand on the issue of the military as we have seen. Ferdinand's response alarmed Pallotto. The emperor indicated to Saxony that he was willing to discuss the implementation of the Edict but, significantly, not a modification of it.[100] Pressure began to build up among the Catholic electors for some form of compromise, with Mainz taking the lead. Lamormaini requested special prayers from the whole Society.[101] Maximilian hesitated to follow Mainz's lead. There must have taken place at this time a conversation reported by Schoppe. Maximilian and the Spanish ambassador, Tursi, approached Lamormaini in an attempt to convince him to incline Ferdinand toward flexibility on the Edict. According to Schoppe, Lamormaini "closed his eyes and answered them: the Edict must stand firmly, whatever evil might finally come from it. It matters little that the emperor because of it

---

[95] The full title of this manuscript was "Ars servandi animas Regum ac Principum. Accessit Lucerna scrutandae Principum conscientiae seu secretum examen." Schoppe exhorted rulers not to be the "succubi" of their confessors. See Mario d'Addio, *Il pensiero politico di Gaspare Scioppio e il Machiavellismo del Seicento* (Milan, 1962), 195-7.
[96] D'Addio, 195-8.
[97] Lamormaini to the emperor, Sept. 18 and Aug. 14, 1630, in Dudik, 337-9.
[98] HHStA, Religion. 32, f. 103; report of the committee of councillors, Jul. 10, ibid., Kriegs. 88, ff. 26-7.
[99] Emperor to Saxony, Aug. 23, 1630, HHStA, RTA 100a (iii), ff. 70-74; BANF 5, 677-8.
[100] Emperor to Saxony, Sept. 19-20, 1630, ibid., 100a (iii), ff. 66-71; Pallotto to Barberini, Oct. 5, 1630, cited in Repgen 1: 1: 224, n. 128; BANF 5: 679.
[101] Vitelleschi to Lamormaini, Nov. 23, 1630, ARSJ, Aust. 4I, f. 355, responding to Lamormaini's letters of Oct. 5, 14, and 20.

loses not only Austria but all his kingdoms and provinces and whatever he has in the world, provided he save his soul, which he cannot do without the implementation of his Edict."[102] In the text, it is not clear whether Tursi and Maximilian went to Ferdinand together or separately. So Maximilian was well aware of Lamormaini's stand, which was almost certainly, he must have thought, that of Ferdinand. Much later, Maximilian asserted that at Regensburg it was the confessors, especially Lamormaini and Contzen, who had persuaded Ferdinand and the Catholic electors that concessions on the Edict were unacceptable to conscience and that God would enable the Catholics to triumph if only they trusted in Him. Thus they refused to compromise on the Edict.[103]

The Catholic electors met on October 21. Maximilian refused to take any responsibility for a modification of the Edict and so acted against the advice of some of his own councillors.[104] At this same meeting, he initiated the compromise that resolved the dispute over the military, and so he drew closer to Ferdinand. The Peace of Regensburg had been concluded only eight days previously, thus seeming to make possible the transfer of troops from Italy to meet the advance of Gustav Adolph, and it ended another source of contention between Ferdinand and the electors. They were closing ranks. On October 22, the deputies of the Catholic electors met with a group of imperial councillors that included Stralendorf, Trautmannsdorf, and Abbot Anton Wolfradt, but not Eggenberg. Mainz's representative explained that the Edict was the chief cause of a war that the exhausted states could no longer maintain, and he urged that talks with the Protestants begin at Regensburg about its modification.[105] The following day the imperial councillors agreed to recommend to Ferdinand that he permit such talks subject to his ratification. The Catholic electors, they felt, could be trusted "to proceed with care and caution, since it was their interests above all that were at stake." The suggestion of the councillors that Ferdinand seek a statement from the electors in writing "as a permanent record" manifested their intention to make clear to posterity who was responsible for concessions.[106]

During the next two or three days, Mainz spoke directly with Eggenberg and then with Ferdinand himself. He reported back to the Catholic electors on October 26 that Eggenberg favored the start of conversations with the Protestants in Regensburg. Ferdinand approved talks with the Protestants

---

[102] This quotation and its context are taken from a manuscript prepared for the elector of Trier in 1636 entitled "De praesentibus Sacri Romani Imperii calamitatibus earumque causis et remediis." It is cited in d'Addio, *Il Pensiero Politico di Scioppio*," pp. 197–8, n. 193, from Schoppe's "De Vita Sua," Florence, Biblioteca Mediceo-Laurentia, Codici Scioppiani 223, ff. 60–71. A similar passage is found in Schoppe's Philoteca, ibid., 243, f. 446; see also f. 450.
[103] "Discurs uber des Reichs statum" (after 1637), published in Albrecht 1, 379–81; see Bireley 1, 222–3.
[104] Minutes, BANF 5: 643–6. [105] Minutes, BANF 5: 646–8.
[106] Minutes of the meeting of the imperial councillors, BANF 5: 648–9.

but affirmed that he was not interested in a change of the Edict nor a new Peace of Religion. The electors then decided that it would be better now to assure the emperor that they had no intention of departing from the Peace of Religion or the Edict and not send him a detailed report of talks with the Protestants.[107] Undoubtedly Ferdinand's position restrained the electors. At Maximilian's initiative they determined that any discussion at Regensburg should only deal with arrangements for later talks, not with the issues themselves. So Mainz suggested Frankfurt to Landgrave George of Hesse-Darmstadt as the place to gather February 3 to discuss interpretations of the Peace of Religion. Ferdinand approved this.[108] But a few days later, to dispel rumors that the Edict might be suspended, he instructed the imperial commissioners charged with its enforcement to proceed with their task.[109] On this note, the convention came to a close on November 12.

A look at the policy of the Curia at Regensburg requires that we distinguish between its substance, about which not even the nuncios were fully informed, and its perception by Ferdinand, Lamormaini, and the imperial councillors. Urban's brief of May 5, 1629, had seemed to indicate the pope's firm backing of the Edict. Pallotto outdid himself to accommodate the emperor, and he urged the pope to push Ferdinand not to modify the plans for the restitution of church lands. If the pope "did not obtain the satisfaction and glory of achieving such a great good, he would not lose that of having pursued it with all his energy, in the best manner, nor [would he lose] the merit with God of having completely satisfied the part of a holy and zealous pastor."[110] Ferdinand's whole career revealed a special providence God had for him that went beyond human understanding.[111] Rocci did not work so closely with Lamormaini as had Pallotto, but after the conclusion of the Treaty of Regensburg, he assumed that a charge of his was to discourage concessions on the Edict, an issue that he took up with imperial ministers including Eggenberg.[112]

In substance, papal policy was complex and ambivalent. A primary concern of Urban was juridical. Rocci was instructed to avoid any statements that might imply papal approval of either the Edict or the Peace of Augsburg, both of which had conceded rights to the heretics in the Empire. He was, however, to call attention to Protestant violations of the Peace and the need to remedy

---

[107] Minutes of the conference of the delegates of the Catholic electors, BANF 5: 652–4; see also the minutes of the meeting of the Bavarian privy council, Oct. 28, 1630, ibid., 654–5.
[108] In his instruction to his delegates to the Frankfurt Conference, Jan. 27, 1631, HHStA, RTA 101a(I), ff. 5–8, Ferdinand stated clearly that he had approved talks with the Protestants at Frankfurt.
[109] Emperor to Franz Wilhelm von Wartenberg and Johann von Hyen, HHStA, Religion. 35iv, ff. 66–6v.
[110] Pallotto, Vienna, to Barberini, Aug. 2, 1630, Repgen 1: 2, #15; see the discussion in 1: 1, 203–4.
[111] *Status particularis regiminis S.C. Majestatis Ferdinandi II* (Leiden, 1637), The author refers to an undated (final?) relation of Pallotto that I have been unable to locate.
[112] Rocci to Barberini, Sept. 2 and Oct. 21, 1630, BL 6967, ff. 39–48 and 169–72.

them. Should he not be able to prevent all concessions on the Edict, he should do all that he could to secure the most advantages for the Catholics.[113] But Urban was not at all ready to give Ferdinand's program for Germany complete support, unwilling as he also was to see the growth of Habsburg power. The pope's policy on the election of young Ferdinand was disingenuous. Rocci was to give the impression in Regensburg that Rome favored it while intimating to Maximilian and the other electors that the pope could hardly oppose the emperor's intent but that he really favored Maximilian as a candidate.[114] Secret negotiations, promoted by Urban and without Rocci's knowledge, took place at Regensburg between Father Joseph and Maximilian's councillors toward the formation of a Franco-Bavarian alliance that would lead to a Catholic balance to Habsburg power. In May 1631 they would result in the secret Treaty of Fontainebleau between France and Maximilian.[115]

At Regensburg, Lamormaini clearly won out over the other councillors, and especially over Eggenberg, but with disastrous results for the emperor in the long run. Lamormaini himself may have tacitly acknowledged this in his later *The Virtues of Ferdinand II, Emperor of the Romans*, when he never once mentioned the Edict of Restitution and its aftermath. The confessor now was satisfied, to say the least, with the results of the convention.[116] Wallenstein's dismissal eliminated the major source of conflict between the emperor and the Catholic electors, and the differences that remained over the organization of the military were not likely to grow to the point that they would drive the two parties apart. The Treaty of Regensburg with France removed another source of conflict with the electors; it secured the recognition of Ferdinand's jurisdiction in Italy, and for Lamormaini pointed to an approaching cooperation with the Most Christian King. Even Richelieu's refusal to ratify it did not seem to discourage him; he expected a new settlement soon. Ferdinand still wanted peace in Italy, and after the news arrived of Richelieu's rejection of the terms of the Treaty of Regensburg, he informed the nuncio that he had dispatched a courier to Italy directing his general there to refrain from any hostile acts.[117] Frederick of the Palatinate's rejection of any compromise regarding the restitution of lands to him forestalled any disagreement between Ferdinand and Maximilian on this issue. Above all, the Edict stood; all suggestions of concessions had been warded off. In addition, Ferdinand had shown himself generously supportive of the ambitious plan developed by Lamormaini for

---

[113] See above, n. 79; see also Barberini to Pallotto, Aug. 10, 1630, NBD 4, *Nuntiaturen des Pallotto und Rocci*. #74.2 (pp. 242–3).
[114] Albrecht 1, 282–4; see also Barberini to Rocci, Nov. 9, 1630, ibid. #126.2 (p. 353 and n. 3).
[115] Ibid., 253–7, 303–4.
[116] Vitelleschi to Lamormaini, Dec. 14, 1630, ARSJ Aust. 4I, f. 373.
[117] Rocci to Barberini, Nov. 11, 1630, NBD 4, *Nuntiaturen des Pallotto and Rocci*, #127.2 (pp. 355–7).

the foundation of Jesuit colleges, especially in Lower Saxony, to be financed by the income from recovered church lands.[118]

Regensburg represented a defeat for a number of imperial councillors and especially for Eggenberg. For him it was the low point of his influence with Ferdinand. The councillors made known at Regensburg their dissenting views. This emerges clearly from later criticism they leveled against the "theologians" and remarks that they later made that they had pointed out the way to peace for Ferdinand before "the unhappy trip to Regensburg."[119] But the evidence indicates less vigorous opposition than passive discontent combined with helplessness to hinder the course of events, for his colleagues if not for Eggenberg himself. Ferdinand gave Eggenberg permission to absent himself from some conferences at Regensburg and then in February or March to return to Graz. Eggenberg's bitterness showed through in April when at Ferdinand's request he gave his opinion on a new treaty with France. The "apostasy of the electors," he wrote, "nearly broke my heart." He had not failed to speak out at Regensburg, he added, and he still had much to say about events there.[120]

Eggenberg considered the convention a surrender to the electors and a humiliation of the emperor, a view with which the Spaniards concurred. Eggenberg had acquiesced reluctantly in the dismissal of Wallenstein; this had initiated the unhappy course of events. Eggenberg and Tursi had opposed the Treaty of Regensburg in vain. No serious discussion had been allowed about the election of the king of the Romans. Eggenberg had advocated further talks with the Protestants at Regensburg and seems to have wanted some compromise on the Edict. Tursi certainly did; the Spaniards wanted compromise on the Edict for the sake of peace in Germany, so that Ferdinand would be free to aid them in Italy and perhaps even in the Netherlands. This contrasted directly with Lamormaini's policy, and indeed following the convention of Regensburg Olivares with encouragement from Eggenberg tried, unsuccessfully, to force Vitelleschi to remove him from his post as confessor to Ferdinand.[121] The close of the convention left Eggenberg discouraged and hurt.

An amount of opposition had surfaced among the Catholic electors to Lamormaini's and Contzen's policy on the Edict. Mainz favored modest concessions and seems to have influenced Cologne and Trier in this direction. Even Maximilian wavered briefly. Yet it would be unfair to attribute the failure to reach an understanding with the Protestants solely to the militants in the Catholic camp. There existed a wide gap between moderates on each

---

[118] Bireley 2, 133–5.
[119] Position paper of the imperial councillors, Oct. 18, 1631, BAGW, 1: #393. Though a list is given of those present at this session of the privy council, it is impossible to tell which individuals endorsed it, though certainly a majority did; see also AF 11: 1126–7, 1438.
[120] Eggenberg to Ferdinand, Apr. 20, 1631, printed in H. Von Zwiedineck-Südenhorst, *Hans Ulrich Fürst von Eggenberg* (Vienna, 1880), 192–7.
[121] Bireley 2, 178–80.

side. This emerges from a comparison of the "Hessian Points," which represented a moderate Protestant position unacceptable to Saxony and Brandenburg with the "Catholic Response" which circulated at Regensburg as the answer to the "Hessian Points" from a group of moderate Catholics, including Mainz. A Bavarian privy councillor remarked upon reading the "Hessian Points" that the Protestants could not have asked for more had they just achieved a major victory on the battlefield; prior to the convention he had affirmed the need for an understanding with the Protestants.[122]

Two basic differences separated Lamormaini from his adversaries in Vienna, and they were increasingly recognized at the time. One was theological, the other political. Ferdinand, according to the confessor, had been given a mission by God to restore Catholicism in Germany within the parameters of the Peace of Augsburg. Divine providence would assist him, as it had in the past, when the odds looked to be against him from a human or rational perspective. There remained, to be sure, a remote possibility that his forces might be defeated. But Ferdinand had to answer the call of the Lord. If it meant his ruin, that was God's will. To yield to the Protestants was to reject God's call and to fail in confidence in God. The confessor had no problem in acknowledging in theory that in cases of necessity Ferdinand could concede many points. But precisely to admit to this necessity was to reveal a lack of trust in God. Shortly after the conclusion of the Convention of Regensburg, Lamormaini wrote Cardinal Barberini: "Little remains; God promises us the victory; he is active for it. It is as easy for God to give us victory when we are weak as when we are strong. Let the giants, the sons of Enoch, or the Goliaths, not strike fear in us. With God's aid we will devour them. Let us stand firm, and he will fight for us. If we should do otherwise and allow heresy to live, and again ally with the heretics, that course will certainly lead to ruin and to scandal."[123]

Lamormaini wrote in the tradition of the holy war of the Hebrew Scriptures, as did Contzen with appropriate adaptation for Munich. The opposition began to attack this theology by denying the parallel with the Hebrew Scriptures. An anonymous Dominican professor at the University of Cologne developed this position in a paper for the elector of Cologne.[124] In the Old Testament, he elaborated, God did guarantee victory to his people through a special revelation. What the militants were doing was to assert, at least implicitly, a divine revelation in support of their position. But there was no evidence for

---

[122] Bireley 1, 140. For a discussion of the "Hessian Points" and the "Catholic Response," see ibid., 139–41. They are published in BANF 5: 680–90.
[123] Jan. 11, 1631, BL 7054, ff. 78–9.
[124] "Consilium Theologicum cuiusdam Monachi Dominicani et celebris professoris," Munich, Bayerisches Hauptstaatsarchiv, Kriegsakten. 242, 22 folios. The probable author was Cosmas Morelles, a Spanish Dominican, professor of theology at the University of Cologne and apostolic inquisitor for Cologne, Mainz, and Trier. On him, see "Morelles, Cosmas," *Enciclopedia Universal Ilustrada* 36 (Madrid, n.d.), 993–4.

this, God had not provided any assurance of victory. Human prudence not appeals to divine providence ought to govern policy. Drawing at length on an argument from natural law developed by Thomas Aquinas, he showed that in the current situation prudence permitted concessions to the Protestants. The Catholics could surrender church lands without violating their consciences. Indeed, such a policy would benefit both Church and Empire by establishing peace and so a stable situation in which the Church could grow and religion flourish. Nothing in the Scriptures nor in canon law stood in the way of this. So the theological issue gradually became human prudence versus an alleged revelation in the formation of policy. How was the decision on the Edict to be made, on the basis of human prudence and rational consideration or on that of a special revelation regarding Ferdinand's divine vocation? The author's answer was clear.

His attitude toward France constituted Lamormaini's chief political difference with his opponents. He refused to admit that in the long run Louis XIII, if not Richelieu, would not come to Ferdinand's assistance in his efforts for Catholicism in Germany. The Most Christian King would, eventually, at least remain neutral and at best join with the Catholic forces in the Empire. This was not completely unrealistic. As the Convention of Regensburg ended, Richelieu's enemies stood on the verge of his overthrow and the appointment of one of their own in his place. On November 10, the "Day of Dupes" in France, Marie de Medici was already distributing offices to her *dévot* friends. But Louis XIII, after hesitation, renewed his support of the cardinal, and Richelieu's main rival Michel de Marillac was imprisoned. Marie found herself isolated, and in late July she fled to the Spanish Netherlands. From then on, Richelieu's status was more secure. But the dévots, his enemies, had come within a hair's breadth of seizing power in France.[125]

But Richelieu's opposition at home did not disappear. Louis XIII remained childless until 1638 when the future Louis XIV was borne after twenty-two years of married life. Until then Louis's brother, Gaston d'Orleans, was heir to the throne, an unpredictable figure who resented Richelieu and was engaged in several attempts to remove him. Lamormaini's belief that France would eventually revise its policy was not so unrealistic as Eggenberg and the Spaniards imagined.

[125] D.P. O'Connell, *Richelieu* (London, 1968), 228–42.

Chapter 7

Setback, 1631–1632

At the close of the Electoral Convention of Regensburg on November 12, 1630, Ferdinand and the Catholic electors agreed to participate in a conference at Frankfurt, to start the following February 3, to discuss interpretation and implementation of the Religious Peace. Unofficial efforts mediated by Mainz to close the gap between Catholics and Protestants had failed, and neither Saxony nor Brandenburg approved the Protestant position as laid out by Landgrave George of Hesse-Darmstadt. Saxony then followed through with its plan for a conference of Protestant states, which met from late February until early April in Leipzig. So the opening of the Frankfurt Conference was postponed until August 3. Meanwhile Gustav Adolph, fortified by subsidies granted him by the French in the Treaty of Bärwalde of January 23, 1631, continued his advance in the north. By mid-April, he had occupied Pomerania and much of Mecklenburg and Brandenburg. The dismissal of Wallenstein and the continuation of the war in Italy after Richelieu's rejection of the Peace of Regensburg prevented the emperor and the League from confronting him more effectively. Brandenburg was forced to conclude a provisional agreement with Gustav Adolph on May 14 which was confirmed on June 20. The Spaniards sought to persuade the emperor to compromise with the Protestants on the Edict, in order to form a joint Catholic-Protestant German front against the invading Swedish force and to continue to support them in Italy against the French. Ferdinand's ratification on June 19 of the Peace of Cherasco, which revised the Peace of Regensburg to the benefit of the French and ended his intervention in Italy, was a victory for Lamormaini and for Maximilian and the other electors, and a defeat for the Spaniards and, at court in Vienna, for Eggenberg.

Gustav Adolph's route of the heretofore undefeated Tilly, then, at the crucial battle of Breitenfeld near Leipzig on September 16, 1631, reversed the whole course of the war. It led to a low point for Ferdinand similar to the period following the Defenestration of Prague more than ten years earlier. But he never faltered. Gustav Adolph swept through much of central and south Germany, occupying Munich in May and June 1632. Tensions and finger-pointing grew between the two cousins, Ferdinand and Maximilian, especially over policy toward France. Ferdinand looked for help from Rome and Spain, and the influence of the Spanish party in Vienna expanded significantly. Wallenstein was recalled in late 1631 to assume his second generalate. The death of the charismatic Gustav Adolph at the battle of Lützen in November 1632, where his army fought to a draw with Wallenstein's, then provided Ferdinand with new hope.

The battle over policy on the Edict continued in Vienna after the Electoral Convention of Regensburg through the winter and spring, and then into the summer of 1631. Lamormaini, fearful that the upcoming conference with the Protestants might lead to concessions, sought to secure support from Rome. To Barberini he wrote on January 11 asking him to persuade Pope Urban to urge the Catholic electors to remain steadfast.[1] Ferdinand himself had told him, he related, that he was willing to risk everything to maintain the Edict, provided the electors and especially Maximilian did not falter. Bishop Knöringen of Augsburg, as well as the militant Franz Wilhelm von Wartenberg, Maximilian's cousin and bishop of Osnabruck since 1625, also made efforts to garner active support for the Edict in Rome.[2] Urban responded with a series of briefs, to Ferdinand, to Empress Eleonore, to the king of the Romans, to Eggenberg as well as to the Catholic electors and other Catholic princes expected to participate in the conference at Frankfurt. He exhorted them not to compromise. He not only hoped for but he demanded that Ferdinand "not ... permit anything to be decreed that is contrary to the divine law or canonical authority."[3] Both Rocci and Pier Luigi Carafa in Cologne were instructed to attempt to prevent the conference at Frankfurt, and should this not be possible, to hinder any concessions at it, and Rocci was told to cooperate with Lamormaini, who had every reason to think that the pope stood with him.[4] Yet Urban threatened no ecclesiastical censures should the Catholic princes yield; Lamormaini had not suggested these. Perhaps Urban's attitude was revealed as much by his refusal to grant the funds requested by Ferdinand and by the minimal grant that he made to the Catholic League.[5]

---

[1] BL 7054, ff. 78–9.
[2] Knöringen to Urban VIII, Dec. 12, 1630, Repgen, 1: 2: #28; P.L. Carafa to Barberini, Liège, Jan. 3, 1631, Repgen 1: 1: 243, communicated Wartenberg's views to Rome.
[3] All were dated Feb. 10, 1631, Repgen 1: 2, ##33–44 (pp. 79–86, citation on p. 79).
[4] Barberini to Rocci, Feb. 8, 1631, Repgen 1: 2, #32; for the letter to P.L. Carafa, see the notes to #32.
[5] Dieter Albrecht, "Zur Finanzierung des Dreissigjährigen Krieges," in *Der Dreissigjährige Krieg: Perspektiven und Strukturen*, ed. Hans Ulrich Rudolf (Darmstadt, 1977), 389–91. Wege der Forschung, 451.

On March 11, Rocci personally presented the papal brief to Ferdinand. The emperor assured Rocci "that to the extent this was possible, he would not consent to anything prejudicial to religion." He had already several times risked his states and his own life for the sake of religion.[6] Eggenberg, too, reassured Rocci that "the Emperor would remain steadfast in not permitting for his part anything prejudicial to the Catholic religion; he would rather lose the Empire and his own life." But it was necessary that the electors also held firm.[7]

Ferdinand had already chosen as his chief delegate to Frankfurt Count Johann Casper von Stadion, a former president of the war council, currently Grand Master of the Teutonic Knights, and at least a nominal privy councillor who shared Lamormaini's position on the Edict. An early draft of the instruction for Stadion dated January 29, 1631, maintained a hard line. It showed Ferdinand unwilling to compromise but ready to talk about the manner of the Edict's enforcement. His delegate should see to it that there was no agreement on any measures not in line with the Peace of Augsburg and the Edict, so that Ferdinand would not be saddled with the odium of rejecting them.[8] The instruction had been discussed at a privy council session of January 11 at which both Ferdinand and Eggenberg were present, and no serious objections to it had been registered.[9] Ferdinand had ordered that the instruction be shown to Lamormaini and to Lucas Fanini, Jesuit confessor to Empress Eleonore, and both had approved it.[10] About this time Eggenberg departed for Graz, grumbling that Ferdinand no longer listened to him.[11] Copies of the instruction were sent to Maximilian and to Mainz on February 15 along with a letter stressing the need for Catholic unity. Soon it became evident that the Leipzig Conference called by Saxony would compel the postponement of the conference planned for Frankfurt. Only a few minor changes were made in the final instruction for Stadion dated July 8.[12]

Princes and delegates from more than forty Protestant states assembled in Leipzig on February 20 in order to formulate a common policy regarding the Edict, the coming Frankfurt Conference, the advance of the Swedes, and the depredations of the imperial military. The success of the conference was limited, but the first convention of Protestant states in ten years alarmed the Catholics. Letters to the four Catholic electors and to the emperor of April 3 and 7

---

[6] Rocci to Barberini, Mar. 15, 1631, BL 6968, ff. 74–84; see Repgen 1: 1: 260–1.
[7] Rocci to Barberini, Mar. 8, 1631, ibid., ff. 69–73.
[8] Emperor to Stadion, Jan. 29, 1631, HHStA, RTA 101a(I), ff. 9–9v; instruction for the delegates to the Frankfurt Conference, Jan. 27, 1631, ibid., ff. 5–8.
[9] Minutes of the privy council, Jan. 11, 1631, HHStA, RTA 101a (ii), ff. 32–32v.
[10] See also Vitelleschi to Lamormaini, Mar. 29, 1631, ARSJ, Aust. 21, ff. 439–40.
[11] A letter of Eggenberg to Wallenstein, dated Mar. 28, 1631 from Graz, shows that Eggenberg was there by then; see H. von Zwiedineck-Südenhorst, *Hans Ulrich Fürst von Eggenberg* (Vienna, 1880), 101.
[12] See note 7; the instruction was rewritten in the margins of the earlier copy to serve as the register copy.

Setback, 1631–1632

demanded not only that the enforcement of the Edict cease but that all ecclesiastical properties reclaimed by the Catholics by virtue of it up to that point be returned.[13] The states assembled at Leipzig then declared that they would no longer supply funds, troops, or quarters for the imperial army, and they announced their intention to form their own army of 40,000 in self-defense.[14] This was a serious blow to Ferdinand, who counted on the support of the Protestant states against the Swedes. Implied was Protestant resistance to further attempts to carry out the Edict. Beyond this John George of Saxony was not prepared to venture. As it was he only cooperated reluctantly with the Calvinist states at Leipzig, and no preparations were made to raise the Protestant army.

A new awareness of impending danger arose in Vienna as a result of the Leipzig Conference, but there was little movement toward concessions. Seifried Breuner, governor of Lower Austria and a privy councillor of increasing importance, laid out his position regarding the expanding war with Sweden in a memorandum of late March or early April.[15] It differed little from Lamormaini's.

Breuner realized that the Protestant states would probably ally with Sweden and receive support from the English and the Dutch. The threat from France he tended to discount especially in view of the expected conclusion of a revised peace in Italy. The emperor and the Catholic states had to work in harmony, he insisted, if they were to avoid Protestant dictation. Their only hope was a bold military stroke and quick victory. Concretely, this meant that Tilly prosecute with vigor the siege that he had undertaken against Magdeburg. The strategic city had been one of the first German states to go over to Gustav Adolph the previous year, and it now was waiting anxiously for him to relieve the siege. Its reduction by Tilly would intimidate Saxony, hinder Protestant recruitment of troops in the Lower Saxon Circle, and make possible the enforcement of the Edict in the area. Breuner, who was noted for his financial acumen, insisted on the need to draw more funds from the Austrian lands, especially Anterior Austria and the Tyrol and from the Catholic states of the Bavarian Circle that did not belong to the League. The monasteries themselves had to contribute more; "the major cause of the present war is the ecclesiastical lands," he asserted. But the Catholics could not long bear such a burden. If God did not concede them a major victory in the coming year, he wrote, "we will have to accept the best

---

[13] The Protestant Estates assembled in Leipzig to the Four Catholic Electors, Apr. 3, 1631, Michael Casper Londorp, *Der romischen kayserlichen Majestät . . . Acta publica und schriftliche Handlungen* (Frankfurt, 1668) 4: 134–5; the same to the Emperor, Apr. 7, 1631, ibid., 136–43.
[14] Resolution of the Protestant Estates assembled in Leipzig, Apr. 12, 1631, ibid., 144–6; this was sent to the emperor on Apr. 14.
[15] Undated, HHStA, RTA 100b, ff. 276–7. A notation on f. 278v reveals Breuner as the author at some time during the Leipzig Conference.

conditions we can get, unless the good God chooses to provide us with other resources we cannot at this time foresee with our human reason."

Ferdinand deputed a committee of councillors to assess the situation anew after news arrived of the pressure that the Swedes were putting on Brandenburg and especially of the Treaty of Bärwalde of January 23, 1631, by which Richelieu guaranteed generous subsidies to the Swedish king for five years for his campaign against the emperor. One article of the treaty provided that Gustav Adolph refrain from attacking those German Catholic states that did not oppose him. Whether this article was known in Vienna cannot be said, but it indicated Gustav Adolph's intent to direct his campaign against the emperor.

The names of the members of the committee are not known. In their report of March 17, they stressed the danger of the current situation and made a number of recommendations but without suggesting concessions to the Protestants.[16] All the emperor's enemies were coming together against him. Trouble could be anticipated from the English and the Dutch as well as the French, and now from the Turks, too. The committee feared that the Protestants at Leipzig would join the advancing Swedes and that the states of the Lower Saxon Circle would rise up. The war was devastating the Empire, resources drying up, the people overwhelmed. To meet the deteriorating state of affairs, the councillors recommended first of all the formation of the Habsburg alliance that Spain was now promoting, to include the emperor, the Archduchess Isabella in the Netherlands who now governed after the death of her husband, Archduke Albert, Archduke Leopold in Innsbruck, the Catholic states in Germany, and the Spaniards.[17] Second, they called for the buildup of the army such as Tilly had advocated at Regensburg. Third, a mission should be sent to Munich to elicit suggestions about sources of new revenues and means to a peaceful settlement with the Protestants. But the privy council thought it wiser to await the outcome of the Leipzig Conference before taking decisive action. Accordingly, Ferdinand wrote Maximilian and Mainz on March 19 instead of dispatching an emissary, and his letter lacked the sense of urgency in the committee's report.[18]

Once the communications from the Leipzig Conference reached Vienna, the opposition to Lamormaini in the privy council grew. This is clear from an incomplete memorandum dated May 4, 1631, that may never have reached the emperor.[19] The authors who constituted a group within the privy council, called themselves the emperor's "most loyal councillors." They identified explicitly with Eggenberg, who had now returned to Graz, and they were wary of

---

[16] HHStA, Kriegs. 91 (March), ff. 41–4.
[17] Heinrich Günter, *Die Habsburger Liga, 1625–1635. Briefe und Akten aus dem General-Archiv zu Simancas* (Berlin, 1908), 33–6; Albrecht 1, 232–40.
[18] HHStA, Kriegs. 91 (March), ff. 45–9.   [19] Ibid., 92 (May), ff. 44–7.

the Catholic states. They reminded Ferdinand that following the Electoral Convention of Mühlhausen, in early 1628, they had urged a peaceful settlement in the Empire and warned of a religious war. Their statement implied lack of commitment to the Edict and certainly disappointment over the failure to modify it at Regensburg.

Ferdinand should now use his response to the Leipzig resolution of the Protestant states to initiate negotiations toward a settlement with them. The sharp language of the resolution pointed to peril. The councillors also suspected that the Catholic states would make their own arrangement with the Protestants that would allow them to take credit for movement toward peace and saddle Ferdinand with the odium of having opposed peace until the end. He would have no choice but eventually to go along with such an agreement. Richelieu intended to entice the Catholic states into a neutrality agreement with the Swedes, they pointed out correctly. Ferdinand should dispatch emissaries to Saxony and Brandenburg, and lest the Catholic states become suspicious, send a copy of the instructions for the emissaries to them. The councillors approached the topic of Stadion's instructions for Frankfurt with caution. They were "too limited" and would hinder future talks. Ferdinand ought to consult the theologians once again, in order to ascertain the concessions that might be made to the Protestants "without compromising conscience."

These "most loyal councillors" were almost certainly Stralendorf, Trautmannsdorf, and Anton Wolfradt, now prince-bishop of Vienna and no longer abbot of Kremsmünster. Back in January 1628 they had collaborated along with Eggenberg on position papers calling for the conciliation of Saxony and Brandenburg and caution in pursuing the goals outlined by the Catholic electors at Mühlhausen. The three were moderates on the religious issue. Stralendorf, in addition, had recently clashed with Lamormaini on the issue of the distribution of the ecclesiastical lands to be recovered by the Edict.[20] Bishop Anton Wolfradt was close to Eggenberg, and he had recently received high marks from Jacques Bruneau, a veteran diplomat in Spanish service.[21] Two further members of the group may have been Johann Baptista Verda von Werdenberg and Cardinal Dietrichstein. Both were privy councillors. Werdenberg owed his advancement from a modest background in Gorizia to the rank of count to Eggenberg; he had served as the chancellor of the Austrian chancery since its formation in 1620.[22] Dietrichstein, a friend of the Spaniards, was soon to emerge as an advocate of a moderate policy.

---

[20] Bireley 2, 142, 145. [21] Günter, 47.
[22] On Werdenberg see Schwarz, 122, 383–5, and Harald Tersch, "Gottes Ballspiel. Der Krieg in Selbstzeugnissen aus dem Umkreis des Kaiserhofes (1619–1650)" in *Zwischen Alltag und Katastrophe. Der Dreissigjährige Krieg aus der Nähe*, ed. Benigna von Krusenstjern and Hans Medick, 2 ed. (Göttingen, 2001), 499–505.

He had been chosen to meet the Infanta in Genoa in early 1630 and conduct her to her wedding with the King of Hungary in Vienna.[23]

Ferdinand did dispatch two envoys to Saxony and Brandenburg, Hans Hegenmüller, a court councillor, to Saxony and Karl Hannibal von Dohna, a Silesian nobleman, to Brandenburg.[24] Their instruction was dated May 6. But it allowed for no significant compromise on the Edict which allegedly only aimed at the restoration of true justice, the only basis for a genuine peace.[25] The emperor confirmed his intention to send a delegation to Frankfurt, with a view to remedying abuses in the enforcement of the Edict and so come to an understanding. The states at Leipzig were abandoning him in his hour of need, his delegates were to complain, and they had no right to raise troops without his consent. Secret instructions for Hegenmüller directed him to sound out John George about his mediation of an armistice, but without undermining Tilly's current siege of Magdeburg.

The imperial councillors found Saxony's response to Hegenmüller's mission encouraging; it was significantly milder than the resolution of the Leipzig states had been.[26] John George was 'perplexed," as Hegenmüller reported, caught between Gustav Adolph and Ferdinand. The elector affirmed that he felt obliged to challenge Ferdinand's claim to interpret the Religious Peace. Yet he agreed to attempt to secure an armistice with the Swedes, and he expressed a strong desire for peace which encouraged Vienna. Dohna's mission to Brandenburg achieved nothing; George William was compelled to hand over several garrisons to Gustav Adolph on May 14.

Stubborn Magdeburg finally fell to Tilly on May 20. Te Deums were chanted in Prague and in Vienna.[27] Gustav Adolph had been unable to save his ally. The city was devastated, and nearly 20,000 perished in a fire that broke out after the imperial forces entered it.[28] Ferdinand, in his next communication to Saxony of June 14, encouraged John George not to attempt an armistice with Gustav Adolph but to seek to persuade him to retreat from the Empire.[29]

---

[23] Günter, 79.
[24] On Hegenmüller, see Schwarz, 246–7; on Dohna, Arno Duch, "Dohna, Karl Hannibal von," *Neue Deutsche Biographie* 4 (Berlin, 1959): 51.
[25] HHStA, Trautmanndorfarchiv, 101ii. 161–78, with a secret supplement, ff. 179–80; on Dohna's mission, see Johannes H. Gebauer, *Kurbrandenburg und das Restitutionsedikt von 1629* (Halle, 1899), 176. Hallesche Abhandlungen zur neueren Geschichte, 38.
[26] Saxony to the emperor (given Hegenmüller), May 20, 1631, HHStA, Traut., 101ii, ff. 190–215, and a handwritten note, ibid., Friedens. May 20, 1631, ff. 3–4v; The position paper of a deputation of councillors dealing with Saxony's response and Hegenmüller's oral report is in ibid., 9 cii, ff. 18–27v.
[27] Entries for May 29 and 30, 1631, *Die Diarien und Tagzettel des Kardinals Ernst Albert von Harrach (1598–1667)*, ed. Kathrin Keller and Alessandro Catalano (Vienna, 2010) 2: 46, 47.
[28] Michael Roberts, *Gustavus Adolphus: A History of Sweden, 1611–1632*, vol. 2: 1626–1632 (London, 1958), 495–6.
[29] HHStA, Traut., 101ii, ff. 217–26v.

While Hegenmüller was in Torgau with John George, the young imperial court councillor Ferdinand Kurz von Senftenau represented the emperor at a meeting of the Catholic League in the Swabian town of Dinkelsbühl during the first three weeks of May where they discussed their response to the Leipzig Conference and the Swedish advance.[30] Kurz found his initial skepticism about the League's willingness to stand with Ferdinand to have been unwarranted. The League states joined Ferdinand in his firm stance on the Edict while agreeing that continued negotiations at Frankfurt would be useful. Ferdinand expressed his satisfaction to Maximilian and to Mainz that the League was ready to go to the limit with him for Empire and religion.[31] While indicating a surprising readiness to promise contributions to the war effort, they followed Maximilian's advice not to launch a preventive attack against Saxony; they were not adequately prepared nor did they want to allow a myth to develop that the Protestants had taken up arms only in self-defense. Tilly, on the other hand, after the reduction of Magdeburg pushed for decisive military action before the Protestant forces could regroup.[32]

By mid-June the emperor, the Catholic states, and Saxony had all agreed that the conference planned for Frankfurt should begin on August 3. The emperor and the Catholic states seemed to be in agreement on the Edict. Still, it was only on July 28 that Maximilian and Mainz explicitly expressed their agreement with Ferdinand regarding the instruction for Stadion that he had sent them back in February.[33] Points of difference remained between Ferdinand and Maximilian along with the states of the League. One regarded continuing disagreements over the organization of the military, another Maximilian's suspected contacts with France. A Spanish spy had made his way into the apartments of Bagno, the departing nuncio in Paris, in early 1631. There he came upon papers that revealed the secret negotiations being carried on between Maximilian and Richelieu with the encouragement of the Curia. The discovery seemed to confirm Spain's long suspicions. Maximilian did sign, on May 8, the secret Treaty of Fontainebleau with France that prohibited either party from attacking the other either directly or indirectly and committed each to clear measures of defensive assistance in the event of attack by a third party. France promised to defend Maximilian's position in the Palatinate, a matter of great concern to him. The treaty was to last for eight years.

---

[30] On the Dinkelsbühl Conference, see Bireley 1, 149–53.
[31] Kurz von Senftenau to the emperor, Dinkelsbühl, May 15, 1631, HHStA, Traut. 101ii, ff. 61–8; Kurz von Senftenau's report on the Dinkelbühl Conference, undated, ibid., ff. 89–96; Emperor to Maximilian and Mainz, Jun. 9, 1631, ibid., ff. 78–81. On Kurz von Senftenau, see Schwarz, 260–3.
[32] Bireley 1, 159–60.
[33] Maximilian and Mainz to Ferdinand, Jul. 28, 1631, Munich, Bayerisches Hauptstaatsarchiv, Kriegsakten 236 I, f. 97.

Maximilian had carefully safeguarded his obligations to the emperor in the treaty, and he certainly considered it to benefit the Empire in that it committed France to come to his defense in the event of a Swedish attack. Adam Contzen, Maximilian's Jesuit confessor, was even more optimistic about French intervention to assist the Catholics in Germany than was Lamormaini, and he judged the treaty to be a step in this direction. But in Vienna most councillors were certain to interpret the treaty as fostering Richelieu's plan to neutralize Bavaria and through it the League; it looked like betrayal. In early August, Maximilian sent an emissary to Vienna who admitted to a treaty with France which, he stated, had been approved by the pope, a fact never conceded by Rome, and who explained the elector's position. Ferdinand allowed himself to be convinced and put up a good front, but the result was new mistrust between the two courts. The Spanish party used Maximilian's association with the French as an argument for a more flexible policy toward Saxony on the part of the emperor.[34]

Negotiations for the marriage of Ferdinand's son with the Spanish Infanta Maria Anna, sister of Philip IV, had begun in 1625 once the prospective bridegroom had acquired the title of king of Hungary. Maria, born in 1607, had been wooed as a teenager by Charles, the prince of Wales for the ill-fated "Spanish Match" between Spain and England. A contract for the marriage with Ferdinand Ernst had been worked out, and the two were married by proxy in 1629 in Madrid as the emperor was preparing to send troops to Italy. Maria Anna only departed from Spain the following spring, landing in Genoa on June 18, 1630. Delays and detours followed, partly due to the spread of plague in north Italy. Finally, she made her formal entrance into Vienna on February 26, 1631, as wife of Ferdinand and queen of Hungary. Festivities that greatly surpassed those at Innsbruck in 1622 at Emperor Ferdinand's marriage with Eleonore surrounded the celebration of the union from late February until late March of that fateful year. On March 9, the first Sunday of Lent, a genuine opera was staged, appropriately entitled "The Happy Catch" (*La caccia felice*). During the two intermissions ballets were performed, the first featuring pages dressed in African costumes in a Turkish dance, the second young boys in Asian costumes in a dance.[35] A new bond had been created between Vienna and Madrid.

Along with Maria Anna came her confessor, Don Diego de Quiroga, a Spanish Capuchin.[36] Emperor Ferdinand had taken measures through his

---

[34] Proposition of the Bavarian emissary to Vienna, presented Aug. 7, 1631, BAGW 1: #332; emperor to Maximilian, Aug. 9, 1631, ibid. #333; Eggenberg to Maximilian, Sept. 1, 1631, Kschw 131, f. 37; Albrecht 1, 256–62; Bireley 1, 167–9.

[35] Herbert Seifert, *Die Oper am Wiener Kaiserhof im 17. Jahrhundert* (Tutzing, 1985), 32, 128–9. Wiener Veröffentlichungen zur Musikgeschichte, 25.

[36] On Quiroga, see Buonaventura de Carrocera, "El Padre Diego de Quiroga, diplomatico e confessor de reyes, 1574–1649," *Estudios Franciscanos* 50 (1949): 71–100.

ambassador in Madrid to convince Maria Anna to bring a Jesuit with her as confessor, but the young queen, backed by the Spanish government, insisted on the Capuchin Quiroga.[37] The Spaniards had long considered Lamormaini a major opponent of their policy. His persistent support for peace with France and his championship of the Edict earned him their hostility. They aimed to combat his influence at court through Quiroga. Almost as soon as the Capuchin arrived, he became a significant political force in Vienna – "for eighteen years the person at the court of Vienna in whom Philip IV, Olivares and Spanish ministers had the most confidence"[38]– as did Maria Anna herself, and so a rival of Lamormaini. But if Maria Anna did succeed in bringing her own confessor with her, the emperor successfully prohibited her from including two Spanish musicians in her entourage, and Spanish influence on the cultural life of the court was minimal. The new queen of Hungary had planned a performance of Lope de Vega's "Feast of the Golden Fleece," *(Fiesta del vellocino de oro)* for her husband's birthday in July 1631 but it was postponed and only staged two years later.[39]

But even bolstered by the presence of Quiroga and Maria Anna in Vienna, the Spanish party was unable to prevent the renegotiation of the Treaty of Regensburg that brought peace between the emperor and France in Italy. France was still working out the terms of the Treaty of Bärwalde with the Swedes in January 1631, when the French emissary Brûlart de Léon arrived in Vienna to resume talks. Vienna aimed at ratification of the treaty concluded at Regensburg, as it stood. Nuncio Rocci assured Lamormaini that the Curia was doing all that it could to obtain this goal despite its lack of leverage in Paris.[40] A courier arrived in Vienna in mid-April with terms worked out on the scene in Cherasco in Italy on April 6 and approved conditionally by the imperial negotiators there. The new terms made some adjustments for Italy, but they eliminated a French commitment to refrain from assisting Ferdinand's enemies in Germany which for Vienna had been a principal feature of the original Treaty of Regensburg.[41]

The conflict over ratification now engaged Lamormaini and Rocci against the Spanish party, reinforced by Quiroga. At a banquet at the residence of the

---

[37] Henar Pizarro Llorente, "La eleccion de confesor de la infanta Maria de Austria in 1628," *La Dinastia de los Austrias: Las relaciones entre la Monarquia Catolica y el Imperio* (Madrid, 2011) 2: 785–99; Bireley 2, 161.

[38] Carrocera, 85.

[39] Andrea Sommer-Mathis, "Ein 'picaro' und spanisches Theater am Wiener Hof zur Zeit des Dreissigjährigen Krieges," *Wien im Dreissigjährigen Krieg. Bevölkerung, Gesellschaft, Kultur, Konfession* (Vienna, 2001), 672, 677, 684. Kulturstudien 32.

[40] Rocci to Barberini, Mar. 22, 1631, NBD 4, *Nuntiaturen des Giovanni Battista Pallotto und des Ciriaco Rocci (1630–1631)*, ed. Rotraud Becker (Tübingen, 2009): #167.2 (pp. 440–2.).

[41] Auguste Leman, *Urbain VIII et la rivalité de la France et de la Maison d'Austriche de 1631 à 1635* (Paris/Lille, 1920), 7–8.

imperial general Baltasar de Marradas in late April, Rocci and Ottavio de Villani, a senator of Milan and Spanish official in Vienna nearly came to blows.[42] The privy council was divided, with the majority favoring acceptance for two reasons. The emperor could not afford to alienate the electors who continued to oppose the intervention in Italy, and he needed to free troops to confront the persistent advance of the Swedes in the north. Ferdinand could not come to a decision himself, and he determined to seek the opinion of Eggenberg who remained in Graz at the time.[43]

On April 21, a special courier delivered the opinion of Eggenberg, who now complained that the emperor no longer consulted him. "The oracle of Graz," as Rocci called him,[44] rejected the revised agreement, and he implored the emperor to insist on the original terms of the treaty, "vigorously, persistently, heroically, and imperially." This clearly included the crucial first article, even though Eggenberg did not name it explicitly, as well as articles regarding the territorial settlement. Already aware of the Treaty of Bärwalde, he gave voice to his disappointment, almost his disgust, with the way the privy councillors had once again capitulated to the electors. Not long ago, presumably at Regensburg, he had discussed the matter with Lamormaini, "to whom I entrusted my soul for many years," and with other Jesuits. They had all agreed that the Treaty of Regensburg met every standard of justice, and that "nothing more could be demanded from you, whatever God might send according to his holy and divine will." He clearly wanted to forestall any argument of Lamormaini that Ferdinand was required to bend still further to retain the support of the electors and to bring peace to Italy.[45]

Ferdinand now came down on the side of Eggenberg and the Spaniards. He ordered the reopening of negotiations with the French, and Kurz von Senftenau, scarcely returned from Dinkelsbühl, was dispatched to Paris in early June, his task to persuade the French to ratify the original terms of the Treaty of Regensburg and to inquire about "rumors" of an agreement between Louis XIII and Gustav Adolph. Kurz von Senftenau was to assure the French king that Ferdinand desired to work with him for peace in Europe and the advancement of the Catholic religion.[46] In the meantime changes were introduced into the terms agreed upon at Cherasco that seemed to meet Eggenberg's objections to their territorial provisions but did not address the issue of France's support of Ferdinand's enemies in Germany. Ferdinand ratified the terms of the second

---

[42] Entry for April 29, 1631, *Diarien Kardinals Harrach* 2: 46.
[43] Emperor to Eggenberg, Apr. 18, 1631, in H. von Zwiedineck-Südenhorst, *Hans Ulrich Fürst von Eggenberg* (Vienna, 1880), 191–2; see also pp. 94–5.
[44] Rocci to Barberini, Apr. 26, 1631, NBD 4, *Nuntiaturen des Pallotto und Rocci*, #178.1 (pp. 464–6).
[45] Eggenberg to the emperor, Apr. 20, 1631, Zwiedineck-Südenhorst, 192–7.
[46] Instruction for Kurz von Senftenau's mission to Paris, Jun. 8, 1631, HHStA, Staaten, Frankreich, Berichte und Weisungen 24.

Treaty of Cherasco on June 19, to the satisfaction of the electors and to the bitter resentment of the Spaniards. This ended the Mantuan War.[47]

Upon returning from Paris, Kurz von Senftenau reported that Louis XIII acknowledged that he aided Sweden and that he justified it by Ferdinand's intervention in Italy.[48] This seemed to make it evident that Richelieu would not renounce his intent to assist the emperor's enemies. The French did assure Kurz von Senftenau that they would abide by the settlement for Italy and that they would be accommodating in the developing dispute over the three prince-bishoprics on the western border of the Empire: Metz, Toul, and Verdun. The Treaty of Cateau-Cambrésis of 1559 provided for their cession to France, but whether they remained imperial fiefs and so in some way subject to the emperor was disputed.[49] But Kurz von Senftenau was justifiably wary of French assurances. As a result of a secret treaty that Richelieu made with Savoy, France received back the commanding fortress of Pinerolo and so obtained its entry into Italy.[50]

The Spaniards in Vienna increasingly argued, in that spring and summer of 1631, for a joint imperial and electoral front against the oncoming Swedes and eventually against the French. Protestant cooperation was a necessity, and to secure this, so was a compromise on the Edict. The alternative was a religious conflagration that would encompass all Christendom. Philip IV wrote directly to Ferdinand on June 19 suggesting that "he find a more opportune outlet for his piety and holy zeal." Those envious of his greatness, by which Philip meant Maximilian of Bavaria, took advantage of his zeal for religion, in order to cause trouble in the Empire and weaken him.[51] The Spaniards acknowledged that Ferdinand needed Maximilian and the League; yet the Bavarian elector, whose contacts with the French had now been revealed, remained the villain. And Lamormaini colluded with him.[52]

So the Spaniards determined to win over Lamormaini to their side, or if this were not possible, to moderate or end his influence with Ferdinand. Philip IV directed the duke of Guastalla, now Spanish ambassador at the court of Ferdinand, to gain the favor of the confessor "at any price," even that of a cardinal's hat.[53] In May Spain raised the issue with Vitelleschi in Rome.

---

[47] Romolo Quazza, *La guerra per la successione di Mantova e del Monferrato, 1628–1631* (Mantua, 1926) 2: 303–5.
[48] Report of Kurz von Senftenau, Jul. 31, 1631, HHStA, Staaten, Frankreich, Berichte und Weisungen 23, ff. 49–56.
[49] D.P. O'Connell, *Richelieu* (London, 1968), 159, 203, 213
[50] Ibid., 259–61; Leman, 21–2, 27, 34.
[51] Philip IV to the emperor, Jun. 19, 1631, Günter, #48.
[52] Philip IV to the Duke of Guastalla (Spanish ambassador in Vienna), Apr. 22 and Jun. 19, 1631, Günter, ## 43, 49; Philip IV to the Marquis of Cadereyta (second Spanish ambassador in Vienna), May 28, 1631, ibid. #47; see also pp. 75–7.
[53] Apr. 22, 1631, ibid., #43.

Cardinal Borja, still the Spanish resident at the papal court, complained to the superior general about Lamormaini's activities. But the Spanish strategy backfired. Vitelleschi wrote directly to Ferdinand and to the king of Hungary asking them to vouch for Lamormaini's allegiance to the king of Spain.[54] Ferdinand interpreted the Spanish move as interference in his government, and both he and his son defended the Jesuit. To his own surprise, then Vitelleschi found out – he did not reveal his source – that it was Eggenberg who had provoked the vigorous Spanish complaints against Lamormaini. The confessor was accused, Vitelleschi informed Lamormaini, of transmitting confidential information to Maximilian, countering Habsburg interests in Italy, and, more generally, mingling unduly in political matters; "since he [Eggenberg] often differs with you, you with your diligent zeal draw the other councillors to your position with the result at times that this difference of views between the two of you on matters of great moment renders the emperor himself uncertain and perplexed."[55]

Eggenberg had returned to Graz in late March, and he did not return to Vienna until the end of June, and then only when summoned by Ferdinand with a handwritten note.[56] During this time he must have determined to make a vigorous effort to counter Lamormaini's influence with Ferdinand. His threats to resign, as Vitelleschi remarked, were evidently meant to force Lamormaini's departure. Vitelleschi recommended that Lamormaini neither write nor say anything that might be construed as hostile to Spain. But the confessor could not do this without abandoning his whole project. Unfortunately, we do not have either his response to Vitelleschi nor his reaction to the revelation about Eggenberg.

Madrid undertook another attempt in September to secure support in Vienna.[57] The list of those the ambassadors were to cultivate indicates those whom besides Eggenberg and Cardinal Dietrichstein Madrid thought to be influential in Vienna: Stralendorf, Trautmannsdorf, the bishop of Vienna, and Werdenberg. Also named were Maximilian von Dietrichstein, young nephew of the cardinal who served as *Hofmeister* of Empress Eleonore, and Count Christoph Simon von Thun-Hohenstein, who was close to the king of Hungary, having overseen his education and was later to become his *Obristhofmeister*. One should speak frankly to Empress Eleonore if necessary; she should be reminded that after the death of Ferdinand her fate would depend not on France or the pope but on Spain and the king of Hungary. "I feel certain," King Philip wrote, "that the confessor of the emperor will be more difficult

---

[54] Vitelleschi to Ferdinand II, Oct. 25, 1631, ARSJ, Germ. 113 2II, f. 467; Vitelleschi to the king of Hungary and Bohemia, Oct. 15, 1631, ibid., ff. 466–7.
[55] Vitelleschi to Lamormaini, Oct. 18, 1631, ARSJ, Aust. 4I, ff. 532–4.
[56] Walther E. Heydendorff, *Die Fürsten und Freiherren zu Eggenberg* (Graz, 1965), 114–16.
[57] Philip IV to the Marquis of Cadereyta, Sept. 15, 1631, Günter, #53; Philip IV to the Duke of Guastalla, Sept. 15, 1631, ibid., #55. 56; see also pp. 79–80, 86.

to win over, although he is the most important because of the temperament of His Imperial Majesty and the ease with which he allows himself to be guided by him."[58] The Spaniards also planned another assault on Vitelleschi through Cardinal Borja threatening retaliation against Jesuits in Spain if the superior general did not act.[59]

Military successes in the late spring and early summer inspired new confidence in Vienna.[60] Magdeburg had fallen to Tilly, though little was left but a shell after the disastrous fire. Once peace was concluded with France on June 19, troops returning from Italy were easily able to disperse the Protestant militias assembling in Württemberg and to secure the submission of the duke. But Gustav Adolph was not inactive. New recruits – Scottish, English, but mostly German – joined his forces. His new treaty with Brandenburg on June 20 allowed him to occupy fortresses there and to recruit widely. The Catholic forces were being maneuvered out of Mecklenburg by Gustav Adolph with the help of the troops raised by the two dislodged dukes. Maximilian ordered Tilly to withdraw from Hesse-Cassel lest he provoke Landgrave Wilhelm. Tilly saw the greater danger coming at the moment from Saxony as it built up its army, and he persistently sought permission from Maximilian and Ferdinand to undertake a preventive attack against John George. Following up on two earlier communications of June 14 and July 16, Ferdinand wrote on July 20, asking Maximilian and Mainz what ought to be done in this extremely difficult situation. Military necessity as expressed by Tilly's conviction of the need to forestall Saxony's buildup of forces clashed with the political goal of a last-minute understanding with John George. Then, on July 30, Ferdinand instructed the general to attempt once more to negotiate with John George. If this should fail, he authorized Tilly to attack at his own discretion.[61] A pause in the action ensued. Maximilian hesitated; on August 12 in a communication to Mainz he still opposed an attack on Saxony without, however, showing a readiness to make concessions on the Edict, which alone would make an agreement possible. Neither he nor Mainz had as yet responded to Ferdinand's request for advice.[62]

Rome continued to exhort the emperor to stand firm on the Edict, but it held out little hope for positive assistance. On May 7 Ferdinand instructed Prince Paul Savelli, his agent in Rome, to seek an extraordinary audience with Pope Urban to plea for funds. Great dangers threatened the German Catholics, and if they should succumb, Savelli was to convey forcefully to the pope, the Italians

---

[58] Philip IV to the Duke of Guastalla, Sept. 15, 1631, ibid., #55.
[59] Philip IV to Pedro de Axpe (Spanish secretary in Naples), Oct. 7, 1631, ibid., #61.
[60] Rocci to Barberini, Jul. 26, 1631, NBD 4: *Nuntiaturen des Pallotto und Rocci*, #205.2 (pp. 520–2).
[61] Albrecht 2, 786–7; Ritter, 496, dates this letter of Ferdinand July 23. [62] Bireley 1, 159–60.

would soon experience the fury of the oncoming Swedish Protestant forces. Ferdinand asked for one-half the income from the church lands recovered by the imperial armies. The emperor also requested that Urban grant him a regular monthly subsidy as other popes had, and if it were necessary, to dip into the papal reserves stored in the Castel San Angelo for the funds.[63] Upsetting to Vienna, in addition to Rome's unclarified role in Richelieu's negotiations with Maximilian, was Urban's intense focus on a matter of papal and Barberini family interest at a time when the fate of Catholicism in Germany seemed to be at stake. The prefect of Rome had died in April, and Urban now aimed to bestow this office on his nephew Taddeo. The pope planned to upgrade this position to the status that it had possessed in the Middle Ages. Papal dispatches regularly directed the nuncio to win the support of the emperor for this plan so that, for example, on ceremonial occasions in Rome the prefect, Urban's nephew, would precede the imperial and other ambassadors.[64]

The conquest of Magdeburg did elicit from Urban an effusive brief for Ferdinand. "On such a great benefit of heaven we congratulate Your Majesty, whom the Almighty seems to have chosen to destroy heresy, the nurse of perpetual sedition, in the Roman Empire, the protector of the Roman Church."[65] The victory certainly presaged greater things to come. Urban exhorted Ferdinand to remain firm in his intent not to permit "that any harm be inflicted on the Catholic Religion in any deliberation about the affairs of Germany." Another brief two weeks later communicated the same message.[66] But Vienna expected more from the pope than exhortations.[67]

From the start the Frankfurt Conference was doomed. Neither Catholics nor Protestants had shown any significant inclination to compromise since Regensburg. Stadion, the imperial delegate, arrived on August 4 accompanied by Konrad Hildbrant, a court councillor. Thirteen Catholic princes, ten of them ecclesiastical, sent delegates in addition to the emperor. Maximilian's stood out as most important. The Catholic delegates began to meet on August 11 in order to formulate a common position. The weekly reports of the imperial delegation back to Vienna showed them to be content with the stance of the delegates from the Catholic states.[68] Only on August 19 did the Saxon delegates arrive, and then with instructions not to participate in any negotiations until those of Brandenburg turned up. By then it had become apparent to most delegates that no compromise was in sight. On his way back from the election of a bishop in

---

[63] Emperor to Savelli, May 7, 1631, HHStA, Staaten, Romana 53; Rocci to Barberini, May 10, 1631, *NB 4: Nuntiaturen Pallotto und Rocci*, #183 (pp. 474–6).
[64] Albrecht, "Finanzierung des Dreissigjährigen Krieges," 553–4; Repgen, 1: 1, 290–1.
[65] Jun. 28, 1631, BL ff. 113v–14v.   [66] Jul. 12, 1631, ibid., f. 123.
[67] Rocci to Barberini, Aug. 9, 1631, NBD 4: *Nuntiaturen des Pallotto und des Rocci*, #210.2 (528–30).
[68] These are found in HHStA, RTA, 101a.

Würzburg. Pierre Luigi Carafa, the nuncio in Cologne passed through Frankfurt where he exhorted the Catholic delegates to steadfastness.[69]

By September 4, the Catholic delegates were aware of the substantial points of the Saxon instruction which went well beyond the position taken by the Protestants at the Leipzig Conference. It called for a suspension of the Edict and the designation of the year 1620 as normative for the adjudication of all disputes regarding church properties or rights. Such an agreement would have allowed the Protestants to retain all the church lands that had come into their hands from the Peace of Augsburg until the start of the war. It amounted to a new religious peace. When they heard this, some Catholic delegates advocated a postponement of the conference. The delegation from Brandenburg finally arrived on September 12, with a position more extreme than Saxony's.[70] The conference finally opened on September 15 with the reading of the uncompromising imperial statement[71] The Catholics then had to wait over a week for the Protestant response, but no Catholics departed lest they be held responsible for the breakdown of the conference. The Protestant response of September 24 showed no intention of yielding concessions. So the two parties remained deadlocked when the news began to arrive of Gustav Adolph's decisive defeat of Tilly's forces at Breitenfeld.[72]

Imperilled on the flank by Saxony as well as threatened from the front by the Swedes, Tilly had on August 29 formally enjoined John George to cease the recruitment of troops and to transfer those under arms to the emperor's service. He repeated the injunction on September 3, and when he received no response, he crossed the border into Saxony and headed for Leipzig. John George then sent a request to Gustav Adolph for assistance, and on September 11 the two formed an alliance, a development that the Catholics persistently had hoped to prevent. Tilly took Leipzig on September 15, but two days later the combined Swedish and Saxon armies, with their 42,000 troops providing a clear numerical advantage, crushed Tilly at Breitenfeld outside Leipzig. This was the first major Protestant military victory of the German war, and it shattered the myth of Catholic invincibility.

Reports of the Swedish–Saxon victory encouraged the Protestants at the Frankfurt Conference, though it took a while before they realized its scope. Negotiations continued without success. On September 30, the imperial delegates reported that the Catholic states were not wavering, a fact that satisfied them as well as Ferdinand.[73] Two weeks later the bishop of Würzburg reported that Gustav Adolph had taken his fortress at Königshofen and was advancing

---

[69] Because of a dispute over protocol, Carafa did not talk directly with Stadion but wrote him a letter, Frankfurt, Aug. 27, 1631; see Repgen 1: 2: #48; on Carafa's visit in Frankfurt, see Repgen 1:1: 268–72.

[70] Gebauer, 181–5, 188, 192–6.   [71] HHStA, RTA 101, ff. 13–14v.   [72] Bireley 1, 162.

[73] HHStA, RTA 101, ff. 24–24v; emperor to the delegates in Frankfurt, Oct. 8, 1631, ibid., ff. 64–64v.

along the Main River. The next day, October 14, the Catholic delegates left Frankfurt. The fortunes of war had shifted to back Gustav Adolph in his triumph.

Gustav Adolph and John George quickly followed up their victory. John George retook Leipzig within a few days and then marched through Bohemia to Prague which he seized on November 15, to the delight of the Bohemian exiles. Gustav Adolph turned to the west. By mid-October, the bishopric of Würzburg had fallen into his hands. In mid-November, after taking Frankfurt, he invaded the archbishopric of Mainz, and he entered the city of Mainz on December 23, in time to celebrate Christmas there. The precipitous military activity then slowed down for the winter while Gustav Adolph consolidated his position. So the Catholics had the opportunity to regroup. Archbishop Anselm Casimir of Mainz, disillusioned by the failure of Maximilian and the Catholic League to protect his territory from the onslaught of Gustav Adolph, now looked to the Habsburg Ferdinand for support. Soon he would become a firm ally of the emperor, immune to overtures from France.[74]

The defeat at Breitenfeld created for Ferdinand a crisis comparable to that following the Bohemian rebellion. The Empire seemed to be collapsing. Tilly's defeat was the general's first since the start of the war, and it delivered a severe blow to morale. Gustav Adolph seemed now to have acquired the aura of invincibility. The Catholic armies were in disarray. But Ferdinand faced adversity head on. Concern for his conscience and his reputation prevented him from accepting, much less initiating, concessions. Had not God saved him in apparently desperate situations before? His principal privy councillors, aware of the need for eventual concessions but also of Ferdinand's mentality, were cautious in proposing them, and even the moderates recognized that they would not be able to satisfy the demands of Gustav Adolph, now at the peak of his power. Before an acceptable peace could be reached, a military and political balance had to be established.

Tension grew between Vienna and Munich after Tilly's defeat, but their common religious goals and realization of mutual dependence always prevented a break. On the one hand, Vienna feared a secret arrangement between Maximilian and France and then Sweden; even before Breitenfeld, Maximilian had in fact concluded the secret Treaty of Fontainebleau with France. On the other, Munich was afraid of a deal between Ferdinand and Saxony, at the expense of Maximilian and his understanding of Catholic interests; this was precisely what Spain and a soon-to-be rehabilitated Wallenstein advocated. In addition, Vienna was greatly vexed by Maximilian's claim in a letter to John George that he had not approved Tilly's advance into Saxony. The claim was

---

[74] Franz Brendle, *Der Erzkanzler im Religionskrieg. Kurfürst Anselm Casimir von Mainz, die geistlichen Fürsten und das Reich 1629 bis 1647* (Münster, 2011), 299–300, 339–46.

Setback, 1631–1632

literally true, but as Ferdinand pointed out to the Bavarian elector, Maximilian had not responded to a query about a major decision that could not wait.[75] The situation recalled that back in 1625 when Tilly and to a certain extent Maximilian had forced a hesitant Ferdinand's hand and invaded Lower Saxony. Cooler heads prevailed in Vienna, and the matter was dropped but not forgotten.

A deputation of councillors, including Eggenberg, convened to discuss the new situation on October 6.[76] They did not think it probable that in the circumstances Saxony would yield on the position that it had taken at the Leipzig Conference. They probably were not yet aware that at Frankfurt Saxony had raised its demands substantially. Any terms consistent with his conscience and reputation that Ferdinand might offer would not be acceptable to John George, they thought. The councillors did recommend, however, that indirect contacts be pursued with John George through Wallenstein and Hesse-Darmstadt, who undertook to organize another Catholic-Protestant meeting after the failure of the Frankfurt Conference became evident. Eggenberg authorized Wallenstein to make contact with Saxony through Hans Georg von Arnim, Wallenstein's former general who had gone over to Saxon service.[77]

A Bavarian emissary soon arrived in order to plan for a military buildup and to discuss negotiations with Saxony. But Maximilian hesitated to suggest concrete concessions. The committee of councillors deputed to evaluate his position interpreted this reluctance as an attempt to avoid responsibility.[78] They hoped for an initiative from Maximilian that would edge Ferdinand toward accommodation, at least with Saxony, but Maximilian was as hesitant to lead in this direction as was Ferdinand.[79] The councillors implicitly criticized Ferdinand himself and expressed their lingering bitterness over the outcome of Regensburg when they remarked that they had at that time explained the difficulty of continuing the war. Now to secure acceptable terms would be much more difficult. They added a slap at Lamormaini when they asserted that whenever Ferdinand asked the theologians to evaluate terms for a settlement, they always found serious disadvantages in it even in purely political matters. But despite their pessimism, the councillors recognized the need for further negotiations with Saxony.

The privy councillors now strongly advocated that Ferdinand participate in the conference promoted by Hesse-Darmstadt, now scheduled for mid-

---

[75] Maximilian to the emperor, Sept. 26 and Oct. 3, 1631, BAGW 1: ##365, 374; Emperor to Maximilian, Oct. 8 and 11, 1631, ibid. ##378, 380.
[76] Position paper, BAGW 1: #376.
[77] Georg Irmer, *Die Verhandlungen Schwedens und seiner Verbündeten mit Wallenstein und dem Kaiser, 1631–1634*, 1 (Leipzig, 1888): xxviii. Publikationen aus den Preussischen Staatsarchiven, 35.
[78] Oct. 18, 1631, BAGW 1: #393. [79] Bireley 1, 174–6.

December in Mühlhausen, but they too were unwilling to suggest a concrete position on the Edict, recommending that this be decided in concert with the Catholic electors.[80] Two drafts of a communication to the Catholic electors revealed the differences in Vienna. The first stated explicitly that it might be wise to discuss concessions on the Edict, which had driven the Protestants into an alliance with Sweden. In the revision this suggestion was eliminated; it called only for a general discussion of the means to peace and stressed the need for cooperation between the two "chief pillars" of the Catholic religion in Germany, the emperor and the Catholic states. Both drafts affirmed that neither bore the responsibility for the disaster of Breitenfeld. It "was to be left to the hidden judgment of God, which was always at work and which undoubtedly had been provoked to inflict such a punishment by serious sins of all types committed by the undisciplined soldiery."[81] This comment was obviously a theological explanation. It is similar to a long paper drawn up by Maximilian's confessor, Adam Contzen, "A Consideration of the Persecution of the Church in Germany," which attributed the dire situation of the Catholics in the Empire to their sins; its publication was prohibited by his Jesuit superior.[82]

On November 13, as the date for the conference at Mühlhausen approached, the imperial councillors, bypassing Lamormaini, secretly convoked a group of six theologians to inquire whether the emperor might make concessions similar to what the Protestants at Leipzig had demanded. Among them were two Spaniards – the Jesuit Ambrosio Peñalosa, a member of the entourage of the queen of Hungary, and a Dominican professor at the University of Vienna, Juan de Valdespino – and the Italian Franciscan, Ottaviano da Ravenna. The following week they presented their separate opinions orally to a committee of councillors that included Cardinal Dietrichstein, Bishop Anton Wolfradt of Vienna, and Stralendorf. Only Ottaviano's paper survives; the others probably signed on to his view. Generally speaking, he accepted the principle of the lesser evil, the same position to which Becan had appealed back in 1620: if the alternative was the ruin of the Catholic religion in Germany, Ferdinand might suspend and even cancel the Edict; whether this was truly the case, he left up to the councillors to decide. But for the surrender of church property he needed the pope's permission, which he might presume in case of a severe emergency. His closing remarks, then, included sentiments that one would have expected from Lamormaini. Was the situation truly as extreme as the councillors painted

---

[80] Position paper, undated, HHStA, RTA 100b, ff. 142–7v. There are two versions of the paper here that date from about Nov. 1.
[81] This letter seems never to have been sent. Both drafts are found within an undated paper of the privy council, HHStA, Friedens. 46g, ff. 407–11.
[82] "De Persecutione Ecclesiae Christi per Germaniam Consideratio," Munich, Bayerisches Hauptstaatsarchiv, Jesuitica 81, ff.126–226; see Bireley 1, 177–8.

It, the only alternative the suppression of Catholic worship and the resulting humiliation of the Empire? Hope in God was necessary.[83]

Ottaviano's insistence on papal approval for the surrender of church property put Rocci on the spot, and he wrote for instructions to Rome. Barberini responded on December 13. Under no conditions would Urban sanction concessions. Following his general policy, he would not give up the juridical rights of the church. But Rocci should not make an issue of the matter, and if he could do so credibly, act as if he knew nothing of it. If he could not do this, he ought to convey the pope's disapproval but make no effort to forestall the concessions. The one development that the pope wanted to avoid was a direct request from Ferdinand since he would have to deny it. Otherwise, he was ready to allow Ferdinand to make the decision that he considered the best for the Church.[84] But Ferdinand was not yet ready to exercise such independence.

By mid-December it became evident that Gustav Adolph would not permit the meeting of Catholics and Protestants at Mühlhausen, so that a need for papal approval dropped from mind in Vienna, to the relief of Rome.

But the Catholic states planned to hold their own meeting at Ingolstadt; Ferdinand dispatched as his delegate the court councillor Hermann von Questenberg who had participated in the Frankfurt Conference. His task was to secure a clear statement from the states on the lengths to which they would go in making concessions. Questenberg was to inform the states that, for his part, Ferdinand was ready, with them, "to persevere through good and evil to the end of this war, that we therefore look for nothing else than the same from them, that they stand by us courageously with the unchanging loyalty that is their duty."[85] Ferdinand, Questenberg was to make clear, was confident that they would not enter into a neutrality agreement on their own. The suspicion behind this was based on fact. Hercule de Charnacé, a veteran French diplomat, had begun talks with Maximilian on December 3.[86]

Questerberg found only a handful of delegates when he arrived in Ingolstadt on December 21. Only after Maximilian had assented to the draft of a neutrality agreement with Sweden did the Bavarians turn up six days later. Two weeks before, troops of Archduke Leopold had intercepted communications between Maximilian and Paris that revealed the presence of Charnacé in Munich. Copies were sent to Questenberg for his information and to Maximilian with a request for an explanation.[87] Questenberg noted the perplexity of the Bavarians. They had grown despondent; measures they might take toward concessions, they thought, would offend God and measures to continue the war were

---

[83] Repgen 1: 2: #49II; ibid., 1: 1: 276–81.   [84] Repgen 1: 1: 281–7.
[85] Instructions for Questenberg's mission to Ingolstadt, Dec. 6, 1631, HHStA, RTA 100b.
[86] Bireley 1, 170–3.
[87] Emperor to Maximilian, Dec. 21, 1631, BAGW 1: #473; emperor to Questenberg, Dec. 21, 1631, ibid., #475.

simply beyond them. At one point, then three delegates approached Questenberg privately to inform him that they considered French mediation the only way out of the situation. Bavaria had already begun negotiations with Paris, they acknowledged adding that the bishop of Würzburg would soon embark on a trip to Paris. Would Ferdinand approve this initiative?

Questenberg responded in words that Ferdinand later endorsed. In light of the Franco–Swedish alliance, negotiations with France were tantamount to negotiations with the enemy. For more than a century, the French policy of weakening the Empire had not changed. And even if France sincerely intended to help the German Catholics, there was little that it could do in light of the present military superiority of the Swedes. Rather, Questenberg pointed out, it was necessary to discuss concessions with the Protestants, but on this issue neither Questenberg nor the representatives of the Catholic states were prepared to become specific. So nothing came of the meeting in Ingolstadt.[88]

Vienna had its own plan to meet the advance of the Swedes. Eggenberg and other councillors now envisioned Wallenstein's return to military command and then to negotiations with Saxony. As early as the winter of 1630–1631, Ferdinand had begun to regret the general's dismissal and to seek advice from him. Wallenstein, for his part, had made contact with Matthias Thurn, the principal figure of the Bohemian exiles, and through him with Gustav Adolph himself. What took place between them remains unknown.[89]

In mid-October Eggenberg and Gerhard von Questenberg, Herman's brother and war councillor, began to recommend that Wallenstein be recalled to service. From his retirement in Friedland, the general rebuffed Ferdinand's first approach, but by mid-November he agreed to discuss terms with Eggenberg. The two finally meant at Znojmo (Znaim) in Moravia on December 10. Wallenstein agreed to take up the army command once again but for only three months, time enough to reorganize the army and bring it up to strength but not to take it into battle. Both Ferdinand and Philip IV promised substantial financial support of the army, and Maximilian promised to pay his part, too. The Spanish party in Vienna had proposed that the young king of Hungary, who was eager to show his mettle on the battlefield, be invested with the formal command of the army of which Wallenstein would in effect be in charge, and Ferdinand himself went along with this proposal. But Wallenstein rejected it out of hand and it was quickly set aside at Znojno. Wallenstein was given explicit assurances that restrictions would be placed on Lamormaini's influence at court. Neither he nor other political clerics would be allowed to interfere with Wallenstein's activity through their "varying

---

[88] Questenberg to the emperor, Dec. 22, 1631 and Jan. 1, 1632, HHStA, RTA 100b; emperor to Questenberg, Jan. 7, 1632, ibid.; on the meeting in Ingolstadt, see Bireley 1, 175–6.
[89] Golo Mann, *Wallenstein* (Frankfurt, 1971), 764–71; Ritter, *Deutsche Geschichte* 3:525.

and ill-founded principles," according to Ferdinand's instruction, probably prepared under Eggenberg's own direction.[90]

Wallenstein had long considered the Edict disastrous for the emperor and for Germany, and he blamed it first of all on Lamormaini's influence. He made its eventual revocation and a return to the status of church lands in 1629 a condition of his acceptance of the military command.[91] Eggenberg accepted this stipulation, it can be assumed, since it nearly corresponded to what the six theologians had considered acceptable three weeks before. Whether Ferdinand explicitly approved it cannot be determined; most likely he did not. The previous fall Ferdinand had encouraged Wallenstein's secret correspondence with King Christian of Denmark in the hope of enlisting him against Christian's enemy and rival, Gustav Adolph. But Ferdinand had rejected the general's recommendation that Christian be promised several north German bishoprics to which his family had earlier held title. This could not be allowed without papal approval.[92] Eggenberg most likely believed that he would be able to persuade Ferdinand to accept these terms when the time for a decision came. For the moment there was no need to take a position on the Edict because the Mühlhausen Conference had been cancelled, and nearly all in Vienna agreed that no serious negotiations with the Protestants could take place until a balance of forces had been established. In the meantime, Eggenberg would continue to make efforts to have Lamormaini dismissed as Ferdinand's confessor.

On December 24, Charnacé departed from Munich for Mainz, there to present Gustav Adolph with a tentative neutrality agreement to which Maximilian had agreed, even though the elector knew that it would bring him into ill repute in Vienna. The Swedes already held several Catholic states, including Mainz and Würzburg. Bavaria lay defenseless before them. Tilly's army was in disarray, and Ferdinand could spare no troops to help him. So, under these circumstances, Maximilian agreed to observe neutrality with Gustav Adolph provided the king consented to allow the practice of the Catholic religion in the Catholic states that he occupied, to respect the borders of the member states of the Catholic League, and to restore their rightful rulers to the states of the League that he had overrun. These were unrealistic terms, and one wonders whether Maximilian really expected Gustav Adolph to agree to them. Maximilian realized that the terms would probably divert the brunt of the Swedish offensive against the Habsburg lands, but he reasoned that they would preserve religion in the Empire and enable the League quickly to recover and hasten to Ferdinand's aid. Maximilian even attempted to include Ferdinand in the agreement. Charnacé guaranteed that should Gustav Adolph refuse the terms, France would break with Sweden and come over to the Catholic side. This

---

[90] Dec. 10, 1631, BAGW 1: #450; Mann, 785–6; Ritter 3: 525–6.
[91] Leopold von Ranke, *Geschichte Wallensteins*, 3 ed. (Leipzig, 1872), cited in Repgen 1: 1, 288.
[92] Mann, 773.

would amount to the achievement of a goal that many including Maximilian and Lamormaini had long envisioned. Indeed, Maximilian's real goal may have been to put pressure on the French to rescue the German Catholics. His error lay not in the belief that Gustav Adolph would consent to the agreement but that France would abandon Sweden if he did not.[93]

Maximilian's high chancellor, Joachim von Donnersberg, journeyed to Vienna in mid-January to defend the elector's policy; there the government, now under Wallenstein's increasing influence, was much less inclined to listen to his message. Donnersberg was also instructed to promote harmony between Paris and Vienna; Swedish success had shown the need for Catholic unity. But a committee of councillors made up of Trautmannsdorf, the bishop of Vienna, Stralendorf, and Hermann von Questenberg rejected Donnersberg's defense of Maximilian's negotiations for neutrality with Sweden.[94] Public opinion in Vienna manifested little sympathy for him.[95] Meanwhile, Gustav Adolph rejected out of hand the terms of neutrality and offered much more stringent ones in their place which would require that Maximilian sacrifice some states of the Catholic League and compromise the practice of the Catholic religion in Swedish-occupied lands. Maximilian turned them down. By mid-February, it had become evident that France would not break with Sweden despite Charnacé's promises. So Maximilian was compelled to turn more completely to Vienna. Donnersberg returned to Munich at the end of March, the differences with the emperor having been papered over but not forgotten.[96]

In the aftermath of Breitenfeld, Spanish influence in Vienna rose dramatically. Spain appeared to many as the rock of salvation at this time of crisis. More at his initiative than Spain's, Ferdinand renewed the secret Oñate Treaty on October 20, 1631; this reaffirmed the bonds between the two branches of the House of Habsburg.[97] Madrid realized that Ferdinand badly needed its assistance; it aimed to exploit the situation in order to attain those elusive goals of Spanish policy, an alliance with the emperor and German states that would commit them to aid Spain in its war with the Dutch and to support it in its conflict with France[98] But there were limits to what Spain could hope to achieve. A paper drawn up by the aforementioned four councillors, without the participation of Eggenberg, showed that they did not accept the Spanish position that France had to be excluded from German affairs at any cost. Under suitable circumstances, they were prepared to accept Maximilian's recommendations that France serve as a mediator at a European peace conference.[99]

Ferdinand signed a treaty of alliance with Spain on February 14 in Vienna. But its ambiguity admitted of an interpretation that explains Lamormaini's

---

[93] Bireley 1, 172–4. [94] Position paper, Jan. 28, 1632, BAGW 2: #604.
[95] Albrecht 1, 341. [96] Bireley 1, 179, 181–6.
[97] Walter Platzhoff, *Geschichte des europäischen Staatensystems 1559–1660* (Munich, 1928), 193.
[98] Günter, 98–105. [99] See above, n. 88.

satisfaction with it.[100] Spanish influence can be detected in the de-emphasis of the religious element in the statement of its goal, the defense of the Empire rather than the faith, and the invitation to Protestant states such as England, Denmark, and the Protestant electors to join. But a principal purpose was to put an end to the hostility between the House of Habsburg and Bourbon France, on the unrealistic basis, to be sure, of the Treaty of Regensburg and the return of Pinerolo to Savoy; at least some in Vienna came to see it as the foundation of a grand Catholic alliance against the heretics and even the Turks. So Cardinal Pazmany thought whom Ferdinand sent to Rome in late February to secure Pope Urban's participation.[101]

What the Spaniards found most difficult to swallow was the mission of Baron Peter von Schwarzenberg to Paris, in early March, to invite Louis XIII to join the alliance. Schwarzenberg's instruction, corrected by Ferdinand himself, encouraged the French king to send an agent to Vienna.[102] Meanwhile, Philip IV refused to ratify the alliance because it did not call for imperial intervention in the Netherlands or eventual war with France, and the Spanish ambassador who had signed the alliance was recalled. But Spain sent an army down from the Netherlands to operate along the Mosel and in the Palatinate on the left bank of the Rhine, and so to help in the defense there against the Swedes.

During the autumn of 1631, the Spanish government once again took measures to reduce the influence of Lamormaini and if possible, to have him removed from court. Olivares denounced the confessor to Vitelleschi as an enemy of the House of Habsburg, and he summoned to Madrid in November seven prominent Spanish Jesuits to whom he issued dire threats against the Society in Spain if something were not done to remedy the situation in Vienna. Vitelleschi called the accusations against him to the attention of Lamormaini without identifying himself with them, and Lamormaini defended himself in a letter to the king of Spain. But the confessor came under criticism from many others as well, including fellow Jesuits. The superior of the Jesuit house in Vienna where Lamormaini resided informed Vitelleschi that many in the city blamed Lamormaini and the Jesuits for the war and the suffering that it brought them[103] Lamormaini lay low during the first half of 1632, sick in bed for a number of weeks. But he had not lost his influence with Ferdinand. On January 21, the emperor wrote him in his own hand, "I hope in my God, and I await the confusion of his enemies and of all the

---

[100] Vitelleschi to Lamormaini, Mar. 29, 1632, ARSJ, Aust. 4II, ff. 599–600.
[101] Pazmany to the emperor, Pressburg, Feb. 10, 1632, Peter Pazmany, *Epistolæ Collectæ*, ed. Franciscus Hanuy, 2 (Budapest, 1911): #712; Günter, 107–9.
[102] Mar. 2, 1632, HHStA, Friedens. 18, ff. 19–27v; see also Khevenhüller, *Annales Ferdinandei* 12: 310–12, and Leman, 95, 112–4, who attributes part of the initiative for Schwarzenberg's mission to the new nuncio in Paris, Allesandro Bichi.
[103] Nicholas Jagnitorius to Vitelleschi, Jan. 3, 1632, ARSJ, Aust. 21, f. 55.

political councillors."[104] The message would not have pleased Eggenberg nor would Lamormaini's remark to Ferdinand that the emperor could count on him alone to give disinterested advice. Their own ambition for advancement and wealth colored to a greater or lesser extent the opinions of all the other councillors.[105]

Wallenstein's original commission lapsed at the end of March. Ferdinand sent Eggenberg to Göllersdorf near Vienna to negotiate with the general the terms of his continued service. In his memorandum for Eggenberg Ferdinand recognized the wrong that the general had suffered at his hands, and he gave Eggenberg complete freedom in working out the terms for Wallenstein, though he did not mention the Edict.[106] In a conversation on April 13 at Göllersdorf, Eggenberg and Wallenstein reached an agreement about his continued service. The agreement appears to have been unwritten, and it has been open to varying interpretations.[107] At the least the general was granted widespread control of appointments in the imperial army and of its movements and quarters. He was guaranteed regular funds from Spain and from the hereditary lands, with supplements from confiscated lands. Ferdinand renewed his authority to negotiate with Saxony and through it with other Protestant states. Made over to him personally was the Silesian principality of Grossglogau and a sum of 400,000 gulden. Full payment for his services and for compensation for the loss of Mecklenburg was left to the future. The general almost certainly received renewed assurances against a repetition of his dismissal and against the interference of ecclesiastics in political affairs. Wallenstein was not happy with the Edict of Restitution, he told an agent of Rocci who brought him a papal brief congratulating him on his return to imperial service; he would war rather with Turks than heretics.[108] Lamormaini had tried to improve relations with him in

---

[104] Published in Dudik, 275; Two other handwritten notes from Ferdinand to Lamormaini, dated Jan. 11 and 12, 1632, ibid., 274–5, are too cryptic to be completely intelligible. But they point to Lamormaini's involvement in the formation of policy toward France.
[105] "Vita Lamormaini," 63–63v. It is impossible to date this statement, and it may well stem from another period of Lamormaini's tenure as confessor. In the margin of the Roman copy of the "Vita Lamormaini" someone wrote, "Caution here; better to omit this," presumably in any biography of Lamormaini or history of the Society. On this paragraph, see Bireley 2, 178–82.
[106] Memorial for Eggenberg, Apr. 12, 1632, in *Quellen zu Geschichte Wallensteins*, ed. Gottfried Lorenz (Darmstadt, 1987), 228–30. Ausgewählte Quellen zur Deutsche Geschichte der Neuzeit, 20.
[107] Much has been written about the Göllersdorf agreement, but as Georg Lutz, "Wallenstein, Ferdinand II und der Wiener Hof. Bemerkungen zu einem erneuten Beitrag zur alten Wallensteinfrage," *Quellen und Forschungen aus italienischen Archiven und Bibliotheken* 48 (1968), 227–8) has remarked, modern research has not been able to establish what the terms were or whether they were ever written out. I have followed Mann, 826–34. See also the discussion in *Quellen zu Geschichte Wallensteins*, 228–37.
[108] Rocci to Barberini, Feb. 14, 1632, BL 6970, ff. 78–88.

an effusive New Year's greeting, and when this failed to elicit a response, in a subsequent Easter greeting. But Wallenstein turned a deaf ear to both.[109]

During the last months of 1631 and the first half of 1632, Ferdinand's relationship with Rome grew more tense, this despite Barberini's directive to the new nuncio in Paris, Alessandro Bichi, to cease efforts to detach Bavaria from the emperor and to remonstrate with Richelieu about French support for Sweden. Rome now acknowledged that the preservation of Catholicism in Germany required that Ferdinand and Maxmilian stand together.[110] Vienna continued to seek funds from Rome as well as a commitment to the Habsburg cause in Germany. Ferdinand found it difficult to understand why Urban did not come out against the French given France's known aid to the Swedes. In December the pope did approve a monthly subsidy of 5,000 scudi each for Ferdinand and for the Catholic League, but Ferdinand considered the sum paltry when it was compared with the monies Urban assigned to advance the interests of the Barberini family, and he resented sharing the funds with the League.[111]

In February 1632, Cardinal Pazmany was sent on a mission to Rome to attempt to pry funds loose there and to persuade the pope to take a leading role in the alliance of which the treaty between the emperor and Spain of February 14 was the foundation and which was now presented as against the heretics and the Turks. Pazmany impressed upon Urban that the war in Germany was a religious one. Its principal cause was the Edict of Restitution, "which," he told the pope,"Your Holiness praised so highly."[112] Ferdinand was fighting for the church, and the pope had the obligation to aid him, especially by persuading France to cease its subsidies to the heretics. Now was the time for Urban to show the leadership that great popes had in past crises.

His journey to Rome left Pazmany disillusioned. He made his grand entrance into the Eternal City on March 28, three weeks after the Spanish Cardinal Borja made a dramatic protest against papal policy in a famous consistory of cardinals on March 8.[113] But one could not win over Urban with such methods. Pazmany's audiences with the pope and his sessions with other curial officials soon revealed that Urban would not participate in the alliance because of his fear of France. The most he could do, Urban told Pazmany, was to continue

[109] Jan. 2 and Apr. 9, 1632, published in Beda Dudik, *Waldstein, von seiner Enthebung bis zur abermaligen Übernahme des Armee-Ober-Commando* (Vienna, 1858), 194.
[110] Albrecht 1, 339–40.
[111] Rocci to Barberini, Dec. 27, 1631, BL 6969, ff. 219–25; Albrecht, "Zur Finanzierung des Dreissigjährigen Krieges," 555–6.
[112] Statement presented to Pope Urban by Pazmany, Apr. 6, 1632, *Epistolæ Collectæ* 2: #725; this is an enclosure with Pazmany to the emperor, Apr. 10, 1632, ibid., #727 where Pazmany stated that it was a nearly verbatim account of what he told the pope in his audience and later presented in writing. On the mission of Pazmany see also Leman, 146–66.
[113] On this incident, see Leman, 146–66.

urging France to cease aiding the Protestants. And, in truth, the fear of a French schism did haunt the pope; the Anglican schism of the previous century remained a painful memory in Rome.[114] Urban later gave Pazmany a further reason for not joining the alliance: the goal to defend the Empire included the maintenance of the Peace of Religion with its recognition of Protestant rights. Urban probably would send more funds, Pazmany reported, but he would not open up the treasure of Castel San Angelo.[115]

What stunned Vienna was that after the cardinal reminded Urban in an audience that the war was a religious one and that the pope had praised the Edict, Urban denied that he had ever done so. In fact, Urban contended, the Edict had not pleased him, as the documents would show, "unless perhaps (which he said was accustomed to happen often) the secretaries had written something more [than they should have]." Perhaps, Urban went on, the losses suffered by the German Catholic princes were a divine punishment for their failure to return the recovered church properties to their rightful owners.[116] Here the pope alluded to the dispute between the monastic orders on the one hand and the bishops and the Jesuits on the other over possession of recovered monastic lands in which Ferdinand generally favored the latter.[117] There was, as we have seen, some basis in fact for Urban's claim that he had not approved the Edict, but Ferdinand could hardly have been expected to interpret otherwise the flowery missives from Rome lauding his zeal and often communicated to him by supporters of the Edict like Pallotto and Lamormaini. As Ferdinand wrote Pazmany, Vienna could not be expected to know that papal officials did not accurately represent the mind of the pope. Copies of a number of papal communications to the emperor including the brief of May 6, 1629, were forwarded to Pazmany in Rome to demonstrate that the pope had supported the Edict and that he had approved the emperor's disposition of ecclesiastical lands.[118]

But Ferdinand needed papal aid, and he had no intention of acting in pique. Pazmany was told to redouble his efforts, and when he returned in July, he did not come back empty-handed. He undoubtedly succeeded in confirming Rome's decision taken at Bavarian suggestion prior to his arrival, namely, to dispatch extraordinary nuncios to the three capitals – Madrid, Paris, and Vienna – with the goal of reconciling the respective rulers and eventually uniting them in an alliance.[119] When Girolamo Grimaldi, the extraordinary

---

[114] See, for example, Girolamo Grimaldi (extraordinary nuncio in Vienna) to Barberini, Nov. 5 and 26, 1633, BL 6980, ff. 172–6v, 185–90v.,
[115] Pazmany to the emperor, Apr. 10, 16, 24, May 1, 1632, *Epistolæ Collectæ* 2: ##727, 731, 734, 756.
[116] Pazmany to the emperor, Apr. 10, 1632, *Epistolæ Collectæ* 2: #727.
[117] On this dispute, see Bireley 2, 133–50.
[118] Emperor to Pazmany, Apr. 28, 1632, HHStA, Staaten, Romana, 53.
[119] Bireley 2, 84; Ludwig von Pastor, *Geschichte der Päpste im Zeitalter der katholischen Restauration und des Dreissigjährigen Krieges* 13 (Freiburg, 1928): 440–1, 448–51.

nuncio for Vienna, arrived in late June, he brought with him 80,000 talers for the emperor and 50,000 for the League. Several times in the years before the Peace of Prague in 1635, similar modest sums flowed north in addition to the monthly subsidies.[120]

The foundation stone of Urban's policy thus became the promotion of reconciliation among the Catholic states, especially the Habsburg states and France, and the formation of a Catholic alliance. This corresponded to the long-standing design of Lamormaini, who could find a positive note in the French response to Schwarzenberg's mission to Paris. Louis desired peace, he affirmed, and he even showed a willingness to assist the emperor against Sweden should Gustav Adolph turn down reasonable terms. The catch was in the conditions Louis proposed: recognition of French possession of the fortress Pinerolo, acceptance of the French interpretation of the Treaty of Monzon of 1626 with Spain regarding the Valtelline, and acquiescence in French garrisons in Metz and Moyenvic near the French border with the Empire. The emperor was to attempt to persuade Spain to accept these conditions, and should he fail, to remain neutral in any conflict that might ensue between France and Spain.[121] This would, of course, split the two Habsburg states and so achieve a long-standing goal of the French.

How seriously did Richelieu take the Schwarzenberg mission to Paris? He may have wanted to maintain contact with Vienna merely because he had to indicate some interest in the papal plan for the reconciliation of the three crowns. More likely his response to Schwarzenberg was dictated by the new French relationship with Sweden that the unforeseen degree of Gustav Adolph's success had created. The French had not anticipated that Gustav Adolph would stand on the Rhine in December 1631, and they did not want to see him expand his presence there. The French concluded several treaties with an eye on the Swedish king. Two were signed with the elector of Trier. The first in December 1631 guaranteed the elector French protection, and the second the following April provided for French garrisons in the two fortresses on the Rhine, Ehrenbreitsein (opposite Coblenz) and Phillipsburg. They then imposed two treaties on the Duke of Lorraine, who had aided Louis's domestic enemies, in January and June 1632. These conceded broad rights to France in his territories and committed the duke to support French interests.[122] Richelieu seems to have maintained communication with Vienna in order to keep ajar an emergency door through which he might pass and still reach some of his goals in the event that his project for an anti-Habsburg alliance failed or proved to be unmanageable as Gustav Adolph advanced.

---

[120] Albrecht, "Finanzierung des Dreissigjährigen Krieges," 400–6.
[121] "Relatio Summaria," see above n. 95 and Leman, 113–17.
[122] Albrecht 1, 320-2; Leman, 217, 235–6; Hermann Weber, *Frankreich, Kurtrier, Der Rhein, und das Reich, 1623-1635* (Bonn, 1969), 112–13, 121-7, 146, 192-3.

The nuncios now managed most of the communications between Vienna and Paris, and through them Ferdinand tried to persuade Louis to send a representative to Vienna. But Louis claimed that he could not send one until the emperor gave a definite response to his proposals. The posting of a representative would arouse the suspicion of his allies. Ferdinand followed the recommendation of his privy council when in response he explained the reasons for his insistence on the Treaty of Regensburg and requested a clearer statement of the French position.[123] Another turn of events would bring a French negotiator to Vienna in February of 1633.

For many the hope of an understanding between Ferdinand and Louis was an illusion, the product of wishful thinking. But the extraordinary nuncio Grimaldi persisted. He tried hard to explain that the pope could not break with France and still claim to be "universal father" of all Catholics.[124] Among the emperor's councillors, Grimaldi found Trautmannsdorf and Werdenberg open to the possibility of an understanding with France.[125] On the other side were Eggenberg and the bishop of Vienna, who remained at court when Eggenberg returned to Graz in mid-September.[126] Grimaldi was especially critical of several religious at court who vigorously rejected any understanding with France. He pointed at the Capuchin agent of Cardinal Harrach in Vienna, Basilio d'Aire, whom he characterized as "completely Austrian," and even more so Quiroga, who in one meeting, according to Grimaldi, defended all the actions of the Spanish crown since the days of Peter of Aragon, who died in 1381.[127] Lamormaini's name rarely turned up in the nuncios' dispatches in the spring and summer of 1632.

During spring and summer of 1632, the Catholic forces encountered continued adversity. The Swedes crossed the River Lech near Rain into Bavaria on April 15. Tilly was wounded in the fighting and died two weeks later. So the Catholics lost their veteran general. The Bavarians defended the fortress at Ingolstadt successfully and the line along the Danube to Regensburg and Passau, but Gustav Adolph bypassed Ingolstadt and marched to the west through Bavaria ravaging the country. He entered Munich triumphantly on May 17 where he held court until June 7. Maximilian was compelled to move his court and government to Braunau in Upper Austria and to Salzburg

---

[123] Report of the committee of councillors on negotiations with France," Jul. 18, 1632, HHStA, Friedens. 18, ff. 104-5, approved by the privy council, ibid., f. 106.
[124] Grimaldi to Barberini, Jul. 17, 1632, BL 6978, ff. 33-45v.
[125] Grimaldi to Barberini, Jul. 3, 10, Sept. 11, 1632, ibid., ff. 14-20, 22-32, 115-19. On Sept. 25, however, Grimaldi wrote that he thought Werdenberg had lost all hope of an agreement with France, ibid., ff. 132-6v.
[126] Grimaldi to Barberini, Jul. 11, Sept. 11, 1632, ibid., ff. 59-67v, 115-19; Rocci to Barberini, Sept. 18, 1632, BL 6971, ff. 48-57.
[127] Grimaldi to Barbarini, Jul. 10, Aug. 14, 1632, BL 6978, ff. 22-32, 76-80.

Setback, 1631–1632

respectively. Swedish troops had earlier marched into Augsburg, so that they controlled much of south central Germany.

Meanwhile, Wallenstein broke camp from Znomjo on April 23 with the intention of gaining the upper hand in Bohemia. He retook Prague on May 25. His advance forced Gustav Adolph to march eastwards. Otherwise Wallenstein might invade a poorly-defended Saxony, thus making negotiations with the emperor attractive to Elector John George and perhaps cut the Swedish king's supply lines to the north. Wallenstein's troops joined Maximilian's in the Upper Palatinate in July, and soon Gustav Adolph's encamped not far from them outside Nuremberg. There the two armies faced off against each other for the balance of the summer. Maximilian grew impatient with Wallenstein's refusal to take advantage of his numerical superiority to secure the major victory that the Catholics hoped would restore the balance between the two sides. Wallenstein insisted on waiting until shortage of supplies compelled the Swedish king to abandon the defensive and to attack. In early September Gustav Adolph did so, but he was thrown back with heavy losses. So he lost his reputation for invincibility. But Wallenstein did not follow up his victory, much to the disappointment of Maximilian.

Pessimism continued to prevail among the Catholics. No operas or significant musical entertainments were performed in Vienna in 1632.[128] A peasant rebellion flared up in Upper Austria in September and October stirred by hopes fixed on Gustav Adolph. Stralendorf, in a long position paper, lamented that without a major victory before the onset of winter the situation of the Catholics would become desperate.[129] The resources of the Bohemian lands would soon be exhausted. Spain was hard pressed in the Netherlands, and it was only from that quarter that there was hope for human aid. The pope, it seemed, had abandoned Ferdinand; he and other Italian princes still had not forgotten Ferdinand's intervention in Italy. Stralendorf even thought that he detected a note of schadenfreude in a recent conversation with Grimaldi. Ferdinand ought to seek peace on the best terms that he could get in order to avoid total collapse. Wallenstein was the one to undertake the negotiations.

But this raised familiar issues of conscience. Aware of Ferdinand's mind, Stralendorf took them into consideration and proposed the safest course. The emperor ought to take no positive initiative with regard to religious issues, so that it would be clear that he accepted only what necessity imposed. Thus there would be no danger of his alienating God, his sole support. But this way of proceeding prevented the emperor from exercising leadership toward a settlement, and it left the initiative on the Catholic side to the electors, from whom little could be expected

---

[128] Seifert, 434–5. [129] Sept. 24, 1632, BAGW 3: #1304.

Gustav Adolph did approach Wallenstein about negotiations, and the general sent the Swedish king's proposals on to Vienna. Included were the revocation of the Edict, the return to the Protestants of most of the church lands recovered during the course of the war, freedom of religion for Lutherans in the Catholic states, and a major redistribution of territories within the Empire. Neither Gustav Adolph nor Wallenstein could have expected Ferdinand to take them seriously. The emperor did ask Wallenstein's opinion on them, noting that the conditions were extremely hard. He had little confidence that negotiations at this time would lead anywhere, Ferdinand wrote, and talks with Saxony and Brandenburg were decidedly preferable.[130]

Then an unexpected turn of events gave the Catholics new hope. The armies had maneuvered about once again in mid-November. After Wallenstein had moved into Saxony, they faced off against each other anew near Lützen, not far from Leipzig. On November 16, Gustav Adolph personally led a charge. The battle itself was a draw, with both sides taking heavy losses, but in the chaos of the fight Gustav Adolph fell. So the Swedes lost their charismatic leader.[131] For Ferdinand the king's death was a response to his prayer. With confidence in God he had rejected a proposal to assassinate Gustav Adolph, as had Philip IV. Such a deed was unworthy of a Christian and an emperor.[132] In thanksgiving for the removal of Gustav Adolph from the scene, a monastery for the Spanish Benedictines was planned near the Schottentor in Vienna. When the military prefect of the city complained that this would dangerously weaken the city's defenses, Ferdinand assured him that the protection of the Blessed Virgin Mary, to whom the monastery would be dedicated, would more than offset this.[133]

According to Grimaldi, Lamormaini claimed to have persuaded Ferdinand that the death of Gustav on the battlefield represented another example of God's miraculous providence over him. The confessor, Grimaldi reported, now foresaw that the war would persist until the military situation improved notably, then France and other Catholic states would be invited to conclude a settlement on terms that the emperor had up to this point thought to be

---

[130] Emperor to Wallenstein, Oct. 31, 1632, BAGW 3, #1488.
[131] Mann, *Wallenstein*, 875-93.
[132] *Virtutes*, 80. Writing from Vienna to Olivares on Jan. 3, 1632, Quiroga mentioned a plan by a "*cierto personaje*" to assassinate Gustav Adolph. He had talked the matter over with the queen of Hungary and other figures favorable to Spain, he indicated, and he recommended that the sum required by the author of the plan be set aside for him. In his response of Mar. 2, 1632, Günter, *Habsburgerliga*, #70, Philip IV refused to have anything to do with the plan, which was unbecoming a "*rey grande y justo.*" Ferdinand's response, according to Lamormaini, was much the same; the plot was beneath both a Christian and an emperor.
[133] *Virtutes*, 26, 35; see Richard Müller, "Wiens räumliche Entwicklung und topographische Benennung," *Geschichte der Stadt Wien*, ed. Anton Mayer 4 (Vienna, 1911), 378 and Ernst Tomek, "Das kirchliche Leben und die christliche Charitas in Wien, ibid. 5 (Vienna, 1911): 257.

inconsistent with his reputation.[134] In other words, once Ferdinand had achieved superiority over the Swedes and Protestants, he would, from a position of strength, be ready to make surprising concessions to the French for the sake of an enduring peace. Perhaps Lamormaini was thinking of the terms proposed by France in response to Schwarzenberg's mission. This prospect remained an option for imperial policy until the Peace of Prague in 1635. Its weakness lay in the belief that the France of Richelieu would be willing to live at peace with a revived imperial power in Germany.

[134] Grimaldi to Barberini, Dec. 11, 1632, BL 6978, ff. 212–18v.

Chapter 8

Recovery, 1632–1634

Most of the councillors in Vienna recognized that the battle of Lützen had resulted in a draw at best and could be considered a victory only because of the death of Gustav Adolph. A small committee of councillors that included Stralendorf recommended in early December 1632 that the emperor press forward with negotiations for peace while at the same time taking advantage of the momentum gained at Lützen. One could not yet hope for reasonable conditions; for these, one would have to wait for the restoration of a military balance. This would come in fact only with the battle of Nördlingen in September 1634. Total victory was out of the question. The enemy possessed far greater resources as a result of the territory that it held in Germany and its connections with France, the Dutch, Denmark, and England. The report of the councillors suggested that Ferdinand dispatch an emissary to Paris now that, with the death of Gustav Adolph, the French alliance with Sweden had lapsed. This initiative may well have come from Justus Gebhardt, who was close to Lamormaini and may have served as his voice in deliberations in Vienna.[1] Meeting four days later, the privy council rejected this recommendation, preferring to await the arrival of an anticipated French emissary in Vienna. Both the committee and the privy council advised Ferdinand that before he make any decisions, he obtain the views of the Catholic electors, Wallenstein, and Eggenberg, who was absent.[2]

Perhaps wanting to hear from a trusted ecclesiastic, Ferdinand now requested an opinion from Cardinal Pazmany who submitted one dated

---

[1] The author of the "Vita Lamormaini" suggested that a copy of the manuscript be presented to Gebhardt; see Eustachius Sthaäl, S.J. to Florence de Montmorency, S.J., Vienna, Oct. 10, 1649, ARSJ, Vitae 139, f. 2.

[2] Position paper with comments of the privy council, Dec. 5–9, 1632, BAGW 3: #1637.

December 8. He advocated a compromise peace with the Protestants.[3] It was impossible, the cardinal asserted, to defeat the enemy militarily; the hereditary lands were exhausted and Spain faced increasing difficulties in the Old World and the New.

> If there were hope either of completely subduing the Empire or radically extirpating heresy, it would be impious and execrable to raise the question of a settlement. But given the present state of affairs and considering the situation in France, Belgium, Italy, and the Indies as well as the exhaustion of the [Catholic] princes and [hereditary] provinces, it [subjection of the Empire and complete uprooting of heresy] seems morally impossible (divine miracles, reserved to the supreme heavenly council do not enter into the deliberation), whereby the resources of the Empire would be totally destroyed.

Lamormaini was clearly the target of the remark in parentheses. Pazmany did not specify terms of peace in his paper, but according to a later conversation with Lamormaini reported by Grimaldi, the cardinal was ready to accept any agreement that would preserve Catholicism in the Habsburg lands.[4] This was where Pazmany's primary interest lay, as did that of the other two "great and learned prelates" mentioned by Grimaldi, who can only have been Bishop Wolfradt and Cardinal Dietrichstein. They were prepared to go well beyond what the six theologians had sanctioned the previous year. All their lands and jurisdictions, it should be noted, lay in the Habsburg lands.

Pazmany held out no hope of assistance from Rome or Paris or from a Catholic alliance, a fact due perhaps to his frustrating journey to Rome the previous spring. Another concern raised by the cardinal was the apparent decline of Ferdinand's health and the growing possibility that he might die before the election of the king of the Romans. Uncertainty over the succession in the imperial office would only serve to encourage more disruption and foreign interference. Some military leaders, Pazmany noted, apparently prolonged the war for their own benefit; so he made his own a conclusion already reached by others in Vienna from Wallenstein's hesitation to commit his troops to battle and to follow up his victories. Thus the cardinal revealed himself as among the advocates of compromise who were unsympathetic to the general.

Ferdinand's acceptance in late January 1633 of a Danish offer to mediate called forth further consultations in Vienna. Bishop Anton Wolfradt and Trautmannsdorf assisted Stralendorf in the preparation of a long report.[5] The arguments were similar to those of the previous December advocating negotiations and the continuation of the war effort. The councillors lamented the immense benefits the Protestants drew from their one victory at Breitenfeld and the little that the Catholics had to show for all their successes on the field of battle. They attributed this to the more widespread popular support that the

---

[3] Peter Pazmany, *Epistolæ Collectæ*, ed. Franciscus Hanuy 2 (Budapest, 1911): #798.
[4] Mar. 19, 1633, BL 6979, ff. 78–85v.   [5] Jan. 28–Feb. 4, 1633, BAGW 3: #1801.

Protestants enjoyed. As far back as the Electoral Convention of Mühlhausen in 1627, they reminded Ferdinand, they had recommended a policy of caution.

They then took up the religious issue, with a view to Lamormaini, it would appear. They assumed that concessions would have to be made but remained vague on specifics. "But it has already been sufficiently deliberated what can be conceded in this matter by reason of necessity in order to avoid greater evil to religion," they wrote, apparently referring to the position of the six theologians. They seem to have approved implicitly the position that the three prelates had approved, that nearly any settlement was acceptable in the Empire provided that the status of Catholicism in the Habsburg lands was safeguarded. These lands merited their principal attention.

Then for one thing, the paper continued, "it is more beneficial to preserve religion in some fashion after the example of Ferdinand I than in the end to risk absolutely everything." So the writers appealed to the spirit of compromise that Emperor Ferdinand I showed when he signed the Peace of Augsburg and the positive results that this had brought. Between 1555 and the "accursed" Bohemian war, Catholicism had made great progress in many areas of Germany. The current war and especially the last few years had reduced the Church to its worst state since the Reformation. Protestant preachers carried on their activities in areas occupied by the enemy where they had never been seen before. The consequence was the loss of many souls. The three councillors pointed out that God's support of a just cause was revealed as much by his granting of useful counsel as of military victories, "since it is the nature of a rational creature to overcome by prudence and counsel rather than by force," they wrote, citing a commonplace from Cicero.

Yet toward the end of their long paper, in a passage recalling Lamormaini, the three took note of God's providential care for Ferdinand. The death of Gustav Adolph had revealed it once again. The concessions that Ferdinand might make were limited, but these limits were not specified.

Therefore also such a great helper [God] is not at all to be offended by yielding to conditions of the sort that might be opposed to his holy name or divine glory. Rather much more is everything else that the divine omnipotence might decree to be suffered and born in patience, because he is the one who puts to death and raises up again, who in the midst of the greatest danger can easily send His Imperial Majesty the best fortune.

The councillors recommended that the emperor respond positively to the peace initiatives of Denmark and Hesse-Darmstadt, and soon Bishop Anton Wolfradt and Hermann von Questenberg were deputed to talks with the Landgrave of Hesse-Darmstadt planned for Leitmeritz (Litoměřice) in Bohemia in March.

Lamormaini found greater significance in the battle of Lützen than did the councillors, as we have noted. According to nuncio Grimaldi, he assured the emperor that if he remained steadfast in his confidence in God and did not misuse the "miracles" God worked on his behalf, Ferdinand would have the honor of extirpating heresy in Germany, "since in ancient times heresy had

Recovery, 1632–1634

never lasted longer than one hundred years." Ferdinand had promised to consult with him before entering into any agreement with the Protestants, Lamormaini told the nuncio. But Grimaldi doubted that his opinion would prevail over the others.[6] Eggenberg expressed nearly the same sentiment to the Bavarian Donnersberg when he remarked that some ecclesiastics still opposed peace but that Ferdinand and his ministers, aware of the exhaustion of finances and suffering of the people, were strongly inclined to it.[7] In talking with Lamormaini, according to Grimaldi, Ferdinand cited the views of Bishop Wolfradt, Pazmany, and Dietrichstein.[8] But it was too early to count Lamormaini out; he continued to look with hope to France.

Paris did not find Gustav Adolph's death completely unwelcome. His triumphant march through Germany had ended Richelieu's hope to control him. The cardinal had not been able to secure neutrality from him toward Bavaria and the Catholic League. Now that the king had departed, the cardinal planned to fashion an anti-Habsburg alliance that he could control. He planned to continue to support Sweden but he aimed to have Saxony and Brandenburg assume the leadership of the Protestant cause in Germany. It was also important for the cardinal to convince some German Catholic states, especially Bavaria, at least to remain neutral toward the coalition that he was building because this would diminish the religious nature of the war and help silence his domestic opposition. The Marquis de Feuquière was sent to Germany in early 1633 to implement this policy. He was to visit Axel Oxenstierna, the Swedish chancellor who was now Sweden's effective policy maker, and the two electors, John George of Saxony and George William of Brandenburg.

Feuquière met with little success. Saxony had no intention of allying with another foreign power, and Brandenburg, while more receptive, would not do so without Saxony. More interesting to John George were the imminent negotiations with Ferdinand. Oxenstierna turned out to be a much stronger personality than either Paris or Vienna anticipated. Sweden did not collapse. On April 19 at Heilbronn in Swabia, Feuquière and Oxenstierna renewed the Franco-Swedish alliance on nearly the same terms as at Bärwalde. A few days later, Oxenstierna formed an alliance with the newly created Heilbronn Confederation of Upper German Protestant states that recognized him as director of their combined forces and left Sweden in firm control. Feuquière failed to secure any recognition of neutrality for the German Catholic states, and Saxony's efforts to gain influence with the Upper German Protestant states met with no success. The following September 9, France entered an alliance with the Heilbronn Confederation but it did not obtain any significant provisions regarding neutrality toward the Catholic states. Wallenstein's successes in

---

[6] Grimaldi to Barberini, Mar. 5, 1633, BL 6979, ff. 64–9.
[7] Donnersberg to Maximilian, Mar. 16, 1633, BANF 8, #53D, (pp. 57–9); KSchw 132, f.32.
[8] Grimaldi to Barberini, Apr. 9, 1633, BL 6979, ff. 117–22.

the east, meanwhile, led Brandenburg to join the Franco–Swedish alliance on October 28, 1633. Richelieu continued to work at obtaining influence over the south and west German states, Catholic as well as Protestant. The French controlled much of Lorraine by early 1633, and French troops as protectors occupied much of the electorate of Trier where French and Spanish troops had clashed.[9]

Meanwhile, Richelieu maintained his contacts with Vienna with the help of the nuncios. Nicolas de Charbonnière arrived there as a permanent resident in February 1633, bearing with him the outline of a treaty to be presented to the emperor by Grimaldi. The price of an understanding with Vienna had been raised from what had been quoted to Schwarzenberg in Paris the year before. Ferdinand was to accede to French possession of Pinerolo in Italy and to recognize French claims not only to Metz but to the other two disputed bishoprics, Toul and Verdun, as well as the growing French occupation of Lorraine. On the other hand, France would agree to withdraw from some areas that it had occupied in Trier. Completely new was a French demand for a German peace conference where France would serve as mediator and full-fledged participant. This would obviously make possible all sorts of mischief, particularly as long as the issue of the succession in the Empire remained unresolved. Any pact with France would also require a commitment not to aid Spain should a Franco-Spanish conflict break out.[10]

The imperial councillors did not take up Charbonnière's proposal until the end of March. They found little basis in the French offer for an understanding with France or for a peace conference. But Charbonnière remained in Vienna, and Ferdinand assured the nuncios that he was ready to participate in the conference of the Catholic powers that Urban VIII was now promoting to resolve the problems of Europe.[11]

Gustav Adolph's death produced little change in Spanish policy. The Spaniards were more determined than ever to obtain German support in the Netherlands after their loss of the fortress of Maastricht shortly before the battle of Lützen. This was the task entrusted to the marquis of Castañeda, who departed from Madrid in October 1632 to replace the marquis of Cadereyta and the now deceased duke of Guastalla as ambassador in Vienna. Castañeda was to

---

[9] Albrecht 1, 355–61; Berthold Bauestadt, *Richelieu und Deutschland. Von der Schlacht bei Breitenfeld bis zum Tode Bernhards von Weimar* (Berlin, 1936), 74, 79–100, 103; Hermann Weber, *Frankreich, Kurtrier, der Rhein und das Reich* (Bonn, 1969), 230–70. Pariser Historiche Studien, 9.

[10] Richelieu, *Mémoires 1629–1638. Nouvelle collection des mémoires pour servir à l'histoire de France depuis la xiiie siècle jusqu'à la fin du xviiie*, ed. Joseph Michaud and Jean Joseph Poujoulat (Paris, 1857) 22: 449–51; Baustaedt, 72–3; Auguste Leman, *Urbain VIII et la rivalité de la France et de la maison de Autriche de 1631 à 1635* (Lille/Paris, 1920). 272–3.

[11] Position paper with remarks of the privy council, Mar. 31–Apr. 1, 1633, HHStA, Friedens. 18, 1633, ff. 8–14v.; see also Leman, 262–3, 272–3.

continue the effort to create an alliance of Habsburg and German states against the Swedes, the Dutch, and the French. The Spaniards now planned to send an army of 24,000 under the command of the governor of Milan, the duke of Feria, through the Valtelline into the Tyrol, and then along the western border of the Empire, to relieve the Spanish forces in the Netherlands. The expedition was also to escort to Brussels, the Cardinal Infante, Don Fernando, the newly-appointed governor of the Netherlands after the death of the Archduchess Isabella. A section of the army was to remain in the Spanish occupied west bank of the Palatinate, to operate against the French or the Swedes as necessity dictated. In January, the veteran diplomat Oñate returned to Vienna as an extraordinary ambassador entrusted with the task of winning over Wallenstein for this plan.[12]

Madrid continued to rely on Quiroga to exercise influence in Vienna. Eggenberg's health was deteriorating. Quiroga was to try to bind Bishop Anton Wolfradt closer to Spain which saw in him Eggenberg's successor. "It is feared," Philip IV wrote Quiroga, "that Trautmannsdorf cannot be won over."[13] Quiroga was also expected to use his influence with Wallenstein, "his friend," and to try to overcome the differences between Count Thun, who wanted a major military role for his master, the king of Hungary, and Eggenberg who along with Wallenstein opposed this.[14]

Vienna was focused primarily on negotiations with the Protestants during the early spring of 1633. The two moderates, Bishop Anton Wolfradt and Hermann von Questenberg, conducted their talks with Hesse-Darmstadt at Leitmoritz from March 23 to 25. No specific instructions appear to have been prepared for them beyond the January paper of Stralendorf, Trautmannsdorf, and Bishop Anton Wolfradt, probably because the talks were meant to be merely exploratory. Ferdinand expected the two to keep in touch with Wallenstein. The general, for his part, was not inclined to work with the moderate party in Vienna; he felt that they moved too slowly and he wanted to take matters in hand himself.[15]

Nothing resulted from the discussions at Leitmeritz except the agreement to continue with negotiations at Breslau in May with the help of Danish mediation. Even the moderates in Vienna considered the demands of the Protestants exorbitant. They included the revocation of the Edict and the determination of 1612 as the normative year for the possession of Church lands and for the free exercise of religion. This would mean not only the

---

[12] Albrecht 1, 362–3; Alfred van der Essen, *Le Cardinal-Infant et le politique européene de l'Espagne, 1609–1641*, 1 (Louvain/Brussels, 1944): 105–110; Heinrich Günter, 130
[13] Philip IV to Quiroga, Jan. 1, 1633, Günter, #83 and pp. 127–8.
[14] Philip IV to Castañeda, Feb. 10, 1633, ibid., #90, and Philip IV to the count of Monterey, Viceroy of Naples, Sept. 6, 1632, ibid., #78.
[15] Golo Mann, *Wallenstein* (Frankfurt, 1971), 919–21.

surrender of all the lands the Catholics had regained in the war thus far but also the widespread free exercise of religion in Upper and Lower Austria and in Bohemia, a concession that Ferdinand would never even consider. It would deprive him of the right granted all imperial princes by the Peace of Augsburg to determine the religion to be practiced in their lands. Hesse-Darmstadt proposed that Maximilian retain the electoral title until his death, when it would return to Frederick's heirs. All the Palatinate lands would, however, revert to them immediately except the Upper Palatinate which Bavaria would keep permanently. Sweden would have to be granted some territories in Germany in compensation for its labors in the Empire. Hesse-Darmstadt repeated a longstanding Protestant demand when he called for a new body composed equally of Protestants and Catholics to decide issues touching religion in the Empire; such decisions were no longer to be made by majority vote in the diet, either in the council of electors or in the council of princes. In addition, he wanted equal representation of Catholics and Protestants on the two imperial courts, the Imperial Court Council in Vienna and the Imperial Cameral Court in Speyer.[16] Upon the return of Bishop Anton Wolfradt and Questenberg to Vienna, Rocci reported that as far as Vienna was concerned, peace was not in sight.[17] But negotiations were to continue.

During 1632 Lamormaini had attempted, without success, to rebuild his bridges with Wallenstein. Meanwhile in early 1633 following up on information from a source he did not name but was Contzen in Munich, Vitelleschi encourged Lamormaini to take up Wallenstein's alleged astrological practices with Ferdinand; they seemed to explain his reluctance to exploit his military advantage. But Lamormaini responded that he was powerless in the matter.[18] The obvious tension between Lamormaini and Eggenberg made Grimaldi reluctant to urge Urban's matter of the prefect of Rome through the confessor since his support might hurt rather than help the papal cause.[19]

Wallenstein himself engaged in negotiations with the enemy in the late spring and summer of 1633, but their precise character and purpose are not clear. On May 17 he initiated an advance into Silesia, but shortly thereafter he and the Saxon general Arnim concluded an armistice that was regularly renewed except for a few brief intervals until October 2. Wallenstein's failure to attack in the east permitted the enemy to concentrate its efforts to the west, especially in

---

[16] Imperial instructions for the delegates to the conference at Breslau, Aug. 26, 1633, BAGW 4, #2008, where there are many references to Leitmeritz; Donnersberg to Maximilian, Vienna, Apr. 27, 1633, KSchw 132, ff. 127-8; Emperor to Maximilian, Apr. 30, 1633, with attachment, BANF 8, #92 (pp. 150-3). Mann, *Wallenstein*, 92-108.

[17] Rocci to Barberini, Apr. 9, 1633, BL 6972, ff. 98-103.

[18] Vitelleschi to Lamormaini, Feb. 19 and Apr. 26, 1633, ARSJ, Aust. 4II, ff. 765, 799. On Wallenstein and astrology, see Mann, 669-73, 974-6.

[19] Grimali to Barberini, May 14, 1633, BL 6979, ff. 170-75v.

Bavaria. Maximilian could not understand the generalissimo's reluctance to mount an offensive, and he grew suspicious of the general's secret negotiations. In their first talks on June 6, Wallenstein and Arnim seem to have agreed tentatively to the return in the Empire, exclusive of the Habsburg lands, to the ecclesiastical and political status of 1618; this would mean the surrender of the Palatinate by Maximilian. The agreement would then, supposedly, serve as the basis for a union of the imperial and Saxon armies, who would then take action against all who opposed the settlement, German or foreign. But neither Ferdinand nor leading councillors in Vienna were ready for such an agreement, the general soon learned. He communicated this to Arnim, with the result that the Saxon general began to question whether Wallenstein accurately reflected the position of Ferdinand.[20]

Indecision and perplexity afflicted the emperor in June and July, when first Wallenstein's negotiations and then the talks planned for Breslau summoned him to take a position. A struggle was taking place for Ferdinand's mind. Forceful intervention by Lamormaini and the two nuncios Rocci and Grimaldi almost certainly influenced him in the rejection of the terms suggested by Wallenstein. At the least they confirmed him in it. In mid-June, Rocci reminded Lamormaini of his duty as confessor "to warn His Majesty not to agree out of human considerations to a peace so prejudicial to the Catholic religion." Lamormaini assured Rocci that he had spoken "freely enough" with both Eggenberg and Ferdinand, and that "he had found them sufficiently constant on the point of not prejudicing the Catholic religion." Ferdinand would not permit Wallenstein to enter an agreement with Saxony before he, Ferdinand, looked it over carefully and made necessary adjustments. The emperor, Rocci continued, would never accept 1618 as normative for the Habsburg lands. But Ferdinand, and more so Eggenberg, inclined to accept 1618 for the Empire which would compel Maximilian's surrender of the Palatinate. Eggenberg reminded the nuncio that Ferdinand had his own theologians who had recognized the principle of the lesser evil and left its application up to the political councillors. Rome had never accepted the Religious Peace but had tolerated it, Eggenberg explained to Rocci; at the same time he rejected the nuncio's suggestion that Ferdinand pursue more actively an agreement with France.[21]

---

[20] Hermann Hallwich, *Wallensteins Ende. Ungedruckte Briefe und Acten* 2 (Leipzig, 1879), xciv–xcv; see also Gerhard von Questenberg to Wallenstein, Vienna, Jun. 12, 1633, *Documenta Bohemica Bellum Tricennale Illustrantia*, Vol. 5: *Der schwedische Krieg und Wallensteins Ende*, ed. Miroslav Toegel (Prague/Vienna, 1977): #504; Wallenstein's Deputy to Heinrich San Julian (his emissary in Vienna), Jun. 15, 1633, Hallwich, ibid., #476; Eggenberg to Wallenstein, Jun. 20, 1633, ibid., #482. Cf. Mann, *Wallenstein*, 948–51.

[21] Rocci to Barberini, Jun. 18, 1633, in Repgen, 1: 2: #52; Grimaldi to Barberini, Jun. 18, 1633, ibid., #50.

The following week Rocci personally took his case to the emperor, and he reported on July 2 that peace was not as close as some thought.[22] But the situation remained fluid. Ferdinand assured Wallenstein on July 9 that he would follow his recommendations, and a few days later Gerhard von Questenberg was optimistic.[23] Preparations were now under way for the negotiations in Breslau. Trautmannsdorf headed the imperial delegation assisted by Hermann von Questenberg and Justus Gebhardt. The three were to cooperate with Wallenstein, but the general's enthusiasm dipped when he learned who made up the imperial negotiating team.[24] He probably was unhappy that Bishop Anton Wolfradt had declined to serve on it[25] and realized that Gebhardt was close to Lamormaini. The appointment of Trautmannsdorf to the negotiating team also most likely did not sit well with him; the minister had tried to avoid the assignment because he found it difficult to work with Wallenstein.[26] According to Trautmannsdorf, Grimaldi had reported a couple months earlier, he and many others were disgusted with the "impertinences" of the general, and the minister had expressed his support for the young king of Hungary, whom they hoped to convince the emperor to place at the head of the imperial army. According to Trautmannsdorf, Grimaldi reported, "if the emperor were convinced and we were [all] in agreement to dismiss Wallenstein, it would be enough to write the principal captains since he is no less hated in the army than he is feared by all."[27] So it was eventually to turn out with the general. Nor was Trautmannsdorf prepared to consent to a return to the status of 1618 in the Empire as the basis for a settlement with the Protestants.[28]

The three delegates to the conference at Breslau only departed on August 28, with a first stop at Wallenstein's camp.[29] A few days after they had left, the two nuncios delivered to Ferdinand a brief from Pope Urban.[30] The pope encouraged Ferdinand to stand steadfast while dispensing with the rhetorical flourishes of earlier briefs. Perhaps the Curia now checked the work of its secretaries more carefully. The pope continued to maintain his policy up to this point. He made clear that he opposed concessions and so protected the Church juridically; but he made no further effort to pressure Ferdinand to reject terms of peace. Ferdinand, it seems, was being torn apart by the division over policy among his councillors. Rocci related that he displayed "melancholy and much perplexity of soul." The nuncio conjectured that this was caused

---

[22] Rocci to Barberini, Jun. 25 and Jul. 2, ibid. ##55, 57.
[23] Emperor to Wallenstein, Jul. 9, 1633, Hallwich, *Wallensteins Ende* 1: #158; Gerhard von Questenberg to Wallenstein, Jul. 15, 1633, BAGW 4: #1976.
[24] Hallwich, *Wallensteins Ende*, 2: xcv.   [25] Rocci to Barberini, Jul. 2, 1633, Repgen 1: 2: #57.
[26] Grimaldi to Barberini, Jul. 16, 1633, ibid., #62.
[27] Grimaldi to Barberini, May 14, 1633, BL 6979, ff. 176–84v.
[28] Trautmannsdorf to the emperor, Bischof-Teinitz, Oct. 29, 1633, BAGW 4: #2102.
[29] Three delegates to the emperor, Gross-Petrowitz, Sept. 10, 1633, BAGW 4: #2021.
[30] Urban VIII to Ferdinand II, Jul. 9, 1633, Repgen 1: 2: #59; see also Rocci to Barberini, Jul. 30 and Sept. 3, 1633, ibid., ##68, 79.

by his dependence on Wallenstein, but one might attribute it as much to his anxiety over the terms of the peace settlement.[31]

The long delay of the departure of the imperial delegation for Breslau augured poorly for its success. The conference never did convene. But the instructions are important because they outline an imperial negotiating position.[32] Vienna's goal in the negotiations was to forge an agreement between the Catholic and Protestant states, that is, Saxony, Brandenburg, and the other signatories of the resolution issued at Leipzig in April 1631, that would serve as the basis for an alliance to expel the foreigners from the Empire and attract the other German states to join. The delegates were assigned a difficult task when they were directed to coordinate their efforts with Wallenstein and the envoys expected from Bavaria and Mainz. The instructions foresaw Ferdinand as the judge who would pass on any arrangement concluded by the Catholics and Protestants. But he obviously did not want to act one way or the other without the approval of the Catholic electors. If the electors did decide to make concessions, the emperor had no choice but to go along with them, lest he be stigmatized as the obstacle to peace. As it turned out, neither Maximilian nor Mainz responded to the emperor's request for delegates or even for an opinion for the conference.[33] Neither Ferdinand nor the Catholic electors wanted to take the responsibility for either prolonging the war or making religious concessions.

The instructions bore a clear resemblance to what the six theologians had sanctioned in the fall of 1631. They authorized the delegates to agree to the suspension of the Edict until some form of imperial assembly was held, which might or might not be a diet, but for which a date was to be set lest an indefinite delay ensue. The delegates might accept 1629 as the norm for the possession of Church lands, not the free exercise of religion, in the sense that all lands recovered by virtue of the Edict might be returned; this did not apply to properties regained by the ordinary legal procedure and not by virtue of the Edict, whether before or after 1629. Named as belonging to this category were Magdeburg, Bremen, and Halberstadt; they had been claimed for Archduke Leopold William and so constituted a Habsburg special interest. No concessions were to be made regarding them without consulting Vienna. This was a far cry from the norm of 1612 called for by Hesse-Darmstadt or of 1618 (not applicable to the Habsburg lands) acceptable to Wallenstein, and, it seems, to Eggenberg and the three prelates, Bishop Anton Wolfradt, Dietrichstein, and Pazmany. Significant now was the willingness to grant Denmark several north German bishoprics currently occupied by the Protestants in order to win his favor as a mediator. With regard to the bishoprics held by Saxony and Brandenburg the delegates might renew the Mühlhausen guarantee of 1620

---

[31] Rocci to Barberini, Sept. 10, 1633, BL 6973, ff. 97–103.
[32] Aug. 26, 1633, BAGW 4: #2008.   [33] Bireley 1, 197.

that promised that no effort would be made to recover them by force until the case was heard in the courts. If these terms did not satisfy the two Protestant electors, the delegates might go along with whatever the Catholic electors approved.

Where Church lands had to be given up, every effort was to be made to preserve freedom of religion for the Catholics; it was a matter of the salvation of souls. Obviously, the imperial courts would be crucial in the future, and for this reason Hesse-Darmstadt had made several proposals regarding them at Leitmeritz. But the instructions showed no willingness even to discuss the courts. Any concessions on the Palatinate were to be subject to Maximilian's approval, and only a partial restoration of Frederick's lands to his heirs seems to have been envisioned. Unrealistic was the insistence that Sweden receive no compensation and that it be excluded from the negotiations. Ferdinand was inclined to grant an amnesty to those who had broken with him since 1631 and had not gone beyond the position stated in the Leipzig resolution of that year.

The instruction reflected well the state of mind in Vienna, especially the indecision on the religious issue and the intent to avoid responsibility. Ferdinand must have breathed a sigh of relief when he realized that the conference would not convene. On November 26, the delegates were still in Prague waiting for the arrival of the Danish mediators.[34] Partly to blame for the failure of the conference to take place was a rumor of the plague but the principal reason was the opposition of the Swedes and the French, who knew that the negotiations were not in their interests. The Swedes refused to grant passes to the Danish participants.[35]

Wallenstein resumed talks with Arnim after he realized that nothing would come from the negotiations planned for Breslau. Ferdinand appeared to be delighted when he learned that the two were on the verge of agreement, but the talks suddenly collapsed on September 25.[36] A desperate Bishop Anton Wolfradt writing to Trautmannsdorf refused to give up hope for a favorable peace. "God will lead his own just cause to success through other means and show to the world that there is no other who would fight for us than our God." Succession in the Empire as well as the Catholic religion were at stake. The bishop grasped at the hope that Spain, France, and the Empire would unite but realized how unlikely this was.[37]

After returning to combat long enough to win an engagement at Steinau (Ścinawa) and so to gain control of Silesia, Wallenstein preferred to reopen talks rather than to exploit his military advantage. On October 18, Ferdinand

---

[34] Emperor to Trautmannsdorf, Nov. 26, 1633, BAGW 4: #2139. [35] Bireley 1, 197.
[36] Emperor to Wallenstein, Sept. 25, 1633, Hallwich, *Wallensteins Ende* 1: #708; Wallenstein to the emperor, Sept. 29, 1633, ibid., #716; ibid., 2: xcvii; Mann, *Wallenstein*, 963–76.
[37] Bishop of Vienna to Trautmannsdorf, undated (early October, 1633), BANF 8: #215 (pp. 368–9).

approved contacts with Saxony and Brandenburg but wanted a report on the religious settlement Wallenstein foresaw before the general renewed negotiations with Sweden or its other allies.[38] Wallenstein then suggested to Arnim a return to the status of 1618 in the Empire, a position which went beyond that of the emperor as expressed in the instructions for Breslau.[39] Trautmannsdorf did not consider Wallenstein's offer acceptable.[40]

By now Arnim, in addition to Saxony and Brandenburg, began to question whether Wallenstein presented the emperor's position accurately. On November 13, Wallenstein reported to Ferdinand that the talks had once again broken down. At nearly the same time Duke Franz-Julius of Saxony-Lauenburg, who had participated in the negotiations, advised the emperor that Arnim and the two electors wanted to deal directly with his delegates.[41] Wallenstein had now played out his role as a negotiator while alienating those in Vienna who felt that he had been too ready to make concessions and who resented his independence. Still, he maintained contacts with Saxony and Brandenburg.

Opposition to Wallenstein was mounting in Vienna in the fall of 1633. Up to this point Spain had stood behind him.[42] But Spain was moving toward a break with the general; the issue was the Spanish intent to station an army in the west of the Empire. Wallenstein opposed this. The Spanish presence there would upset his delicate negotiations with the Protestants and not sit well with the French. It would also introduce into the Empire a military force independent of him. At first Ferdinand upheld the general. But then the Spaniards modified their plan. Spanish troops would not remain permanently in the Empire, and they would be employed to raise the Swedish siege of the critical fortress of Breisach on the Upper Rhine, whose loss would render south Germany vulnerable to an eventual French invasion. Maximilian, usually wary of Spain, was enthusiastic. So Ferdinand finally consented to the project. But Wallenstein remained adamantly opposed, and his long refusal and then only reluctant concession of troops bordered on open insubordination to the emperor's express orders. Oñate, Spain's extraordinary ambassador in Vienna, now turned against the general and actively sought his dismissal.[43] Rumblings were also heard in Hungary in the late summer and fall of 1633 where the Calvinist Prince of Transylvania Georg I Rákóczy, the successor of Bethlen Gàbor, taking advantage of Ferdinand's vulnerability, was stirring up trouble so that

---

[38] Emperor to Wallenstein, Oct. 18, 1633, Hallwich, *Wallensteins Ende* 2: #793; Mann, *Wallenstein*, 977–9.
[39] Mann, *Wallenstein*, 981; Hallwich, *Wallensteins Ende* 2: ciii–civ.
[40] Trautmannsdorf to the emperor, Bischof-Teinitz, Oct. 29, 1633, Hallwich, *Wallensteins Ende*, BAGW 4: #2102.
[41] Franz-Julius to the emperor, undated, BAGW 4: #2108.
[42] Philip IV to Castañeda, Oct. 4, 1633, Günter, #115.
[43] Philip IV to Oñate, May 18, 1633, Günter, #137; Mann, 954–60, 1015–17.

Ferdinand had to pay attention to the situation there, too. But in early October the prince signed a treaty with Ferdinand whereby he agreed to cease to attempt an insurrection in the kingdom.[44] Yet Vienna always had to keep an eye on Hungary.

The gap between Maximilian and Wallenstein had widened in the course of 1633; old rivalries and especially differences about the conduct of the war were responsible. Maximilian committed his forces to the successful effort to save Breisach even though he knew that this exposed Regensburg in the east to attack from the Swedish ally, the condottiere Bernhard of Weimar. Maximilian alerted Wallenstein and the emperor to the situation. Ferdinand ordered the general to send troops to defend Regensburg. Bernhard did seize Regensburg on November 14, and he then began a foray of pillage into Bavaria. Wallenstein turned a deaf ear to Ferdinand's orders and Maximilian's cries for help. Finally, he started out in the direction of Regensburg, only to turn back. When Maximilian learned of his retreat, he ordered, on December 18, the emissary whom he had just sent to Vienna, his vice-chancellor, Bartholomew Richel, to push actively for the dismissal of the general. He was to seek out others likely to be of similar mind, Lamormaini, Oñate, and Count Heinrich Schlick, now president of the war council.[45] Just four days earlier in Vienna Eggenberg had confided to Richel that his retreat was "the most harmful, the most dangerous, the most unconsidered thing" that Wallenstein had ever done. If the general did not obey, Ferdinand would have to act "so that all would see that His Majesty was master and the Duke of Friedland a servant." People considered him a friend of Wallenstein, Eggenberg continued according to Richel, and so he was, but his religion and his country came first. Ferdinand would not permit his House and that of Bavaria to be destroyed because of Wallenstein.[46] So the general was losing one of his most influential supporters. A month later, much to Richel's surprise, Eggenberg did not dismiss the possibility of an understanding between Spain and France and thus the withdrawal of French support from the German Protestants.[47]

Wallenstein's position was growing shakier. The general decided to quarter troops in exhausted Bohemia and Upper Austria after promising to find a location for them in enemy territory that winter. The result in Vienna was consternation. It grew when the general resisted an order to engage Bernhard of Weimar and simply followed his own plan for the army for the winter. He differed sharply with Eggenberg over the contribution to be levied on Styria, and this further widened the breach between them. Those in Vienna who saw

---

[44] Emperor to Wallenstein, Ebersdorf, Oct. 19, 1633, *Documenta Bohemica* 5: #612.
[45] Maximilian to Richel, Dec. 18, 1633, Georg Irmer, *Die Verhandlungen Schwedens und seiner Verbündeten mit Wallenstein und dem Kaiser von 1631–1634* 3 (Leipzig, 1891): #319. Publikationen aus den preussischen Staatsarchiven, 46.
[46] Richel to Maximilian, Dec. 14, 1633, Irmer, 3: #318; Mann, 984–98.
[47] Richel to Maximilian, Jan. 9, 1634, BANF 8: #272T (pp. 496–8).

the whole year 1633 elapse without either a substantial victory on the field of battle nor progress in peace talks thought that the time had come for the king of Hungary to take command of the army. Trautmannsdorf was among these as was Schlick and young Ferdinand himself.[48] As it was, events were to bear out the assertion of Wallenstein's enemies that under the king of Hungary the situation would improve.

Wallenstein's health had long been deteriorating. Rumors now circulated about his alleged contacts with the Bohemian exiles, France, and Sweden, his slavery to astrology, his ultimate goals. Some had a basis in fact, others were wildly exaggerated; all of them fed on the personal antagonism many felt toward him, often as a result of the general's own past conduct. One could defend some of Wallenstein's military decisions, but he had undoubtedly misunderstood the importance of Regensburg. But given the atmosphere, the general's refusal to obey was certain to be emphasized. By the end of December, Ferdinand had determined to dismiss him.[49] His chief reason was his belief that Wallenstein had become too powerful and was a threat to his rule. Ferdinand would not endure a "Co-Ruler," as the emperor put it.[50] But as was often the case, he was not in a hurry to take action. Two court councillors were sent to the two generals immediately under Wallenstein, Matthias Gallas and Johann von Aldringen, to determine their loyalty and to secure their opinion about the dismissal of Wallenstein. Details of their mission are not known, but subsequent events show clearly that the generals pledged allegiance to Ferdinand.[51]

Meanwhile, Wallenstein was aware that Vienna planned to take action against him. He kept in touch with the two Protestant electors and renewed his contacts with Sweden and France. Forty-nine of his senior officers were summoned to his winter headquarters at Pilsen, where they found the general scarcely able to rise from bed. On January 13, after discussion of the military situation, the officers signed a pledge of loyalty to their general promising not to abandon him or to allow themselves to be separated from him.[52] News of this reached Vienna at the latest on January 20. About ten days earlier, an alarming report from one of Wallenstein's generals, Ottavio Piccolomini, had reached Vienna alleging that the general intended to overthrow the emperor and the House of Habsburg and to reorder the map of Europe.[53] Thus the meeting at Pilsen was interpreted in the worst possible sense. It pointed to treachery. This called for action.

Ferdinand now followed a procedure suggested by Gundacker von Liechtenstein, long an inactive privy councillor who had reemerged as an important figure at court in the course of 1633. His proposal was dated January 13, so

---

[48] Richel to Maximilian, Jan. 18 and 25, 1634, Irmer, 3: ## 361, 386,
[49] Mann. 1001–18; Ritter, 570–2.   [50] Franzl, 334.
[51] Christoph Kampmann, *Reichsrebellion und kaiserliche Acht: Politische Strafjustiz im Dreissigjährigen Krieg und das Verfahren gegen Wallenstein* (Münster, 1993), 114.
[52] Ibid., 102–3.   [53] Ibid., 120.

before news of the meeting of Wallenstein with his officers at Pilsen had arrived in Vienna; it probably was drawn up in December. Liechtenstein stressed the importance of proceeding according to justice.[54] Accordingly, three privy councillors were chosen to review all the information available on Wallenstein and then assess whether he was guilty and what measures were to be taken. Two of them, Eggenberg and Bishop Anton Wolfradt, had long been associated with the general. The third was Trautmannsdorf. They agreed on January 24, first, that Wallenstein was clearly guilty of rebellion and had to be removed from office. His offense was notorious, as had been that of Frederick of the Palatinate and of the princes of the Lower Saxon Circle who had taken up arms against the emperor in 1625. There was no need for a trial.[55] Orders were to be issued dismissing him and releasing the soldiers from their obedience to him. General Gallas was to take over the army until a new commander was named. Those officers who had sworn allegiance to the general at Pilsen would be pardoned except for two of Wallenstein's closest associates, Christian Baron von Ilow, and Adam Count Trĉka. Secondly, the three called for the general to be arrested and brought under guard to Vienna, where he would be given a hearing. Ferdinand would give him a chance to clear himself. If this were not possible, and the councillors certainly thought that it would not be because the general would not submit to arrest, then Wallenstein and his leading fellow conspirators were to be killed as traitors justly convicted. Implementation was entrusted to the three generals: Gallas, Piccolomini, and Johann von Aldringen.[56]

Ferdinand, apparently still uncertain of the proper course of action, that very evening of January 24 sent Bishop Anton Wolfradt to secure the opinion of Lamormaini, and so the confessor seems to have been given a certain veto over the procedure. He gave in writing his clear, affirmative opinion, and Ferdinand took action according to the recommendation of the three councillors confirmed by the confessor. Lamormaini then sought the prayers of the Vienna

---

[54] Published in Oswald von Mitis, "Gundacker von Liechtensteins Anteil an der kaiserlichen Zentralverwaltung, 1606–1654," *Beiträge zur neueren Geschichte Österreichs* 5 (1908), 103–10, also in Gottfried Lorenz, ed., *Quellen zur Geschichte Wallensteins* (Darmstadt, 1987), 364–71, Ausgewählte Quellen zur Deutschen Geschichte der Neuzeit, 20. Liechtenstein was to be a major figure in the government of Ferdinand III. For an exhaustive study of his life, see Thomas Winkelbauer, *Fürst und Fürstendiener, ein österreichischer Aristokrat des konfessionellen Zeitalters* (Vienna/Munich, 1999).
Kampmann and Winkelbauer disagree on the dating of Liechtenstein's proposal. The former dates it to mid-December, 1633 and presented in the privy council on January 13, pp. 117, 126; the latter finds it in a letter of Liechtenstein to Trautmannsdorf, Jan. 26, and discussed in the privy council on Jan. 28, so after Wallenstein's meeting with his generals in Pilsen was known in Vienna; see *Fürst und Fürstendiener*, p. 218, n. 106.

[55] Kampmann, 120–1; Kampmann argues persuasively that the three councillors drew up a judicial and political opinion paper and did not issue a judicial decision based on a secret trial, pp. 125–30.

[56] Ibid., 124–5.

Jesuits and, through Vitelleschi in Rome, those of Jesuits around the world for the favorable outcome of the event.[57] Lamormaini's subsequent letter of March 4 shows that he, along with many others, was convinced that Wallenstein was a present threat to Ferdinand's throne, that he was actively engaged in conspiracy, and that he would resist dismissal and attempt to turn the army against Ferdinand. This helps us understand why the confessor could consent to the killing or execution of Wallenstein if he could not be taken alive.[58]

Ferdinand and his ministers intended to keep the order dated January 24 dismissing Wallenstein[59] limited to as small a circle as possible, including the generals entrusted with implementing it, Gallas, Piccolomini, and Aldringen, the Spanish ambassador, and the king of Hungary, and they were successful in doing so. They feared, reasonably, that the general might turn the army against Ferdinand, or worse yet, join the Swedes and Bernhard of Weimar and take the army with him. War between those loyal to Wallenstein and those loyal to Ferdinand was considered a real possiblity. The plan was to present the army with a fait accompli. The court maintained its normal communications with the general. The emperor's last letter to Wallenstein was dated February 13.[60] Meanwhile, he urged the generals to follow through with the plan to move against Wallenstein. Piccolomini arrived on February 11 in Pilsen with a unit of trusted and armed troops. Gallas was already there. But at the last minute, wary of the direction that the garrison at Pilsen might take, the two generals decided not to attempt to seize Wallenstein. In the next few days they both left Pilsen with the consent of Wallenstein who was unaware of the plot against him.[61]

After this first plan failed, the generals turned to a second strategy. The tight secrecy was abandoned, and they made efforts to assure the loyalty of the major officers and through them of the rank and file for the moment when a second, public order would be issued dismissing the general from his command. In some instances, troops were moved further from Wallenstein's camp in Pilsen. On February 18 at the latest, General Aldringen reported in Vienna the failure of the initial plan to seize the general. Ferdinand and his ministers now became much more directly involved in the revised plan that called for direct military action against the general, precisely that which the first plan had attempted to avoid. That same day the decision was reached to issue a second, public order dismissing Wallenstein and outlining in detail the charges against him in an effort to convince the army and the public of the justice of the action taken against him. It was stated clearly that those soldiers who continued to obey Wallenstein would be considered and treated as rebels against imperial authority.[62]

---

[57] Ferdinand to Lamormaini, Jan. 24, 1634, Dudik, 276–7; Lamormaini to Vitelleschi, Mar. 4, 1634, published in Heinrich Srbik, *Wallensteins Ende*, 2 ed. (Salzburg, 1952), 310–3.

[58] Lamormaini to Vitelleschi, Mar. 4, 1633, in Srbik, 310–13. This long letter of Lamormaini's is a major source for the whole course of events surrounding the death of Wallenstein.

[59] Lorenz, pp. 379–80.   [60] Kampmann, 123, n. 99.   [61] Ibid., 131–4.

[62] Lorenz, pp. 391–6.

Within a few days the emperor's order was published in Vienna and by February 27 in Prague. Meanwhile, on February 20 Ferdinand ordered troops from Lower Austria and elsewhere to southern Bohemia and especially to Prague to guarantee control of the city. At one point, according to Bartholomew Richel, Maximilian's emissary in Vienna at the time, he seemed determined that along with his son, the king of Hungary, he himself – despite his fifty-five years and failing health – would lead troops in person to hold the town of Budweis, so that "he [could] address the officers in person and in the whole army stir up greater heart and courage, loyalty and devotion when they had their emperor and commander so near to them."[63] This would have been the first time that he had taken to the battlefield since the disaster during the Long Turkish War, and it reveals how serious he considered the situation to be. But such a dramatic gesture turned out to be unnecessary. To meet the anticipated fear of the soldiers that with the disappearance of Wallenstein, the emperor would not be able either to supply or pay them, Ferdinand took emergency measures to raise funds from the Lower Austrian and Upper Austrian estates. Loans were obtained from friendly princes, and already measures were under way to seize the property of Wallenstein and his close associates as a source of funds. The soldiers were offered immediate payment of one month's wages in bar.[64]

Wallenstein, sensing trouble, fled Pilsen on February 21 with his close associates Count Wilhelm Kinsky, Count Christian Ilow, and Count Adam Trčka, a few supporters, and a small force, hoping to reach either Arnim or Bernhard of Weimar. They stopped at Eger in western Bohemia. There three subordinate officers loyal to the emperor, after judging it impossible to bring him back alive and taking precautions to prevent rebellion, killed the three counts in a brief fight, and then, as he lay in bed, the general himself. So Wallenstein met his end. The fears in Vienna of resistance to the removal and then death of the general on the part of large segments of the army were not borne out. Very few came to his support, some in Prague and in Troppau (Opava), but they represented no serious threat and were quickly dealt with.[65]

Lamormaini could not help but interpret the elimination of the threat from Wallenstein as another instance of the Lord's providential care for Ferdinand.[66] General Gallas echoed a similar sentiment in a report to Ferdinand. The success of the action against Wallenstein was "a just sign of God, who would not cease to defend and to protect His Majesty, the House [of Habsburg] and the holy

---

[63] Richel to Maximilian, Feb. 22, 1634, Irmer 3: #4770; Kampmann, 145, 153.
[64] Kampmann, 137–48.
[65] For a discussion of the recent literature on the Wallenstein affair and the part of the generals in it, especially Gallas, see Robert Rebitsch, *Matthias Gallas (1588–1647): Generalleutnant des Kaisers zur Zeit des Dreissigjährigen Krieges: Eine militärische Biographie* (Münster, 2006), 70–81.
[66] Vitelleschi to Lamormaini, Apr. 1, 1634, ARSJ, Aust. 4II, ff. 923–4.

Catholic faith."[67] Philip IV likewise saw the outcome of the Wallenstein affair as a sign of God's providence for Ferdinand and for the whole House of Habsburg.[68] Ferdinand himself saw the frustration of the alleged conspiracy as a response to a vow that he had taken, and he proceeded to endow the Jesuit novitiate of St. Anna in Vienna so generously that Lamormaini had to restrain his munificence.[69] "Father Lamormaini," Rocci related, "has returned to a better state of favor with His Majesty." Eggenberg, on the contrary, looked to be in bad health, probably as a result of "sickness of spirit" caused by recent events. But a week later Rocci revised his opinion on Eggenberg. The chief minister appeared to be in good health and to enjoy the favor of the emperor, despite his many enemies.[70] Among them were those who had long advocated that Ferdinand entrust the king of Hungary with the top military command. They would soon have their way.

By early April matters had settled to a good degree, and it had become clear that no serious threat was to come from Wallenstein loyalists. Ferdinand desperately needed funds to make the payment of one month's salary in bar that he had promised the soldiers and especially for the upcoming campaign season. Both Spain and the pope helped out, but not to the degree that Vienna had anticipated. Ferdinand even called on his ministers for loans, 10,000 florins from Eggenberg, 5,000 from Bishop Anton Wolfradt, 3,000 from the other privy councillors, all the way down to 200 from lower officials. The Lower Austrian estates had voted monies at the height of the crisis, and Moravia and Styria were expected to follow suit.[71]

From April 15 to 30, there took place in Vienna a conference of the leading councillors and military figures, along with representatives of Spain and Bavaria. In the course of their talks, it was announced that the king of Hungary would assume command of the imperial army, though Ferdinand did not issue the official order for this until late August. Both political and military figures now considered the major problem to be the creation of confidence in Ferdinand among the soldiers and in the new military leadership after the fall of Wallenstein. To this they gave their attention at the conference and in the following months. Three issues drew their attention: the distribution of the property of those considered notorious rebels, inquiry into the participation of others in Wallenstein's conspiracy so as to clear the air of lingering suspicions and fears of prosecution, a response to the many charges leveled

---

[67] Gallas to the emperor, Pilsen, Feb. 27, 1634, cited in Rebitsch, 98, who notes that this represented the conviction of the general; it was not just a pious remark to please Ferdinand.
[68] Philip IV to the emperor, May 14, 1634, Günter, #137.
[69] "Vita Lamormaini," f. 81; *Virtutes*, 12.
[70] Rocci to Barberini, Apr. 15 and 22, 1634, BL 6974, ff. 148-57v, 159-69v.
[71] Johann Stücklin (Bavarian agent in Vienna) to Maximilian, Mar. 15, 1634, BANF 8: #342 (pp. 652-3); Kampmann, 149, 175-6.

against Ferdinand by his enemies in an onslaught of propaganda that Wallenstein was the victim of arbitrary justice and even murder on the part of an ungrateful emperor.[72]

Ferdinand made the same distinction at this time as he had at the time of the Bohemian rebellion and of the rebellious activity of princes in the Lower Saxon Circle in 1626 and 1627, that is, a distinction between notorious rebels for whom no trial was necessary and those under suspicion of rebellious activity who deserved a fair hearing. The former included Wallenstein himself and his three associates, Kinsky, Ilow, and Trčka. The confiscation and reallocation of their lands constituted another major transfer of property in Bohemia. The intent was to use the property to help finance the army. Already in late February Ferdinand had appointed confiscation commissioners to inventory and seize lands of the notorious rebels. Should they encounter opposition, they might call upon troops stationed nearby. But even before the commissioners could act, Ferdinand had decided to whom the properties of the rebels would be assigned. The chief beneficiary of the allotment of lands turned out to be General Gallas; after receiving Wallenstein's two principalities, Friedland and Reichenberg as well as most of the lands of Kinsky, he became one of the greatest landholders in Bohemia. This was to be sure a reward for his part in the whole Wallenstein affair. But other generals had played a scarcely inferior role. Ferdinand's generosity to Gallas seems to have been dictated by the intent to bolster his credit and thus the confidence in the soldiers that Gallas would be able to pay them as Wallenstein had. The remaining properties of the notorious rebels were assigned to colonels and other officers to reward them but also to enable them to advance payments to the troops under their command. Many soldiers received their payment much later or never.[73]

Others were suspected of participation in Wallenstein's conspiracy, some already arrested and some still free. Despite the objections of some officers, Ferdinand insisted on proper trials for them and prohibited confiscation of their properties until a verdict was reached. Eventually, only six were formally charged, all of high estate, and five were found guilty. Of these Ferdinand commuted the sentences of four to imprisonment, and only Colonel Hans Ulrich von Schaffgotsch was actually executed, on July 23, 1635, in Regensburg.[74] Gallas, Piccolomini, and others involved in the action against Wallenstein later complained that supporters of the general were not adequately prosecuted, even threatening resignation over the matter.[75] But Ferdinand had no taste for this.

Some pamphlets had already appeared in defense of Ferdinand's conduct in the Wallenstein affair, but they were considered inadequate to meet the charges of hostile propagandists. Public opinion did matter. Stralendorf was commissioned to oversee the composition of a "white book" demonstrating that

---

[72] Kampmann, 180, 184, n.45.   [73] Ibid., 180–4.   [74] Ibid., 184–9.   [75] Rebitsch, 111.

Wallenstein was truly guilty of treachery. Justus Gebhardt, along with others, assisted him. They produced a text entitled "A Detailed and Thorough Report of the Past Abominable Treachery of Friedland and his Adherents,"[76] and it was approved by the privy council on July 5, 1634. Ferdinand then sent it to his son, the king of Hungary in the field, asking him to submit it to the generals who had been involved in the affair. After a delay, they approved it, and it was published on October 18. A further question that arose was whether the emperor ought to take further legal action against Wallenstein, either in the form of a condemnatory sentence for which a posthumous trial would have to be held or in the form of a declaratory sentence which would amount to a further statement of his guilt. There was little sentiment for the former; the king of Hungary and his councillors advocated the latter. But Ferdinand rejected this as unnecessary and undesirable. The "Report" explained his position clearly enough. He had dealt with Wallenstein as a notorious rebel according to natural, Roman, and imperial law. There was no need to say more.[77]

During the months of the Wallenstein crisis, from November 1633 to March 1634, Duke Francis Julius of Saxony-Lauenberg had helped keep alive contacts between Vienna and Dresden, even journeying to Denmark to affirm Ferdinand's continued interest in the king's mediation.[78] After Wallenstein's death, the king of Hungary was given formal charge of the peace negotiations as well as command of the imperial army. The memorial drawn up for him in the emperor's name directed him to take advantage of Saxony's willingness to negotiate.[79] Talks began between the imperials and Saxons on June 15, 1634, in Leitmeritz.[80] The imperial delegates were the same as those for Breslau, Trautmannsdorf, Hermann von Questenberg, and Gebhardt, and they took with them the same instruction. Thus began the negotiations that led directly to the Peace of Prague the following year.

The initial Saxon position was similar to the proposals of Hesse-Darmstadt in March 1633. In his effort to split Saxony from the Swedes and the other German Protestants, Ferdinand inclined to be more generous to the former, but he was not ready to concede the initial Saxon demands. These included permanent possession of the two (arch)bishoprics, Magdeburg and Halberstadt,

---

[76] "Ausführlicher und Gründtlicher Bericht der vorgewesten Fridtländischen Prodition..."
[77] Kampmann, 9–11, 190–6, esp. 193. The juridical position of Ferdinand and the court was also expressed in a position paper drawn up by a committee of councillors that is dated variously. Lorenz has published it, pp. 427–35, and dates it April 1634; Kampmann and others date it much later, July 9. Because it deals at length with the issue of whether a condemnatory or declaratory sentence ought to be issued against Wallenstein and his fellow conspirators, and because it refers to the "Ausführlicher und Gründtlicher Bericht," I prefer the later date.
[78] See, for example, the emperor's instruction for Franz Julius, Dec. 17, 1633, BAGW 4: #2174.
[79] May 2, 1634, BANF, 10: 2, #12 (pp. 17–20).
[80] Minutes, HHStA, Friedens. 10v, ff. 1–6. The minutes of the talks were sent back weekly to Vienna along with the reports of the delegates.

and of the two Lusatias which John George still held in lieu of payment of expenses in the Bohemian campaign of 1620. Beyond its private concerns, Saxony considered the two most important points to be adequate compensation for Sweden – the imperial proposition refused discussion of any compensation – and the determination of a normative year for the permanent possession of ecclesiastical properties and privileges. Saxony proposed 1612 and stated explicitly that this was to apply to the free exercise of religion and to be valid for Upper and Lower Austria, the Bohemian lands, and even Hungary which lay outside the Empire. The imperial instruction continued to see 1629 as the normative year, and this with notable exceptions, conditioned upon acceptance by the Catholic states, and valid only until the convocation of some form of imperial assembly that would draw up a final settlement. Saxony was willing to leave the Palatinate electoral title to Maximilian until he died, but the lands would have to be restored to Frederick's heirs at the time of the settlement. John George expected Ferdinand to issue a general amnesty whereas Ferdinand was ready to grant one only to those who had parted from him at the time of the Swedish invasion in 1631.[81]

Negotiations continued at Leitmeritz until July 17, when the Swedish general Baner's invasion of Bohemia forced their transfer to the Saxon town of Pirna.[82] There the two parties came closer on the normative date. Saxony proposed 1620, to be valid for himself permanently and for the other Lutheran states for 100 years. The counterproposal of the imperial delegates was November 12, 1627, to be valid for Saxony and Brandenburg for forty years and for the other Lutheran states for fifteen years. Trautmannsdorf had recommended this date to Ferdinand. He thought that in addition to providing for Catholic possession of most of the (arch)bishoprics and the protection of Bavaria in the Palatinate, this date was likely to win the support of Saxony and Brandenburg because it returned to the point where all the electors had cooperated, that is, to the date of their joint request, at the end of the Electoral Convention of Mühlhausen of 1627, that the emperor render a decision about the grievances regarding the observance of the Religious Peace.[83] Eventually this would be the date accepted in the Peace of Prague. However, events on the battlefield affected the talks shortly after they resumed on August 28 following another break.

The fall of Wallenstein did not seriously affect Spanish policy. Spain continued to advocate a settlement with the Protestants that would permit Ferdinand and the German princes, Catholic and Protestant, to come to Spain's aid against the

---

[81] Minutes of the talks at Leitmeritz, Jun. 16–17, 1634, ibid., ff. 31–40, 43–52; Saxon memoranda presented Jun. 16–17, ibid., 41–41v, 53–8, 59–61v, 63–5v, 68–70.
[82] Imperial delegates to the emperor, Jul. 17, 1634, BANF 10: 2, #42 (pp. 72–4).
[83] Imperial delegates to the emperor, Jun. 21 and Jul. 5, 1633, BANF 10: 2, ##25 (pp. 31–3) and 33 (pp. 55–61).

Dutch and the French who were becoming increasingly active militarily as well as diplomatically. The Spaniards still considered their enemies in Vienna to be Lamormaini and the nuncios with their vision of Habsburg-Bourbon rapprochement.[84] Spanish efforts at an alliance continued to fail because of the unwillingness of Maximilian and the League to commit themselves to war against the Dutch or the French. But the removal of Wallenstein encouraged closer cooperation among the Spanish, imperial, and League armies. The Spanish ambassadors were wise enough to accept this development without the formalization of an alliance. This led, first, to the recapture of Regensburg by the imperials on July 26, 1634. Later in the summer, another Spanish army marched over the Alps under the leadership of the Cardinal Infante, Don Fernando. The conjunction of the two armies of Don Fernando and the king of Hungary was to lead to one of the decisive battles of the Thirty Years War.[85]

The papacy continued to urge doggedly but unsuccessfully the reconciliation of the three crowns. Richelieu encouraged the Protestant states against the emperor. The appearance of the Spanish army of Feria in the Empire provoked the French, as Wallenstein had foreseen. Under the guise of protecting Alsace against both the Swedes and the Spaniards, Richelieu began to seize areas of it. In September 1633, he occupied Lorraine completely, whose Duke Charles had long been a thorn in the side of the French because of his assistance to dissident elements in France.[86] In October, Ferdinand designated Sebastian Lustrier, a canon of Olmütz, to be imperial resident in Paris where he arrived only the next February. His instructions were very limited, as he told Grimaldi.[87] Nevertheless, in November 1633, just as the Wallenstein affair was coming to a head, Ferdinand and Eggenberg expressed through the nuncios a readiness to yield on the issues of Pinerolo and Moyenvic, fortresses in Savoy and Lorraine, provided the French government guaranteed Spain a clear route from Italy to the Netherlands. For a short time there appeared to be hope of progress, but it fell through because of the counter demands of Richelieu, the renewal of confidence in Vienna after the resolution of the Wallenstein crisis, and Spanish pressure.[88]

Grimaldi had been growing discouraged at the prospects for the peace that he had been sent to promote as extraordinary nuncio. The ministers in Vienna remained skeptical, he reported, when he assured them that the

---

[84] Philip IV to Castañeda, May 18, 1634, Günter, #138; Philip IV to Oñate, May 18, 1634, ibid., #140.
[85] Albrecht 1. 370-1; Ritter, 577-80; Günter, 169-71. Spain and the emperor concluded an alliance on Oct. 31, 1634, but it appears that it was never ratified in the same form by both; see Günter, 190-5, 198, 210; Leman, 522.
[86] Ritter 3: 585-6; Baustaedt, 103.
[87] Grimaldi to Barberini, Oct. 8, 1633, BL 6980, ff. 151-7; the prescription (not strictly instruction) for Lustrier was dated Sept. 14, 1633, HHStA, Staaten, Frankreich, Berichte und Weisungen, 24. On Lustrier's mission, see Leman, 364-9. Lustrier was close to Cardinal Dietrichstein and later served as his chancellor and represented him in Rome.
[88] Leman, 360-70, 375-6.

pope was doing all in his power to prevent the French from aiding heretics. Once he asked whether they really thought the pope ought to resort to ecclesiastical censures against Richelieu or Louis XIII, and not one of them considered that this would be a wise move. They were well aware of the "unhappy" effects of Clement VII's excommunication of Henry VIII of England in the previous century. Eggenberg was always polite, he added, but he held rigidly to the Spanish position.[89] Shortly before Christmas 1633, Grimaldi informed Ferdinand that the pope could no longer afford to maintain two nuncios in Vienna and that he was being recalled. He departed for the south, convinced the Austrians' mistrust would never permit serious negotiations with the French.[90]

Rocci remained in Vienna for nearly another year. His successor, Malatesta Baglioni, did not turn up until November 25, 1634. Baglioni's instructions represented no change of policy. He was directed to establish contact with Lamormaini among others; the confessor was "always well-affected toward the Holy See."[91] But Rocci considered that the favorable outlook for an agreement with Saxony now kept the imperial councillors from dealing seriously with France. This was the case, he reported, even after Bishop Anton Wolfradt told him the Austrians were ready to negotiate despite the French renewal of their alliance with the Dutch on April 15, 1634.[92]

Then came the long hoped-for military victory for the Catholics. In early September, the combined forces of the king of Hungary and the Cardinal Infante overwhelmed the Swedes outside Nördlingen in Swabia. This restored the military advantage to the emperor and his Spanish allies once again. They gained control over most of Upper Germany east of the Rhine including Württemberg. The victory was sure to influence the talks in Pirna. But it also confirmed Richelieu in his decision that France would have to enter the war openly. Only in this way could he reach his anti-Habsburg objectives; there was now no chance that Vienna would consider peace with France on the terms under discussion. Richelieu continued to establish French control over the west bank of the Rhine. A new alliance between France and the Heilbronn Confederation on November 1, 1634, made France the dominant partner. In December a French army even marched across the Rhine to defend Heidelberg against the Catholic forces, a move that enraged Munich as well as Vienna. But the

---

[89] Grimaldi to Barberini, Nov. 5, 1633, BL 6980, ff. 172–6v.
[90] Grimaldi to Barberini, Dec. 24 and 31, 1633, BL 6980, ff. 204–12v, 213–20v; Repgen 1:1: 325.
[91] Instruction for Baglioni, Jul. 2, 1634, NBD 7, *Nuntiaturen des Malatesta Baglioni, des Ciriaco Rocci und des Mario Filorardi. Sendung des Allessandro d'Ales. 1634–1635*, ed. Rotraud Becker (Tübingen, 2004), #1 (pp.1–20, quote on p. 17).
[92] Rocci to Barberini, Aug. 12, 1634, BL 6975, ff. 9–17v; Leman, 397. As a result of this new agreement with France, the Dutch broke off peace talks with Spain.

cardinal delayed formal entrance into the struggle until he could extract the highest possible price from his Swedish and German allies.[93]

From the battle of Lützen and the death of Gustav Adolph on November 16, 1632, to the imperial-Spanish victory at Nördlingen on September 6, 1634, Ferdinand's fortunes gradually improved. One sees this reflected in the number of court dramatic entertainments. After a nearly complete blackout during the difficult year 1632, due also to the deaths of King Sigismund of Poland, Ferdinand's brother-in-law – his sister, Constance, the queen of Poland had died the previous year – and of Archduke Leopold – the entertainments returned at normal intervals in 1633.[94] Negotiations with Saxony picked up in the spring of 1633 and continued intermittently, with the hope that a victory on the battlefield would give the emperor the upper hand once again that would make an agreement feasible. Spanish influence continued to grow, pushing for a settlement with Saxony and then with the other German Protestant states. Yet contacts with France were not broken off even as the French edged aggressively into the Empire from the west. Pope Urban continued to urge an understanding among the Catholic powers, and the nuncios promoted this in Vienna and at the other Catholic courts. In Vienna, Lamormaini championed this policy, having recovered to a degree the influence at court that he had lost after Breitenfeld and persistently encouraging Ferdinand to trust in his providential mission. Ferdinand himself was torn between the two policies and especially over the need to modify the Edict in order to win over Saxony. Then there erupted the Wallenstein crisis. Ferdinand, to his mind, acted decisively, morally, and legally. Now that the victory at Nördlingen over the Swedish army had tipped the military balance in favor of the emperor, Vienna could negotiate with Saxony from a position of relative strength.

The scene was now set for a final confrontation in Vienna over the Edict. On one side was Lamormaini, who continued to oppose concessions to the Protestants and to promote rapprochement with the French as the basis for, at least, French withdrawal of support for the Protestants. He stood nearly alone, with some support from the nuncios, but he retained a firm hold on the emperor. For him the victory at Nördlingen amounted to another manifestation of the Lord's care for Ferdinand. It was a "miraculous victory" which gave solid reason for not making peace with Saxony; so Rocci cited the confessor.[95] Against Lamormaini were aligned Pazmany, the court Capuchins, and the leading privy councillors, Stralendorf, Trautmannsdorf, Bishop Anton Wolfradt, and Cardinal Dietrichstein. All of them felt that the time had come for a compromise peace with Saxony and the more conservative

---

[93] Ritter, 579–81; Baustaedt, 128–9, 142, 149.
[94] Andrea Sommer-Mathis, "Ein 'picaro' und spanisches Theater am Wiener Hof zur Zeit des Dreissigjährigen Krieges," *Wien im Dreissigjährigen Kriege. Bevölkerung, Gesellschaft, Kultur Konfession*, ed. Andreas Weigl (Vienna, 2001), 686–7. Kulturstudien 32.
[95] Rocci to Barberini, Sept. 30, 1634, BL 6975, ff. 60–9.

Protestant states followed by a campaign to drive the foreigners from the Empire and deal with the recalcitrant German states.

One of the principal actors, however, was to be absent from the final scene. Eggenberg died on October 18, 1634, in Ljubljana, where he was taking the baths after having left Vienna for the last time in late June. His last year had been a difficult one, with the painful Wallenstein affair, a loss of favor with the Spaniards for remaining loyal to the general as long as he did, and continually failing health.[96] Despite rumors to the contrary, he died on the best of terms with Ferdinand, though not with the king of Hungary, whose appointment to the command of the imperial army he had long opposed. Letters from Ferdinand to Eggenberg in the last two years of the minister's life, when he was frequently absent from court, show the emperor's desire to have him with him in Vienna for his counsel and for his friendship. Ferdinand wrote him of the birth of his grandson, Ferdinand Franz, and even related how he had shot seventeen stags in his latest hunt. In a letter of July 11, 1634, thus after the conclusion of the Wallenstein affair and in the face of charges that Eggenberg had profited unduly from his support of the general, Ferdinand assured him that "I continue towards you that old, upright trust and love that has always been present between us and with the help of God will continue until the end."[97]

---

[96] Walther E. Heydendorff, *Die Fürsten und Freiherren zu Eggenberg und Ihre Vorfahren* (Graz, 1965), 136–8; see Philip IV to Oñate/Castañeda, Aug. 14, 1634, Günter, #147.

[97] Ferdinand to Eggenberg, Jul. 11, 1634, published in Franz Mareš, "Beiträge zur Geschichte der Beziehungen des Fürsten Johann Ulrich von Eggenberg zu Kaiser Ferdinand II und zu Wallenstein," *Sitzungsberichte der kgl. böhmischen Gesellschaft der Wissenschaften, Classe für Philosophie, Geschichte und Philologie Jahrgang 1892* (Prague, 1893), 34–5. The article includes seven other letters from Ferdinand to Eggenberg in 1632 and 1633.

Chapter 9

Settlement and Death, 1635–1637

The battle of Nördlingen readjusted the political landscape in the Empire. On December 7, 1634, the imperial negotiating team of Trautmannsdorf, Hermann von Questenberg, and Gebhardt returned from Pirna to Wiener Neustadt, not far from Vienna, where the court had moved because of a threat of the plague. They carried with them the draft of a treaty with Saxony, the Pirna Points, that had been worked out in the weeks following Nördlingen. The imperial representatives were expected to return to the Bohemian town of Aussig (Ústí nad Labem) on January 13 with the emperor's ratification for the final conclusion of the agreement.[1] But that was not to be the case. Only after lengthy consultations in Vienna were the imperial negotiators able to return, to Prague now not Aussig, where the peace was concluded that brought Saxony and then Brandenburg and other Protestant states back to the side of the emperor. Meanwhile the papacy continued to urge talks among the three crowns, the emperor, France, and Spain, but in vain. More significant was the convening of another electoral convention in Regensburg in November 1636 which continued into late January of the following year. It, too, took on the character of a European peace conference, if not to the extent of the convention of 1630. At this conference Ferdinand finally reached his long-term goal, the coronation of his son Ferdinand as king of the Romans, and thus guaranteeing a Catholic, Habsburg succession in the Empire. This came about just in time. Ferdinand II died after his return to Vienna from Regensburg, on February 15, 1637.

There were now three papal representatives in Vienna. In addition to Rocci, who did not depart until April 1635, and his replacement Baglioni, Alessandro d'Ales, an Italian Capuchin with long experience in political affairs, had come

---

[1] Imperial delegates in Pirna to the emperor, Nov. 23, 1634, HHStA, Friedens. 10iii, ff. 128–28v.

to Vienna the previous April as a personal representative of Cardinal Francesco Barberini. Like the nuncios, he had an audience with Ferdinand nearly every week. But he found life difficult in the Capuchin convent in Vienna where the Spaniard Quiroga dominated and Alessandro was dubbed "il papalino."[2] On December 2, shortly before the return of the delegates from Pirna, Alessandro reported to Rome conversations he had had with Ferdinand II himself and with Werdenberg. Ferdinand expressed his disappointment, Alessandro reported to Barberini, at the little progress that the pope's plans for peace among the king of France, the king of Spain, and himself had made. But Alessandro then succeeded in awakening in him a renewed hope for the papal project so that Ferdinand told Alessandro, "you have, father, preached me a good sermon."[3] So Ferdinand seemed swayed in the direction of Lamormaini's policy.

Two other interconnected issues arose in the conversations: the recognition of the precedence of the Barberini prefect of Rome before the ambassadors of foreign countries in ceremonies there, and the promotion of Bishop Anton Wolfradt to the cardinalate. Alessandro brought up once again the issue of the prefect of Rome so dear to the pope and Cardinal Barberini. Ferdinand agreed to bring the issue once again to the privy council, and he did. But he would still not act in this matter until he learned the position of the king of Spain. Philip IV, angry at the pope's apparent tilt toward France, after a long delay did not support this project nor then did Ferdinand. Alessandro intimated to Barberini that Rocci needed to be more generous in doling out gifts to councillors in order to move the matter of the prefect forward.[4] Werdenberg, for his part, pointed out to Alessandro that there was nothing better that the pope could do for "this good old emperor" than to bestow the red hat on Bishop Anton Wolfradt. He had become Ferdinand's "intimate councillor," and the emperor wanted to accord him the formal title of director of the privy council that Eggenberg had held, but he could not do so unless Anton Wolfradt were made a cardinal. But Ferdinand's efforts on behalf of the promotion of the bishop never succeeded because the pope thought that Anton Wolfradt had not exerted himself sufficiently and had indeed failed to obtain Ferdinand's clear support for the recognition of the status of the prefect of Rome, and perhaps because he did not want to give Ferdinand another cardinal in addition to Dietrichstein, Pazmany, and Harrach. These two issues continued to cloud the relationship between Vienna and the Barberini pope. Meanwhile, the nuncios Rocci and Baglioni regularly reported on the deteriorating health of the emperor as he aged, especially his increasing weight and apparent kidney disease, neither of which, however, kept him from the hunt.

---

[2] Alessandro to Barberini, Jan. 20, 1635, NBD 7, *Nuntiaturen des Malatesta Baglioni, des Ciriaco Rocci und des Mario Filonardi. Sendung des P. Alessandro d'Ales (1634–1635)*, ed. Rotraut Becker (Tubingen, 2004) #9* (p. 674); Baglioni to Barberini, Jul. 7, 1635, BL 6992, f. 3.
[3] Alessandro to Barberini, Dec. 2, 1634, ibid., #2* (pp. 657–9).
[4] Alessandro to Barberini, Dec. 9, 1634, ibid., #3* (pp. 659–64)

The Pirna Points represented a compromise between Ferdinand and John George of Saxony. Ferdinand came out ahead. But the Points amounted to a virtual revocation of the Edict and so the surrender of Lamormaini's program for a Catholic restoration in Germany. The agreement accepted in principle the historical development of the eighty years since the Peace of Augsburg that the Edict had attempted to overturn. The date proposed earlier by Trautmannsdorf, November 12, 1627, was to serve as the normative date for the enjoyment of disputed ecclesiastical properties, rights, and privileges, including the free exercise of religion. What obtained on that date was to be valid for the next forty years. So, strictly speaking, Ferdinand was not permanently giving up Catholic claims. A body composed equally of Catholics and Protestants was to work out a definitive settlement during this period. Should their efforts fail, the time period might be extended. If agreement still was not reached, both sides reserved the right to take the case to the imperial courts. For the courts, however, the discussion of any changes in structure or confessional balance was postponed indefinitely. Meanwhile, both sides renounced any resort to force. Thus the emperor gave up his claim to issue or enforce a decision. The status of 1627 could easily become permanent.[5]

Concretely, this settlement represented the restoration and/or preservation for the Catholics of the imperial church lands in the south and west of the Empire; many of these including the archbishopric-electorate of Mainz were still occupied by the enemy. It also seemed to provide – there was some vagueness here – for the return to the Catholics of the most important (arch) bishoprics in Lower Saxony that had been held by the Protestants for decades prior to the war and were now in hostile hands. The archbishopric of Magdeburg was an exception. It was granted to John George's son, August, for life. According to the normative year, the Protestants would enjoy religious freedom in these territories, such as Halberstadt, which was assigned to Leopold William.[6] To the northeast the terms recognized the status quo, a concession the imperialists had long been willing to make in favor of Saxony and Brandenburg. Most significant for Ferdinand was the confirmation of his right of reformation in the Austrian and Bohemian lands where John George gave up his demand for freedom of religion for Protestants. From the start Ferdinand had considered this non-negotiable. Excepted was the city of Breslau and several Silesian principalities, where the Protestants were granted free exercise

---

[5] There is a manuscript copy of the Pirna Points in HHStA, Friedens. 16, ff. 170–210; they were printed in the anonymous *Pirnische und Pragische Friedens Pacten, susampt angesteller Collation und Anweisung der Discrepantz und Unterschieds* [sic] *zwischen denenselben* (n.p., 1636). For a good summary, see Ritter, 588–94.

[6] Of the Lower Saxon bishoprics, only Magdeburg and Halberstadt were mentioned explicitly in the Points. According to the position paper of the privy council, Jan. 20, 1635, BANF 10: *Der Prager Frieden 1635*, ed. Kathrin Bierther (Munich, 2007) 2: *Korrespondenz*, #107 (pp. 162–9), Vienna foresaw the return of Minden. Bremen and Verden were not mentioned, though the list was explicitly incomplete.

of religion. With respect to territorial church lands, the compromise allowed many Protestant states, especially in north Germany and in Franconia and Swabia to retain ecclesiastical lands that they had acquired since 1555.

Special concessions were granted to John George and to George William of Brandenburg. They were to retain unchallenged the lands that they had acquired since 1555 for fifty years instead of forty. Besides the allotment of Magdeburg to John George's son for life, Ferdinand also assigned to the Saxon elector as an imperial fief the two Lusatias. John George still held these in lieu of the payment owed him for his part in the suppression of the Bohemian rebellion. Here the Catholics were to enjoy freedom of religion. The solution of the delicate Palatinate question was left to future arbitration, though the Saxon negotiators intimated John George's intention to yield on it provided the Catholics accepted the rest of the agreement. Taken for granted in the subsequent deliberations of the imperial councillors was Maximilian's retention of the Upper Palatinate permanently and the electoral title for life.[7]

The Pirna Points aimed to settle the internal problems of the Empire and to prepare for the expulsion of foreign powers from Germany, preferably peacefully but by force if necessary. The terms foresaw that the other German states, Protestant and Catholic, would ratify the agreement and ally with the two principals. But the draft offered full amnesty and restitution to their territories only to those secular princes and states that had taken up arms against the emperor after Gustav Adolph landed on German soil in 1630. To enforce the peace, a unified imperial army was to be formed, in which Saxony would have a major command. Furthermore, apart from family agreements approved by the emperor, the peace prohibited for the future all alliances among imperial states. This would put an end to the Catholic League as well as to the Heilbronn Confederation. The leading foreign powers were also invited to associate themselves with the agreement, but a chief cause for the eventual failure of the Peace of Prague was the neglect to provide compensation for Sweden. Saxony had initially insisted on this. To expect the Swedes to pack up quietly and return home after five years of war in Germany was unrealistic. The victory at Nördlingen was not that overwhelming.

Ferdinand himself was handed an abstract of the Points on December 11.[8] Copies were dispatched with a request for their opinions to the three Catholic electors – Maximilian, Mainz, and Cologne – but not to Trier because it was felt that he had broken with the other Catholic princes when he allied with France in 1632 and subsequently entered a neutrality agreement with Sweden.[9]

---

[7] Emperor to Maximilian, Dec. 13, 1634, HHStA, Friedens. 10iv, ff. 21–4; see also the position paper of the privy council cited in the previous note.
[8] HHStA, Friedens. 10iv, ff. 3–16.
[9] Hermann Weber, *Frankreich, Kurtrier, Der Rhein und das Reich, 1623–1635* Bonn, 1969), 192–6. 245–6, 388. Pariser Historische Studien, 9. The elector of Trier, Philip Christoph von Sötern,

A significant change was introduced into the original draft of the covering letter to Maximilian.¹⁰ In the final copy Ferdinand informed the elector, who had been kept abreast of the negotiations all along, that this was the best that his negotiators could do; he requested that should Maximilian find the terms unacceptable, he suggest where the resources might be found to continue the war. But a long passage intended to impress upon Maximilian the need for peace was deleted. The change revealed a division between Ferdinand and the councillors who had drawn up the draft. Rocci reported that nearly all the emperor's advisers favored the peace, but Lamormaini opposed it. He was "the cause that the emperor showed little inclination to accept it."¹¹ More time would be required to reach a decision on the peace.

Papal policy generally supported Lamormaini but "with prudence," as Barberini instructed Rocci.¹² A principle of papal policy remained the refusal to approve formally any concessions to the Protestants. Yet Urban had no intention of supporting the German militants either with a greater financial commitment or with positive political or ecclesiastical pressure, such as the threat of a formal protest against concessions. He seems, as the last resort, to have been willing to allow the emperor to make the best political arrangement that he could for the Church. At the same time, papal diplomacy kept up its efforts to reconcile the three Catholic powers, but Rome was losing hope.

Both Spanish ambassadors in Vienna and Quiroga continued to advocate peace with Saxony and an imperial break with France. After the renewed French commitment to the Dutch in April 1634, Madrid was convinced that only the bribery of imperial ministers could account for the emperor's failure to act in the manner that it wanted.¹³ This sentiment grew as French diplomatic and military activity increased, itself partly the reaction to the expanding Spanish presence in the Empire in the form of Feria's army in 1633 and the Cardinal Infante's the following year. By the summer of 1634, as we have seen, Richelieu was convinced that France would have to enter the war openly. He concluded a new treaty with the Heilbronn Confederation on November 1, 1634, and he sent French troops across the Rhine to relieve Heidelberg in December. At the same time, he arranged treaties with a number of the German Protestant princes of southwest Germany so that by year's end the French controlled the left bank of the Rhine from Basel to Coblenz and they occupied the fortresses of Ehrenbreitstein and Philippsburg on the right bank.¹⁴ The Spaniards could only gnash their teeth at Lamormaini's persistent advocacy

---

was captured by Spanish troops when they took the city of Trier on Mar. 26, 1635, and he spent most of the rest of the war in detention, first in the Spanish Netherlands and then in Vienna.

[10] Emperor to Maximilian, Dec. 13, 1634, HHStA, Friedens. 10iv, ff. 21-4.
[11] Rocci to Barberini, Dec. 30, 1634, BL 6945, ff. 208-11.
[12] Barberini to Rocci, Oct. 23, 1634, cited in Repgen, 1: 1: 335, n.121.   [13] Günter, 182.
[14] Berthold Baustaedt, *Richelieu und Deutschland. Von der Schlacht bei Breitenfeld bis zum Tode Bernhards von Weimar* (Berlin, 1936), 149-51.

of reconciliation with France and rejection of peace with Saxony. He must be, they suspected, in secret contact with Richelieu.[15] According to Baglioni, imperial ministers openly asserted that Lamormaini would not have been a less suitable choice for the emperor's confessor had he been appointed by the king of France himself.[16]

The wheels of government in Vienna now turned even more slowly than usual. The emperor had to ask Saxony for a postponement of the return of his delegates. Finally, on January 20, a lengthy position paper prepared under Stralendorf's direction was read before the emperor at a session of the privy council.[17] The paper argued the case for peace persuasively.

For the greater good of both Empire and Church concessions had to be made, the paper contended. The political and military advantage still belonged with the enemy, especially in view of the increasing French activity along the Rhine. They enjoyed a clear financial and material superiority. The states of the Catholic League were either occupied or devastated, and little could be expected from the ravaged lands recovered after Nördlingen. Of the Habsburg territories, only the Austrian lands could still supply funds, and they were approaching their limits; Bohemia and Moravia lay ruined. Foreign aid always enabled the Protestants to come back after a defeat, whereas one more defeat like Breitenfeld would mean collapse for the Catholics and much more severe terms. Nor could Ferdinand expect significant foreign assistance, the paper continued. The aid received from the pope and friendly Italian states amounted to little, and the Spaniards, though still eager to help, were themselves on the brink of exhaustion. The enemy presently controlled the Lower Saxon and Westphalian Circles, and they enjoyed the support of the imperial and Hansa cities. This assured them funds, "the sinews of war," as well as effective lines of supply. France guaranteed them control of the Rhine. In addition, they could count on Dutch aid and according to reports, both the English and the Danes were preparing to send troops. Even from the Turks a threat seemed to be materializing. In Constantinople, French and Swedish envoys were attempting to mediate a peace between the Turks and the Persians so that the Turks could launch an offensive against the emperor. The enemy enjoyed considerable popular support in the Empire. Discipline and a firm structure had still not

---

[15] Philip IV to Oñate, Feb, 16, 1535, Günter, #157; see also pp. 203–4. Lamormaini had exchanged letters with the Jesuit Jean Suffren, confessor of Louis XIII, in 1629–1630 at the time of the Mantuan War. Suffren would not have carried on this brief correspondence without the approval of Richelieu; see Robert Bireley, *The Jesuits and the Thirty Years War: Kings, Courts, and Confessors* (Cambridge, 2003), 101–5.

[16] Baglioni to Barberini, Jan. 20, 1635, Repgen 1: 2: #94.

[17] Jan. 20, 1635, BANF, ibid., #107 (pp. 162–9). Adam Wandruszka, *Reichspatriotismus und Reichspolitik zur Zeit des Prager Friedens von 1635* (Graz, 1955), 23–5, discusses an undated German version of this Latin position paper.

been fully reintroduced into the imperial army, the paper stated, and mutiny among the troops remained a possibility.

To conquer Germany simply was not possible, the paper continued, implying what the council considered to be the only alternative to acceptance of the Pirna Points. Not even the Romans could accomplish this. A few more victories would change little, "since the German spirit would never allow itself to be subdued by force of arms." But even if complete victory were possible, the Catholic courts, that is, Paris and Rome, would never stand for the increase of power that the emperor would thereby acquire. The French showed no sign of readiness to come to an agreement with the emperor. The councillors raised a major issue when they took notice of Richelieu's clear intent to intervene in the contest for the succession should Ferdinand die before his son was elected king of the Romans. Ferdinand's early death could lead to an interregnum allowing the two Protestant electorates, Saxony and the Palatinate, to exercise their functions as imperial vicars. So the House of Habsburg would lose the imperial throne. This would be a disaster for Catholicism, since the House was evidently "the fulcrum of the Catholic religion" in Germany.

Concessions to the Protestants would be more than offset by the advantages to be won: the exclusion of Protestantism from the Habsburg lands, the restoration of the exiled ecclesiastical princes especially along the Rhine, the reacquisition of imperial church lands especially in Lower Saxony, and the retention of the Palatinate by Maximilian, thus solidifying the five-to-two Catholic majority in the electoral college. Charles V had made even greater concessions for peace, Ferdinand was reminded.[18] He was urged to consider those who favored peace. These were the "well-affected" cardinals and ministers in Rome, the estates and loyal subjects in the Habsburg lands as well as the Empire, the king of Spain along with his ministers. In Vienna itself there were religious of various orders as well as "High Cardinals," clearly a reference to Pazmany and Dietrichstein. The emperor's generals and the war council, the Imperial Court Council, all the emperor's loyal servants favored the peace. At its conclusion the paper described vividly the sufferings of the common people that simply could not be permitted to continue. Families had lost their all to pillaging troops. Women and girls had been raped, and thousands of orphans created. Schools were closed, and the education of the youth neglected. Churches lay in ashes. Such conditions could not help but stir in the heart of every patriot an intense longing for peace.

Indeed, a rational analysis pointed to the acceptance of the Pirna agreement. But several remarks in the paper betrayed a fear that the decision would not be

---

[18] Usually those in favor of peace pointed to the precedent of Ferdinand I who accepted the Peace of Augsburg. Those opposed to concessions normally cited with favor the example of Charles V who was believed to have abdicated largely because of his unwillingness to accept concessions to the Protestants. Thus both sides claimed for themselves the imperial tradition. On the abdication see Heinrich Lutz, *Christianitas Afflicta* (Göttingen, 1964), esp. pp. 412–15.

based on such an analysis. They were directed to the arguments of Lamormaini. "Human reason" must dictate the decision, not alleged divine revelation. If ultimate victory were certain, then we should continue to fight despite the cost. But in fact, the outcome was known to God alone. The emperor's championship of justice, the glory of God, and the Catholic religion did not guarantee him victory. The Bible provided many examples where God had ordered a holy war but then had punished the Israelites with defeat because of the misconduct and idolatry of their soldiers. In the Christian era, justice on the side of the Christians had not prevented the loss to the Church of the Eastern Empire, not to mention extensive areas of Africa and Asia. Victory did not always go to the virtuous in this world.

But the time had not yet come for a decision. The Catholic electors had yet to be heard from. Ferdinand also had made known, after the return of the delegates from Pirna, that he intended to convoke a committee of theologians to evaluate the terms of the projected peace. He now asked Cardinal Dietrichstein to chair the committee and to select for it theologians "who were not only learned and conscientious but also loyal and honestly inclined to see Our good and that of Our House."[19] On February 5, the theologians convened in Vienna. Once again the return of the imperial delegates to meet with the Saxons had to be postponed. Twenty-four theologians took part, members of eight different religious orders and one diocesan priest.[20] Their charge was to discuss the terms of the peace among themselves. Each individual or group from a religious order was then to submit its own opinion. They were not to work out a common opinion, presumably because Ferdinand realized that this would have put too much pressure on him to act accordingly or perhaps because he realized that to expect them to come to a common position was unrealistic. As the deliberations began, the Capuchin Alessandro d'Ales, who was not a participant, reported that the emperor inclined strongly toward peace but that Lamormaini told him that he could not in good conscience accept the terms of the Pirna Points. For this reason, Ferdinand was "very sad."[21]

Ferdinand faced a critical decision, perhaps the most important one of his life. Certainly neither he nor his councillors were thinking in terms of the establishment of absolute rule in the Empire. Three times he formulated the terms of the questions to be put to the theologians, and he eventually reduced them to two. The theologians were not asked to judge whether the present situation constituted a sufficient state of necessity to justify the concessions to the Protestants; that determination presumably was up to the political councillors. They were asked rather whether any provisions in the treaty regarding religion were intrinsically evil and so could not be permitted under

---

[19] Emperor to Dietrichstein, Jan. 20, 1635, BANF, ibid., #105 (pp. 154-6).
[20] For a list of all the theologians who participated, see Bireley 2, 278-80.
[21] Alessandro d'Ales to Barberini, Feb. 3, 1635 (two letters), Repgen 1: 2: ##104, 105.

Settlement and Death, 1635–1637

any circumstances without mortal sin. Secondly, if the terms of the peace were acceptable, what was the most appropriate language in which to clothe them? Any concessions had to be seen as essentially a passive tolerance extorted from him by necessity; his conscience and his reputation required this. A third question, obviously loaded against Lamormaini, had been dropped: if the emperor could agree to the peace with a good conscience, was he bound to do so? Or could he rather, in the hope of a miracle, submit the Catholic states, the Empire itself, the Habsburg territories, and his most August house to evident danger, or was this to tempt God?[22] As a basis for their discussions, the theologians were given a copy of the ecclesiastical terms of the peace and the position paper of the privy council of January 20 as well as other papers in favor of peace. The imperial negotiators Hermann von Questenberg and Gebhardt were made available to answer questions that the theologians might have. The conference lasted until February 16, and in the following days the individual opinions were delivered to Dietrichstein.[23] Lamormaini spoke more frequently at the conference than any other participant but did not submit a written opinion.

All the theologians including Lamormaini agreed that there was nothing intrinsically evil in the terms and thus prohibited under any circumstances. Many of the participants thought that it would be enough to affirm the principle that in case of necessity the proposed concessions might be admitted and to leave its application up to the imperial councillors. This is what the councillors wanted. But Lamormaini vigorously maintained that this would be insufficient as a guide for the conscience of the emperor for which he bore the responsibility. To the dismay of Cardinal Dietrichstein, he then secured from Ferdinand further information about the terms which the councillors, for security reasons, had wanted to withhold from the theologians, and he then persuaded most of them to render a decision whether a state of necessity actually existed.[24] Nevertheless, thirteen of the sixteen written opinions affirmed that if better conditions could not be obtained, Ferdinand could accept the terms as they stood.

---

[22] Imperial decree for the theologians' conference, Jan. 20, 1635, HHStA, Friedens. 11a, ff. 64–5v; questions for the theologians' conference, enclosure with emperor to Dietrichstein, Feb. 9, 1635, Brno, Dietrichstein Archive, Karton 90, f. 114; questions for the theologians' conference, enclosure with emperor to Dietrichstein, Feb. 10, 1635, ibid., ff. 115, 120.

[23] The sixteen written opinions are found in HHStA, Friedens. 11a, ff. 214–87. Repgen 1: 1: 355–56, discusses these briefly. For a summary of the written opinions drawn up for the emperor see *BANF*, ibid., #121 (pp. 206–13). Also important for the conference is the material found in the Dietrichstein Archive, Karton 90, which includes the proceedings, "Compendium Gestorum in Congregatione Theologorum" (henceforth "Compendium"), twenty-six clearly and closely written folios signed by the Capuchin Basilio d"Aire.

[24] Compendium, ff. 42v-3, 46–7v, 64–64v; Dietrichstein to the emperor, Feb. 5 and 7 (with enclosure), *BANF*, ibid: #112 (pp. 173–4), #116 (p. 177); emperor to Dietrichstein, Feb. 7, 1635, ibid., #114 (p. 175). Ferdinand was staying at Sopron during the conference.

Two principal factions are discernible among the participants. One comprised the three Capuchins and the other Lamormaini and four of the other seven Jesuits who took part. Quiroga headed the Capuchins. With him stood Valeriano Magni, who was back in Vienna on a mission for King Wladyslaw of Poland at whose court he was now serving, and Basilio d'Aire, an Irish Capuchin who had replaced Magni as an adviser to Cardinal Harrach and correspondent for the Congregation for the Propagation of the Faith in Rome. Quiroga and Basilio both declared in their papers that the emperor could not only accept the terms of the peace but that if he did not do so, he would sin mortally.[25]

Though Lamormaini did not say so with complete clarity, he obviously thought that no state of necessity existed sufficient to justify the concessions to the Protestants, and he implied – to the embarrassment of the other theologians (according to Basilio who kept the minutes) – that the information supplied by the councillors was unreliable. Gebhardt, who sympathized with the confessor, agreed when he stated that Saxony intended to retain the ecclesiastical lands permanently and accepted the limitation to forty or fifty years only to make the terms palatable to the Catholics, but Questenberg, the other imperial representative, disagreed with his colleague.[26] Now was the time for "heroic action," Lamormaini asserted in a long, final address to the group. He still envisioned an agreement with France, as the proceedings reveal.[27]

> Given equally unfavorable conditions, ought one not rather attempt peace with the Frenchmen, who is at least Catholic, than with those whose firm purpose is to destroy Catholics and Catholicism? This, he said, could be considered according to the principle so often cited in the conference, the lesser of two evils is to be chosen. For the Saxon seeks our possessions and our souls, the Frenchman at least not the souls. About this, nevertheless, he said, I make no judgment, I only discourse.

The other Jesuit participants, whether they stood with the confessor or not, as well as the Capuchins realized that they needed to address the idea that God would come to the aid of the emperor in a special way. The Jesuit Blase Slaninus, rector of the Jesuit academy in Olmütz, asserted that even if he could yield licitly to the Protestants, why could Ferdinand not continue the war since, according to the belief of all peoples and nations, he possessed a pledge of divine protection and was thought to have been called by God to eliminate heresy in the north of Europe.[28] The Spanish Jesuit Peñalosa, close to the queen of Hungary and so to Quiroga, had little difficulty with Ferdinand's ratification of the terms, and he contended that God's special care for Ferdinand would show itself in the guidance that he gave him to make the right decision.[29]

The Capuchin Quiroga claimed that the emperor was not excused from the obligation to accept the terms "by a fiducial faith in God, even though this was

---

[25] HHStA, Friedens. 11a, ff. 262–3, 257–9.   [26] Compendium ff. 40–1.
[27] Ibid., f. 63v.; the final folios of the Compendium contain Lamormaini's last address to the group.
[28] HHStA, Friedens. 11a, ff. 226–7.   [29] Ibid., ff. 221–3.

based on long experience of benefits by which Divine Providence had preserved, defended, and protected His Imperial Majesty." Ferdinand had more than satisfied his duty as Defender of the Church.[30] Basilio emphasized that it would be presumption and temerity to rely on divine assistance in the absence of a clear divine revelation such as Gideon had received, according to the Book of Judges. Human reason had to prevail.[31]

A point touched upon by most of the theologians was whether positive papal approval was necessary for any concessions to the Protestants. The question had been raised back in 1631, but circumstances had made it easy subsequently to overlook the response of the theologians then. In October, Urban had responded negatively when asked directly by an emissary of Mainz and Cologne whether he would approve concessions, and they had communicated this to Vienna.[32] The issue was never as important in Vienna as it was to the Catholic electors. Lamormaini brought it up in the theologians' conference, but he never made it central to his argument. Only the two Capuchins, Basilio and Valeriano, realized that Urban preferred not to be put on the spot and for this reason encouraged the emperor to move ahead without consulting him.[33]

By the time the conference of theologians came to an end, the opinions of the three Catholic electors had arrived. Father Alessandro expected that these would carry more weight than the views of the theologians.[34] Contrary to all past experience, they split. Mainz and Maximilian, after encouraging Ferdinand to secure all possible improvements in the terms, agreed to accept the Pirna Points if there was no alternative. Cologne disagreed. All three had agonized over their decision. Mainz asserted in his defense the two maxims: no one was bound to the impossible and the lesser of two evils was to be chosen. His people had borne the brunt of the Swedish invasion and simply could no longer support the war. His suspicions of French intentions – he wrote of French plans to dismember the Empire – subsequently confirmed him in his decision.[35] Maximilian's justification for his break with militant policy was the same argument as that of the imperial councillors. For the sake of the greater good, the Catholics could make concessions to the Protestants. In addition, the French defense of Heidelberg had infuriated him, and he now feared more than ever what an interregnum in the Empire might bring. Important, too, was the stand taken by Mainz, of which the cautious Maximilian was informed

---

[30] Ibid., ff. 262–3.   [31] Ibid., ff. 247–9, 258–61.
[32] Cologne and Mainz to the emperor, Oct. 2, 1634, BANF, ibid. #349 (pp. 790–5).
[33] HHStA, Friedens. 11a, ff. 247–9, 277–87.
[34] Alessandro d'Ales to Barberini, Feb. 17, 1635, Repgen 1: 2: #110.
[35] Mainz to the emperor, Jan. 8, HHStA, Friedens. 11a, ff. 13–4; Jan. 23, BANF, ibid., #380 (pp. 866–7), Apr. 2, 1635, ibid., #427 (pp. 966–7); Mainz to Trautmannsdorf, Mar. 26, 1635, ibid., #423 (pp. 959–62).

before he made his final decision. If an ecclesiastic took the initiative, then he was safe in conscience and reputation.[36]

Cologne, Maximilian's brother, sharply rejected the Pirna agreement, however.[37] Necessity did not justify it. Cologne had benefitted from French protection against the advance of the Swedes, and did not fear French encroachments along the Rhine. The long-term concession of the free exercise of religion in many areas and the surrender of church lands amounted to a new religious peace. The emperor was not empowered to conclude such an agreement without the approval of the pope and of the German Catholic states. The recent victories that God had granted the Catholics, the elector affirmed, gave grounds for new confidence. Where would the Church be if Constantine and Charlemagne had shown such timidity?

The division among the electors unsettled Ferdinand. The opinions of Mainz and Maximilian were welcome in Vienna, but Ferdinand went out of his way to reassure Cologne that the terms were only tentative and that negotiations would continue.[38] That Cologne's arguments were taken seriously is shown by the draft of a lengthy, detailed answer to his charges that apparently was never sent.[39] The emperor had no intention of approving anything involving the electors without their approval, it stated; but the military activity along the Rhine disrupted communications. Most theologians consulted on the matter had agreed that the terms could be accepted for the greater good and for the avoidance of the imminent dangers to Church and Empire. What would the princes answer to God if because of "scruples of this sort" they let Church and Empire perish? The projected treaty had its shortcomings, the author granted, but no human work was perfect. Once again reference was made to the Peace of Augsburg. It, too, had yielded on a number of points to the Protestants, but as a result the Catholic religion had made great progress in the second half of the previous century.

Now that the opinions of the electors had arrived and the results of the theologians' conference were available, Ferdinand, back in Vienna, summoned eight "intimate" (*intimi*) councillors to draw up a final evaluation of the Pirna Points. Included in the group were four clerics, Lamormaini, the two cardinals, Pazmany and Dietrichstein, and Bishop Anton Wolfradt, and four secular councillors, Stralendorf, Trautmannsdorf, Werdenberg, and Heinrich von

---

[36] Maximilian to the emperor, Feb. 14, 1635, *BANF*, ibid., #395 (pp. 902–5).
[37] Cologne to the emperor, Dec. 24, 1634, *BANF*, ibid.; #362 (pp. 809–10). Cologne exhibited the rationale for his position in a set of "Considerations" drawn up by his theologians and sent to Maximilian and the emperor, undated, ibid., #363 (pp. 811–32).
[38] Emperor to Mainz and Cologne, Feb. 21, 1635, *BANF*, ibid.: #119 (pp. 203–204); Richel (who had presented Maximilian's response to Ferdinand in Vienna) to Maximilian, Feb. 28, 1635, ibid. #407 (pp. 926–8).
[39] Undated, HHStA, Friedens. 15, 329–65.

Schlick, chairman of the war council. They met from February 27 to March 10. Ferdinand was perplexed in conscience, a Jesuit in Vienna confided to a correspondent in Munich.[40] One side told him that there were neither soldiers nor funds to continue the war, the other that the war could still be won. Before committing the matter to the eight, Ferdinand stressed for them its importance; it touched the salvation of his own soul. He charged them to state only that for which he and they could take responsibility before the judgment seat of God.[41]

Lamormaini now stood alone in his opposition to the Pirna Points. His recommendation of special missions to Paris and Rome showed that he still hoped for an alliance of the Catholic powers. Shortly before the councillors convened, a courier arrived from the nuncio in Paris with word that France was prepared to send a delegate to the peace conference proposed by the pope, provided Spain and the emperor did the same. This encouraged the papal representatives in Vienna as well as Lamormaini, even though the same courier brought news of a French military buildup and preparations for war. Baglioni reported that the confessor was "most inclined" towards peace with France, and he added that the Spaniards were upset by the new development. Lamormaini and Quiroga had engaged in a sharp exchange.[42]

The paper finally submitted by the intimates argued that "this opportunity to obtain once again and to extend a just peace was to be seized upon effectively and not let go." Twice before the emperor had permitted the opportunity for a just peace to slip by, once when he enjoyed a clear advantage in the Empire, probably an allusion to the Electoral Convention of Regensburg in 1630, and again after Gustav Adolph fell at Lützen; for the second squandered opportunity they blamed Wallenstein.[43] The same mistake was not to be repeated. The councillors showed no confidence in alleged French willingness to negotiate, and they called attention to French efforts to divide the Empire for over 800 years. If Ferdinand rejected Saxony, John George himself would turn to France. Just then French emissaries were bombarding him with offers of an alliance.[44]

[40] Ludwig Crasius, professor of theology at the Jesuit academy in Olmütz and a member of the theologians' conference, to an unidentified correspondent in Munich, Feb. 24, 1635, Munich, Bayerisches Hauptstaatsarchiv, Jesuitica 704, f. 14.
[41] Position papers on the Pirna Points, Mar. 5 and 10, HHStA, Friedens. 11a, ff. 313–23, 325–43, 345–55. Folios 288 to 310v include miscellaneous minutes of the discussion held between Feb. 27 and Mar. 10; see BANF, ibid., #124 (222–37). A paper of Pazmany is found in his *Epistolæ Collectæ*, ed. Franciscus Hanuy 2 (Budapest, 1911): #951. Also present at some of the sessions were Gebhardt and Johann Söldner, a court secretary.
[42] Baglioni to Barberini, Feb. 24 (two letters) and Mar. 3, 1635, Repgen 1: 2: ##113, 114, 117; Alessandro d'Ales to Barberini, Feb. 24, 1634, ibid., #115.
[43] The allusion here is not completely clear. It seems to refer to no one event but to the failure of Wallenstein both militarily and politically during the whole year 1633.
[44] Alessandro d'Ales to Barberini, Feb. 3, 1635, Repgen 1: 2: #104; Trautmannsdorf reported that the French were putting great pressure on Saxony; see also the imperial delegates in Prague to the emperor, Mar. 21, 1635, BANF, ibid., #129 (pp. 290–1).

That would mean the end for the Habsburg succession in the Empire, and the succession was now emerging as a major issue as Ferdinand's health deteriorated.

The position paper argued the pros and cons of the terms as had the opinion of January 20, and with the same result. But several additions and new emphases were aimed at the emperor's conscience. Eighteen theologians had voted that the emperor could accept the peace in good conscience. The people were crying for peace, and "the voice of the people is the voice of God." Peace with Saxony would not betray pusillanimity on Ferdinand's part. True, it was written in 2 Paralipomenon (Chronicles) 25 that if one placed his trust in the strength of his army alone, God would send him to defeat at the hands of his enemy.[45] But Christ himself in Luke 14 cautioned a king not to start a war without first calculating his own strength and that of his enemy. The emperor's cause was certainly just, but God's judgments were inscrutable. Sometimes misfortunes overtook those fighting in holy causes, as was clear in the case of St. Louis of France, who suffered defeat in his first expedition to liberate the Holy Land and fell victim to the plague during the second. One had no evidence that God would lead the emperor to victory. Policy could not be based on anticipated miracles but had to be determined rationally. And if misfortune struck once again as it had at Breitenfeld, that would be the end for Ferdinand in Germany and in the Habsburg lands.

So the councillors came out clearly in favor of the peace with Saxony. But partly as a result of the prodding by the electors and theologians, they encouraged Ferdinand to secure as many further concessions as he could. Lamormaini aimed to preserve as much of the Edict as possible. In the discussions, he called for the explicit exclusion of the Calvinists and the clear recognition of the emperor's right to make a final decision on the ecclesiastical issues after the lapse of the forty-year period. The councillors worked both of these points into their final report in a modified form. They drew up a scale of demands for the imperial negotiators. At first they were to attempt to restrict the normative date of November 12, 1627, to Saxony alone. To this end, all the concessions intended for his private satisfaction were to be granted. The intent was to split John George from the other Protestant states. The normative date would be extended to other Protestant states only until the foreigners had been expelled and an imperial diet or convention determined the status of church lands for the future. Should this be unacceptable to John George, the imperial negotiators were gradually to extend the normative date to other Protestant states and the period of its validity to forty years until John George was satisfied. The paper stressed the need to assure that Maximilian retained the electoral title and lands but they were willing, if necessary, to subject the issue to further discussion. Maximilian had agreed to this provided that he held the title and the lands in the interim.

---

[45] The reference is to events in the reign of Amaziah, king of Juda.

Ferdinand accepted these position papers at the privy council sessions of March 5 and 10 as the basis for the instructions for the imperial representatives to be sent to Prague where the negotiations had been moved. But he added important comments and qualifications. The negotiators were to work diligently to secure the modifications advocated by the council, especially those regarding the Edict. Gebhardt noted in his own hand the remarks of Ferdinand. "The emperor makes this formal statement: I place my trust in you (meaning the delegates), that you keep your oath and your duty in mind and that you zealously take into consideration all [your instructions.]" They were to insist on both the temporary nature of the concessions and Ferdinand's power of ultimate decision, lest he be burdened with "an odium with all Catholics." In particular he wanted the delegates to broaden his power to exclude from amnesty.[46] Three considerations motivated Ferdinand's intent to expand his authority to exclude individuals from amnesty and from restitution to their lands: his sense of justice, his desire to retain as many lands as possible for the Church, and his ability to satisfy his creditors and compensate his supporters for their losses in the war.[47] To the text of the instruction for the delegates, dated March 12, were added in the margin the following words: "Our delegates should make every effort to secure the limitations and modifications herein urged, since they concern the glory of God and his Church, so that we cannot be accused of yielding excessively on points touching the Church's and the Catholic [states'?] interests or of not taking their rights sufficiently into consideration."[48]

With this instruction, Ferdinand finally broke with the position long successfully affirmed by Lamormaini, that the emperor's providential mission to restore Catholicism in Germany assured him of special divine aid and forbade him to make concessions to the Protestants that went beyond the Peace of Religion of 1555. Policy was to be decided on the basis of rational considerations, not on the basis of an alleged divine revelation. When a month later nuncio Baglioni in an audience with the emperor remonstrated with him about the terms of the agreement with Saxony as Barberini had instructed him to do, Ferdinand's response revealed his mind a month earlier. He could, he told Baglioni, take responsibility before God for the decision that he had made. According to the nuncio, Ferdinand went on to affirm that he had heard from France that the goal of that kingdom was to humble the House of Austria.

---

[46] The remarks of the emperor at the session of March 5 are found in HHStA, Friedens. 11a, ff. 343v-4v, as well as in several annotations throughout the paper. The session of March 10, with the emperor present, dealt with more strictly political matters including the Palatinate Question.

[47] See, for example, two petitions for payment presented in Vienna by agents of Cologne, March 1635, BANF 9: *Juni 1634–Mai 1635*, ed. Kathrin Bierther (Munich, 1986), # 247a (pp. 597-601) and #247b (pp. 601-2).

[48] HHStA, Friedens. 11a, ff. 383-94v, 433-87, quotation on 445-445

He had served the Church by expelling the heretics from his own lands, he declared to the nuncio, and he would have done so in the Empire had it not been for the French. Despite Baglioni's caution that Urban would resent his words, the emperor continued, and here Baglioni cited him, that "he did not understand how this theology of the French goes." Richelieu scandalized him. So Ferdinand vented his feelings toward the French, and indirectly toward the pope. He rejected Lamormain's hope in them. Yet he agreed to continue to support Urban's efforts toward peace, but Baglioni began to fear a break between emperor and pope.[49]

Meanwhile, by March 14 the imperial delegation was on its way to Prague. The rising court councillor Ferdinand Kurz von Senftenau, Stralendorf's successor as imperial vice-chancellor under Ferdinand III, replaced Hermann von Questenberg, who had asked to be excused from yet another diplomatic mission and requested reimbursement for his expenses.[50] The negotiations dragged on for another two months, largely because of difficult communications. Gebhardt implicitly criticized Trautmannsdorf when he wrote the court secretary, Johann Söldner, in late March that he did not share the minister's confidence in the good faith of the Saxon negotiators and thought the imperials could obtain better terms than they probably would receive.[51] Bavarian troops intercepted a letter of the magistrates of Nuremberg in mid-March which showed how ardently they desired peace. Seeing this, Maximilian suggested that the imperial cities be excluded from the normative year so that they would have to accept the Edict, that is, the status of 1555, if they wanted to be included in the peace. But Vienna rejected this. Ferdinand and his councillors were particularly eager to include Nuremberg in the peace with its wealth, prestige, and central geographical position.[52]

Surprisingly, John George acceded to nearly all Ferdinand's demands. He did insist that the normative date apply formally to the whole Empire. But the implicit exclusion of Calvinists, which Saxony welcomed, and recognition of a broad imperial right to exclude from amnesty allowed Ferdinand to achieve many of his goals, especially regarding Church property in Württemberg which was nearly completely occupied by the imperials. The normative date was to apply to only four imperial cities in the Upper German Circles: Nuremberg,

---

[49] Baglioni to Barberini, April 21, 1635, Repgen 1: 2. #128 (pp. 183–5); Baglioni to Barberini, Apr. 28, 1635, NDB, *Nuntiaturen Filonardi, Rocci, und Baglioni*, #48.5 (p. 289).
[50] Questenberg to the emperor, Jan. 30, 1635, HHStA, Friedens. 11a, ff. 122–4; emperor to Ferdinand Kurz von Senftenau, Feb. 9, 1635, ibid., ff. 174–5; Gebhardt to Trautmannsdorf, Mar. 14, 1635, HHStA, Traut., 102iii, f. 173. Trautmannsdorf and Kurz were already under way; Gebhardt soon followed.
[51] Mar. 28, 1635, BANF 10: 2, #138 (pp. 299–300).
[52] Bireley 1, 218; minutes of the privy council meeting, Mar. 30, 1635, HHStA, Friedens 15ii, ff. 6–8v; position paper of the committee of councillors, Apr. 30, approved by the emperor, May 1, 1635, BANF, ibid., #159 (361–4).

Frankfurt, Strasbourg, and Ulm. All others had to accept the Edict if they wanted to participate in the peace. A special arrangement was made to accommodate Augsburg.[53] Saxony also agreed that the terms meant the return of the Lower Saxon bishoprics Minden, Verden, and Bremen to the Catholics.

Two further points stood out. Saxony accepted Maximilian's permanent retention of the Palatinate electoral title and the lands on the right bank of the Rhine. References to a possible extension of the forty-year period were eliminated, and John George recognized the emperor's final jurisdiction over ecclesiastical matters after the lapse of forty years if no satisfactory solution was worked out by then. This provision was clearly intended to prevent the status of 1627 from automatically becoming permanent.

Finally, on May 30, the imperial and Saxon delegates signed the Peace of Prague. Eleven days earlier Richelieu had formally issued a declaration of war on Spain in Brussels. But even with the concessions wrung from Saxony, the peace amounted to the final renunciation of Lamormaini's plans for the restoration of Catholicism in Germany. Several days later news of the peace unleashed spontaneous popular rejoicing in Vienna, where Bishop Anton Wolfradt ordered that it be proclaimed from the pulpits and that services of thanksgiving be conducted despite the request of the nuncio not to allow this.[54] But Ferdinand's reluctance to allow a Te Deum to be sung in the churches betrayed a lingering degree of dissatisfaction with the religious terms of the peace.[55] In late April, shortly before the peace was announced, a peasant rebellion had erupted around the town of Cilli (Celje) in Styria, an area generally spared the war's destruction and devastation. Several hundred peasants took up arms as a result of complaints against the noble landowners and excessive taxation. They burned down two castles and a residence of the bishop of Ljubliana and generally engaged in pillage and robbery until troops were sent to quiet the area.[56]

Pope Urban's reaction to the Peace of Prague turned out to be much more positive than Vienna had expected, but it remained in line with papal policy up to that point. Ferdinand notified the pope of the conclusion of the Peace in a communication of June 2. The Peace was a product of necessity, Ferdinand wrote, which he nevertheless hoped would benefit both the Church and the

---

[53] For the text of the Peace of Prague, see BANF 10, 4: *Vertragstexte* (Munich, 1997). See also *Pirnische und Pragische Friedens Pacten, susampt angesteller Collation und Anweisung der Discrepantz und Unterschieds* [sic] *zwischen denenselben* (n.p., 1636).
[54] Baglioni to Barberini, Jun. 9, 1635, NBD, *Nuntiaturen Filonardi, Rocci und Baglioni*, #60.4 (pp. 363-4).
[55] Bishop of Vienna to Trautmannsdorf, Vienna, May 13, 1635, BANF *10*: 2: #163 (p. 367).
[56] See Baglioni to Barberini, May 19, 1635, NBD, ibid., #54.5 (p. 319); A Mell, "Der windische Bauernaufstand des Jahres 1635 und dessen Nachwehen," *Mittheilungen des historischen Vereins für Steiermark* 44 (1896): 205-87.

Empire even if it did not obtain for the Church all the advantages for which both he and the pope would have hoped. The pope knew to whom its shortcomings could be attributed; Ferdinand did not mention either France or Richelieu by name, and he forewent judging them leaving that up to God.[57] Shortly afterward he forwarded to his resident in Rome, now Scipione Gonzaga, prince of Bozolo, a long justification of the Peace that was then published as a broadsheet.[58] As the prince neared the end of his presentation to Urban, the pope complained that the resident was reporting only the advantages and not the shortcomings of the agreement. When told that this was not the case, the pope acknowledged that the terms were much more favorable to religion than he had expected them to be.[59] On July 22, a brief drawn up by the German humanist and convert Lucas Holstein was sent to Ferdinand that recognized Ferdinand's efforts and zeal for the Church but avoided anything that could be interpreted as approval of the concessions to the Protestants.[60] Thus Urban upheld the juridical position of Rome as his successor, Innocent X, would do following the Peace of Westphalia.[61] Urban continued to work for peace among the Catholic powers despite the French declaration of war on Spain. Having secured agreement in principle from the emperor, Louis XIII, and Philip IV to hold a peace conference at an as yet undetermined location, in August 1635 he named Mario Ginetti cardinal-legate to represent him.[62]

The Peace of Prague did not end the war in Germany; yet despite its flaws, it amounted to a significant achievement for Ferdinand and a major shift in his thinking, and it marked a milestone in German history. Brandenburg and most of the German princes invited to do so eventually joined the alliance of Ferdinand and Saxony, and a military reorganization took place that brought Catholic and Protestant forces together, however imperfectly. In doing this, the settlement greatly reduced the religious nature of the war. The most militant phase of the war in Germany, characterized by the Edict of Restitution of 1629,

---

[57] Ferdinand to Urban VIII, June 2, 1635, Repgen 1: 2, #136 (pp. 195–6).
[58] Ibid., #137 (pp. 197–200).
[59] Bozzolo to Ferdinand II, Jul. 23, 1635, ibid., #138 (pp. 200–1).
[60] Urban VIII to Ferdinand II, July 22, 1635, ibid., #140 (pp. 206–7).
[61] Pope Innocent X did not formally issue a protest against the Peace of Westphalia until the bull "Zelo Domus Dei" was published on Aug. 20, 1650, so after the conclusion of the Nuremberg Agreement on Demobilization; it was backdated to Nov. 26, 1648. The protest was meant to have a juridical not a political effect. The pope did not want to give any reason for prolonging the war nor to bear the odium for resumption of the conflict. The purpose of the bull was to preserve the juridical claims of the church. See Konrad Repgen, "Die Proteste Chigis und der päpstliche Protest gegen den westfälischen Frieden (1648/1650): Vier Kapitel über das Breve 'Zelo Domus Dei,'" *Staat, Kirche und Wissenschaft in einer pluralistischen Gesellschaft: Festschrift zum 65. Geburtstag von Paul Mikat* (Berlin, 1989): 625–47.
[62] Repgen 1: 1: 376–88, 393–4, 530.

was over. Inasmuch as it ended the most aggressive phase of the Counter Reformation in Germany, it constituted a return to the more modest policy of Emperor Ferdinand I at the time of the Peace of Augsburg of 1555 and an anticipation of the Peace of Westphalia of 1648. Ferdinand had been convinced that he had been especially designated by God and promised divine assistance to restore Catholicism in Germany to its status at the time of the Peace of Religion of 1555. This conviction had its roots in his dealing with the Inner Austrian estates in the early years of his reign there, was confirmed by the apparently miraculous victory at the White Mountain, and then greatly encouraged and fostered by Lamormaini. It had often if not always played a role in the formulation of policy. This was no longer to be the case. The anti-Protestant crusading spirit that had already abandoned Rome and Madrid now departed from Germany. This does not mean that the emperor, neither Ferdinand II nor Ferdinand III, would overlook the welfare of the Church in the future. But the principle had been established, or perhaps reestablished, that religious concessions could be of greater benefit to Church and Empire than conflict and war, or in other words, that they constituted the lesser evil. When rational analysis showed this to be the case, they could be made without fear of betraying an alleged divine revelation or failing to trust in the Lord.[63]

Lamormaini, while remaining an active figure in Vienna after the Peace of Prague and personally close to Ferdinand, saw his influence on politics diminish. The Jesuit Johannes Gans, a native of Würzburg who had served as preacher for the court of the king of Hungary, became confessor to Ferdinand III shortly after he was crowned emperor. Ferdinand III, while perhaps no less religious than his father, greatly restricted the political role of ecclesiastics, and this policy suited the new confessor who did not attempt to assert himself in politics.[64] At the Electoral Convention of Regensburg in 1641, when asked by the delegates of Mainz whether the elector might agree to further concessions to the Protestants regarding church lands, Gans replied that the consensus of the theologians' conference of 1635 provided a clear precedent. They had sanctioned surrender of ecclesiastical lands for the sake of winning Protestant states over to the emperor's side.[65] Gans subsequently called the Edict of

---

[63] Perhaps it is not an accident that in 1633 two years before the Peace of Prague, the Galileo affair came to a head with the condemnation of the scientist. In both cases the role of revelation was at issue, in politics and in science. In the case of the Peace of Prague, in Vienna an alleged revelation was dismissed as irrelevant for the formation of political policy. In the affair of Galileo, the Church asserted that biblical revelation did have a place in the practice of science.

[64] On Gans, see Robert Bireley, *The Jesuits and the Thirty Years War: Kings, Courts, and Confessors* (Cambridge, 2003), 209–11, 216–17, 219–21

[65] Kathrin Bierther, *Der Regensburger Reichstag von 1640/641* (Kallmunz, 1971), 132–4. Regensburger Historische Forschungen. In note 236 Bierther cites at length the conversation of the Mainz delegates with Gans and another unidentified Jesuit.

Restitution the principal source of all the trouble in the Empire, the creature of zealous and well-meaning but politically inept imperial councillors.[66]

The Peace of Prague marked a retreat from an aggressive assertion of imperial authority in Germany, especially in the compromise on the Edict. But Ferdinand had never aimed at the creation of an absolute, hereditary monarchy in the Empire as his enemies and some modern historians have charged. What Wallenstein at one time may or may not have intended is not clear and remains a historical enigma. Ferdinand aimed at the restoration of imperial authority to what it had been prior to the troubles brought about by the conflict between his predecessors Rudolf and Matthias and especially in service of his religious goal, the restoration of Catholicism in Germany within the constraints of the Peace of Religion. Imperial authority was required to achieve this goal. The instances where he was thought to have stretched the imperial constitution, especially the investiture of Maximilian with the electoral dignity and the promulgation of the Edict, were closely connected with the advancement of Catholicism and were supported by the Catholic electors. Even the bestowal of the duchy of Mecklenburg on Wallenstein had a religious aspect to it, inasmuch as it strengthened the position of the Church in north Germany. The prohibition of alliances spelled the dissolution of the Catholic League and the Heilbronn Confederation. Vienna had long pursued this goal, and it seemed to strengthen the emperor's position. But the anticipated military reform with the imperial, Bavarian, and Saxon armies under a unified command was not intended to be a step toward a German monarchy but rather to provide a smoother functioning of the forces fighting for the emperor, and it was never effectively implemented.[67] The Peace also represented a victory for Spain and the Spanish party in Vienna including Oñate, Quiroga, and the queen of Hungary. The Spaniards had long pushed Ferdinand to restrain his Counter-Reformation zeal and modify the Edict with a view to securing peace and unity in the Empire between Catholics and moderate Protestants, so that Ferdinand could then come to the aid of the Spaniards in their contest with the Dutch and the French.

Even before the defeat at Breitenfeld, leading councillors had pointed out to Ferdinand the impossibility of dominating Germany and the necessity of concessions in the Empire for the sake of consolidation of his position in the Habsburg lands. Stralendorf, Trautmannsdorf, Bishop Wolfradt, and the two cardinals Dietrichstein and Pazmany had all taken this position. Eggenberg, too, had called for concessions, but he did this more out of support for the Spanish position in the Empire. One measure on which neither Ferdinand

---

[66] Bernhard Duhr, *Geschichte der Jesuiten in den Ländern deutscher Zünge* 2: 1 (Freiburg, 1913), 473–4.
[67] Hainer Haan, "Kaiser Ferdinand II und das Problem des Reichsabsolutismus: Die Prager Heeresreform von 1635," *Historische Zeitschrift* 207 (1968), 297–345 (rpt. in Hans Ulrich Rudolf, ed., *Der Dreissigjährige Krieg*, Darmstadt, 1977, 208–64). Wege der Forschung, 451.

nor the councillors ever considered compromise was the maintenance of Catholicism as the exclusive form of Christianity in the Habsburg lands (except in Hungary). Once it became clear to Ferdinand, as it did in 1635, that it was not possible to achieve his religious goals in the Empire and that he was no longer bound to pursue them, his imperial activism waned. It was not an accident that on August 8, 1635, Ferdinand added a second codicil to his testament in which he confirmed his intent that all the lands that he possessed be maintained as a single, indivisible inheritance and in which he stated explicitly that this held for all other lands that might come into his possession by inheritance, conquest in a just war, or in any other way.[68] The Peace of Prague showed the increasing priority the German Habsburgs were to give in the future to the monarchy over the Empire.[69] Ferdinand's achievement was to lay the foundation of the monarchy on the three pillars: the dynasty, the aristocracy, and the Church. Despite all its setbacks, Austria emerged from the Thirty Years War as a major European power.

One reason for the failure of the Peace of Prague to bring peace to the Empire was the exclusion of some states from amnesty and the harshness of the terms imposed on others in order to qualify for the amnesty. Among these were the Elector Palatine Karl Ludwig, son of the now-deceased Elector Frederick, Duke Eberhard of Württemberg, whose restoration was conditioned upon his surrender of the many ecclesiastical lands scattered throughout his principality, and the Calvinist Landgrave of Hesse-Kassel, who was of singular importance because of the modest army under his control. Hesse-Kassel soon allied with France. The condottiere Bernhard of Weimar along with his largely German army went over from Swedish to French service in exchange for the promise of a principality in Alsace.

The main reason that the Peace did not succeed was the continuing presence of Sweden in the Empire and the increasing activity of France. The terms of the Peace allotted only financial compensation to the Swedes. They were not about to return home after five years of war in Germany without some territorial gain. For a time it appeared that imperial negotiations with the Swedes might remove them from the war. But on September 20, 1635, at Stuhmsdorf in Prussia, Richelieu mediated a renewal of the armistice between Sweden and Poland that enabled the Swedes to continue to focus on the war in Germany, and three years later he renewed the French alliance with Sweden on a still firmer basis at the Treaty of Hamburg.[70] Meanwhile he supported Hesse-Kassel and Bernhard of Weimar, and he remained allied with the Dutch in their war against Spain. The

---

[68] Gustav Turba, *Die Grundlagen der Pragmatischen Sanktion*. 2: *Die Hausgesetze* (Vienna/Leipzig): Appendix 10, pp. 359–61. Wiener Staatswissenschaftliche Studien 11: 1.

[69] For the relationship of the Habsburg Monarchy to the Empire after 1648, see R.J.W. Evans, *The Making of the Habsburg Monarchy: An Interpretation, 1550–1700* (Oxford, 1979), 274–308, and Charles Ingrao, *The Habsburg Monarchy 1618–1815* (Cambridge, 1994), 48–52.

[70] This was a ratification of the Treaty of Wismar of March 30, 1636.

appearance of Catholic France on the side of Sweden, the dissident German Protestants, and the Dutch lessened significantly the religious character of the war, but it greatly expanded the conflict into a war between France and the Habsburg states for hegemony in Europe. Meanwhile, the war took an increasingly devastating toll on the population. Members of an English delegation to the Electoral Convention of Regensburg in 1636 wrote of the utter desolation of the country as they traveled up the Main River from Mainz to Frankfurt. Some inhabitants of Mainz so suffered from hunger that they could scarcely crawl to receive the handouts that the traveling party offered them. One village that they passed through along the Danube had been pillaged eighteen times in the previous two years. Berlin's population dropped from 12,000 to 7,500 between 1618 and 1638, and in some rural areas the decline reached 40 percent.[71] Jacques Callot's realistic series of etchings, "Miseries of War," published in 1633, and Grimmelhausen's picareque novel, *Simplicissimus*, published in 1669, illustrate vividly the horrors of the war, as we have seen.

A new personal relationship drew the Houses of Habsburg and Wittelsbach closer together during these months. Maximilian's wife, Elizabeth of Lorraine, died childless on January 4, 1635. Maximilian, aged sixty-two, still vigorous in contrast to the younger Ferdinand whose health was deteriorating and desirous of an heir, now wed Ferdinand's eldest daughter, the twenty-five-year-old Maria Anna, whom several years earlier nuncio Carafa had singled out for her beauty, her judgment, and her general bearing. The wedding took place in Vienna in the small Loreto chapel of the Augustinian church, and it was celebrated by Cardinal Dietrichstein who traveled from Olmütz for the event. Nearly forty years earlier, the cardinal had married the bride's parents, Ferdinand and his first wife, Maria of Bavaria. Many festivities accompanied the marriage. It was a wedding that inevitably had a political aspect. Both the French and the Spaniards were unhappy with it. Ferdinand hoped to tighten the bond between the two Catholic dynasties and to draw the German princes and especially Maximilian to himself, thus weakening their ties with France and rendering himself less dependent on the Spaniards.[72]

Pope Urban, as we have noted, in 1635 was planing to convene a peace conference, and the emperor, France, and Spain had all agreed in principle to attend. The popular suffering and widespread devastation horrified the pope. His juridical position prevented him from negotiating directly with heretics but it did not prevent some indirect contact with them as in his later encouragement of Ferdinand to allow France to bring its Protestant allies to the table at the conference.[73]

---

[71] Geoffrey Parker, *The Thirty Years War*, 2 ed. (London. 1997), 146–8.
[72] Baglioni to Barberini, May 12, 1635, NBD, *Nuntiaturen Filonardi, Rocci und Baglioni*, #52.1 (pp. 312–14.); Albrecht 2, 937–40.
[73] Repgen, 1: 1:, 397–9.

Nuncio Baglioni strove to convince Ferdinand to follow through on his commitment to send a delegate, but Lamormaini told the nuncio that it would be hard to persuade the emperor to trust the French.[74] Later, difficulties arose regarding the location of the meeting. France, for the sake of its Dutch allies, insisted on either Cologne or Liège, but the emperor initially resisted these two cities as hostile to the Habsburgs and too far from Vienna. Nor was Vienna inclined to allow France to dictate the site of the conference. In mid-March 1636, Vitelleschi, certainly at the request of the pope, urged Lamormaini to convince the emperor to accept one of the two Rhenish cities as the location for the meeting.[75] Ferdinand then did agree to Cologne as a result of secret interventions in Vienna, according to the nuncio Baglioni in his report of May 17, 1636,[76] activity that we may attribute to Lamormaini, it seems, still exercising some influence with Ferdinand and hoping for reconciliation with France. Both the emperor and Philip IV did dispatch emissaries to Cologne in 1637. Early that year at the conclusion of the Electoral Convention of Regensburg, Ferdinand's two delegates, Hermann von Questenberg and Johann Krane, an imperial court councillor, headed for Cologne from Regensburg.[77] But the French never did send delegates, largely because they hesitated to accept the terms on which their Swedish and Protestant allies would be received at the conference, so the conference never got off the ground and it was later transferred to Münster in Westphalia, to become the first step toward the Peace of Westphalia.[78]

Ferdinand had long hoped to avoid war with France. He never did officially declare war on France despite the urging of his son, the king of Hungary, nor did Louis XIII declare war on him, though the emperor did eventually issue a justification (*Kriegsmanifest*) for the use of imperial arms against the French in June 1635. On October 31, 1634, he had concluded the Treaty of Ebersdorf, a suburb of Vienna, with Spain that brought him desperately needed subsidies from Madrid and committed him to aid the Spaniards in the Netherlands against the Dutch. But the two parties interpreted this commitment differently, and Ferdinand never sent more than token aid to the Spaniards in the Netherlands.[79] The imperial envoy departed from Paris in August 1635, and the

---

[74] Baglioni to Barberini, Jun. 23, 1635, BL 6991, ff. 139–45.
[75] Vitelleschi to Lamormaini, Mar. 15, 1636, ARSJ, Aust. 5I, ff. 72–3.
[76] Cited in August Leman, "Urbain VIII et les origines du Congrès de Cologne," *Revue d'histoire ecclésiastique* 19 (1923): 382.
[77] Hainer Haan, *Der Regensburger Kurfürstentag von 1636/1637* (Münster, 1967), 255.
[78] Konrad Repgen, "Negotiating the Peace of Westphalia: A Survey with an Examination of the Major Problems," *1648: War and Peace in Europe*, ed. Klaus Bussmann and Heinz Schilling, 1 (Münster, 1999), 356.
[79] Peter H. Wilson, *The Thirty Years War: Europe's Tragedy* (Cambridge, MA, 2009), 555, 559; Klaus Malettke, "France's Imperial Policy during the Thirty Years' War and the Peace of Westphalia," *1648, War and Peace in Europe*, 1: *Politics, Religion, Law and Society*, ed. Klaus Bussmann and Heinz Schilling (Münster, 1999), 182–3.

French agent in Vienna was only expelled in March, 1636.[80] Initially after the Peace of Prague the military situation of the imperials improved, but only briefly. Not even waiting for the marriage of his sister to Maximilian, in June 1635 the king of Hungary took command of the imperial army of the Rhine with General Gallas as the head of his staff, and their forces succeeded in driving the last Swedish forces along with those of Bernhard of Weimar from the Upper Rhine, and the following year they pushed in to Alsace. That year Spanish forces invaded the north of France from the Netherlands, and on August 16, 1636, they took Corbie, only 75 miles north of Paris, causing panic in the capital. But the French counterattacked and retook Corbie on November 14, just as the Electoral Convention of Regensburg reached its mid-point. And the French recovered to the south as well. Sweden had by now seen its forces in the south and west of Germany defeated, and after the Peace of Prague, John George of Saxony sought to convince the German soldiers in the weakened Swedish army in the north to cross over to the emperor by appealing to their patriotism. At one point Swedish officers mutinied and briefly held Oxenstierna captive until they were reassured of their wages. The Swedish chancellor entered briefly into negotiations with John George and through him with Ferdinand, but both sides held out for unrealistic terms.[81] The French then rescued their Swedish allies. The aforementioned Treaty of Stuhmsdorf of September 20, 1635 – mediated by France to prolong the truce between Sweden and Poland – allowed the Swedes to transfer troops from the Polish front to Germany. The next year the Franco–Swedish alliance was renewed and provided new French subsidies to the Swedes. Then on October 4, 1636, as the king of Hungary traveled from the battle front in the west to Regensburg, the Swedes decisively defeated a combined imperial-Saxon army at Wittstock in southern Pomenania, one of the crucial battles of the whole war. A Swedish loss would have destroyed their last remaining army in Germany.[82] Neither foreign power, neither Sweden nor France, had been forced to leave the field.

On June 15, 1635, only two weeks after the signing of the Peace of Prague, Johann Christoph von Stadion, Grand Master of the Teutonic Knights and a privy councillor, addressed a letter to Anselm Casimir, archbishop-elector of Mainz and arch-chancellor of the Empire, calling for the convocation of the electoral college in order to elect young Ferdinand, already king of Hungary and Bohemia, king of the Romans and so successor-designate of his father, the emperor.[83] Emperor Ferdinand saw this clear establishment of the succession as the natural follow-up to the Peace of Prague on the way to peace and order in the Empire, confirmation of the position of the Church, and stability in the Habsburg lands to which he increasingly devoted his attention. Aware of his

[80] Wilson., 559. [81] Ibid., 573–5. [82] Ibid., 580–2. [83] Haan, ibid., 26.

own declining health, the emperor feared that an interregnum would degenerate into instability and even chaos and would probably lead to French intervention in the Empire and possibly an attempt to secure the imperial dignity for Louis XIII. The electors, Protestant and Catholic, shared this fear for the most part. During the coming months Mainz sounded out the other electors about a meeting of the electors to choose a king of the Romans and about the agenda for such a meeting. It soon became evident that whereas Vienna's interest focused nearly exclusively on the election of the king of the Romans, the electors also wanted to take up a number of other issues, foreign and domestic, having to do with peace in the Empire. Finally, on March 6, 1636, Mainz summoned an electoral convention to open on June 15 in Regensburg.

That winter Ferdinand suffered from declining health and showed signs of melancholy. In order to cheer him up, during Carnival Empress Eleonore and the king of Hungary together organized festivities and competitions. On January 30, after the great hall of the Hofburg was cleaned and plushly decorated, many cavaliers and ladies of the court were invited to come dressed in any style that they wanted for a grand feast. A large company of ladies made an imposing entrance into the hall led by Empress Eleonore herself and the queen of Hungary, and they danced a gracious ballet. Then from the other side there entered a company of cavaliers with the king of Hungary and Prince Casimir, brother of the king of Poland, in the lead who in turn danced a ballet. Subsequently, thirty-seven groups formed – some dressed elegantly, others comically – and each group presented to the emperor a note interpreting their dress and dance. Ferdinand took great delight in the event as he did in the parade and mock battle in the square outside the Hofburg the next day and then in a second ballet and ball that evening. Dr. Johann Heinrich von Pflummern, agent of the city of Überlingen in Vienna, recorded in his diary that the events of Carnival must have cost 50,000 florins, and he noted with bitter irony the display amidst the suffering and hunger of the people. It was, as it were, a dance over the abyss.[84] Further festivities had to be cancelled when Leopold William showed signs of the chicken pox, and soon thereafter the king of Hungary returned to the front in the west. Throughout all the events of Carnival, Ferdinand kept up with the business of government.[85]

On May 19, Ferdinand boarded ship in Vienna, taking his time as he headed up the Danube towards Linz and then Regensburg. He halted at the great monastery of Melk to participate in the Corpus Christi procession, and then he remained in Linz for nearly three months, waiting for the electors to arrive before he continued his journey. Tears came to his eyes as he watched the townspeople piously attending Mass in the city which had been a Protestant

---

[84] Harald Tersch, "Freudenfest und Kurzweil. Wien in Reisetagebüchern der Kriegszeit (ca. 1620–1650)," *Wien im Dreissigjährigen Krieg*, ed. Andreas Weigl (Vienna, 2001), 217, 220.
[85] *AF* 12: 1876–8.

nest only twenty years before.[86] Shortly before he left Vienna, a Brandenburg diplomat reported that the emperor was scarcely recognizable as the same person who had been present at Regensburg only six years before: "His thigh was greatly swollen, his body and his face ... puffy... he [is said] to have three times suffered an accident similar to a half-stroke that left him unable to speak for two to three hours."[87] But his health appears to have improved that summer in Linz where he undertook pilgrimages to nearby monasteries and indulged his passion for the hunt.[88]

While on the way to Regensburg and once there, he kept in touch with Count Breuner, whom he had left to assist Leopold William with the government in his absence. From Enns he commended Breuner for his efforts to forestall a threatened attack of the plague, and from Linz he indicated that Leopold William would know now to deal with the brawls between students and the municipal guard in Vienna.[89] The wine in Regensburg did not satisfy his taste, and he asked Breuner shortly after he arrived there to send quickly a better vintage made from the grapes from around the Neusiedler Lake, and in the same letter he summoned three musicians to Regensburg whom he had not brought with him.[90] Later he also requested peaches and pears.[91] Several letters dealt with the case of a woman who had allegedly taken no food nor drink for a long period of time.[92]

Ferdinand finally arrived in Regensburg on August 7 and settled in the episcopal residence. With him came a grand retinue. His wife, Empress Eleonore, and his daughter, Archduchess Cecilia Renata, took personal care of him. The names of the councillors who accompanied Ferdinand to Regensburg showed a gradual change among their numbers. Trautmannsdorf had emerged as the leading minister alongside Bishop Anton Wolfradt after the death of Eggenberg, and he also was named *Obristhofmeister* of the king of Hungary after the resignation and then death of Count Thun. He was to remain the most influential minister at court until his death shortly after the completion of his great work, the Peace of Westphalia, in 1649. Stralendorf came to Regensburg ill, and he died in mid-March, 1637, shortly after the conclusion of the convention. Also present was the rising court councillor Ferdinand Kurz von Senftenau. Of importance at the convention, too, was the court councillor Justus Gebhardt, who would long play a significant role in Vienna. Count Meggau and Bishop Anton Wolfradt seem to have kept low profiles. Neither of the two cardinals, Dietrichstein and Pazmany, came to Regensburg and both were

---

[86] Franzl, 356. [87] cited in Haan., ibid., 93. [88] Franzl, 355–6.
[89] Emperor to Breuner, May 21, Jun. 9 and 25, 1636, "Aus dem Gräflich Breuner'schen Archive zu Aspern an der Zaya," *Notizenblatt: Beilage zu Archiv für Kunde österreichischer Geschichte* 1 (1851).
[90] Emperor to Breuner, Aug. 22, 1636, ibid., 156.
[91] Emperor to Breuner, Sept. 11, Oct. 7, ibid.
[92] Emperor to Breuner, Wels, July 26, Regensburg, Aug. 27, Oct. 31, 1636, ibid., 156–7.

Settlement and Death, 1635–1637

about to pass from the scene; Dietrichstein died at Brno on September 29, 1636, and Pazmany at Pressburg on March 19, 1637. Lamormaini remained close to Ferdinand and traveled with him to Regensburg, but was much less prominent than he had been there in 1630. The king of Hungary, summoned from the battlefield in the west, arrived only on October 15 as the election approached. As he neared Regensburg, he encountered his father's hunting party, and he was joined by his wife, the queen of Hungary, who had arrived from Vienna with a large party three days earlier.[93]

In the imperial retinue there also came Oñate and Castañeda, two veteran Spanish ambassadors. They exercised the increasing Spanish influence at the imperial court also by virtue of the Spanish subsidies that helped to finance the participation of both the emperor and the Catholic electors at the convention.[94] Nuncio Baglioni, too, traveled in the imperial party. This time, as opposed to the convention in 1630, the nuncio received clear instructions to support wholeheartedly the election of the king of Hungary. Pope Urban now recognized the importance of his election for the Catholic cause in the Empire, and he resisted Richelieu's attempt to persuade him to prevent the choice of the Habsburg candidate.[95]

Three of the Catholic electors came in person to participate in the convention. Maximilian was the first to arrive, on August 19. He returned to Munich in September to be with his wife at the birth of their first-born son but was back in December for the actual election; meanwhile he was ably represented by his long time vice-chancellor, Bartholomew Richel. Anselm Carimir of Mainz turned up on August 24. Ferdinand of Cologne did not enter the city until October 22, but his delegation had preceded him. The fourth Catholic elector, Philip Christoph of Trier, was excluded from the convention because of his agreement with the French back in 1632 at the time of the Swedish advance to the west. He received French protection from the Swedes in exchange for French occupation of part of his territory, including the two fortresses on the Rhine, Phillipsburg and Ehrenbreitstein. The Spaniards had arrested him when they drove the French out of most of Trier in 1635. Soon he was transferred to Vienna where he remained in confinement under the care of the nuncio until the end of the war. Neither of the two Protestant electors, John George of Saxony and George William of Brandenburg, came to Regensburg in person but they sent delegations in their place. Other representatives came from England with special interest in the Palatinate issue, the Dutch Republic, Denmark, and Poland, the two last-named seeing themselves as potential mediators. No one turned up from Paris.

The convention finally opened on September 15 with the reading of the emperor's proposition. Ferdinand would have preferred to limit the business

---

[93] Haan, ibid., 94–6.   [94] Ibid., 110.
[95] Auguste Leman, "Le Saint-Siège et l'élection imperiale du 22 Décembre 1636, *Revue d'histoire ecclésiastique* 34 (1938), 543, 549.

of the convention to the election of his successor, but Anselm Casimir convinced him that the meeting would have to take up other issues as well. The emperor was determined to maintain the provisions of the Peace of Prague; on the other hand, he showed sufficient flexibility on the surface so as not to provoke an opposition from the electors that might endanger the candidacy of his son. The electors first took up the question of whether an election would take place at all, leaving the actual choice until later. The Catholic electors all favored an election but the Brandenburg and Saxon delegates hesitated at first for tactical reasons, well aware that they could not hinder the election nor did they really want to do so. Lamormaini visited the Brandenburg delegation to inform them that it would be to their own benefit not to stand in the way of the emperor's goals,[96] and they soon received word from the elector himself that they were to support the emperor. The elector instructed his delegates that they were to keep the emperor's favor, perhaps with a view to difficult negotiations with Sweden that lay ahead. John George's affirmative vote arrived only after some delay and with the firm recommendation, though not as a condition, that the amnesty issue be revisited.[97] The vote to carry out an election at Regensburg pointed implicitly to the election of the king of Hungary, since no other candidate had been put forward.

Ferdinand aimed at Regensburg as with the Peace of Prague to unite the German princes against the foreigner French and Swedes. But his position on amnesty often worked against this goal. The amnesty issue came up for considerable discussion at Regensburg, and it would only be fully resolved at the Peace of Westphalia. In 1636–1637, three principalities were chiefly involved: Württemberg, Hesse-Kassel, and the Palatinate. Saxony felt a special obligation to Württemberg as a fellow Lutheran state and saw its reputation involved in the matter. Duke Eberhard of Württemberg, as we have seen, had been excluded from the Peace of Prague until he agreed to surrender permanently the monastic lands that the Catholics had recovered by virtue of the Edict. They amounted to about one-fourth of his duchy. In addition, some lands in the duchy had been assigned to imperial supporters. Lamormaini advocated vigorously for the retention of the lands by the various monastic orders.[98] The Imperial Court Council at first voted against concessions to Württemberg but then after taking account of the Saxon intercession for Duke Eberhard, it divided more or less evenly on the issue. Both sides made juridical as well as political arguments. Those for the concessions stressed the need to conciliate John George. Ferdinand then submitted the issue to the electors in early October, so that they too would bear responsibility for the decision. The Catholic electors opposed concessions to the duke, as did Brandenburg again

---

[96] Haan, ibid., 137.   [97] Ibid., 133–8.
[98] Heinrich Günter, *Das Restitutionsedikt von 1629 und die katholische Restitution Altwirtembergs* (Stuttgart, 1901), 287–93, 308.

with a view to retaining Ferdinand's good will. Saxony eventually joined the majority, John George having decided that he had done all that he could on behalf of the duke.[99] So Württemberg was denied any concessions.

Hesse-Kassel constituted a special case in that it possessed a significant if relatively small military force active in the Westphalian Circle against Ferdinand.[100] Even before the convention had opened, Ferdinand had determined to impose the imperial ban on Landgrave Wilhelm. When he notified his two sons, the king of Hungary and Archduke Leopold William, of his decision, they both surprised him with their opposition to it. Both of them, joined by Trautmannsdorf, spoke for negotiations with the Landgrave in order to win him over for the campaign against the foreigners. But the emperor remained firm in his decision, also because of his commitment to Landgrave George of Hesse-Darmstadt, who figured to gain at the expense of his cousin and rival.[101]

Negotiations also resumed once again over the crucial issue of the Palatinate, but no progress was made. The English nobleman Thomas Howard, Earl of Arundel, joined by Jacob Rusdorf, a representative of Karl Ludwig, had journeyed first to Linz in June and then to Regensburg to lobby for restitution for the heir of Frederick. Charles I was committed to his nephew's cause. Ferdinand's concern to keep England from joining with France in another anti-Habsburg alliance rendered him sympathetic to Howard's case. Oñate also favored the cause of Karl Ludwig. Even Maximilian realized that despite the assurance that he had received from the Peace of Prague, his position in the Palatinate would never be fully secured until the Palatinate party also recognized it. He wanted a final settlement with the heirs of Frederick so that he would have no more challenges to face. Indeed, at one point he was ready to agree to return the Lower Palatinate to Karl Ludwig, and there was talk of alternation of the electoral title should Maximilian's direct line die out; his son had not yet been born when the talks began. There was even talk of the creation of an eighth electorate as was eventually provided at the Peace of Westphalia. But this issue would have to wait for resolution until 1648.[102]

On November 8, the emperor suffered a stroke that prevented him from speaking, hearing, or seeing; he recovered his faculties after two hours, but the event stirred the electors to move ahead to the election.[103] Finally, it was scheduled for December 9 but postponed until December 22, partly to enable Maximilian to return from Munich for the event. He then, the newly-created elector, proved most aggressive in imposing greater restrictions on the emperor, especially in favor of the electors. Neither Saxony nor Brandenburg showed great interest in the issue. The election capitulation aimed to secure more control for the electors over the emperor, and it listed a number of instances

---

[99] Haan, ibid., 176–99.   [100] Wilson, 572–3.
[101] Haan, ibid., 199–208.   [102] Ibid., 233–51.   [103] AF 12: 1899.

where the emperor had exceeded his authority. In the future, the emperor was expected to act in consort with the estates and especially with the electors before entering alliances, introducing taxes, or committing troops for deployment outside the Empire. He had already agreed to associate representatives of the electors with him in negotiations at Cologne and with the Swedes, though little came of this.[104] With regard to an issue that had arisen in the case of the Palatinate, the Lower Saxon estates, and Mecklenburg, that is, the emperor's right to impose the ban, it was asserted that in most cases he could not act without the approval of the electors. Even in notorious cases where the offender persisted in his activity, it was expected that the emperor communicate with the electors before rendering a decision but not necessarily obtain their approval.[105] So the legality of Ferdinand's actions in this regard seemed to be confirmed. Yet nothing was said about the enforcement of these restrictions nor was the suggestion that electoral conventions be held on a regular basis acted upon. The council of princes resented the predominance of the electors in the capitulation;[106] eventually, at the Peace of Westphalia they, too, will be allotted a greater say in imperial affairs.

Finally, in the high point of the convention, young Ferdinand was unanimously elected king of the Romans on December 22 and then crowned king of the Romans by the archbishop-elector of Mainz on December 30, both events taking place in the cathedral of Regensburg. Emperor Ferdinand remained then in Regensburg for another month as negotiations continued on other matters. He waited to participate on January 21 in the coronation as queen of the Romans of Maria Anna, the Spanish Infanta and wife of young Ferdinand, before leaving the city for Vienna on January 23, his health steadily worsening. Empress Eleonore had planned a "great masquerade" for January 20 to cheer up the fatally ill Ferdinand, but it had to be cancelled.[107]

Ferdinand had achieved his two principal goals at the electoral convention. First, he saw his son elected king of the Romans and with this the firm establishment of the imperial succession in the House of Habsburg. This he considered to be essential for both the health of the Empire and the Church. There would be no interregnum with the likely confusion and possible chaos that would result from it. Secondly, he had reaffirmed the terms of the Peace of Prague which he considered to be the way to peace in the Empire. In the amnesty question, he refused to make any further concessions to the Protestants, a position that probably was influenced by Lamormaini though it is difficult to prove except in the case of Württemberg. He also would not officially declare war on France, and despite his mistrust of the French, he dispatched emissaries to the anticipated conference at Cologne. In his last years, he had refocused his attention on the Habsburg lands where it had been directed in the earlier years of his reign as emperor before the issue of

[104] Haan, ibid., 172.   [105] Ibid., 219.   [106] Ibid., 280–1.   [107] Tersch, 214.

Settlement and Death, 1635–1637

the Palatinate and then the successes of Wallenstein and especially the fateful Edict had led him deeper and deeper into imperial politics. His renewal of his testament in 1635 promoted the unity of the Habsburg lands in Central Europe and greatly brought forward the formation of the Habsburg Monarchy as a major European power even without the full incorporation of Hungary and Anterior Austria and the Tyrol.

The imperial party stopped at Straubing down the Danube from Regensburg for the night of January 25. That evening Ferdinand sent Lamormaini a brief note in his own hand asking for a dispensation from his usual hour of prayer while traveling. Otherwise he would have to rise at 4 a.m.[108] Finally after arriving in Vienna on Sunday, February 8, Ferdinand first venerated the shrine of Our Lady of Loreto in the Augustinerkirche and then received the petitions of folks who approached him. Tuesday he began taking prescribed medicines. His head remained clear as he continued to take part in conciliar activity, but his body was obviously weakening. Saturday found him writing a long letter to his son, explaining the state of his health and spending a good deal of time with Lamormaini. He wanted to live, he stated, until his son returned from Regensburg, but only if this was the will of God in whose hands he rested. The newly-elected king of the Romans had remained in Regensburg for discussions with the electors of Mainz and Cologne. On Saturday Ferdinand arranged for Lamormaini to return to hear his confession. At supper he appeared to be comfortable, and he retired after prayers at about 9 p.m. But after about two hours, he awoke coughing and breathing only with difficulty. He would die the next day, he told Empress Eleonore, and he bid her farewell. Lamormaini then arrived for confession, asking that the assembled princes and courtiers leave the room briefly. After confession, Ferdinand prayed for God's mercy and the assistance of Mary, his Angel Guardian, and St. Ignatius. He asked Lamormaini to say Mass for him there in the room, but the chief doctor did not think that he would last through the Mass, so a host was brought to him from the chapel for Holy Communion; then he was anointed. Though he said nothing after receiving Holy Communion, the doctor thought that he remained conscious. Finally he expired at 9 a.m. on Sunday February 15, peacefully and holding a blessed candle in his hand. Lamormaini immediately said Mass for him in the bedroom with all those present gathered around the bed. They included Leopold William, Prince Maximilian von Dietrichstein, nephew of the cardinal, Ferdinand's daughter Archduchess Cecilia Renata, Werdenberg, and seven Jesuits. At the time, some remarked that Ferdinand, "now blessed, will obtain from God through his intercession the public and universal peace which he always desired but was never able to secure."[109]

---

[108] Emperor to Lamormaini, Straubing, Jan. 25, 1637, Dudik, 278.
[109] This account of Ferdinand's death is based on an anonymous manuscript in the Österreichische Nationalbibliothek in Vienna, "Relatio Obitus Ferdinandi." The same account is found in *AF* 12 (Leipzig, 1726): 2361–5.

Ferdinand's body was immediately embalmed and, according to custom, laid out in his ante-camera in the Hofburg for two days, then was moved to the court chapel and finally to the Augustinerkirche. Only on February 22 did his son Ferdinand arrive back in Vienna from Regensburg. The solemn funeral took place on Tuesday, March 17, in the Augustinerkirche with the nuncio presiding. Four days later his body began the journey to Graz where it was laid to rest in the chapel that he had commissioned de Pomis to build back in 1614 to house his remains. Later in the century it would be completed as the Mausoleum by Johann Bernhard Fischer von Erlach, the great Austrian Baroque architect. Over his grave in the crypt read the words *Vitæ et Armorum Sanctitate Clarus* (Renowned for the Sanctity of His Life and his Arms).

Conclusion

Emperor Ferdinand II deserves to be counted a leading and highly influential ruler of the seventeenth century, as well as a religious and moral man. More than any other individual, Ferdinand contributed to the formation of the Habsburg Monarchy on the pillars of the dynasty, the Catholic Church, and the aristocracy. At the Peace of Westphalia at the end of the Thirty Years War, the Monarchy emerged under his son, Ferdinand III, as one of the European powers, and it avoided in the 1640s the upheavals that convulsed France, Spain, and England. Ferdinand stabilized the dynasty after the weak and ineffectual reigns of Emperors Rudolph and Matthias, and he practiced a moderate form of absolutism that incorporated the estates of his territories into his government. As Hans Sturmberger pointed out, Ferdinand's preservation of the estates fostered in the Habsburg territories a sense of regional identity and a federalist system of government that characterized the Monarchy and still does the Republic of Austria today.[1] In the Empire he firmly established the Habsburg succession, so crucial to the position of the Catholic Church in Germany. The Counter Reformation and Catholic Reform in Central Europe owed more to him than to any other secular ruler. But he erred seriously with the Edict of Restitution and more so in maintaining it at the Electoral Convention of Regensburg in 1630 and subsequently. This undoubtedly helped to prolong the Thirty Years War. Had he been ready earlier and more extensively to compromise on the Edict, he might have been able to protect Germany from the Swedes and the French.

A genial and humane individual, Ferdinand enjoyed a happy domestic life. His first wife, the Wittelsbach Maria Anna, remained in the background while

---

[1] Hans Sturmberger, "Der absolutistische Staat und die Länder in Österreich," *Der österreichische Föderalismus und seine historische Grundlagen* (Vienna, 1969), 75–6.

bearing him seven children, four of whom survived into adulthood; his second wife, Eleonore Gonzaga, brought forth no children but proved to be a loving companion – her care for him in his last years is touching – while participating actively in the cultural and even the political life of the court. He generally got along with his brothers Leopold and Carl though especially with the former there were difficult moments, and he provided well for his surviving children Ferdinand, Leopold William, Maria Anna, and Caecilia Renata, who would marry Wladyslaw, king of Poland, in 1637.

Ferdinand was undoubtedly a genuinely religious and moral person in both his personal and his political life. Nuncio Carafa called him a "saint," with a confidence in God similar to King David's. His Wittelsbach mother, Archduchess Maria, his father Archduke Carl, who greatly regretted the concessions that he had made to the Protestants in the Pacification of Brück of 1578, and after his father's death in 1590, his uncle, the Bavarian Duke William V, all influenced the development of his religious orientation. The Jesuits fostered it further, starting with his years at Ingolstadt. A firm desire to submit to and to carry out God's will as he understood it characterized him from his earliest years, along with an equanimity in times of favorable and ill fortune. Ferdinand took seriously his obligation to foster the salvation and the religious welfare of his subjects. Beyond this, he came to believe that God in His providence had assigned him a mission to restore Catholicism, first in his own lands and eventually in much of the Empire. Twice at least he made a vow to the effect that he would do all in his power to advance the cause of the Church, first with regard to Inner Austria when he visited Loreto in 1598, and later in 1624, more generally after Lamormaini became his confessor. His sense of mission and his confidence in God led him to undertake measures despite warnings from his councillors that they were imprudent and beyond his resources. This was the case first when he successfully expelled the Protestant preachers and teachers from Inner Austria in 1598. Subsequently he and many others saw the hand of God over him, for example, in his "miraculous" rescue from the Protestants in Vienna in June 1619 by soldiers of Buquoy, and then in his many military victories, some of them unexpected, into the late 1620s. Yet he did not always take the riskier course. At the time of his election as king of Bohemia in 1617, acting on the principle of the lesser evil with the approval of the Jesuits he consulted, he agreed to honor the Letter of Majesty, and two years later, with the support of his confessor Becan, he acted in a similar fashion when he agreed to concessions to Lower Austrian Protestants in order to secure their recognition of him as their ruler.

But once he became Ferdinand's confessor in 1624, his long-time friend the Jesuit Lamormaini further encouraged him in his sense of a providential mission. Should Ferdinand not respond to this divine summons, he endangered his own salvation. This attitude contributed to the Edict of Restitution, the attempt to reclaim all the properties seized by the Protestants since 1555. The measure revealed most clearly the religious nature of the war, and at one

Conclusion

time Ferdinand characterized it as the goal of the whole conflict. One could make a solid legal argument in support of it, but not of its political wisdom. More significant than the issuance of the Edict was the refusal to compromise on it when such a compromise might have kept Saxony and even Brandenburg from allying with Gustav Adolph. An issue regularly debated in the council in Vienna came to be the theological one, whether one could base a policy on an alleged divine revelation as seemed to be involved in Lamormaini's position or whether policy had to be founded on a rational evaluation of its pros and cons. Only at the Peace of Prague did the latter position win out, and Ferdinand acted on the principle of the lesser evil once again.

Ferdinand proved to be a stickler for legality, and he inclined toward clemency for his enemies. The Edict he considered to be legal, especially after the publication of Laymann's *The Way to Peace*. In his dealings with the various estates he adhered to agreements and to traditions, though in contested or ambiguous cases he could stretch the law in his favor. He aimed at fairness in the procedure that led to the attempted arrest and death of Wallenstein. In the case of the Bohemian rebels, of those who took up arms against him in the Lower Saxon Circle in 1625, and of the supporters of Wallenstein, notorious rebels were punished peremptorily and legally, but those who came under suspicion were given a fair hearing.

One theme that runs through Ferdinand's reign as emperor was where his priority lay, in his hereditary lands or in the Empire. The two were intertwined. Effective control of his hereditary lands provided the territorial base necessary for him as emperor, and his status as emperor strengthened his position in the hereditary lands. With his testament of 1621, after the rebellion in Bohemia had been quelled, Ferdinand showed his intent to consolidate his Austrian and Bohemian territories; he established primogeniture, took measures to recatholicize his lands, and negotiated with or dictated to the estates while promoting an aristocracy loyal to the dynasty that controlled the estates. The acceptance of the Bohemian crown by Frederick of the Palatinate had already extended the conflict into the west of the Empire. Maximilian's claim to the Palatinate and Ferdinand's support of it involved Ferdinand further in the conflict to the west. Maximilian first encouraged Ferdinand to commission an army under Wallenstein in 1625 – some of Ferdinand's councillors opposed this – and then he pressured Ferdinand the following year to allow Tilly to invade Lower Saxony in order to deal with the buildup of hostile forces there. So to a degree, Ferdinand was pulled further into the conflict to the west by Maximilian. At this point, a committee of unnamed councillors warned against an attempt to conquer the Lower Saxon Circle and advised him to look to defense against Bethlen and the Turks in the East and to the consolidation of the Habsburg territories. They represented a return to the policy of Klesl who had advocated compromise with the Protestants in the Empire in order to bolster defenses in the east, especially against the Turks. But by the winter of 1627–1628, Wallenstein's military victories had brought Ferdinand to the peak of his power in the Empire, and preparations were under way for the Edict. The Edict then called for a still greater commitment to the Empire; but the goal of this commitment was not the establishment of an absolute monarchy in the Empire, which Ferdinand never intended, but the provision of justice to the Church for its losses in the Empire. At the same time Ferdinand attempted to exercise his authority as emperor in the dispute over Mantua. Ferdinand stuck to the Edict, again in the face of passive resistance from councillors, and only after the victory of Gustav Adolph at Breitenfeld in 1631 did negotiations gradually begin to modify the Edict, and they resulted eventually in the Peace of Prague in 1635. One of the factors pushing Ferdinand in this direction was the need to focus on his territorial lands where he refused to permit any toleration of Protestants. In 1635, he once again renewed his testament of 1621. The Peace of Prague obviously did not represent a withdrawal from the Empire; Ferdinand strengthened the position of the emperor there. But it did tip the balance toward the Habsburg Monarchy.

Ferdinand was said to be indecisive by both Carafa and the Venetian ambassador, and was sometimes characterized by others as "perplexed" when he was faced with a major decision, especially over religious matters. This may have resulted from a delicate conscience or even some scrupulosity; his own salvation could be at risk. Lamormaini wrote in the *Virtues of Ferdinand II* that the emperor thought it best to follow the advice of his councillors, and he regularly consulted ecclesiastics, his confessors in particular but also the Cardinals Dietrichstein and Pazmany. But Ferdinand could and did make decisions. His councillors often disagreed, as in the relative weight to be assigned the Empire or the Habsburg lands, and he had to decide between the parties. They disagreed over the Edict and over the intervention in Italy at the time of the Mantuan War. In this context there belong the differences between Lamormaini and Eggenberg who both in addition to their positions as confessor and chief minister enjoyed a genuine friendship with Ferdinand dating back to his early years in Graz. One could see in each of them, perhaps, a father figure for Ferdinand. But he was not dominated by either of them. Initially, the two seem to have been on good terms, Eggenberg stating at one time that he had also entrusted his conscience to Lamormaini and joining Ferdinand in his vow in 1624 to undertake all that was possible for the good of religion. But they fell out over the intervention in Italy and the Edict, and perhaps also over Wallenstein. Lamormaini tended to favor France; Eggenberg generally stood with Spain. Ferdinand sided with Eggenberg in the invasion in Italy and with Eggenberg's position – he was dead by then – at the Peace of Prague, but with Lamormaini on the Edict and on the many efforts to find an agreement with France.

Ferdinand navigated more or less successfully between his Wittelsbach cousin and later son-in-law in Munich, Maximilian, and his brother-in-law, Philip III and later his nephew, Philip IV, in Madrid, both in turn head of the House of Habsburg. He was dependent – financially, militarily, and politically – on the Bavarian elector and the Spanish kings. But none of them dominated him, and overall he tended to side with Maximilian because of their common commitment to the cause of the Church in the Empire. Maximilian, slightly older, he knew personally from his early years at Ingolstadt, but they cannot be said to have been close. He had no direct personal contact with the kings of Spain. Maximilian drove a hard bargain with Ferdinand in the Treaty of Munich of 1619 for his assistance after the Bohemian rebellion, and Ferdinand generally supported the Bavarian on the Palatinate issue despite the frequent opposition of the Spaniards. Maximilian was named as a member of Ferdinand's regency committee when the emperor drew up his testament in 1621. Ferdinand and Maximilian stood together in their militance against the Protestants and on the Edict, whereas the Spaniards generally favored a less militant policy so as to unite Germany and to secure the support of the emperor in Italy, the Netherlands, and ultimately against France. Both Ferdinand and Maximilian stepped back from their militance at the Peace of Prague, a move welcomed by the Spaniards.

Ferdinand had smoothed out his difficulties over the succession in the Habsburg lands in Central Europe prior to the outbreak of the war, in the Oñate Treaty of 1617. The Spaniards came to Ferdinand's support in the wake of the Bohemian rebellion, out of dynastic loyalty to be sure but also out of their awareness of the need for a Habsburg power in Central Europe to maintain their position in the Netherlands and Italy. Ferdinand never did aid them significantly in the Netherlands, but he did do so, eventually, in Italy in 1629–1631, to the consternation of Maximilian and the German states. But this venture was relatively short-lived, and the second Treaty of Cherasco in 1631 disappointed the Spaniards. Ferdinand long remained open to the possibility of a European peace agreement with the French mediated by the papacy, a goal long fostered by Lamormaini, and he never did officially declare war on the French.

Ferdinand greatly advanced the cause of the Counter Reformation and the Catholic Reform in the Habsburg Monarchy. But the policy of recatholization did not reach its high point in the Austrian and Bohemian lands until the reign of Leopold. Ferdinand has been called a precursor of Josephinism in the Habsburg lands; certainly the tendency in this direction dated from the Middle Ages. Lamormaini had written that "piety can only be restored by a powerful authority," and he emphasized the duty of the Christian ruler to suppress heresy. Except for the earliest ones in Inner Austria, the reformation commissions employed by Ferdinand were controlled by the government. Ferdinand long supported the Jesuits in their dispute with Cardinal Harrach over control of the university in Prague. His testament of 1621 as well as the *Princeps in Compendio* attributed to his court stressed the prince's responsibility to foster the religious life of his subjects, but neither of them mentioned attachment to or obedience to the pope. Ferdinand was discouraged by the lack of papal financial aid for the Church in Germany, and he was certainly provoked by the conduct of Urban VIII including his tilt toward France and his intense desire to elevate the status of the prefect of Rome for his nephew. But Ferdinand did retain his respect for the papacy, and he continued to cooperate with Urban's efforts to reconcile the rulers of Catholic Europe.

Many funeral orations across Catholic Europe lauded Ferdinand after his death. In a service held in Prague on April 6, 1637, the Jesuit Peter Wadding set Ferdinand alongside Constantine and Charlemagne, and only one day previously, in a sermon given at a memorial at the papal court and addressed to the pope, the Jesuit Silvestro da Pietrasanta saluted Ferdinand as "the exemplar of Christian princes," comparing him not only to the Christian emperors but also to Alexander the Great and Tiberius.[2] But Lamormaini created the most lasting memorial to Ferdinand with his the *Virtues of Ferdinand II, Emperor of the Romans*, which was to become a Baroque classic in the tradition of the *Pietas Austriaca* and was to exercise a significant influence in the Habsburg Monarchy. It appeared in early 1638, just a year after Ferdinand's death, in a Latin edition, in both quarto and duodecimo formats, in Vienna, Antwerp, and Cologne,[3] as well as in German, Italian, and Flemish translations, and in 1639 in a French edition.[4] A number of editions followed, including one in Spanish in 1640.[5] Lamormaini stated in the preface that he had two goals in writing the book: to honor Ferdinand and to hold up his virtues for imitation; and to impress upon his son and successor, Ferdinand III, the need to maintain the policy of his father and to imitate his virtues.[6] His plan, Lamormaini indicated, was to write a four-volume biography of Ferdinand, the first to deal with his genealogy, education, and youth; the second with his years of government in Inner Austria; the third with his tenure as emperor; and finally the fourth, with his virtues. Only the final volume has survived, and it makes sense to have composed it first if Lamormaini wanted to influence the reign of Ferdinand III. Whether the other volumes were ever written or were written but then withheld from publication for political reasons remains uncertain.[7]

---

[2] Petrus Wadding, S.J., *Oratio funebris dicta cum clerus et proceres regni exsequias celebrarent Ferdinandi II Romanorum imperatoris et Regis Bohemiae* (Vienna, 1638), and Sylvester a Pietrasanta, S.J., *Oratio funebris habita ad Urbanum VIII. Pont. Max. dum insta exsequiarum Ferdinandi II imperatori persolverentur* (Rome, 1637).

[3] *Virtutes*.

[4] *Ferdinandi Secondi Römischer Kheysers Tugenden* (Vienna and Cologne, 1638); *Virtu di Ferdinand II Imperatore* (Vienna, 1638); *De Deuchden von Ferdinandus II* (Antwerp. 1638); *Le narré des vertus de Ferdinand II* (Mons, 1638); see Carlos Sommervogel, *Bibliothèque de la Compagnie de Jésus* 4 (Brussels/Paris, 1893, rpt. 1960): 1429–31

[5] See below.

[6] *Virtutes*, preface and dedication. I cite the edition published at Vienna in 1638 in the quarto format unless otherwise indicated.

[7] See Robert Bireley, "The Image of Emperor Ferdinand II (1619–1637) in William Lamormaini, S.J.'s *Ferdinandi II Romanorum Imperatoris Virtutes (1638)*," *Archivum Historicum Societatis Jesu* 78 (2009): 120–1.

A lively style characterizes the *Virtutes of Ferdinand II*, which includes many anecdotes and vignettes that hold the reader's attention. Such details, Lamormaini states, often reveal a person's true character. The author states that in his text of 112 pages divided into twenty-seven chapters, he will deal first with Ferdinand's virtues regarding his relationship with God and the saints, then those regarding the perfection of his own soul, and finally those regarding his treatment of others. But in fact the line between these divisions blurs as does that between private and public virtues. Five virtues or perhaps more correctly five sets of virtues figure most prominently in Lamormaini's portrait: zeal and determination to defend and spread the faith, confidence in God and His providential care, prudence in government, the classical princely virtue of liberality, and piety in the twofold sense of reverence for family and forebears and of devotion to God. But Lamormaini turned to other virtues, too. In his discussion of Ferdinand's zeal for the faith, Lamormaini describes his efforts at restoring the faith in his own lands; for this he deserves the title "Apostolic Emperor." But the author does not mention the Edict of Restitution in this context. This may well have amounted to an admission that Ferdinand erred grievously with the Edict and that it told against a reputation for prudent government. It came up only obliquely later in a reference to Ferdinand's patience toward those who opposed it.[8] Under the virtue of charity, Lamormaini returned to Ferdinand's measures to eliminate heresy. No one would have undertaken the burdens and faced the opposition that Ferdinand did in this regard unless he cared for his subjects. It would have been much easier to tolerate heretics. "Non-Catholics," he cited Ferdinand, "consider me unfeeling in my prohibition of heresy. I do not hate them but love them; unless I loved them, free from any concern I would leave them in their error."[9]

In the last three chapters, Lamormaini appeared to suggest that Ferdinand be considered for eventual canonization. In 1625 and 1634, Urban VIII had issued bulls regulating the procedures for canonization and stating that no causes could be introduced until fifty years after the death of the individual involved. He laid down three requirements for sainthood: heroic virtue, miracles, and a reputation for holiness.[10] Without adverting to the papal bulls, Lamormaini covered these three areas in the last chapters. Here for the first time he called Ferdinand "holy" and referred to his virtues as "heroic." The second to last chapter took up God's "singular divine providence" for Ferdinand, and the last displayed the testimonies of "the greatest men" to Ferdinand's virtue, but before turning to individuals, it recounted how in Vienna at Ferdinand's death

---

[8] *Virtutes*, 4, 5, 61. [9] Ibid., 77.
[10] Marcus Sieger, *Die Heiligsprechung: Geschichte und heutige Rechtslage* (Würzburg, 1995), 208–12, 253–60. Forschungen zur Kirchenrechtsgeschichte 23; W. Bois, "Canonisation dans l'église romaine," *Dictionnaire de Théologie catholique* 2: 2 (Paris, 1905): col. 1643–8; Pierre Delooz, "The Social Function of the Canonization of Saints," *Consilium: Models of Holiness*, ed. Christian Ducpuoc and Casiano Floristán (New York, 1997): 14–24.

the people proclaimed with one voice that "the emperor has died of whom no previous age has seen the equal in holiness, piety, integrity, and mercy." Summoned to the bar here among many others was the nuncio Carafa, whom Lamormaini cited as saying that "after Constantine there had been no emperor equal to Ferdinand."[11]

The title of the 1638 Cologne edition showed the intent to assimilate the *Virtues of Ferdinand II* to the mirror of princes genre. It read *The Form of a Christian Prince* (Idea Principis Christiani): *The Virtues of Ferdinand II, Emperor of the Romans.* So it proposed Ferdinand as the model of a Christian ruler. The Spanish version of 1640 deserves special attention. It was sponsored by Sor Dorothea de la Cruz, illegitimate daughter of Emperor Rudolf II and marquise of Austria who resided in the convent of the Discalced Franciscans in Madrid, and it was translated by José Pellicer de Tovar, the official chronicler of Philip IV. The full title, *The Virtues and Spiritual Life of Ferdinand of Austria, the Second of this Name Emperor of the Romans* (Virtudes y vida espiritual de Ferdinand de Austria, segundo del nombre emperador de Romanos), suggests that the volume was intended more as a guide to the spiritual life than as a handbook for a ruler. Pellicer de Tovar, having claimed to have read the lives of many great kings and rulers, declared Ferdinand the equal of any. God had worked prodigious miracles through him, and the emperor had combined the political with the evangelical to the benefit of many. Subsequent versions of the *Virtues of Ferdinand II* considered the emperor to be both an exemplary Christian and model prince, as in the *Ideal Form of a Man and of a Christian Prince* (Idea exemplaris et hominis et Principis Christiani), published at Feldkirch in 1657.

The contemporary Austrian diplomat and privy councillor Franz Christoph von Khevenhüller ended in 1646 the last of his *Annals of Ferdinand II* (Annales Ferdinandei) with the full German text of Lamormaini's *Virtues of Ferdinand II.*[12] Khevenhüller, who would have known Ferdinand II and Lamormaini, wrote of Ferdinand's "heroic" virtues, and in a short profile of Ferdinand in an accompanying volume referred to him as "the holy Lord" (der Heylige Herr).[13]

Even in the arts Lamormaini's image of Ferdinand found expression. Twenty-six monumental historical and allegorical oil paintings illustrating themes from the *Virtues of Ferdinand II* decorated the walls of the Habsburg royal castle in Pressburg that was constructed in the 1640's.[14] A beautifully

---

[11] *Virtutes*, 110, 112.
[12] The first nine volumes of the *Annales* appeared in a rare edition at Regensburg from 1640 to 1646; all twelve volumes came out only at Leipzig from 1721 to 1726.
[13] *Conterfet Kupferstich* (Leipzig, 1721), 63.
[14] Géza Galavics, "Reichspolitik und Kunstpolitik. Zum Ausbildungsprozess des Wiener Barock," *Akten des internationalen Kongresses für Kunstgeschichte, Wien, 4–10 Sept., 1983* (Vienna, 1984), 7–12. Galavics sees in this cycle a certain parallel to the Medici cycle by Rubens in the Louvre painted in the early 1620's.

Conclusion 313

illustrated manuscript, "An Austrian Exhibition or a Carefully Arranged Compendium of the Virtues of Austrian Princes" (Theatrum Austriacum seu Virtutum Austriacorum Principum Compendium Concinnatum), dated about 1696 and attributed to the Jesuit Andreas Paur, tutor of the future Emperor Charles VI, contains an illustration of Ferdinand's vow at Loreto to extirpate heresy in Inner Austria in 1598, with a lengthy citation from Lamormaini's *Virtues of Ferdinand II*.[15]

Subsequent versions of the small volume came out at Linz in 1678, Graz in 1715, Tyrnau, in 1737, and the last at Vienna in 1857. So Ferdinand's memory remained alive.

---

[15] This is found in the Newberry Library in Chicago, allegedly a copy of manuscript 12800 in the Nationalbibliothek in Vienna. I am grateful to Prof. Howard Louthan of the University of Florida for calling my attention to this piece.

For further representations, most from the early 1620s, see Štépán Vácha, *Der Herrscher auf dem Sakralbild zur Zeit der Gegenreformation und des Barock. Eine ikonologische Untersuchung zur herrschlichen Repräsentation Kaiser Ferdinands II. In Böhmen* (Prague, 2009).

Genealogical Overview of the Austrian Habsburgs

THE OLDER GENERATION

Ferdinand I, Emperor (1503–1564) oo Anna of Bohemia and Hungary (1503–1547)
15 children including the following 4

1. Maximilian II, Emperor (1527–1576)
oo Maria of Austria (1528–1603)
16 children including
Anna (1549–1580)
oo Philip II of Spain (1527–1598)
Rudolf II, Emperor (1552–1612)

Ernst (1554–1595)

Elizabeth (1554–1592)
oo Charles X of France (1550–1574)

Matthias, Emperor (1557–1619)
oo Anna of Tyrol (1585–1618)
Maximilian of the Tyrol (1558–1618)
Albert (1559–1621), Regent of the Netherlands
oo Isabella Clara Eugenia of Spain (1566–1633)

3. Ferdinand of the Tyrol (1529–1595)

2. Anna (1528–1590)
oo Albrecht V of Bavaria (1528–1579)
7 children including
William V, Duke of Bavaria (1548–1628)
oo Renata of Lorraine (1544–1602)
Ferdinand (1550–1608)
oo Maria Pettenbeck (1573–1619)

Maria (1551–1608)
oo Carl of Inner Austria (1540–1590)

Maximiliana (1552–1614)

Ernst (1554–1612). Elector of Cologne

4. Carl of Inner Austria (1540–1590)

Genealogy

oo 1. Philippine Welser (1527–1580)
oo 2. Anna Caterina Gonzaga (1566–1621)
7 children including
Anna (1585–1618)
oo Matthias, Emperor (1557–1619)

oo Maria of Bavaria (1551–1608)
15 children (see next table)

THE CHILDREN OF CARL OF INNER AUSTRIA AND MARIA OF BAVARIA

Ferdinand (+1572)

Anna (1573–1598)
oo Sigismund of Poland (1566–1632)

Maria Christierna (1574–1621)
oo Sigismund Báthory of Transylvania
(1572–1613), divorced 1599

Catherine Renata (1576–1595)

Elisabeth (1577–1586)

Ferdinand II, Emperor, (1578–1637)
oo 1. Maria Anna of Bavaria
(1574–1616)
(for children, see below)
oo 2. Eleonore Gonzaga (1598–1655)

Carl (1579–1580)
Eleonora (1582–1620)
Margaret (1584–1611)
oo Philip III of Spain (1578–1621)

Gregoria Maximiliana (1581–1597)
Maximilian Ernst (1583–1616)
Leopold of the Tyrol (1586–1632)
Bishop of Passau, Bishop of Strasbourg
oo Claudia de Medici (1604–1648)

Constance (1588–1631)
oo Sigismund of Poland (1566–1632)
Carl (1590–1624)
Bishop of Breslau
Bishop of Brixen

Maria Magdelena (1589–1631)
oo Cosimo II de Medici (1590–1621)

CHILDREN OF FERDINAND II AND MARIA ANNA OF BAVARIA

Johann Carl (1605–1619)
Ferdinand III, Emperor (1608–1657)
  1. Maria Anna of Spain (1606–1646)
  2. Maria Leopoldine of Tyrol (1632–1649)
  3. Eleonora Gonzaga-Rethel (1630–1686)

Maria Anna (1610–1665)
oo Maximilian of Bavaria (1573–1651)
Cecilia Renata (1611–1644)
oo Wladyslaw of Poland (1595–1648)
Leopold William (1614–1662)
Archbishop of Magdeburg
Bishop of Halberstadt

Index

Agnelli-Soardi, Vincenzo, bishop of Mantua, 187
Albert, archduke, co-ruler of the Netherlands, candidate for emperor, 47
   and succession in the Empire, 48, 68, 75, 124
Aldringen, Johann, general, 261, 262, 263
Alexander d'Ales, Capuchin, 273–74
Anna Maria, queen of Poland, 15
Anselm Casimir Wamboldt von Umbstadt, archbishop-elector of Mainz, 232, 300
   and Ferdinand, 257
   and Pirna Points, 283
   at Regensburg (1630), 203, 209, 210
Anton Wolfradt, abbot of Kremsmünster, prince-bishop of Vienna, privy councillor, 127, 133, 228, 258, 289, 298
   and cardinalate, 274
   and the Edict, 210, 234–35, 257
   and France, 238
   on imperial policy, 159, 197, 221–22, 249–50, 274, 292
   and Pirna Points, 284–86
   and Wallenstein, 262
Arnim, Hans Georg von, general, 233, 254, 255, 258
Augsburg, Peace of, 3, 22, 49–50, 54, 55, 73, 194, 250
Austria, proposed kingdom of, 131–32
Aytona, Francisco de Moncada, marquis de, Spanish ambassador in Vienna, 190, 191

Baglioni, Malatesta, nuncio in Vienna, 270, 287, 299
Bagno, Giovanni Francesco Guidi di, nuncio in Paris, 192, 223
Baltic venture, proposed, 163, 166
Barberini, Francesco, cardinal, 142, 200, 201, 203
Bärwalde (1631), Treaty of, 216, 220, 225, 226, 251

Basilio d'Aire, Capuchin, 244, 282–83
Bassevi, Jakob, Jewish financier, 134
Báthory, Sigismund, prince of Transylvania, 15, 45, 71
Becan, Martin, Jesuit, confessor of Ferdinand, 105
   and execution of Bohemian rebels, 119–20
   and the Palatinate Question, 152, 155, 156
   and toleration in Lower Austria, 107
Bellarmine, Robert, cardinal, 94
Bernhard, duke of Weimar, general, 260, 263, 293, 296
Bethlen Gàbor, prince of Transylvania, 71, 74, 83, 101, 104, 105, 108, 109, 117, 136, 157, 162, 163, 259
Blyssem, Heinrich, Jesuit, 9
Bocskay, István, prince of Transylvania, 45, 46
Bohemia, confiscations, 144–45, 266
   Counter Reformation in, 145–50
   estates of, 65–66, 69, 74, 83–4, 136
   exiles, 232
   renewed constitution (*Verneuerte Landesordnung*), 164–65
Bohemian campaign, 112–17
Bohemian Confederation, 69, 100, 107, 108, 109, 117
Borgia y Velasco, Gasparo, cardinal, 103, 228
Botero, Giovanni, political writer, 23, 125, 133
Brandenburg, electorate, *see* George William
Breisach, fortress, 259
Breitenfeld (1631), battle, 231, 234
Brenner, Martin, bishop of Seckau, 9, 21, 32, 35, 39
Breslau, abortive conference at, 253, 257–58
Breuner, Seifreid Christoph von, imperial councillor, governor of Lower Austria, 202, 219, 298
Bruck, pacification of, 1, 5, 7, 8, 9, 10, 22, 37, 38, 60

Index

Brüderzwist (Brothers' Quarrel), 46–9, 53–7, 65, 67–71
Brûlart de Léon, Charles, French diplomat, 203, 206–207, 225
Bucquoy, Charles, count, general, 95, 97, 113, 114, 115, 116, 117, 144

Caetano, Antonio, nuncio in Prague, 51, 86
Callot, Jacques, artist, 113, 294
Capuchins, 40
Carafa, Carlo, nuncio in Vienna, 141, 147, 152
   and Lamormaini, 146, 147, 150
   on Ferdinand, 179–80, 181, 183–83
Carafa, Pier Luigi, nuncio in Cologne, 201, 217
Carl, archduke, father of Ferdinand, 1, 2
   death, 10
   and Protestants 1, 3, 5–6, 7–9
   testament, 10, 14
   and Turks, 6–7
Carl, archduke, brother of Ferdinand, bishop of Breslau, bishop of Brixen, grand master of the Teutonic Order, 87, 125, 131–32
Casal, Peter, secretary of Ferdinand in Graz, 25, 16, 28, 30
Castañeda, marquis de, Spanish diplomat, 252
Catholic League, 56, 62, 66, 67, 72, 93, 112, 206
   proposal of Ferdinand for, 62–5
   reconstituted, 74, 101, 109, 111
   end of, 276, 292
Charbonnière, Nicolas de, French resident in Vienna, 252
Charles V, emperor, 1, 2, 76, 279
Charnacé, Hercule de, French diplomat, 235, 237
Cherasco (1631), Treaties of, 225–27
Christian IV, king of Denmark, 158–59, 237, 257
Christian of Anhalt, prince, 53, 100, 114
Cilli (Celje), town in Styria, peasants' revolt, 289
Clement VIII, pope, 19, 21, 27–8, 48
Collalto, Ramboldo, count, general, president of the war council, 128
   and the Edict, 199, 201
   and Mantuan War, 192, 193, 201
   and war in Lower Saxony, 159
Cologne, archbishopric-electorate, see Ferdinand, archbishop-elector of Cologne,
Cologne, city, projected peace conference, 294–295

Constance, queen of Poland, 25, 105, 271
Constantine, emperor, 86, 130, 165
Contzen, Adam, Jesuit, confessor of Maximilian of Bavaria, 133, 195, 203, 205, 208, 210, 224, 234
Counter Reformation, see Counter Reformation in Bohemia, Inner Austria, Upper Austria

Dampierre, Henri count, general, 97
Defenestration of Prague, 90–91
Dessau Bridge (1626), battle, 162
Dietrichstein, Franz von, bishop of Olmütz, cardinal, privy councillor, 42, 107, 116, 122, 127, 134, 147, 298, 299
   on imperial policy, 160, 221–22, 234–35, 249, 257, 271, 292
   and Pirna Points, 279, 284–86
   chair of Theologians Conference, 280, 281
Dinkelsbühl (1631), conference of the Catholic League, 223
Dohna, Karl Hannibal von, imperial diplomat, 222
Domenico à Jesu Maria, Carmelite, and battle of the White Mountain, 115, 116
   mission to Vienna, 193
Donauwörth, town in Swabia, 50, 57
Donnersberg, Joachim von, Bavarian official, 152, 238

Eberhard, duke of Württemberg, 293, 300, 301
Ebersdorf (1634), Treaty of, 295
Edict of Restitution, 63, 286, 287, 288, 291–92, 311
   origin, 194, 197–202, 306, 307
   at Regensburg (1630), 207–211
   revocation, 275, 289–90
Eggenberg, Hans Ulrich von, first minister, 20–21, 26, 95, 127, 138, 292
   death, 272
   and the Edict, 200, 210, 218, 220, 255, 257
   and Ferdinand, 53, 67, 200–201, 217
   and France, 244, 255, 260, 269
   and Lamormaini, 150, 228
   and the Mantuan War, 190, 191, 192, 226
   and second marriage of Ferdinand, 129–30
   and Palatinate Question, 153
   and Prague Consortium, 134
   at Regensburg (1630), 210, 213–14
   and Spain, 21, 79, 163
   and war in Lower Saxony, 160

Eggenberg, Hans Ulrich von, first minister (cont.)
  and Wallenstein, 160, 233, 236, 240, 241, 260, 262, 265; *see also* Cherasco, Treaties of
Eleonore, empress, second wife of Ferdinand, 11, 165, 193, 228, 297, 302, 303
  marriage, 129-31
  music, 131
  and Mantuan War, 190, 192,
Ernst, archduke, regent of Inner Austria, 14, 19
Esterhazy, Miklós, Hungarian palatine, 157

Fanini, Lucas, Jesuit, confessor of Empress Eleonore, 218
Ferdinand I, emperor, 1, 2, 7, 124
Ferdinand II, emperor, 1, 2, 72, 113, 264
  absolutism, 37, 38-9, 125, 135-37, 144, 161, 197, 280, 292, 305, 308
  king of Bohemia, 84-7
  and Bohemian rebels, 93, 95, 118-21
  and Brandenburg, 257
  and the Church, 29, 99-100, 138-40, 146, 309-10
  and projected Cologne peace conference, 295
  death and funeral, 302-304
  and Defenestration of Prague, 91
  and the Edict, 194-96, 199, 203-204, 206-11, 217, 275, 305, 307
  and Eggenberg, 20-21, 26, 53, 127, 205, 213, 226, 228, 272, 308
  election as emperor, 99
  and the Empire, 61, 123-24, 157, 307-308
  finances, 44-5, 133-35, 137, 265
  and Gustav Adolph, 246
  and France, 112, 235-36, 239, 244, 269, 295-96, 302
  funeral orations, 310
  and the Habsburg Monarchy, 123-26, 293, 302, 305, 308
  health, 16, 179, 274, 297, 298, 301
  the hunt, 12, 99, 179-80, 181, 182-83, 274
  at Ingolstadt, 10-13, 15-17
  and the Jesuits, 16-17, 40, 43, 86, 102, 125-26, 140, 144
  and the Jews, 116
  and removal of Klesl, 77-78, 84, 93-4
  journey to Italy, 25-30
  legality, 86, 98, 110, 136, 152, 262, 266-67, 302, 307
  and Letter of Majesty, 86
  and Maria his mother, 23, 26, 29, 58-60
  marriages, 22, 25, 40-41, 42, 129-31, 306
  and Matthias, 47, 48, 54, 55, 56, 57, 65
  and Maximilian of Bavaria, 13, 16, 42, 45, 52, 54, 55, 57, 98, 101-102, 125, 151-58, 159-62, 206, 223, 224, 232, 233, 234, 238, 257, 276-77, 294, 307, 308-309
  and mercy, 119, 121, 312
  method of government, 126-29
  mission, 35, 37, 214, 271, 291, 306
  music, 10, 130, 179, 180, 181-82
  personality and daily order, 179-83, 308
  piety of, 10-11, 11-12, 13, 16, 34, 35, 37, 89-90, 97, 124, 128-39, 142, 246, 306, 312
  and Peace of Prague, 287, 289, 290, 300
  and Pirna Points, 276-77, 280-81, 284, 285
  at diet of Regensburg (1608), 49-57
  at electoral convention of Regenburg (1630), 202, 203, 211
  at electoral convention of Regensburg (1636-37), 297-303
  and Emperor Rudolph, 17, 25, 53, 55
  as ruler in Inner Austria, 20, 22-24, 31-39
  and Saxony, 87, 107, 111, 129, 151, 165, 222, 229, 257, 267-68, 271
  and Spain, 25, 75, 78-80, 154, 188-92, 213, 228, 309
  summation, 305-310
  testament (1601), 43
  testament (1621), 124-26
  testament (1635), 293, 303
  and toleration, 85-7, 95, 102-103, 105-10
  and the Turks, 25, 43-5, 108, 163
  and Urban VIII, 146, 229-30, 241-43, 252, 288-89
  vow at Loreto, 28-9
  and Wallenstein, 82, 97-8, 159-60, 163-64, 166, 204-205, 236, 240, 246, 256, 261-64
  and war in Lower Saxony, 159-62
  and Duke William of Bavaria, 14, 15, 18-19, 54-5, 57, 76
  early youth, 10-12;
    see also Brüderzwist (Brothers' Quarrel), Counter Reformation, Palatinate Question,
Ferdinand III, emperor, 89, 124, 236, 265, 267
  king of Hungary, 157, 270, 291, 296
  king of Bohemia, 165
  marriage, 224-25
  succession in the Empire, 196-97, 296, 299, 302

Index

Ferdinand, archduke, ruler of Anterior Austria and the Tyrol, 2, 14
Ferdinand, archbishop-elector of Cologne and the Pirna Points, 284
Feria, Gómez Suárez de Figueroa y Cordóba, duke of, general, 253
Fernando, cardinal-infant of Spain, 253, 269, 270
Fitzsimmons, Thomas, Jesuit, confessor of Bucquoy, 117
Fontainebleau (1631), Treaty of, 223–24, 232
France, 112, 214, 215, 227, 247, 258, 289
  invasion of Italy, 191–92
  second invasion of Italy, 193
  and Sweden, 220, 243, 251, 252, 296; *see also* Louis XIII, Richelieu
Frankfurt Conference (1631), 230–31, 231–32
Frederick, Elector Palatine, king of Bohemia, 76, 98, 100, 113–14, 115, 162
  ban of, 110
Fürstenberg, Wratislaw, count, diplomat, 112

Gabrieli, Giovanni, musician, 27
Gallas, Matthias, general, 296
  and Wallenstein, 261, 262, 264–65, 266
Gans, Johannes, Jesuit, confessor of Ferdinand III, 291–92
Gebhardt, Justus, imperial councillor, 185, 248, 256, 267, 281, 282, 287, 288, 298
George William, elector of Brandenburg, 111, 153, 203, 207, 231
Ginetti, Mario, cardinal, legate, 290
Gonzaga, Eleonore, empress, second wife of Ferdinand, 129–31, 143, 165, 180, 182, 202, 218, 297, 298, 302, 303
  and the Mantuan War, 187, 190, 192, 193, 228
  patron of opera, 131, 181
Geheim Protestantismus, 40
Gradisca, war of, 80–83
Graz, city, 2, 3, 5, 33, 104
Graz, Jesuit college, 7, 9, 40
Graz, nunciature, 8
Gregory XV, pope, 152
Gregory of Valencia, Jesuit theologian, 12, 16
Greiffenklau, Georg Friedrich von, archbishop-elector of Mainz, 199, 203; *see also* Mainz
Gretser, Jakob, Jesuit, 16, 102
Grimaldi, Girolamo, extraordinary nuncio in Vienna, 242, 244, 245, 255, 269–70
Grimmelshausen, Hans Jakob Christoffel von, author, 113, 294

Guarini, Giovanni Battista, dramatist, 30
Gustav Adolph, king of Sweden, 159
  death, 246
  and France, 216, 226
  invasion of the Empire, 203–204, 216–17, 229, 232, 244–45

Habsburg alliance, 220, 238, 241, 253, 269
Hague, League of the, 158
Haller, Richard, Jesuit, 16
Harrach, Carl von, privy councillor, 153
  and war in Lower Saxony, 160
Harrach, Ernst von, archbishop of Prague, cardinal, 145–46
Hegenmüller, Hans, imperial councillor, 222
Heilbronn Confederation, 251, 276, 277, 292
Heinrich-Julius, duke of Brunswick, 67, 68
Henry IV, king of France, 64, 65, 66, 70
Herberstorff, Adam von, governor of Upper Austria, 140, 143
Hesse-Darmstadt, Landgrave George of, 211, 214, 253, 258, 301
"Hessen Points," 214
Höchst (1622), battle, 154
Homberger, Jeremias, Protestant preacher, 9
Hungary, 2, 53, 87–8, 91, 108–109, 131, 136, 141
Hungary, king of, *see* Ferdinand III
Hyacinth da Casale, Capuchin, 152, 153

Imperial Court (or Aulic) Council (Reichshofrat), 126, 128, 129, 133, 197, 198, 254
Ingolstadt, Jesuit college, university, 12–13
Ingolstadt (1631), abortive conference of Catholic League, 235–36
Inner Austria, 2
  Protestants in, 4–5, 135
  Counter Reformation in, 9, 23, 24, 31–40, 139, 165
  Instruction for the Conduct of Government, 24

James I, king of England, 101, 111, 153
Jessenius, Johannes, rector of the University of Prague, 121
Jesuits, in Inner Austria, 7, 9, 40
  in Bohemia, 145; *see also* Ferdinand and the Jesuits
Jews, 116, 150–51
Johann Carl, archduke, eldest son of Ferdinand, 69, 72, 89
  death, 104

John George, elector of Saxony, 87, 222, 275, 276, 296
 and Bohemian rebellion, 109–110
 and the Leipzig Conference, 218–19
 and the Palatinate Question, 147;
  see also Saxony
Joseph du Tremblay, Capuchin, 203, 206–207
Josephinism, 138
Jülich-Cleves crisis, 66–7

Kanisza, (Nagykanisza), fortress town, 25, 43, 45, 71, 74
Karlovac (Karlstadt), 7
Keller, Jakob, Jesuit, 102, 117
Kepler, Johannes, astronomer, 30, 31
Klesl, Melchior, bishop of Vienna, cardinal, director of the privy council, 28, 65, 67, 70, 74, 88, 94
 arrest of, 83–4
 and the *Brüderzwist*, 46, 67
 composition in the Empire, 70, 72, 73, 75, 89
 conversion to a *politique*, 70
 and Defenestration of Prague, 92–3
 and Letter of Majesty, 70
 and the Diet of Regensburg (1613), 71–74
 and succession in the Empire, 75, 76
 and the Turks, 72, 75
 and War of Gradisca, 81, 82
Knöringen, Heinrich von, prince-bishop of Augsburg, 198, 217
Komorn (Komàom) (1618), Treaty of, 74
Kufstein, Hans Ludwig von, governor of Upper Austria, 138
Kurz von Senftenau, Ferdinand, imperial councillor and diplomat, 223, 288, 298
 mission to France, 226, 227

Lamormaini, William, Jesuit, confessor of Ferdinand, 105, 132, 141–42, 300
 and Bohemia, 146, 147–50
 criticism of, 150, 220, 228, 233, 239, 272
 and Treaty of Cherasco, 216
 and projected Cologne peace conference, 295
 and the Edict, 195, 197, 200, 208, 209, 210
 and Eggenberg, 142, 191, 213, 226, 237, 228, 254
 and Ferdinand, 20, 135, 142, 147, 166, 205, 209, 239, 246, 250–51, 262–3, 264, 265, 271, 277, 291, 295, 299, 303, 304, 308
 Ferdinandi II Imperatoris Romanorum Virtutes, 310-12
 and France, 192–93, 212, 214–15, 243, 247, 251, 285
 and heretics, 106, 141, 148
 and Lower Austria, 105–107
 and Mantuan War, 190–91, 192
 and the Pirna Points, 284–86
 at Regensburg (1630), 205, 208, 210, 212
 at the Theologians Conference, 281–82
 and Upper Austria, 141
 and Urban VIII, 190–91, 200, 201, 217
 and Wallenstein, 184, 205, 236–37, 254, 263
Laymann, Paul, Jesuit, 198–99, 200
Leipzig Conference (1631), 209, 218–19
Leitmeritz (Litoméice), negotiations at, 250, 253, 267–68
Leopold, archduke, bishop of Passau, prince-bishop of Strasbourg and ruler of the Tyrol and Anterior Austria, 23, 27–8, 41, 58, 65, 66, 68, 69, 271
 candidate for emperor, 49, 68
 and Ferdinand, 69, 71, 125, 131–32
Leopold William, archduke, 257
Letter of Majesty, 65–6, 69, 83, 85, 90, 95
Lieben (Lebeň) (1608), Treaty of, 57
Liechtenstein, Gundacker von, imperial councillor, 127, 138, 153
 and imperial finances, 133
 and war in Lower Saxony, 159
 and Wallenstein, 261–62
Liechtenstein, Karl von, prince, governor of Bohemia, 116, 118, 119, 121, 138, 144
 and Prague Consortium, 134
Lipsius, Justus, humanist, 23, 125
Lobkowitz, Wilhelm Popel von, 119
Louis XIII, king of France, 112, 157, 243;
  see also France, Richelieu, cardinal,
Lower Austria, 4, 65
 estates of, 83, 96–7, 135
 toleration in, 102, 107, 165
Lübeck (1629), Peace of, 164
Lustrier, Sebastian, imperial diplomat, 269
Lutter am Barenberg (1626), battle, 162
Lützen (1632), battle, 246, 248

Magdeburg, archbishopric, 72, 73, 275
Magdeburg, city, 219, 222, 223, 229
Magni, Valeriano, Capuchin, and Counter-Reformation in Bohemia, 145–46, 148–49
 at Theologians Conference, 282, 283
 and Wallenstein, 184, 186
Mainz, archbishop-elector of, *see* Anselm Casimir von Wambold; Greiffenklau,

Index 321

Georg Friedrich von; Schweikardt von Kronberg, Johann,
Malaspina, Germanico, nuncio in Graz, 4, 8, 9
Mantua, city, 193
Mantuan War, 183, 187–95, 206–207, 225–27
Margaret, archduchess, queen of Spain, 35
Maria, archduchess, mother of Ferdinand, 2, 3, 10, 14, 15, 19, 32, 41
   death and testament, 59–60
   and Ferdinand, 10, 12, 14–15, 17, 35, 36, 53, 58–60
   journeys. 15, 24–5, 35
   and Protestants, 5, 11, 15, 36
Maria Anna, archduchess, first wife of Ferdinand, 22, 40–41, 42, 43, 58, 89
Maria Anna, Spanish Infanta, wife of Ferdinand III, 225–26, 302
Maria Christierna, archduchess, princess of Transylvania, 15
Maria Magdelena, archduchess, 58
Marradas, Balthasar, general, 82, 226
Martinitz, Jaroslav, count, imperial councillor, 86, 90, 118
Matthias, archduke, emperor, 4, 48, 55, 69
   death, 95
   elected emperor, 71
   and Defenestration of Prague, 91, 92, 93
   support for Ferdinand's succession, 76, 77, 85; *see also* Brüderzwist
Mausoleum, 304
Maximilian II, emperor, 2, 4
Maximilian, archduke, regent in Inner Austria, ruler of Anterior Austria and the Tyrol, 19, 20
   death, 94
   and removal of Klesl, 77–8, 84, 93–4
   and succession in the Empire, 47, 48, 75
Maximilian, duke and elector of Bavaria, 11, 44, 51, 62, 67, 72, 107, 115, 299, 301
   and Bohemian rebellion, 96, 118
   and the Edict, 194–96, 199, 206–11
   and France, 112, 223, 232, 235–36
   and Gustav Adolph, 235, 237, 238
   and the Pirna Points, 283
   and Saxony, 223, 229
   and Upper Austria, 113, 140–41
   and Wallenstein, 184–85, 245, 255, 260; *see also* Ferdinand and Maximilian, Palatinate Question, and war in Lower Saxony
Maximilian Ernst, archduke, brother of Ferdinand, 23, 65, 72, 89

Mecklenburg, duchy, 113, 185
   transfer to Wallenstein, 166, 186
Meggau, Leonhard Helfried von, imperial councillor, 84, 128, 298
   and war in Lower Saxony, 160
Milensio, Felice, papal agent, 52
Military Border, 5, 6, 7
Mitterndorf, parish in Styria, 31
Monzon (1626), Treaty of, 158
Morelles, Cosmas, Dominican theologian, 214
Mühlhausen, convention of (1620), guarantee, 109–11
Mühlhausen, electoral convention of (1627), 195–96
Mühlhausen, abortive conference of (1631), 234, 235
Munich Conference (1579), 8
Munich (1619), Treaty of, 101–102, 151

Nevers, Charles de, duke of Mantua, 187, 188, 189, 190, 191, 203, 207
Nikolsburg (Mikulov) (1621), Treaty of, 117
Ninguarda, Felician, papal diplomat, 7–8
Nördlingen (1634), battle, 270, 273
Nuremberg, city, 288

Olivares, count-duke of, 158, 163
   and Lamormaini, 191, 192, 213, 225, 239; *see also* Philip III, Spain
Oñate, Iñigo Velez deGuevara y Tasis, count de, Spanish diplomat, 79, 80, 155, 253, 259, 299, 301
   and Defenestration of Prague, 92, 93, 96
   and Peace of Prague, 292
Oñate Treaty (1617), 80, 238
Ottaviano da Ravenna, Franciscan, theologian, 234–35
Oxenstierna, Axel, Swedish chancellor, 251, 296

Palatinate Question, 102, 151–57, 161–62, 165, 206, 254, 258, 276, 301; *see also* Maximilian, duke and elector of Bavaria; Munich (1619), Treaty of; Regensburg (1623), convention of princes,
Pallotto, Giovanni Battista, nuncio in Vienna, 166, 188, 191, 203
   and the Edict, 198, 201, 211
Passau, prince-bishopric of, conflict over, 27–8, 41–2; *see also* Leopold, archduke
Paul V, pope, 46, 52, 57, 63, 64
   and Klesl, 70, 93–4

Paul V, pope (cont.)
  subsidies, 95, 103, 104
  and toleration, 103
Pazmany, Peter, archbishop of Esztergom, 88, 128, 157, 298, 299
  mission to Rome, 241–43
  on imperial policy, 248–49, 257, 271, 292
  and Pirna Points, 279, 284–86
Peñalosa, Ambrogio, Jesuit, 234, 282
Philip III, king of Spain, 25, 35, 47, 75
Philip IV, king of Spain, 124
  and the Edict, 227
  and death of Wallenstein, 265
Philippi, Heinrich, Jesuit, confessor of the king of Hungary, 147, 149
Piccolomini, Ottavio, general, 261, 262
Pietas Austriaca, 138-39
Pirna Points, 273, 275–77
Pomis, Giovanni Pietro de, court artist, 26, 40, 104, 135
Portia, Girolamo, count, nuncio Graz, 21, 23, 26, 31
Prague Blood Court (Prager Blutgericht), 118–19, 120–21
Prague Consortium (Prager Münzconsortium), 133–34
Prague (1635), Peace of, 267–68, 286, 289, 290–91, 292, 293–94, 307–308, 309
Prague, university, 140, 145–46
Princeps in Compendio (The Essential Prince), 126
Priuli, Giovanni, composer, 130
Protestant Union, 56-7, 61, 65, 66, 67, 101, 111, 112, 154

Questenberg, Gerhard von, imperial councillor, 236
Questenberg, Hermann von, imperial diplomat, 235–36, 238, 267, 281, 282, 288
Quiroga, Don Diego de, Capuchin, confessor of the Infanta Maria Anna, 224–25, 244, 253
  and Peace of Prague, 286
  at Theologians Conference, 282–83
  and Wallenstein, 253

Radkersburg, town in Styria, 25, 32, 39
Rákóczy, Georg, prince of Transylvania, 259–60
Regensburg, convention of princes (1623), 154–56
Regensburg, diet of (1608), 49–57
Regensburg, diet of (1613), 71–72, 72–74

Regensburg, electoral convention of (1630), 197, 202–215, 285
Regensburg (1636–37), electoral convention of, 273–296, 303
Richel, Bartholomew, Bavarian minister, 260–64
Richelieu, Armand-Jean du Plessis, cardinal, 157, 158, 252
  and Ferdinand, 243
  anti-Habsburg policy, 158, 192, 243, 251, 269, 270–71, 277, 293
  and the Treaty of Regensburg (1630), 207;
  see also France, Louis XIII
Rocci, Ciriaco, nuncio in Vienna, 203, 226, 256
  and the Edict, 211, 217, 235, 255
Rudolf II, emperor, 2, 35, 36, 45, 47, 66
  death, 71
  and Ferdinand, 14, 17, 20, 43, 51, 54, 55;
  see also Bruderzwist

Santa Maria della Vittoria, church in Rome, 116
Savelli, Paul, prince, imperial representative in Rome, 229
Saxony, electorate, 50, 51, 55, 72, 94
  and the Edict, 94, 154, 230–231
  and Peace of Prague, 276, 288–89
  at Regensburg (1630), 203, 206, 207
  at Regensburg (1636–37), 300, 301;
  see also John George, elector of Saxony
Schaffgotsch, Johann Ulrich von, colonel, 266
Schlick, Heinrich count, general, president of the war council, 85, 119, 260, 284–86
Schoppe, Gaspar, polemicist, 62, 103
  mission to Rome (1609), 63–5
  at diet of Regensburg (1608), 52, 53, 56
  at electoral convention of Regensburg (1630), 208–209
Schrottel, Georg, Jesuit, confessor of Ferdinand of Cologne, 208
Schrottenbach, Balthasar von, minister in Graz, 11, 12, 13, 17, 26
Schwarzenberg, Peter von, baron, diplomat, 239, 243
Schweikard, Johannm, von Kronberg, elector of Mainz, 51, 62, 72
  and the Edict, 194
  at election of Ferdinand, 99
  and Palatinate Question, 152, 155;
  see also Mainz
Scultetus, Abraham, Calvinist preacher, 114
Senj (Zengg), port, 81, 82
Sigismund II, king of Poland, 15, 105, 163, 271

Index

Silesia, 144
Sissek, fortress, 19, 43
Slawata, Vilém, imperial councillor, 86, 90,
    118, 122, 128, 160
    and war in Lower Saxony, 160;
    see also Defenestration of Prague
Sonnabenter, Lorenz, pastor in Graz, 32
Sotern, Philip Christoph von, archbishop-
    elector of Trier, 153, 252, 276, 299
Spain, 47, 253
    and Ferdinand, 76, 78–80, 213, 216, 227,
    238, 289
    and Lamormaini, 227–28, 229, 239, 269,
    277–78
    and the Mantuan War, 183, 187–94
    and the Palatinate Question, 153, 154
    and the Pirna Points, 277
    and the Peace of Prague, 292
    and Wallenstein, 259; see also Philip IV, king
    of Spain, Olivares
"Spanish Road," 79, 153
Stadion, Johann Caspar von, Grand Master of
    the Teutonic Knight, imperial councillor,
    218, 230, 296
Steinau (1632), battle, 258
Sternberg, Adam von, Bohemian nobleman, 84,
    85, 298
Stralendorf, Peter Heinrich von, vice-chancellor
    of the Holy Roman Empire, privy
    councillor, 128, 298
    and the Edict, 198, 199, 200, 210, 234–35
    and France, 238
    and imperial policy, 153, 197, 221–22, 245,
    248, 249–50, 271, 292
    at the Electoral Convention of Mühlhausen
    (1627), 195–96
    and Maximilian. 128, 199
    and the Pirna Points, 278, 284–86
    and the electoral convention of Regensburg
    (1630), 210
    and Wallenstein, 204, 266–67
    and war in Lower Saxony, 160
Stobäus, Georg, von Palmburg, bishop of
    Lavant, 9, 21, 32–3, 42, 44
"Sturmpetition" (Stormy Petition), 96–7
Sturmsdorf (1635), Treaty of, 293, 296
Suffren, Jean, Jesuit, confessor of Louis XIII,
    192

Tanner, Adam, Jesuit, theologian, 16
Theologians Conference, 280–83
Thomas Aquinas, theologian, 215

Thurn, Heinrich Matthias count, general, 85,
    90, 91, 92, 96, 97, 98, 117, 236
Thun-Hohenstein, Christoph Simon von,
    councillor of the king of Hungary, 288, 298
Tilly, Johann count, general, 45, 154, 206
    and Bohemian campaign, 112, 115, 117
    and war in Lower Saxony, 161
    and Saxony, 229, 231
Trautmannsdorf, Maximilian von, privy
    councillor, 92, 127–28, 253, 256, 298
    and the Edict 200, 210, 256
    and France, 238, 244
    mission to Rome, 102–104
    and imperial policy, 197, 221–22, 249–50,
    271, 292
    on the Palatinate Question, 153
    and Peace of Prague, 267–68
    and Pirna Points, 284–86
    and Wallenstein, 256, 259, 262
Trier, archbishop-elector of, see Sotern, Philip
    Christoph von,
Turkish Waar, Long, 19, 43–6
Twelve Years Truce, 92, 153, 158

Ulm (1620), Treaty of, 112
Upper Austria, 4, 140–41
    Counter Reformation in 142–43, 153, 165
    estates of, 65, 83, 96, 113, 116, 136, 140–41,
    143
    Peasants Rebellion (1626), 143
    Peasants Rebellion (1632), 245
Urban VIII, pope, 146, 158
    and a Catholic alliance, 242, 269, 271, 277
    and peace conference in Cologne, 290,
    294–95
    and the Edict, 201, 211, 212, 217,
    235, 242
    and Ferdinand, 146, 217, 230, 256
    and Franco-Bavarian alliance, 192, 203
    and Mantuan War, 187–88, 190–91
    and Peace of Prague, 277, 289–90
    and the prefect of Rome, 230, 274
    and succession of Ferdinand III, 212, 299
Uskoks, 6, 21, 81–3

Valdespino, Juan de, theologian, 153, 252,
Venier, Sebastian, Venetian ambassador, on
    Ferdinand, 179–81
Verospi, Fabrizio, extraordinary nuncio in
    Vienna, 94, 152
Vienna, city, 132
    Jesuit church, 166

Vienna, city (cont.)
  siege of (1619-20), 96-7, 104-105;
    see also "Sturmpetition" (Stormy Petition)
Vienna, Peace of (1624), 136, 157
Vienna (1606), Treaty of, 46, 48, 56
Viller, Bartholomew, Jesuit, confessor of
    Ferdinand, 21-2, 26, 29, 32, 41, 51, 54,
    82, 97
  influence on Ferdinand, 20, 22
  and Letter of Majesty, 95
  resignation, 102
Vitelleschi, Muzio, superior general of the
    Jesuits, 117
  and Lamormaini, 228, 254
  and Spain, 227-28, 229
Vlach Statute (Statuta Valachorum), 163

Wallenstein, Albrecht Wenzel Eusebius von,
    159, 236, 253
  death and aftermath, 163-67
  and the Edict, 201, 237, 240, 257
  first generalate, 160-61, 163-64, 166, 204
  second generalate, 236-37, 240, 245,
    254-55, 258-65
  and Lamormaini, 205, 236-37
  and treasury of Moravian estates, 97-8

  and War of Gradisca, 82
  and Prague Consortium, 133-34
Wartenberg, Franz Wilhelm von, prince-bishop
    of Osnabruck, 217
Werdenberg, Johann Baptista Verda von, privy
    councillor, 228
  and France, 244
  on imperial policy, 221-22
  and Pirna Points, 284-86
White Mountain (1620), battle, 115
William, Duke of Bavaria, 50, 54, 55
  oversight of young Ferdinand, 11, 12, 14, 17,
    20
  mirror of princes, 18-19
  warning about concessions to Protestants,
    96
Wimpfen (1622), battle, 154
Witte, de, Hans, financier, 134
Wittstock (1636), battle, 296

Ziegler, Reinhard, Jesuit, confessor to electors
    of Mainz, 194, 195, 203, 208
Zsitvatorok (1606), Treaty of, 46, 48, 56, 57,
    71, 74, 108, 117
Zuñiga, Balthasar de, Spanish diplomat and
    minister, 69, 75, 76, 78, 96

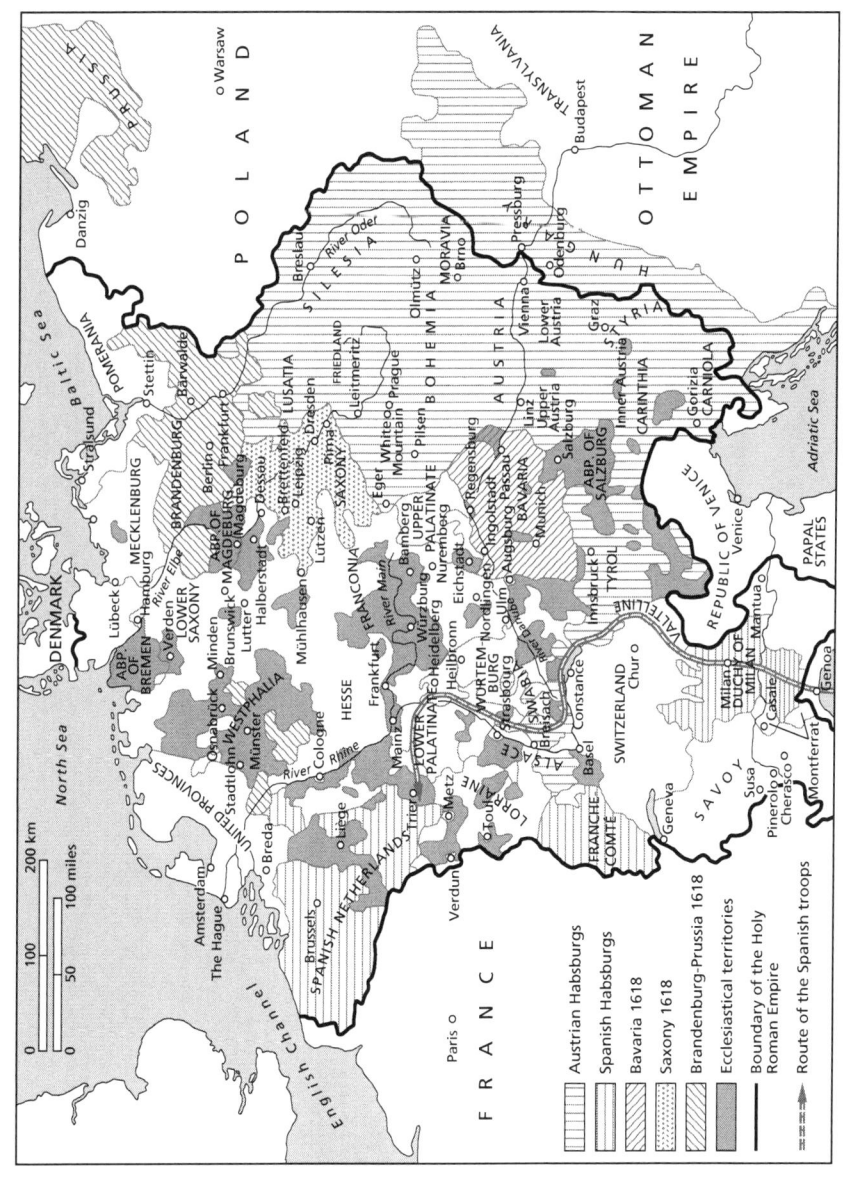

Map of the Holy Roman Empire during the Thirty Years War.

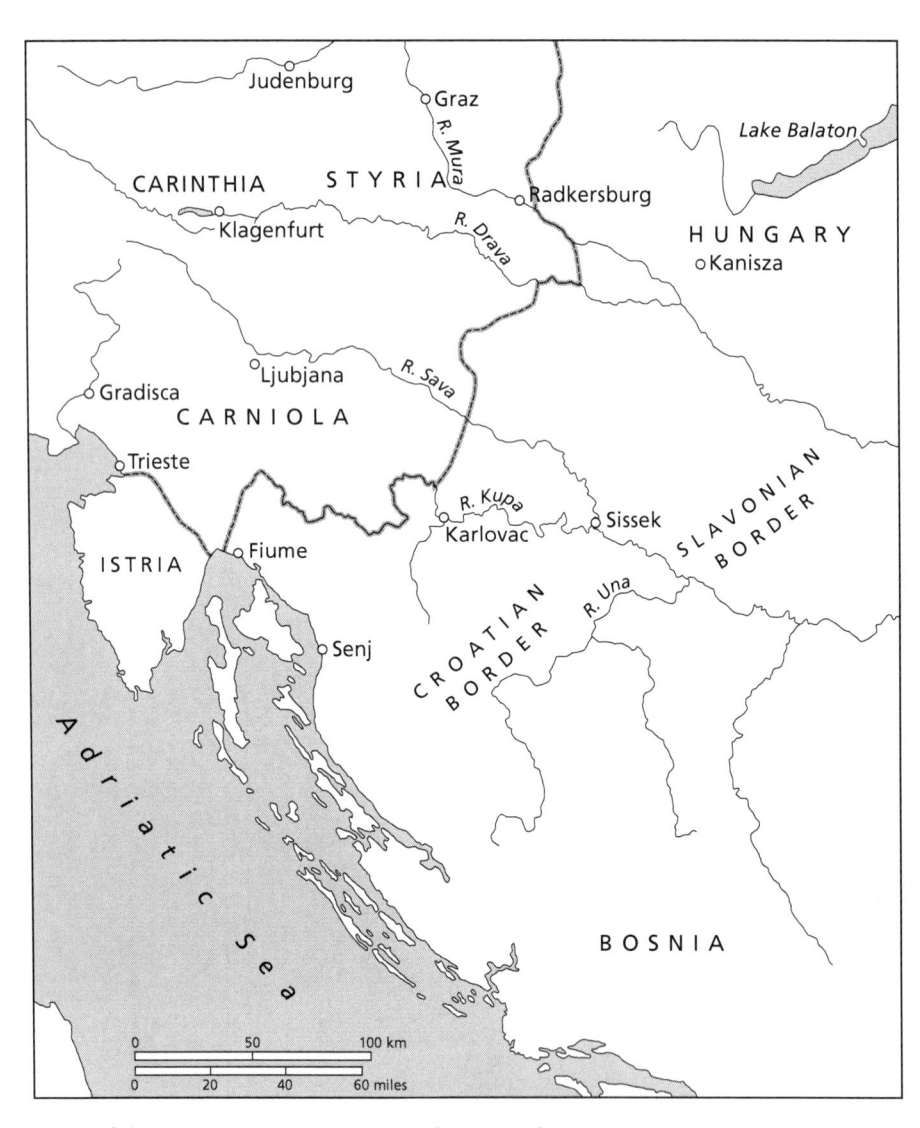

Map of the Inner Austrian-Croatian Military Border.

18623287R00183

Printed in Great Britain
by Amazon